Good Reason for Writing

A TEXT WITH READINGS

Vincent Barry

Bakersfield College

Wadsworth Publishing Company
Belmont, California
A Division of Wadsworth, Inc.

For
JEANNINE

English Editor: Kevin Howat

Production Editor: Sally Schuman

Designer: Patricia Girvin Dunbar

Copy Editor: William Waller

Cartoons: Erkii Alanen

Calligraphy: Maureen O'Lone

Printed in the United States of America

2 3 4 5 6 7 8 9 10—86 85 84 83

ISBN 0-534-01232-9

_____

Library of Congress Cataloging in Publication Data

Barry, Vincent.
  Good reason for writing.

  Includes index.
    1. English language—Rhetoric.   2. Reasoning.
  3. College readers. I. Title.
  PE1431.B37   1983   808'.0427   82–10869
  ISBN 0–534–01232–9

_____

Preface

In recent years the teaching of composition has increasingly focused on thinking and writing as interrelated processes. One facet of the thinking process—reasoning—has received special attention, together with the type of writing to which it most applies—argumentation. Composition instructors have responded commendably to this new focus (and, in some cases, requirement) by devising courses intended to sharpen students' argumentative skills. Such courses go by various names: Critical Thinking, Thinking for Writing, Argumentative Writing, Argument and Persuasion, and the like. Whatever the name, these courses share the purpose of trying to link sound reasoning with argumentative writing.

Instructors choosing this approach have largely had to select from among a category of texts that can be termed "informal logics," books that introduce the students to the basics of logic, giving special attention to commonplace fallacies. As good as these texts are, they are designed primarily to make the student a critical reader and thinker. Although the abilities to read and think critically are powerful aids to composing sound arguments, they are not in themselves sufficient. Students must also learn to recognize and use underlying rhetorical patterns that structure the thinking process and argumentative essay. They must learn not only how to distinguish the good argument from the bad but also how to compose sound argumentative essays. It is these assumptions that have given rise to the present text.

Good Reason for Writing is a text/reader that focuses on the most common rhetorical patterns that structure the thinking process and the argumentative essay. Specifically, this text has four main objectives: (1) to teach argumentative writing; (2) to develop and refine critical thinking and rhetorical skills, especially as they pertain to extended arguments; (3) to impart basic principles of research and offer guidelines for doing a research paper; and (4) to develop informed opinion. What distinguishes this text from others in the field, then, is that *Good Reason for Writing* places writing squarely in the center of things. Yes, the text introduces basic principles of correct reasoning as well as over 50 common fallacies. And yes, the text trains students to be more perceptive and searching readers and thinkers. But it gives writing the preeminent position warranted by the needs and desires of its audience.

A glance at the table of contents will reveal this book's coverage and structure. But a word is in order about certain topics that underscore the centrality of writing. Chapter 2, for example, deals with the primary ingredients of the argumentative essay: thesis, main points, and organization. It also stresses the importance of audience and persona. Chapters 3–6 concern specific patterns used in developing argumentative essays. Chapter 10, although not intended to be a research primer, includes the steps involved in and guidelines for writing effective research papers. This chapter serves as a capstone to the book. It shows how all the elements of sound thinking, perceptive reading, and deliberate writing coalesce in the lengthy, argumentative essay based on organized research.

As for its structure, the text is organized to allow diverse approaches. Thus, apart from doing Chapters 1 and 2 first, instructors and students can hopscotch around, making minor adjustments as they do. Just as important, Part 3, "Troubleshooting for Fallacious Arguments," is written so that instructors can feel secure assigning it for independent study, or even omitting it.

Beyond this, *Good Reason for Writing* has several other features geared to make students better writers, readers, and thinkers. One is its many topical examples and illustrations. Another is its numerous in-chapter and end-of-chapter exercises, again of a contemporary character. Still another is its essay models and sample research paper, as well as suggested theme topics.

But perhaps its single most useful tool, from both an instructional and a financial view, is its reading selections. Although most texts of this kind take up the extended argument, very few offer enough of the right kind of examples to reinforce the coverage. As a result, instructors are left in the lurch, often having to increase students' costs by assigning a supplementary anthology. In contrast, *Good Reason for Writing* has 21 extended argumentative essays for student evaluation and classroom discussion. In format these pieces range from editorials to letters to formal essays. In content they embrace an array of important and controversial current issues: privacy and videotapes, the draft, the New Right, "whistle-blowing," abortion, teenage pregnancies, patriotism, and so on. An extensive Instructor's Manual is available on request.

The ideas and talents of many people have gone into the making of *Good Reason for Writing*. Wadsworth's English editor Kevin Howat deserves my thanks for having solicited and helped shape the work. Also of enormous assistance were the reviews of William Harlan, Diablo Valley College; George F. Hayhoe, Virginia Polytechnic Institute; Nancy W. Johnson, Northern Virginia Community College, Annandale campus; Robert Keefe, University of Massachusetts at Amherst; Larry McDoniel, St. Louis Community College at Meramec; Rosemary Ortman, University of Louisville; Annette Rottenberg, University of Massachusetts at Amherst; and Stafford H. Thomas, University of Illinois at Urbana.

Vincent Barry

Contents

CONTENTS

CONTENTS

CONTENTS

PART THREE

Troubleshooting for Fallacious Arguments

CONTENTS

PART FOUR

Research

Chapter Ten
THE RESEARCH PAPER 339

PART ONE

Argument and the Argumentative Essay

I. Argument

*W*hat do you think the following assertions have in common?

1. I'm going to study medicine, because studies indicate that there will be ample job opportunities in medical fields for the indefinite future.

2. Of course we're the league champions. We won the play-offs, didn't we?

3. The best reason for going to college is that it increases one's earning potential. That's why I'm in college and why I'm determined to graduate.

4. Capital punishment should be permitted, because it deters crime.

5. Insofar as women have the right to determine what happens to their bodies, they have a right to elective abortion.

6. Life probably exists someplace else in the universe. After all, it's most

likely that life-sustaining conditions similar to those found on earth exist outside our planet.

7. Guns kill people; that's why handguns should be banned.

8. Since women are not by nature as ambitious and aggressive as men, they aren't equipped to succeed in business.

9. Given the evidence, it's safe to say that cancer is caused by a virus.

10. Many people believe that megavitamin therapy helps ward off disease. Reason enough, then, to start taking heavy doses of vitamins.

11. People who drink and drive imperil their own lives and those of others. That's why I don't drink and drive.

12. If angle A of a triangle is seventy degrees and angle B is sixty degrees, then angle C must be fifty degrees.

13. It's not likely to rain on the Rose Parade next year, because, as always, the parade will be held in sunny Pasadena.

14. Inasmuch as tension between the superpowers is increasing, we can expect military confrontations in places such as the Middle East.

15. Most people favor the legalization of marijuana. So it should be legalized.

16. Any social policy that discriminates on the basis of sex is inherently unfair. It follows that a military draft that excludes women is unfair.

Each of these utterances is an argument, a subject that will concern us throughout this book. As you can readily see from the preceding examples, arguments abound. Sometimes people formulate them, as they might in deciding which courses to take, books to read, political positions to hold, and social viewpoints to endorse. At other times people have arguments thrust on them. At school or work, for example, somebody may serve up an argument and expect us to react. Or while reading a newspaper or magazine we may confront an argument on some burning social issue. At still other times people are called on to present a rather lengthy, well-developed argument, as for a class assignment or occupational task. And then there are those times when we simply want to speak up and be heard, as in writing a letter to the editor or stating a position before a city council. Arguments abound, and our success depends in part on an ability to handle them.

This book will help you deal with arguments. It is especially designed to help you read and write longer pieces of argument, the kind that you often confront in college and afterward. In order to read or write a long argument intelligently, you first must know what an argument is. In part this knowledge includes an understanding of an argument's structure and an ability to recognize arguments and distinguish two kinds: inductive and deductive. Also essential is familiarity with the nature of generalizations.

A good way to learn about argument is to consider specimens—that is, short argumentative passages such as the sixteen above. That's what we'll be doing in this chapter—carefully inspecting specimens in order to learn about the anatomy of an argument. In subsequent chapters we will build on this foundation in order to distinguish good argument from bad and to learn how to write sound argumentative essays.

ARGUMENT

The word *argument* calls up a number of impressions. For some people an argument is a fight. For others it's a discussion. For still others an argument is something to be avoided or won. In our study we will not use *argument* in any of these senses. Rather, we will follow the conventions of logic and rhetoric and use this definition: an *argument is a group of propositions* (that is, true or false statements), *one of which is held to follow from the others.*

Here's a simple example of an argument:

> *All students in the class are members of the debate team.*
>
> *Annie is a student in the class.*
>
> *Therefore, Annie is a member of the debate team.*

The statement "Annie is a member of the debate team" is held to follow from the other two statements; the first two statements presumably entail the third. Taken together, these three statements make up an argument. Of course, the statements could appear as a single sentence and still be an argument, as in:

> *Since all students in the class are members of the debate team and Annie is a student in the class, Annie is a member of the debate team.*

An argument, then, can take the form of individual sentences or just a single sentence. In any event, an utterance is an argument when (1) it consists of a group of propositions and (2) one of the propositions is held to follow from the others.

Propositions

A *proposition is a true or false statement,* or what is commonly termed a declarative sentence. To understand this definition fully, you need a clear idea of what propositions are and how they are related in arguments.

These are propositions: "Sacramento is the capital of California." "Bees make honey." "Humans are not vertebrates." "Ronald Reagan was not elected president in 1980." "Life exists outside our solar system." "Vitamin C helps prevent the common cold." They are statements that are either true or false. In some cases their truth is not in question (for example, "Sacramento is the capital of California"); in others their falsehood is not in question (for example, "Humans are not vertebrates"); and in other cases their truth is uncertain (for example, "Life exists outside our solar system"). But all are statements that are either true or false. Such statements are termed propositions.

Clearly, not every sentence is a declarative sentence—that is, a proposition. Often we ask questions, express exclamations, or give orders. "Where are you going?" "Good grief!" and "Close the door after you" are not true or false statements. When an utterance functions strictly in a nondeclarative way, it is not a proposition and thus cannot be considered part of an argument.

But a question, exclamation, or command may serve a multiple function in a sentence. In addition to its usual function of asking, exclaiming, or commanding, it may also be expressing a statement. Take the example "When did William Faulkner, the great American writer, live?" Besides asking a question, this utterance says that Faulkner was a great writer. Similarly, "You let the cat out!" may be implying that letting the cat out was not a good idea. And "Attend every class if you want to pass" not only expresses a command but asserts a condition for passing the class: You are required to attend every class in order to pass. When nondeclarative utterances make a statement, they can be part of an argument.

To illustrate, suppose that Fred and Fran are discussing government control of advertising. Fred argues that there should be considerably more control, or else consumers will be increasingly victimized. In response, Fran says: "But don't you realize that such intervention is an insult to the whole concept of free enterprise? And that's precisely why we should have less, not more, government control." Embedded in Fran's question is the statement "Intervention is an insult to the whole concept of free enterprise." In her view this proposition is part of her argument for less government control. Fran is arguing, and her question functions as a statement used to support her contention.

Relating Propositions

An argument, as noted, not only consists of propositions but also relates them in such a way that one is held to follow from the others. *Follow from* is the key phrase.

Often we assert things without maintaining that one assertion follows from the others. "Washington is the capital of the United States," "The Golden Gate Bridge is in San Francisco," and "Denver is 'The Mile-High City' " are mere assertions; they are not internally connected. No one of these statements is held to follow from the others. Taken together they do not constitute an argument.

Besides making mere assertions, we often offer explanatory information in propositional form. Here are two such statements: "The child was amused by the kitten's play" and "We moved the 'jazzercise' class to another room to accommodate the large enrollment." Such explanatory assertions often appear in a group of statements, as in this paragraph:

> *The joints of our bodies are particularly susceptible to mechanical wear and tear. The ends of the long bones must rub against each other without destroying themselves and must bear the weight of the body. The joints are surrounded by tough connecting tissues, ligaments and muscles which bind the bones together in a tough but flexible unit while permitting movement often against great force. When any of the tissue in and around the joints fails, arthritis is said to be present.*[1]

Like all explanatory assertions, this one helps explain some phenomenon, in this case arthritis.

The difference between explanations and arguments lies primarily in the purpose of the discourse. If writers and speakers want to prove a contention, then they are arguing. But if they regard the truth of a contention as unproblematic and wish to show why or how it is the case (rather than that it is, in fact, the case), they are explaining. Accordingly, in "Susan looks better since her vacation," the speaker is not trying to establish that Susan looks better but rather explaining why Susan does in fact look better. In contrast, in "Susan ought to get a raise, since she has worked so hard," the speaker is trying to establish the contention that Susan in fact deserves a raise. Again, *if writers intend to establish the truth of a proposition, they are arguing; if they are trying to show why or how something is the case, they are explaining.*

There are occasions, of course, when a series of statements is both argumentative and explanatory. In the following passage from a Sherlock Holmes classic, *The Hound of the Baskervilles,* the master detective not only demonstrates to Watson the truth of a contention but also explains how he arrived at it:

> **Holmes:** *You have been at your club all day, I presume.*
>
> **Watson:** *My dear Holmes!*
>
> **Holmes:** *Am I right?*
>
> **Watson:** *Certainly, but how—*
>
> **Holmes:** *. . . A gentleman sets forth on a showery and miry day. He returns immaculate in the evening with the gloss still on his hat and his boots. He has been a fixture, therefore, all day. He is not a man with intimate friends. Where, then, would he have been? Is it not obvious?*

---

[1]Abraham Hoffer. "Good Nutrition + Supplements + Minerals: Three Way Attack on Arthritis." *The Health Quarterly*, vol. 4., 1981, p. 30.

With these introductory remarks behind us, let's now consider the structure of an argument.

STRUCTURE OF ARGUMENTS

Many aspects of an argument fall under its structure. We will limit ourselves to four: premises and conclusions, signal words, unexpressed premises, and premise support.

Premises and Conclusions

From the simple examples of arguments that we have already seen, one thing is clear: *Arguments express a point of view that is supported.* Arguments tell not only what writers believe but also *why* they believe it.

In the study of argument, what writers or speakers advocate is termed the conclusion of the argument. *The conclusion of an argument is the statement that is held to follow from the premises.* In the argument "Capital punishment should be permitted, because it deters crime," "Capital punishment should be permitted" is the conclusion.

The support that the person offers for advancing a particular contention is termed the premise (or premises). *The premise of an argument is the statement (or statements) that is held to entail the conclusion.* Premises are the reasons, evidence, or considerations that support the conclusion. In the preceding example, "it [capital punishment] deters crime" is the argument's premise. Here are additional examples (premises are italicized, conclusions are not):

> *Most people favor the legalization of marijuana. This is why* marijuana should be legalized.
>
> The defendant may still be innocent, *for possession of a murder weapon does not necessarily establish guilt.*
>
> *Although not all films have educational value,* the upcoming National Geographic special must be educational, *because it has been endorsed by the National Education Association and is being televised by public broadcasting.*

Notice that premises and conclusions can occur anywhere in an argument. Premises needn't appear at the beginning; conclusions needn't appear at the end.

Signal Words

Of help in detecting the presence of arguments are signal words. *A signal word indicates the presence of a premise or conclusion.* In English we have an

array of premise signals, among which are *since, as, because, for, inasmuch as, for the reason that, moreover, also, and, but, in addition to,* and the like. Similarly, we have many conclusion signals, such as *so, thus, it follows that, therefore, consequently, as a result, hence,* and *finally.* Accordingly, we write: "Inasmuch as the time is short, I shall forego the introductions"; "Since all triangles have three sides, it follows that this four-sided figure cannot be a triangle"; "Cancer is an insidious disease, for it often defies early detection."

Although useful in indicating the presence of arguments and their premises and conclusions, signal words can be misleading. For example, the statement "Susan looks better *since* her vacation" is not an argument, despite the presence of "since"; for the "since" in this case connects things in time. In contrast, in "Susan should get a raise, *since* she has worked so hard," "since" signals a reason, a premise that is offered to justify a contention. The only way to differentiate between the meanings of *since* and other such words is from context. The point is that, although signal words are useful in locating arguments, they are no substitute for a close inspection of the context in which the discourse occurs.

Although all arguments have premises, the premises are not always explicit. Sometimes they go unexpressed. Moreover, the arguments we commonly come across and formulate sometimes offer support for premises. So we should look at these two additional features of the structure of an argument: unexpressed premises and premise support.

Exercise

1.1   Determine which of the following are arguments and which are not. Explain your answers. In the case of arguments, indicate premises and conclusions, and list signal words where appropriate.

1. Most people I know prefer foods with no preservatives added. So I guess such foods are good for you.

2. Insofar as the president has expressed a view, the issue is closed.

3. Your aunt's arrival has been delayed by inclement weather.

4. Nobody likes to take orders, but everybody likes to give them. Clearly, giving orders is preferable to taking them.

5. Of course vitamin C helps prevent colds. Hasn't a Nobel laureate said so?

6. It's little wonder we dislike others as much for their strengths as for their weaknesses. We naturally dislike whatever makes us despise ourselves.

7. Inflation cannot be controlled by voluntary means. Only strict government regulation of prices and wages will work.

8. "It is worth saying something about the social position of beggars, for when one has consorted with them, and found that they are ordinary human beings, one cannot help being struck by the curious attitude that society takes toward them." (George Orwell. Down and Out in Paris and London. New York: Berkley, 1967, p. 125.)

9. "In bureaucratic logic, bad judgment is any decision that can lead to embarrassing questions, even if the decision was itself right. Therefore ... no man with an eye on a career can afford to be right when he can manage to be safe." (John Ciardi. "Bureaucracy and Frank Ellis." In Manner of Speaking. New Brunswick, N.J.: Rutgers University Press, 1972, p. 250.)

10. "Even the most productive writers are expert dawdlers, doers of unnecessary errands, seekers of interruptions—trials to their wives or husbands, associates, and themselves. They sharpen well-pointed pencils and go out to buy more blank paper, rearrange [their] office, wander through libraries and bookstores, change words, walk, drive, make unnecessary calls, nap, day dream, and try not 'consciously' to think about what they are going to write so they can think subconsciously about it." (Donald M. Murray. "Write Before Writing." Quoted by Morton A. Miller in Reading and Writing Short Essays. New York: Random House, 1980, p. 275.)

11. "You and I are far from that stage of mastery (of the exacting writer), but we are none the less obliged to do some rewriting beyond the intensive correction of bad spots. For in the act of revising on the small scale one comes upon gaps in thought and—what is as bad—real or apparent repetitions or intrusions, sometimes called backstitching." (Jacques Barzun. "All Good Writing Is Rewriting." In Simple and Direct. New York: Harper & Row, 1976, p. 184.)

12. "Names are far more than mere identity tags. They are charged with hidden meanings and unspoken overtones that profoundly help or hinder you in your relationships and your life." (Christopher P. Andersen. The Name Game. New York: Simon & Schuster, 1977, p. 1.)

13. "It isn't surprising that many athletes have discovered the benefits of

taking vitamin E regularly. The vitamin is in short supply in most of our diets. Vitamin E is an essential part of the whole circulatory mechanism of the body, since it affects our use of oxygen." (Ruth Adams and Frank Murray. Vitamin E: Wonder Worker of the 70's. New York: Larchmont Books, 1972, p. 17.)

14. *"There is nothing in the biorhythm theory that contradicts scientific knowledge. Biorhythm theory is totally consistent with the fundamental thesis of biology, which holds that all life consists of the discharge and creation of energy, or, in biorhythmic terms, an alteration of positive and negative phases. In addition, given that we are subjects to a host of smaller but nonetheless finely regulated biological rhythms, it seems reasonable that larger rhythms will also come with play."* (Bernard Gittelson. Biorhythms: A Personal Science. New York: Warner Books, 1977, p. 146.)

Unexpressed Premises

Arguments often depend on premises that the arguers do not state explicitly. These are termed unexpressed premises. Here is a simple example of an argument with an unexpressed premise: "John must be on a diet, because he refused dessert." Clearly, at the very least, the speaker is assuming: If John refused dessert, he must be on a diet. Using wedges (< >) to indicate the unexpressed premise and a solid line to separate the premises from the conclusion, we have:

> <If John refuses dessert, he must be on a diet.>
> John did refuse dessert.
>
> _____
>
> Therefore, he must be on a diet.

Here's another simple example: "Because the rate of violent crimes has increased since capital punishment was discontinued, capital punishment must be a deterrent to crime." In the argument, the arguer assumes that an increase in the violent crime rate following the discontinuance of capital punishment necessarily demonstrates that capital punishment is a deterrent to crime. Thus, the argument is:

> <If the rate of violent crimes increases after the discontinuance of a punishment, then the punishment is a deterrent to crime.>
> The rate of violent crimes did increase after the discontinuance of capital punishment.

————————————

Therefore, capital punishment is a deterrent to crime.

Here are two more examples:

ORIGINAL
ARGUMENT: *Beth is a merit scholar. So she must be smart.*

RECONSTRUCTION: *<All merit scholars are smart.>*
Beth is a merit scholar.

————————————

So Beth must be smart.

ORIGINAL
ARGUMENT: *Obviously the man is a stranger. After all, only a stranger would be in this neighborhood after dark.*

RECONSTRUCTION: *Only a stranger would be in this neighborhood after dark.*
<The man is in this neighborhood after dark.>

————————————

Obviously, the man is a stranger.

An unexpressed premise, then, is an assumption; that is, it is a judgment or opinion that a person takes to be true, even though the person is not certain—and perhaps can never be certain—that it is true. Unexpressed premises play an important part in advancing an argument. In order to understand and evaluate an argument, readers must be able to detect and make explicit its unexpressed premises. By the same token, writers must be aware of their unexpressed premises to ensure solid bases for their claims.

In dealing with unexpressed premises, readers face two big problems: reconstruction and evaluation. Reconstruction involves making the unexpressed premises explicit; evaluation involves assessing the truth of the premises. Since the chapters ahead deal extensively with premise evaluation, we needn't concern ourselves with that issue here. But before we can assess a premise in our own writing or that of others, we must be able to express it—to expose what lies hidden.

Reconstruction is no mean task. Indeed, it's a rather complex process with many pitfalls awaiting the unwary. Mastering the art of reconstruction really requires a formal study of logic, which this text is not intended to provide. But we can examine one quality of a faithful reconstruction that is most useful for writers and readers to keep in mind—relevancy.

Relevant Reconstructions Although a premise may go unstated, it is still a part of an argument. As such it must be directly related to the rest of the argument. If we reconstruct premises that are not relevant—that is, directly related to an argument—we misrepresent the argument.

For example, suppose a father tells his son: "You're going to State U. merely for the social life. Clearly, you won't do well academically." What's the unstated premise here? What is the father assuming to advance his assertion that his son will not do well academically at State U.?

The father may be assuming a number of things: that anyone who goes to college merely for the social life is unwise; that his son does not have the best motive for going to college; that social life should not enter into a person's choice to go to college. Indeed, if asked, the father might very well agree with any or all of these assumptions. But the issue concerns the unexpressed premise, which, together with the stated one ("You're going to State U. merely for the social life"), leads to the assertion that the son will not do well academically. The possibilities listed, in fact, are irrelevant; they are not related directly to the rest of the argument. Only one assumption is: Anyone who goes to State U. merely for the social life will not do well academically. It follows that, since the son is such a person, he will not do well academically at State U.

Take, as another example, an argument expressed by a student in an introductory philosophy course. Asked to state her opinion about the existence of God, Joy writes: "Since there is evil in the world, God does not exist." What must Joy be assuming that, together with the stated premise, entails the conclusion that God does not exist? Again, Joy may be assuming any number of things: that evil is undesirable; that floods, famines, sickness, and death represent evils in the world; that evil has always been in the world; and so forth. But no one of these assumptions, together with the stated premise, entails her contention; none of them represents a *relevant* reconstruction of her unstated premise. Rather, Joy must be assuming that evil in the world is incompatible with the existence of God. Thus, her argument is:

<If there is evil in the world, then God does not exist.>
There is evil in the world.

———————————

Therefore, God does not exist.

Having faithfully reconstructed her argument, we can begin to evaluate it intelligently. Moreover, being aware of her unexpressed premise, Joy should realize that at some point she must support not only the explicit premise (that there is evil in the world) but also the implied one (that evil is incompatible with God). Failing to detect her own unexpressed premise and the need to support it, she leaves her argument open to attack.

While there is no sure-fire way to ensure relevant reconstructions, making the reconstruction adhere strictly to the content of the stated premise and conclusion helps enormously. Notice, for example, that in Joy's argument a connection was established between evil in the world and the nonexistence of God. In the father's argument going to State U. for the social life was related to not doing well academically at State U. You can see the same fidelity to the content of the stated premise and conclusion in the other reconstructions. Adhering strictly to the content of what is expressed, then, is vital to relevant reconstruction. By ignoring or departing from the content we introduce premises that are not directly related to the argument.

Exercise

1.2   State the unexpressed premises in the following arguments. Ensure a relevant reconstruction.

1. I welcome laws protecting the patient's right to informed consent, for such laws serve as guards against malpractice suits.

2. Whatever threatens privacy threatens justice. That's why limitations on the Freedom of Information Act threaten justice.

3. Because dogs eat meat, they are considered carnivores.

4. Since church property is used to make a contribution to society, it should not be taxed.

5. Inasmuch as all participants are adults, some of the people leaving the stadium must not be participants.

6. **Bart:** We should increase our defense spending.
   Bea: Why is that?
   Bart: Because that's the only way to keep up with the Soviets.
   Bea: I see.

7. "Liberty means responsibility. That's why most men dread it." (George Bernard Shaw.)

8. "Yond Cassius has a lean and hungry look; . . . such men are dangerous." (Shakespeare, Julius Caesar.)

9. "The Brethren [referring to Supreme Court justices quoted anonymously in a book by that title] became sources in violation of trust, and so must be considered somewhat untrustworthy." (George F. Will. "The Injudicious Justices." Newsweek, December 10, 1979, p. 93.)

10. "This remarkable book [In the Belly of the Beast, by convict Jack Henry Abbott], unfortunately, will almost certainly allow further indulgence in one of our most inveterate fantasies Americans have so long and deeply romanticized—the loner, the outlaw, the truly tough man—that even when the humdrum horror of such lives is made clear, a residual glamour remains." (Terence Des Pres. "A Child of the State." New York Times Book Review, July 19, 1981, p. 3.)

11. "If you lie still [in the face of iniquitous government] you are considered as an accomplice in the measures in which you silently acquiesce. If you

resist you are accused of provoking irritable power to new excesses. The conduct of a losing party never appears right." (Edmund Burke.)

Premise Support

Consider the structural features of these two arguments, which deal with censorship:

ARGUMENT 1: *Censorship would be acceptable if it could be easily enforced. But censorship cannot be easily enforced. Therefore, censorship is not acceptable.*

ARGUMENT 2: *Censorship would be acceptable if it could be easily enforced. But censorship cannot be easily enforced. The main problem with enforcement is determining which works will not be censored. Therefore, censorship is not acceptable.*

Notice that the argument contained in the two examples is the same:

Censorship would be acceptable if it could be easily enforced.

Censorship cannot be easily enforced.

Therefore, censorship is not acceptable.

However, Argument 2 differs from Argument 1 in offering some support for the second premise. In effect, the arguer is saying that, if we take into account the problems inherent in identifying works not to be censored, there is good reason to regard censorship as unacceptable. Such support for an individual premise is another structural feature that many arguments have, and it really functions as a "mini-argument" within the main one.

Premise support is crucial in argument, because it underpins the premises, which, in turn, support the conclusion. If the premise support is inadequate, then the premises that undergird the conclusion collapse, and so does the conclusion itself. To a large degree, then, evaluating and formulating sound arguments depend on the strength of premise support.

Sometimes the support offered for a premise is inadequate. For example, in Argument 2 the support offered ("The main problem with enforcement is determining which work will not be censored") is minimal at best. It is unlikely that the audience will endorse such a controversial claim on the basis of such skimpy support. In contrast, consider the same argument with more developed support, as represented by the passage (not italicized) in the following paragraph:

15

> *Censorship would be acceptable if it could be easily enforced. But censorship is not easily enforced.* The main problem is determining which works will not be censored. For example, some have said that the "classics" will and should be exempt from censorship. But what is a "classic"? Any traditional definition probably would exclude new works, since a work usually cannot be recognized as a classic until some time after its release. That means that the censor must determine which works will become classics, surely an impossible task. As a result, censors will have little choice but to ban those "nonclassics" that smack of smut. If you think this is an idle fear, recall that plenty of works of art and literature that today are considered classics were once banned. Works by Chaucer, Shakespeare, Swift, and Twain are just a few. More recently William Faulkner, Ernest Hemingway, and James Joyce found their works banned. *There is no question, then, that determining which works will not be censored is a major, perhaps insurmountable, problem in enforcing censorship. Therefore, censorship is not acceptable.*

Here the author shows why determining which works will be censored is a real and pressing problem. As a result, he or she stands a far better chance of convincing the audience that censorship is unacceptable.

There is no simple way to determine how much support is needed to prop up a premise and, by implication, an argument's conclusion. But surely the more controversial the conclusion, the more support it will need. Premise support is especially vital in extended arguments—that is, the multiparagraph arguments that we commonly encounter in editorials, reviews, and essays and that we are called on to compose. Insofar as the following chapters deal largely with refining analytical and compositional skills, they take up the challenge of evaluating and developing sound premise support. It is enough here, therefore, simply to acknowledge premise support as an important part of the structure of an argument.

Exercise

1.3   Identify the conclusions, premises, and premise support in the following arguments:

1. "Nor is there anything smart about smoking. A woman who smokes is far more likely than her nonsmoking counterpart to suffer from a host of disabling conditions, any of which can interfere with her ability to perform at home or on the job. . . . Women who smoke have more spontaneous abortions, stillbirths, and premature babies than do nonsmokers, and their children's later health may be affected." (Jane E. Brody and Richard

16

Engquist. "Women and Smoking." *Public Affairs Pamphlet 475*. New York: Public Affairs Committee, 1972, p. 2.)

2. "Inundated by information surrounding the phenomenon [the unsolved murders of twenty-eight black persons in Atlanta between July 1979 and September 1981] but starved for hard facts by authorities' rigid 'no comment' posture, reporters sometimes grasped at straws of news. That happened in April, when reporters flocked to a press conference called by veteran civil-rights activist Roy Innis. Holding aloft an envelope that he said contained the photograph of a suspect, Innis refused to divulge the suspect's identity. Police refuted Innis' claim, but TV reported it with a minimum of qualification. Said one reporter in defense, 'When Innis said those things on the steps of City Hall, what did you want me to do—ignore him?' " (Jeff Prugh. "The Murders in Atlanta: Did TV Show Too Much—Or Too Little?" TV Guide, October 17–23, 1981, p. 8.)

3. "Since the mid '50's, for example, scientists have observed the same characteristics in what they thought were different cancer cells and concluded that these traits must be common to all cancers. All cancer cells had certain nutritional needs, all could grow in soft agar cultures, all could seed new solid tumors when transplanted into experimental animals, and all contained drastically abnormal chromosomes—the 'mark cancer.' " (Michael Gold. "The Cells That Would Not Die." San Francisco Chronicle, "This World," May 17, 1981, p. 9.)

4. "One woman told me that brown spots, a bugaboo to older women, were twice as numerous on the left side of her face and arm due to daily use of her car. The right, or interior, side of her face and right arm showed far fewer brown spots. Since these unattractive marks seem to be promoted by exposure to the sun, either cover up or use a good sunscreen." (Virginia Castleton. "Bring Out Your Beauty." Prevention: The Magazine for Better Health, September 1981, p. 108.)

5. "It also appears that suicide no longer repels us. The suicide rate is climbing, especially among blacks and young people. What's more, suicide has been appearing in an increasingly favorable light in the nation's press. When Paul Cameron surveyed all articles on suicide indexed over the past 50 years in the Reader's Guide to Periodical Literature, he found that voluntary death, once portrayed as a brutal waste, now generally appears in a neutral light. Some recent articles even present suicide as a good thing to do and are written in a manner that might encourage the reader to take his own life under certain circumstances. Last year, a majority of Americans under 30 told Gallup pollsters that incurable disease or continual pain confer on a person the moral right to end his life." (Elizabeth Hall with Paul Cameron. "Our Failing Reverence for Life." Psychology Today, April 1976, p. 108.)

INDUCTIVE ARGUMENTS

In speaking of argument, logicians and rhetoricians generally distinguish two kinds: inductive and deductive. We will consider them separately in order to isolate their characteristics, but we should not think of them as opposed. They are, in fact, complementary modes of reasoning and argument. Technically, inductive reasoning leads to probable or likely conclusions; deductive reasoning leads to logically certain conclusions. Considered in a formal sense, then, an inductive argument is one whose conclusion is held to be more or less probable; a deductive argument is one whose conclusion is held to follow from its premises with logical certainty. Although these definitions precisely distinguish between induction and deduction, they are not as useful to the student writer as a more conventional description that links induction and deduction to generalizations and specifics. Therefore, we will not adhere to the technically precise definitions but rather view induction and deduction within the context of forming generalizations.

Forming Generalizations

Broadly speaking, we can define inductive reasoning as reasoning from the specific to the general. In a typical inductive argument, then, the conclusion is always a generalization.

A generalization is a statement that covers many specifics. "When seat belts are used, traffic fatalities decrease." "If detected early enough, most cancers can be cured." "Apple trees grow better in the state of Washington than in Florida." These statements cover the specific instances of wearing seat belts, detecting cancer early, and growing apple trees in Washington and Florida. All are generalizations. Their conclusions are reached only after a few or many specific instances end with the same result.

It is impossible to say precisely how many specific instances are needed before a generalization based on them is warranted. Sometimes just one is enough to establish a good generalization. Thus, running out of gas once is enough to establish a good generalization: When a car runs out of gas, it won't run. Sometimes a few specifics are needed to establish a sound generalization. For example, annoyed with the knock in your car's engine, you switch to a high-octane gasoline. The knock vanishes. You return to using the first gas, and the knock recurs. When you again switch to the higher octane, the knock vanishes. On the basis of these few instances, you can form a generalization: My car performs without a knock with high-octane gasoline.

Sometimes a large number of specific instances are needed before forming a sound generalization. For example, if a company wanted to find out if its commercials affected sales, it would have to undertake an extensive study of specifics to draw an acceptable generalization. Again, if a college wanted to find out if its ethics courses resulted in any behavioral changes for the students who took them, it would have to consider many specifics.

There are even times when no reasonable number of specifics is enough to establish an unqualified generalization. For example, it is sometimes said that women don't make good engineers. But such a generalization about a gender trait is simply unwarranted on the basis of a few specifics. At best a qualified generalization would have to be established. It is important in understanding induction and in writing to distinguish between unqualified and qualified generalizations.

An unqualified generalization is a statement that asserts that something is true of all members of a class. Examples of unqualified generalizations are "All humans are mammals," "Men can't bear children," "No human can remain under water very long without air," "An object maintains its line of direction until acted on by some outside force," "All known life needs oxygen to survive," and "Every instance of human decapitation results in death." In each statement a property is attributed to every member of its class. Sometimes a universal quantifier, such as *all, every,* or *no,* is not stated but implied. Thus, "Humans are vertebrates" and "Voters are citizens" imply that every human or every voter is intended. Because of their categorical application, unqualified generalizations are sometimes termed universal generalizations.

In contrast, *a qualified generalization is a statement that asserts that something is true of a percentage of a class.* Unqualified generalizations never speak of every member of a class but only of some. "Seventy-five percent of the voters favor the president's economic program," "Most of the students in this class are business majors," and "A large number of doctors are opposed to abortion-on-demand" all qualify as qualified generalizations, which are sometimes termed statistical generalizations.

Notice that a qualified generalization is so stated as not to apply to all the specifics that it could cover. The unqualified statement "Women make good nurses" must apply to every individual woman, a patent falsehood. But the qualified versions "Many women make good nurses" and "Women often make good nurses" are easily confirmed by observation of specifics. Generalizations are qualified when they include a word or a phrase such as *many, almost always, sometimes, often, mostly, usually, ordinarily, typically, under certain circumstances, rarely, a few, at times,* and the like. Whether the generalization is qualified or unqualified, it is the product of inductive thinking, which requires some elaboration.

Three Kinds of Generalization

There are basically three kinds of generalization: inductive, pseudoinductive, and noninductive. We use and abuse all three in argument.

Inductive   *An inductive generalization is a statement that is based on observed specifics.* Many inductive generalizations are false, however, because of misrepresentation of evidence, either by a person or a group of people. For example, suppose you find a course in Elizabethan drama boring; so does everyone else who took it. On the basis of these specifics you decide never again to read Shakespeare or perhaps never again to take a course in drama. Even later pleasant experiences with Elizabethan drama (for example, seeing *Hamlet* expertly performed) might not be enough to dislodge from your mind this inductive generalization that you so quickly formed on the basis of a few observed specifics.

Large groups of people also can misinterpret evidence and then form a false inductive generalization. A classic example is found in anthropology. Anthropologists studying a South Seas tribe found its members believing that body lice advanced good health. In fact, every healthy person had body lice, and most sick people didn't. Clearly there was a correlation between having lice and being healthy. But lice didn't promote health. Being healthy caused a person to have lice.

Pseudoinductive   Sometimes people don't misinterpret observed specifics but rather accept as evidence what is irrelevant—that is, what is not evidence at all. This kind of reasoning leads to pseudoinductive generalizations. *A pseudoinductive generalization is one that people think is based on observed specifics but that is not.* For example, a person who spends thirty dollars in a supermarket in ten minutes forms the pseudoinductive generalization that inflation is "out of control." But the time it takes to spend money is no measure of the inflation rate. Obviously, if we had the money, we could spend thousands of dollars in a few minutes on, say, a Mercedes or a Bentley. But that wouldn't indicate how severe inflation was.

Similarly, a politician may base opposition to capital punishment on the fact that a disproportionately large number of minority-group members are sentenced to death. But the observed specifics speak more to a problem of inequity in sentencing than to the legitimacy of the death penalty as a form of punishment.

Noninductive   Besides inductive and pseudoinductive generalizations there are those that people form that are not inductive at all, for they are not based on any observed specifics. These are called noninductive generalizations. *A noninductive generalization can be said to be largely derived from one's cultural system—that is, from assumptions about religion, politics, economics, social behavior, and so on.* We absorb thousands of these assumptions from our society in the process of growing up. Here are some commonly held noninductive generalizations: "Democracy is the best form of government." "Communism and socialism are evil." "There exists a single God who is all good and all powerful and who intervenes in the lives of His creations." "The two-party system is the best way to structure our political system." "We should never intentionally put to death the old and infirm." "If people just try hard enough, they can succeed." "Anybody can grow up to be president of the United States." "People should marry for love, not money." "Nice girls don't go to bed with a boy on the first date, perhaps not before marriage at all." "Women are passive and men, aggressive." "It's OK for males to be promiscuous but not females." The list goes on, but in each case it is not so much observed specifics that lead one to these generalizations but orientation to a particular aspect of culture. Blindly accepting such generalizations leads to selective perception—that is, to seeing only what we want to see.

DEDUCTIVE   ARGUMENTS

Induction involves forming generalizations based on observed specifics. In contrast, *deduction is the reasoning process by which we reach a specific conclusion rather than a generalization.* In a typical deductive argument, then, the conclusion is a specific. Thus, whereas induction ordinarily involves reasoning from the specific to the general, deduction usually moves from the general to the specific. Looked at another way, in deduction we make use of the generalizations that we form by induction.

To distinguish better between deduction and induction and to see how they are complementary reasoning processes, consider this simple example. Suppose you go to the refrigerator wanting something to eat. You see a bag of apples. Picking up an apple and biting into it, you find that it's sour. You notice, too, that it is hard and green. You pick out another and find that it also is hard and green—and sour. You rummage through the bag and find that all the remaining apples also are hard and green. You *induce*—that is, form the generalization—that all the apples in the bag are sour.

Suppose that a little later someone else opens the refrigerator and offers you one of the apples. Your mind, quickly and perhaps unconsciously, reasons this way: "All hard and green apples in the bag are sour. This apple I'm being offered is hard and green and taken from the bag. Therefore, this apple is sour." Not liking sour apples, you politely refuse. In this case you have reasoned *deductively.* You started with a generalization and ended with a specific conclusion.

Although we are rarely conscious of the logical processes involved, each of us daily reaches or acts on hundreds of specific conclusions—deductions— whose origins are the generalizations stored in our minds. The reasoning processes whereby we decide which specific courses to take, films to see, books to read, food to eat, friends to choose, places to visit, causes to support and viewpoints to hold can usually be traced back to the generalizations that we consciously or unconsciously deposit in our minds and draw on when the need arises. The generalizations may be ours, in the sense that we have formed them based on our own direct experience; or they may be somebody else's— that is, generalizations that we have accepted based on the testimony of an outside party. The soundness of these stored generalizations largely determines the soundness of our decisions and greatly affects the quality of our life.

Generalizations and Deductions

To see better the connection between generalizations and deductions and how influential our generalizations are, let's consider a few examples. Suppose that you decide to cut your English class half a dozen times. On each occasion you have reached a specific conclusion, or deduction, that cutting English class won't hurt you very much. Whether or not you're aware of it, at some time in the past you must have (perhaps unconsciously) put into your head the generalization that cutting English class will not hurt you. Your generalization may or may not be sound. Nonetheless, you use it in the process of deduction.

Similarly, another student cheats on a math exam. His cheating is the product of a deduction, but the generalization he started with is that cheating on a math exam will do him some good. Still another student arrives early on the first day of a psychology class to ensure that she gets a seat in the front. She has, in effect, deduced that she should sit up front. But the generalization she started with is that sitting up front in a psychology class (perhaps any class) will benefit her.

Clearly, a good many of our deductions help get us through life safely and successfully. For instance, knowing that driving on a wet pavement can be dangerous, you act when the road is wet on the deduction that you need to drive slowly. Realizing that caffeine keeps you awake nights, you deduce on many occasions that you must decline that inviting second cup of coffee after dinner. Again, recognizing that a college education is valuable in "getting ahead," you deduce that you must complete college at any cost.

By the same token, our deductions can be harmful. For example, a young man disappointed in love deduces that an attractive young woman will eventually hurt him. So he doesn't give the relationship a chance to develop. Likewise, a girl forms the generalization that, if she appears too intelligent, boys won't like her. As a result, she deduces that she ought to suppress her superior intelligence around a boy she's fond of.

We can hurt not only ourselves through faulty generalizations but others as well. A personnel director, for example, may hold the false generalization that there is little point in training women for a job, because they will leave within three years. He deduces that he should not hire Alice Malloy, despite her impeccable qualifications. A dyed-in-the-wool Democrat (or Republican) has formed the faulty generalization that only Democrats (or Republicans) are competent to hold office. From this the party chauvinist deduces that a specific candidate from an opposing party isn't even worth considering for office. In fact, the candidate may be the best qualified of the alternatives. In brief, countless instances of prejudice are really deductions based on false or improperly qualified generalizations that mask sweeping prejudices.

Clearly, generalizations affect our lives. Moreover, rarely do we form a deduction that is not based on a generalization. Induction and deduction, then, are intimately connected. They should not be viewed as antagonistic or

22

incompatible but rather complementary. The legitimacy of our specific applications depends largely on the soundness of our generalizations.

Exercise

1.4   Identify the generalization in the following arguments. Do you think that the writer is forming the generalization (induction) or inferring a specific from the generalization (deduction)? In each case, tell what kind of generalization is being used—inductive, pseudoinductive, or noninductive.

1. Most chain smokers stand a very good chance of getting lung cancer. So I must admit that, since I'm a chain smoker, I run a serious risk of cancer.

2. Children should be seen, not heard. That's why I don't want you to say anything this evening, Joey, when the adults are here.

3. Inasmuch as more than half of all automobile accidents involve drivers under twenty-five, it follows that drivers under twenty-five are probably a greater driving risk than those over twenty-five.

4. The presidential candidate whom Maine selects is usually the one who'll be elected. So it's safe to say, "As Maine goes, so goes the nation."

5. Every class I've taken so far this year has had more females than males in it. I'd venture to say, then, that females probably outnumber males at this institution.

6. If the president stands for reelection, she'll surely win. Nobody even doubts that the president will stand for reelection. Therefore, it's clear that the incumbent will win the election.

7. The likelihood that there are atmospheric conditions similar to earth's elsewhere in the universe are very high. Therefore, extraterrestrial life probably exists.

8. Inasmuch as we can know only our own experiences of things, I can't be sure that this book really exists.

9. It's unwise to exceed posted speed limits, for statistics indicate that speeders have a greater chance of having accidents than those who don't speed.

10. "The coarsest type of humor is the practical joke: pulling away the chair from under the dignitary's lowered bottom. The victim is perceived, first as a person of consequence, then suddenly as an inert body subject to the laws of physics: authority is debunked by gravity, mind by matter; man is degraded to mechanism." (Arthur Koestler. Janus: A Summing Up. New York: Random House, 1978, pp. 122–23.)

11. "Like the American philosophers William James and John Dewey, the existential philosophers are appealing from the conclusions of 'Rational-

istic' thinking which equates Reality with the object of thought, with relations of 'essences,' to Reality as men experience it immediately in their actual living. They consequently take their place with all those who have regarded man's immediate experience as revealing more completely the nature and traits of Reality than man's cognitive experience." (Paul Tillich. "Existential Philosophy." Journal of the History of Ideas, vol. 5, 1944, p. 48.)

12. *Jocasta (speaking to Oedipus):*

> But why should men be fearful,
> O'er whom Fortune is mistress, and foreknowledge
> Of nothing sure? Best take life easily,
> As a man may. For that maternal wedding,
> Have no fear; for many men ere now
> Have dreamed as much; but he who by such dreams
> Sets nothing, has the easiest time of it.
>
> —Sophocles, *Oedipus Rex*

THE STRUCTURE OF A DEDUCTION: THE SYLLOGISM

We have seen that generalizations are used to reach specific conclusions, or deductions. Thus, having formed the generalization that literature courses are interesting, you deduce that you will take the Hemingway course offered in the spring. From this example and some of the others that we've dealt with you might assume that deductions are always a two-part logical process: generalization followed by specific conclusion. Actually, however, deduction is a three-part process, which is termed a syllogism.

A syllogism is a deductive argument that contains two premises and a conclusion. Here is a syllogism we met earlier:

All students in the class are members of the debate team.

Annie is a student in the class.

Therefore, Annie is a member of the debate team.

The first statement in this or any syllogism is termed the major premise. *The major premise typically is a generalization that covers all or some members of a class.* The second statement is called the minor premise. *The minor premise usually identifies some specific as a member of the category covered in the major premise.* The conclusion of the syllogism is the deduction that

24

results from the application of the generalization of the major premise to the specific of the minor premise.

Many times in reasoning and writing we use the deduction of one syllogism as the major premise for another deduction, then use that deduction as the major premise for still another, and so on to the final idea we are seeking. For example, suppose that two persons decide to live together before marriage. Here's how the couple might have reached that deduction:

MAJOR PREMISE: *Any premarital arrangement that allows a couple to learn as much about each other as possible is desirable.*

MINOR PREMISE: *Living together before marriage allows a couple to learn as much about each other as possible.*

CONCLUSION: *Living together before marriage is desirable.*

In relation to its major premise, this conclusion is a specific. But in another sense it is a generalization, though admittedly less broad than the major premise because it is concerned with *one* premarital arrangement rather than *any* premarital arrangement. In this second sense, as a generalization, this conclusion might be used as the major premise of another argument that builds on the first. Thus, the couple might have continued the argument this way:

MAJOR PREMISE: *Living together before marriage is desirable.*

MINOR PREMISE: *We will do whatever is desirable.*

CONCLUSION: *We will live together before marriage.*

The couple's major premise in this second argument is the conclusion of the first deduction. In the same way, the couple might build still another argument, this time using the conclusion of the second argument as, say, the minor premise in a third. Thus:

MAJOR PREMISE: *Couples who live together before marriage should be quite clear about each other's rights and responsibilities.*

MINOR PREMISE: *We will live together before marriage.*

CONCLUSION: *We should be quite clear about each other's rights and responsibilities.*

Here is another example of a multiple syllogism, in which the conclusion of one deduction is used as the premise for another:

MAJOR PREMISE: *Films full of senseless violence are objectionable.*

MINOR PREMISE: *The film showing at the Cinema Six is full of senseless violence.*

CONCLUSION: *The film showing at the Cinema Six is objectionable.*

MAJOR PREMISE: *The film showing at the Cinema Six is objectionable.*

MINOR PREMISE: *I never see objectionable films.*

CONCLUSION: *I will not see the film at the Cinema Six.*

Frequently in arguing, especially in longer arguments, people string together arguments but leave premises unexpressed. For example, someone might say: "The film showing at the Cinema Six is objectionable, because it's full of violence. So I won't see it." Embedded in this assertion are the two preceding arguments. Before the audience or author could evaluate the argument, the unexpressed premises would have to be flushed out; each of the arguments would have to be assessed. Again, suppose someone said: "I don't take tough courses. So I'll have to shop around for another science course besides physics." Embedded in this assertion are two arguments:

MAJOR PREMISE: *I don't take tough courses.*

MINOR PREMISE: *<Physics is a tough course.>*

CONCLUSION: *I'm not taking physics.*

MAJOR PREMISE: *<Whoever doesn't take physics must shop around for another science course.>*

MINOR PREMISE: *I'm not taking physics.*

CONCLUSION: *I'll have to shop around for another science course.*

So the conclusions that we reach through the logical process of deduction often function as premises in other deductions. What's more, people often express strings of arguments in which premises, even conclusions, go unexpressed. In order to assess the argument, then, it is crucial to make what is implied explicit.

Exercises

1.5 *Following are five syllogisms. Use the conclusion of each as either a major or minor premise in another syllogism.*

1. MAJOR PREMISE: *Competition brings out the best in a person.*

    MINOR PREMISE: *Grades encourage competition.*

    CONCLUSION: *Grades bring out the best in people.*

2.   MAJOR PREMISE: American consumers should buy only products made in the United States.

   MINOR PREMISE: BMWs are not made in the United States.

   CONCLUSION: American consumers should not buy BMWs.

3.   MAJOR PREMISE: The Equal Rights Amendment respects traditional American values.

   MINOR PREMISE: The electorate should endorse whatever respects traditional American values.

   CONCLUSION: The electorate should endorse the ERA.

4.   MAJOR PREMISE: The U.N. should oppose all terrorist actions.

   MINOR PREMISE: Terrorist actions include most skyjackings.

   CONCLUSION: The U.N. should oppose most skyjackings.

5.   MAJOR PREMISE: Any educated person knows how to write well.

   MINOR PREMISE: Jones can't write well.

   CONCLUSION: Jones is not an educated person.

1.6   By suppressing premises, compress each pair of the preceding arguments into a sentence or two. For example, suppose this were the pair:

   MAJOR PREMISE: All humans are mortal.

   MINOR PREMISE: Smith is a human.

   CONCLUSION: Smith is a mortal.

   MAJOR PREMISE: Whoever is mortal is subject to the laws of nature.

   MINOR PREMISE: Smith is a mortal.

   CONCLUSION: Smith is subject to the laws of nature.

Compressed: Smith is subject to the laws of nature because, like all other humans, Smith is a mortal.

1.7   Write the two syllogisms that are embedded in each of the following arguments:

1. Students who study argument make good writers, because students of argument are bright and bright people have something to say.

2. Insofar as politicians are opportunistic, they are self-interested. This means that they cannot be expected to do what is best for their constituents.

3. Since "docudramas" are entertainment, they do not report events accurately. Therefore, one should view docudramas skeptically.

4. No law that infringes on the First Amendment is constitutional. That's why the courts will never uphold any law that requires reporters to divulge their sources.

5. Inasmuch as inflation is a serious problem, all workers must be concerned about it. In the final analysis, then, workers should moderate their demands for higher wages.

FALLACIES

A sound argument is one in which (1) the premises are true and (2) the reasoning process is correct—that is, valid. Sound arguments, then, have both truth and validity. Obviously, not all arguments are sound. Sometimes the premises are false or questionable, or the reasoning process is incorrect. Logicians and rhetoricians call an unsound argument fallacious. A fallacy is an incorrect argument—that is, an argument that may seem to be correct but is not. Fallacies may be formal or informal.

Formal

Formal fallacies pertain to incorrect procedures in the reasoning process. When the reasoning process is correct, the premises entail the conclusion, and the argument is said to be valid. But when the reasoning process is incorrect, the premises do not entail the conclusion, and the argument is said to be invalid. Note well that validity refers to the reasoning process or the form of an argument; it does not pertain to the truth of the premises.

Because a proper consideration of formal fallacies is complex, it is best left for the study of logic. But you should pay special attention to the scope of the generalization that you are applying to specific instances. For example, there is an important difference in scope between the following two statements:

NONEXCLUSIVE: All seniors study Shakespeare.

EXCLUSIVE: Only seniors study Shakespeare.

The first generalization includes all seniors, but it doesn't exclude anybody else. Thus, if you learn that Brenda is studying Shakespeare, you can validly infer: "Brenda could be a senior." You would be incorrect, however, to infer that Brenda must be, or necessarily is, a senior. The second generalization ("Only seniors study Shakespeare") is much more restrictive. If you learn that Brenda is studying Shakespeare, then you can correctly infer from the second generalization: "Brenda must be a senior." Indeed, based on the second generalization, you have logical grounds for inferring that Tim, Blanche, Preston, or any other individual studying Shakespeare is a senior.

Valid deductions are entailed by the premises. To draw valid conclusions, then, we must remember that generalizations may apply to some members of a group but not all. They may apply to all members of a group and no one else or to all members of a group and others also. The following arguments alert you to some common problems in applying generalizations to specific cases:

MAJOR PREMISE: *Some students are intelligent.*

MINOR PREMISE: *Marcia is a student.*

INVALID
CONCLUSION: *Marcia is intelligent.*

VALID
CONCLUSION: *Marcia may be intelligent.*

Since the premises speak only of some students, we have no way of knowing whether Marcia is one of those students who is intelligent. Therefore, we have no basis for drawing an unqualified conclusion.

MAJOR PREMISE: *All students are intelligent.*

MINOR PREMISE: *Marcia is intelligent.*

INVALID
CONCLUSION: *Marcia is a student.*

VALID
CONCLUSION: *Marcia may be a student.*

The premises are not speaking of everyone who is intelligent. In other words, although intelligence may be a characteristic of all students, being intelligent does not necessarily make one a student. Therefore, the premises provide no basis for an unqualified conclusion. The best we can say is that Marcia may be a student.

MAJOR PREMISE: *Only students are intelligent.*

MINOR PREMISE: *Marcia is a student.*

INVALID
CONCLUSION: *Marcia is intelligent.*

VALID
CONCLUSION: *Marcia may be intelligent.*

29

The major premise is asserting that all intelligent people are students ("Only students are intelligent"). Even if Marcia is a student, she is not necessarily intelligent.

MAJOR PREMISE: *Only students are intelligent.*

MINOR PREMISE: *Marcia is intelligent.*

INVALID
CONCLUSION: *Marcia may be a student.*

VALID
CONCLUSION: *Marcia is a student.*

Since the major premise asserts that every intelligent person is a student, Marcia must be a student if she is intelligent. Therefore, a qualified conclusion ("may be") is unwarranted.

MAJOR PREMISE: *No students arc intelligent.*

MINOR PREMISE: *Brenda is not a student.*

INVALID
CONCLUSION: *Brenda is intelligent.*

VALID
CONCLUSION: *Brenda may be intelligent.*

Although the major premise excludes intelligence from every student, it does not refer to the nonstudent population. Therefore, we have no basis for drawing the unqualified conclusion that Brenda is intelligent. She may be.

Informal

Informal fallacies are commonplace errors in reasoning that we fall into because of careless use of language or inattention to subject matter. Whereas formal fallacies pertain to the reasoning process itself, informal fallacies refer to the content of our assertions. The soundness of our thinking and argument depends not only on valid procedure but also on using true premises. If either of the premises of an argument is false, then the conclusion is not a sound one. For example, coming across the name of Justice Sandra O'Connor in an article, a student infers that O'Connor must be a male. The student's syllogism might appear as follows:

MAJOR PREMISE: *All Supreme Court justices are males.*

MINOR PREMISE: *O'Connor is a Supreme Court justice.*

CONCLUSION: *O'Connor must be a male.*

Although the student has paid attention to the scope of the generalization (major premise) in applying it, the major premise happens to be false. Not all Supreme Court justices are males. Thus, the argument is valid (that is, the reasoning procedure is correct) but unsound, because one of its premises is false.

But the premises need not be patently false for a deduction to be unsound. Take, for example, the deduction that abortion laws are unjust. The syllogism that leads to this conclusion might appear as follows:

MAJOR PREMISE: *A law that in any way restricts a woman's right to have an abortion is unjust.*

MINOR PREMISE: *Current abortion laws restrict the woman's right to have an abortion.*

CONCLUSION: *Therefore, current abortion laws are unjust.*

Again, there is no problem here with validity: *Assuming* the premises are true, the conclusion is entailed. Nor is the problem with any patent falsehood in the premises. Nevertheless, the major premise is open to question. Why are restrictive abortion laws unjust? Why is it necessarily more just to allow a woman to have an abortion on demand than to prohibit that? Just what is meant by "right" in a "woman's right" to have an abortion? Because one of the premises is open to serious doubt, the soundness of the argument is in question.

There are literally hundreds of ways that informal fallacies creep into arguments. Because writing and evaluating arguments depend in large part on being able to detect and eliminate these commonplace errors, we will thoroughly examine informal fallacies in the pages ahead.

Exercises

1.8   *The following syllogisms may be unsound, because (1) the reasoning procedure is invalid or (2) the premises are false or questionable. Identify the error, if any, and explain.*

1. MAJOR PREMISE: *All eighteen-year-old males must register for the draft.*
   MINOR PREMISE: *Jeff is an eighteen-year-old male.*
   CONCLUSION: *Jeff must register for the draft.*

2. MAJOR PREMISE: *A Republican administration always causes a recession.*
   MAJOR PREMISE: *The Reagan administration is Republican.*
   CONCLUSION: *The Reagan administration will cause a recession.*

3. MAJOR PREMISE: Smoking pot leads to drug addition.
   MINOR PREMISE: Many young people smoke pot.
   CONCLUSION: Many young people will become drug addicts.

4. MAJOR PREMISE: Dramatists usually have vivid imaginations.
   MINOR PREMISE: Neil Simon is a dramatist.
   CONCLUSION: Neil Simon must have a vivid imagination.

5. MAJOR PREMISE: Killing another human is never justifiable.
   MINOR PREMISE: Self-defense sometimes involves killing.
   CONCLUSION: Self-defense sometimes isn't justifiable.

6. MAJOR PREMISE: Thousands of young couples today are living together before marrying.
   MINOR PREMISE: Ted and June are living together before marrying.
   CONCLUSION: Ted and June must be a young couple.

7. MAJOR PREMISE: The brighter a person is, the better grades the person will make in this class.
   MINOR PREMISE: I'm brighter than anyone else in this class.
   CONCLUSION: I will make higher grades in this class than anyone else.

8. MAJOR PREMISE: Whenever the temperature dips below freezing, precipitation takes the form of snow.
   MINOR PREMISE: The temperature tonight is below freezing.
   CONCLUSION: Any precipitation tonight will take the form of snow.

9. MAJOR PREMISE: Most athletes are in super physical condition.
   MINOR PREMISE: A number of the class members are athletes.
   CONCLUSION: A number of the class members are in super shape.

10. MAJOR PREMISE: A square has four sides.
    MINOR PREMISE: This polygon has four sides.
    CONCLUSION: This polygon is a square.

11. MAJOR PREMISE: Many children from broken homes develop emotional problems.
    MINOR PREMISE: Rod is a child from a broken home.
    CONCLUSION: Rod will develop emotional problems.

12. MAJOR PREMISE: *Any good argument is at least understandable.*

    MINOR PREMISE: *What Jan just said was as clear as crystal.*

    CONCLUSION: *What Jan just said is a good argument.*

13. MAJOR PREMISE: *No Christian believes that Jesus was a mere man.*

    MINOR PREMISE: *Many people who consider themselves spiritual believe that Jesus was a mere man.*

    CONCLUSION: *Many people who consider themselves spiritual are not Christians.*

14. MAJOR PREMISE: *Several fruits are highly acidic.*

    MINOR PREMISE: *A grapefruit is a fruit.*

    CONCLUSION: *A grapefruit is highly acidic.*

15. MAJOR PREMISE: *Professor Kinkaid's field is economics.*

    MINOR PREMISE: *Professors are usually competent in their fields.*

    CONCLUSION: *Chances are that Professor Kinkaid is competent in economics.*

16. MAJOR PREMISE: *No male can bear children.*

    MINOR PREMISE: *Sally is not a male.*

    CONCLUSION: *Sally can bear children.*

1.9   Starting with the following conclusions, invent proper major and minor premises to create sound syllogisms. If you wish, you may qualify the conclusions. Following is a sample:

CONCLUSION: *Jack will probably get into the graduate school of his choice.*

MAJOR PREMISE: *Students who graduate from college with a 4.0 grade point average can ordinarily get into the graduate schools of their choice.*

MINOR PREMISE: *Jack will graduate from college with a 4.0 grade point average.*

CONCLUSION: *Jack will probably get into the graduate school of his choice.*

1. Harry is going to fail this course.

2. The Arabs and Israelis will probably be warring again in the near future.

3. A Democrat will be our next president.

4. The Bickersons' marriage won't last long.

5. *Norman will probably major in nursing.*

6. *There will be a brawl at the football game tonight.*

7. *Professor Berenson will teach the American literature course in the fall.*

8. *Unemployment will rise in the next eighteen months.*

1.10 *Prepare full syllogisms for each of the arguments in Exercise 1.3.*

RELIABLE AND EFFECTIVE
GENERALIZATIONS

In the forthcoming chapters we will, in effect, be examining the rules and procedures for checking the reliability of generalizations. But it would be appropriate to conclude this chapter with a few guidelines for recognizing and making reliable and effective generalizations.

First, since a good generalization is always based on observed specifics, always ask how complete the evidence is. What proportion of the total number of relevant cases has been examined? This is especially important when the class referred to includes a vast number of subcategories.

For example, consider the generalization "Most college graduates make more money in a lifetime than noncollege graduates." Even qualified, the category "college graduates" includes many subcategories—that is, individuals who differ from one another in many ways. Thus, there are college graduates who attended an Ivy League college, college graduates who entered a field directly related to their majors, female college graduates, and so on. A sample that overlooks the many subcategories within the group "college graduates" misrepresents the group itself. Deductions based on it are, therefore, logically suspect—even if they turn out to be true.

Second, always make sure that the specifics on which the generalization rests are representative—that is, that the observed cases are typical of the total population of cases. For example, it would be erroneous to infer, on the basis of the salaries of famous actresses, that the average working woman makes about the same as her male counterpart. The sample simply is not typical of working women as a whole.

Although these guidelines are useful when reading, they also apply to writing effective generalizations. Writing argumentative essays, as we will shortly see, requires the skillful use of generalizations. Argumentative writers must reason inductively and deductively and make use of both kinds of argument in presenting their cases. More specifically, argumentative writing largely involves the skillful manipulation of generalizations. Sometimes writers build to a generalization, as they might when arguing the merits of gun control legislation. Thus, having offered a series of reasons, the writer forms the generalization that there ought (or ought not) to be gun control. At other times writers begin with a generalization and attempt to draw a deduction from it. For example, a writer might try to make use of the generalization that people should not injure others in order to deduce that, in at least some cases, euthanasia is not only permissible but obligatory. Whether writers make effective generalizations depends very much on their adherence to the two qualities just mentioned—completeness and representativeness of generalization.

In order to ensure completeness and representativeness, anchor your generalizations to representative examples. Show the reader the connection between your generalization and the observations and experiences from which it was derived. Ideally, you should back up each generalization with a fair sampling of the evidence behind it. Certainly you must take special pains to do this when the contention is a controversial one (for example, "The United States should unilaterally disarm in order to ensure world peace," "All forms of nontherapeutic abortion should be prohibited," "Solar energy is preferable to nuclear energy," and so on). Writers use various ways to support generalizations: by a solid listing of facts and figures; by using outstanding familiar examples; or by citing authentic examples that will strike the reader as typical or representative. Here's an example of each:

USE OF FACTS AND FIGURES: *"The National Commission on Diabetes, a panel appointed by Congress to study the problem, reported in 1975 that diabetes and its complications cause more than 300,000 deaths in the United States each year, making it the third leading cause of death, behind heart disease and cancer. The number of diabetics in the United States is doubling every fifteen years. A newborn child now faces a 1-in-5 chance of developing diabetes. Ironically, this increase is a direct result of improvement in the treatment of the disease. Diabetics who once might have died young or during periods of stress, such as giving birth, are now living relatively normal lives. They are bearing children who are more likely to develop diabetes." (Thomas H. Maugh II. "The Two Faces of Diabetes." Science Year, 1978. Chicago: Field Enterprises Educational Corporation, 1979, p. 58.)*

USE OF OUTSTANDING FAMILIAR EXAMPLES: *"The average athlete begins to wonder when his career is going to end almost as soon as he starts. He knows that it either can be shortened with devastating swiftness by an injury, or eventually reach the point at which the great skills begin to erode. As time goes on, and the broadcasters begin to refer to the athlete as a 'veteran' and the club begins to use high draft choices to acquire young collegians to groom for his position, the player has to decide whether to cut it clean and retire at the top—as Rocky Marciano, the heavyweight champion, did—or wait for some sad moment—Willie Mays stumbling around in the outfield reaches of Candlestick Park—when the evidence is clear not only to oneself but to one's peers that the time is up." (George Plimpton. "The Final Season." Harper's, January 1972, p. 62.)*

USE OF TYPICAL EXAMPLES: *"In our society, food is often connected with recreation. We go out for coffee, invite friends over for drinks, celebrate special occasions with cakes or big meals. We can't think of baseball without thinking of hot dogs and beer, and eating is so often an accompaniment to watching TV that we talk of TV snacks and TV dinners. Just as Pavlov's dogs learned to salivate at the sound of a bell, the activities we associate with food can become signals to eat. Watching TV becomes a signal for coffee and doughnuts; nodding over a book tells us it's time for pie and milk." (Michael J. Mahoney and Kathryn Mahoney. "Fight Fat with Behavior Control." Psychology Today, May 1976, p. 43.)*

Whatever the strategy, the goal is the same—to show the reader the connection between the generalization and the observations and experiences from which it was derived. In the chapters ahead we will inspect these techniques as we explore the argumentative essay.

SUMMARY

This chapter dealt with argument and gave particular attention to the generalization. An argument is a group of propositions, one of which is held to follow from the others. Four elements of an argument's structure are noteworthy:

1. *Premises and conclusions.* The conclusion of an argument is the statement that is held to follow from the premises. The premise is the statement that is held to entail the conclusion. *Reasons* and *evidence* are synonymous with *premises.*

EXAMPLE (WITH PREMISE ITALICIZED): *Most people favor the legalization of marijuana. That's why* marijuana should be legalized.

2. *Signal words.* Signal words are terms that indicate the presence of a premise or conclusion. Some typical premise signals: *since, because, for, for*

the reason that, inasmuch as. Some typical conclusion signals: *therefore, thus, consequently, it follows that, accordingly, hence.*

3. *Unexpressed premises.* Unexpressed premises are assumptions that arguers do not state explicitly but that serve as premises in their arguments.

> EXAMPLE: *Jack must be on a diet, because he refused dessert.*
> *Assumption:<If Jack refused dessert, he must be on a diet.>*

In reconstructing premises it is crucial to ensure relevancy—that is, to ensure that the reconstruction, together with the expressed premise, actually entails the conclusion.

4. *Premise support.* Premise support is material provided to back up a premise.

> EXAMPLE: *Censorship would be acceptable if it could be easily en-*
> *forced. But censorship is not easily enforced. The main*
> *problem is determining which works will not be censored.*
> For example, some have said that the classics . . .

There are two kinds of argument: inductive and deductive. In a typical inductive argument the conclusion is a generalization. A generalization is a statement that covers many specifics. An unqualified generalization is a statement that asserts that something is true of all members of a class (for example, "All humans are vertebrates" or "Men can't bear children"). A qualified generalization is a statement that asserts that something is true of a percentage of a class (for example, "Seventy-five percent of the voters favor the president's economic program" or "Most of the students in the class are business majors"). There are basically three kinds of generalizations—inductive, pseudoinductive, and noninductive.

A typical deductive argument is one whose conclusion is a specific. Although we are rarely conscious of the logical processes involved, each of us reaches or acts on hundreds of specific deductions every day. The origins of these specific conclusions are the generalizations stored in our mind. Used properly, generalizations are useful in ensuring a safe and successful life; used improperly, they can injure ourselves and others.

Deduction is a three-part logical process termed a syllogism. A syllogism is a deductive argument consisting of two premises and a conclusion. The first statement is called the major premise and typically is a qualified or unqualified generalization. The second statement is called the minor premise and usually identifies some specific member of the category covered in the major premise. The third statement is the conclusion. For example:

MAJOR PREMISE: *All students in the class are members of the debate team.*

MINOR PREMISE: *Annie is a member of the class.*

CONCLUSION: *Therefore, Annie is a member of the debate team.*

Often the conclusion of any deductive argument can function as the premise of another argument.

The many ways that an argument can be unsound are termed fallacies. Fallacies—incorrect argument—may be formal or informal. Formal fallacies are incorrect procedures in reasoning. Given their complexity, formal fallacies are best left to a study of logic. In general, though, we must pay careful attention to the scope of generalizations in applying them to specific instances. Informal fallacies are commonplace errors in reasoning that we fall into because of careless use of language or inattention to subject matter. We will focus on informal fallacies in the chapters ahead and show how they undercut argumentative writing.

Finally, reliable generalizations should always be based on complete evidence and specifics that are representative of the entire class sampled. Since writers use induction and deduction in formulating and writing argumentative essays, they must bear in mind these two features of a reliable generalization—that is, completeness and representativeness. In order to ensure completeness and representativeness, writers must take pains to show the reader the connection between their generalizations and the specifics behind them. Three techniques are useful in achieving this: listing facts and figures, using outstanding familiar examples, and citing typical examples. In the chapters ahead, we will discover considerably more about these techniques and, of course, about writing an argumentative essay.

ADDITIONAL   EXERCISES

Identify the structure of each of the following arguments by reference to conclusions, premises, unstated premises, and premise support. Prepare a syllogism (or syllogisms) for each argument.

1. *If there were a God, there wouldn't be evil in the world. But there is evil. First, there are natural evils such as earthquakes, famines, floods, and fires. Second, there are moral evils, ones inflicted by humans themselves: war, murder, robbery, rape, and all sorts of emotional pain. Surely because there is such obvious evil in the world, there is no God.*

2. *Whatever threatens society should be carefully controlled, and certainly pornography qualifies as a threat. After all, at the very least pornography often deals with things such as exhibitionism, voyeurism, prostitution, sadism, child molestation, and other forms of sexual perversion, many of which involve harm to people. Besides, much of the stuff portrayed is illegal. Beyond this, pornography poses a direct and immediate threat to the style and quality of life that we want and value. It follows that pornography should be closely controlled.*

3. "The networks have a shameful record in portraying blacks in prime *C*
time; they portray blacks in stereotypical fashion or overlook their exis- *P*
tence entirely in, say, a series set in midtown Manhattan." *(Robert Guil-*
laume, star of ABC-TV's Benson. Quoted by Jane Hall and Joseph Finne-
gan. "TV Teletype New York/Hollywood." TV Guide, August 1–7, 1981,
p. 32.)

4. "Imagination has just become reality. . . . This is the sound of the future.
Tapes with the widest possible dynamic range. The flattest frequency
response obtainable. And freedom from noise distortion." *(Advertise-*
ment for Fuji cassettes.)

5. "I'm impressed with the Atari 800. Nothing so complex has ever been so
simple. It's as easy to set up as a stereo. It's so easy to operate your kids
can use it." (Gordon Cooper, former astronaut, in advertisement for Atari
computers.)

6. **Creon:** Why did you try to bury your brother? . . .
Antigone: I owed it to him. Those who are not buried wander eternally
and find no rest. (Jean Anouilh, Antigone.)

7. "The curiosity of science and her bent for innovation seem uncontrol-
lable. She pries into every heavenly nook and earthly cranny. She respects neither the ancient sanctity of tombs nor the caressing intimacies
of boudoirs." (R. G. H. Siu. The Tao of Science. New York: Wiley, 1957, p.
4.)

8. "Members of the expert panel approved by Defense Secretary Caspar W.
Weinberger to study alternative plans for deploying the MX nuclear
missile are extremely well qualified for the task. It is disappointing,
therefore, that they are turning out to be of so little help to the Administration in reaching a decision." ("Holes in the MX Plans." Los Angeles
Times, July 19, 1981, part V, p. 4.)

9. "Another kind of man-made destruction would occur if we suffered a
global nuclear war, which would be more destructive, by some orders of
magnitude, than all past wars combined. I dismiss this as a serious threat
because such a war would leave no victors." (Lloyd Motz. "Earth: Final
Chapters." Science Digest, August 1981, p. 81.)

10. "Only in feminist writings are women seen as really important in their
own right, and not just in relation to children or men. In all else, anything
that is associated with women or classified 'feminine' tends to become,
by definition, an ancillary issue, tangential to the really important matters that should concern serious minds." (Diane Eisler. "Women's Rights
and Human Rights." The Humanist, November–December 1980, p. 6.)

11. "One of the interesting ways in which the abortion issue differs from most
other moral issues is that the plausible positions on abortion appear to be
extreme positions. For if a human fetus is a person, one is inclined to say
that, in general, one would be justified in killing it only to save the life of

the mother. . . . On the other hand, if the fetus is not a person, how can it be seriously wrong to destroy it? . . . The upshot is that there is no room for a moderate position on the issue of abortion." (Michael Tooley. "Abortion and Infanticide." Philosophy and Public Affairs, vol. 2, no. 1, Fall 1972, p. 83.)

12. "It's hard to pity doctors, but they deserve it. Never has a priest-class been asked to do so much with so little knowledge. Our fund of medical information has expanded miraculously in this country; so fast, in fact, that many patients truly believe doctors are capable of curing anything. TV's fascination with miracle cures and medical pot-boilers has magnified the medical mystique beyond all proportion. This unrealistic pressure to cure every ill, solve every mystery of disease, places the medical profession under a terrible burden of expectation." (Bill Mandell. "Little Murders in the Hospital: Physician Heal Thyself." San Francisco Sunday Examiner and Chronicle, July 26, 1981, p. A3.)

13. "If there were clear boundaries between the animals and the people, each side having its own territory, friction would be minimized. But that is not the case. Although some of the 5,000 square miles of ecosystem that lie outside the park are protected areas—including neighboring Ngorongoro Conservation Unit and Masai Mara Game Reserve in Kenya—sizable sectors have no conservation status. Consequently, the migratory herds spend a good part of their annual cycle competing with humans for food." (Norman Myers. "The Canning of Africa." Science Digest, August 1981, p. 74.)

14. "Whereas inadequacies of governments and societies to provide the family planning education and services desired by millions of women is one of the obstacles to the socioeconomic development of their countries and the attainment of a better quality of life for their people . . . the World Conference of the United Nations Decade for Women . . . recommends that contributing governments should set aside an appropriate proportion of their resources for population programs." ("Resolution I: Family Planning." Adopted July 30, 1980, by the World Conference of the United Nations Decade for Women: Equality, Development, and Peace.)

15. "Both parties commonly contend that democracy itself is on their side. Each side claims that, in addition to the benefits of efficiency (or fairness, or economy, etc.) to be gained for its mode of enterprise, the making of decisions its way is the more consonant with the nature of democracy. It is well, therefore, to see what can and what cannot be derived from democracy itself on the question of what should be publicly and what privately decided." (Carl Cohen. "How Should We Decide Who Should Decide What Comes Before What?" In Ethical Theory in Business, ed. Tom L. Beauchamp and Norman E. Bowie. Inglewood Cliffs, N.J.: Prentice-Hall, 1979, p. 86.)

2. Argumentative Essay

"What would you think of a man who walked into a hospital room and shot to death a bedridden patient?"

Professor Jenkins's question stunned the class. "Not much!" someone shouted from the back of the room. The others agreed.

The professor went on. "What if I told you that the killer was the brother of the patient, who happened to be dying of an incurable brain disease and had begged his brother to end his misery?"

The class fell silent, but only long enough to allow the professor to read a newspaper item reporting the extraordinary incident. Then bedlam broke loose. Everyone had something to say and wanted to say it. For the next hour the class crackled with opinion—some of it sensible, some of it foolish, but all of it spirited.

As the session ended, Professor Jenkins said, "OK, for next time, write a

500-word essay on voluntary euthanasia, which, as you know, refers to the practice of allowing terminally ill patients to elect to die."

Jackie Watson, a class member who had decided opinions on the matter, couldn't wait to do the assignment. That night, having allowed the issue to rattle around in her head for most of the afternoon, Jackie composed the following essay.

LET THE DYING DECIDE?

Recently a young man walked into a hospital room, pointed a loaded revolver at the patient lying comatose in the bed, and pulled the trigger, killing the patient. The patient, who happened to be dying from irreversible brain damage, was the assailant's brother. In better times, before the auto accident that had left him a "vegetable," the patient had made it quite clear to his brother that he would never want to live "like a vegetable." Thus, the killing. Although the young man's motives were probably noble, and although the plight of countless terminally ill needs no documentation, there are good reasons to resist the legalization of voluntary euthanasia, no matter what its form.

For one thing, euthanasia is killing, and killing is wrong. The Bible is clear on that. So is our society, which historically has taken a dim view of euthanasia. Our traditional religious and social opposition to euthanasia is a good reason for not liberalizing euthanasia laws.

Of course, some will say: "Let the terminally ill patient decide." But is such a person capable of a rational, voluntary decision? Presumably patients should be allowed to die on request when they have developed a tolerance to narcotics. But just when is that? If such patients are to decide when they are drugged, then their decisions surely cannot be considered voluntary. And if they are to choose after the drugs have been withdrawn, then their decisions certainly cannot be voluntary, for excruciating pain would preclude voluntariness. So, whereas it is one thing to insist that the dying should be allowed to decide, it is quite another to show that they are in a position to make a rational, voluntary choice.

But let's assume that a rational, voluntary choice is possible. Is it prudent? Is it wise and merciful to burden the already overburdened patient with the additional pain that having to make a death decision entails? Just think about how many patients are eaten up mentally by the thought that they are financial and emotional drains on their families. Why, doctors and nurses will testify that some of these patients end up actually apologizing for continuing to live! Were they allowed to, such patients easily might choose euthanasia. But could

42

we be sure that they truly wanted to die and not just unload the guilt of remaining alive?

In fact, one such incident occurred in my own family. The attending physician suggested to my aunt's family that, given the woman's terminal condition and the expense of sustaining her, they might want to "let her die." It happened that my aunt was rational enough to be consulted. But who would, or should, do this? Because the family was divided on the question, the upshot was terrible emotional pain for all concerned. Family members turned on one another, some wanting to let my aunt die, others resisting. In the end, nothing was decided. My aunt languished for some time, eventually slipped into a coma, and died. Today some family members still don't speak to others. So what was gained? Nothing. In this case, the family would have been far better off had the physician never offered the mercy-death opinion.

In addition to these concerns, there is the whole matter of mistaken diagnoses. Who hasn't heard of someone's being misdiagnosed? Although rare, mistaken terminal diagnoses do occur. So long as the person is alive, the mistake can be corrected. But once a death decision has been acted on, there is no chance of correction.

None of this is intended to condemn the young man who killed his brother. Surely the impulse that sparked his action was all too human. Nevertheless, in the final analysis far too many reasons argue against the legalization of voluntary euthanasia for us to let our hearts rule our heads.

In the preceding chapter we saw that an argument is a group of statements, one of which is held to follow from the others. For purposes of understanding, we focused on short arguments, ones we might come across in a simple advertisement or brief paragraph. But arguments come in longer, multiparagraph form, such as Jackie Watson's. These can be termed argumentative essays, and they are the concern of this chapter.

We come across argumentative essays all the time. Open a newspaper to the editorial page, tune in the commentary on the evening news, look at an article in some journal—chances are, you will encounter an argumentative essay. Perhaps, like Jackie Watson, you have had to write one to advance some program, policy, or position. Beyond this, you probably will need to evaluate argumentative essays and construct sound ones of your own on the job, because professions such as law, journalism, education, science, and business often require these skills. And you will certainly want to be able to think through and formulate thoughtful positions on issues that face you in your various social roles as parent, citizen, and consumer. In short, the evaluation and formulation of argumentative essays are skills that you can ill afford to lack.

43

Although you may not agree with Jackie Watson that euthanasia should be prohibited, you should recognize in her essay most of the features of argument that we noted in the preceding chapter. Embedded in her essay is a series of short but critical arguments. For example, in the second paragraph Jackie applies a noninductive generalization about religious and social prohibitions against euthanasia to the specific of legislation in order to form the deduction that euthanasia laws should not be liberalized. Expressed in a syllogism her argument might read:

MAJOR PREMISE: *Whatever our religious and social traditions have prohibited should not be legalized.*

MINOR PREMISE: *Our religious and social traditions have prohibited euthanasia.*

CONCLUSION: *Euthanasia should not be legalized.*

Again in the fourth paragraph she applies a noninductive generalization—in this case one about the imprudence of increasing the burden of the terminally ill by forcing them to make a death decision. She forms the deduction that offering a patient a choice is imprudent. Syllogistically, her argument might read:

MAJOR PREMISE: *Anything that adds to the burden of a terminally ill patient is imprudent to permit.*

MINOR PREMISE: *Allowing the terminally ill to make a death decision adds to their burden.*

CONCLUSION: *Allowing the terminally ill to make a death decision is imprudent.*

As support for her minor premise, she refers to patients' worries about money and family and to the testimony of health professionals. She also offers a personal experience.

Beyond this, each of her reasons can be viewed as a deduction that, by implication, functions as a premise in a subsequent argument against the legalization of euthanasia, her main point. In the preceding argument, for example, the conclusion presumably is to serve as the minor premise in an implied syllogism such as this:

MAJOR PREMISE: *<Whatever is imprudent should not be permitted.>*

MINOR PREMISE: *Allowing the terminally ill to make a death decision is imprudent.*

CONCLUSION: *<Allowing the terminally ill to make a death decision should not be permitted (that is, euthanasia should not be legalized).>*

As another illustration, consider the syllogism embedded in the next to last paragraph:

MAJOR PREMISE: *Mistaken terminal diagnoses can be corrected only if the patient is alive.*

MINOR PREMISE: *A death decision that is acted on ensures the death of the patient.*

CONCLUSION: *A death decision that is acted on makes the correction of a mistaken terminal diagnosis impossible.*

Since Jackie is offering this as another reason against the legalization of euthanasia, we can presume that her deduction is to serve as a premise in additional implied arguments. Forming syllogisms, we might get:

MAJOR PREMISE: *<Anything that makes the correction of a mistaken diagnosis impossible should never be permitted.>*

MINOR PREMISE: *A death decision that is acted on makes the correction of a mistaken diagnosis impossible.*

CONCLUSION: *<A death decision that is acted on should never be permitted.>*

MAJOR PREMISE: *<A death decision that is acted on should never be permitted.>*

MINOR PREMISE: *<Legalized euthanasia would allow a death decision to be acted on.>*

CONCLUSION: *<Legalized euthanasia should never be permitted.>*

Were we evaluating Jackie's essay, we might find several of her generalizations questionable. For example, in the second paragraph she generalizes that "killing is wrong." The religious and social traditions she invokes for support, in fact, condone certain forms of killing, as in self-defense, capital punishment, and a just war. At the very best, then, only *some* killing is wrong. The question, then, is: Is euthanasia a form of killing that is wrong? Her unqualified generalization ("killing is wrong") encourages her to miss this point entirely.

Likewise, in generalizing that patients are incapable of a free choice because they are either drugged or in excruciating pain, she overlooks cases of people who, before illness, request that in dire health straits they be permitted some form of euthanasia. In some states these requests take the form of what is called a "living will," which can have the force of law behind it.

By the same token, one might question her seemingly unqualified generalization that permitting a death decision increases the already heavy emotional burden that the terminally ill must carry. Does Jackie overlook cases in which quite the opposite occurs? Does she ignore situations in which the burden is *increased* in the absence of a death decision? Assuming that there are such cases, then all she is logically justified in asserting is: Permitting a death decision *sometimes* increases the burden on patient and family.

We needn't pursue the analysis, for the point should be clear. In this argumentative essay, as in any other, an inspection reveals all the elements present in a short argument: signal words, unexpressed premises, support for premises, and various generalizations that are drawn and applied. Indeed, an argumentative essay can be viewed as a series of subordinate arguments, all of which stand in support of a main contention.

In the preceding chapter we examined the anatomy of the argument. In this one we will inspect the anatomy of the argumentative essay. Although we can't cover every aspect of this rhetorical mode, we will focus on the importance of audience considerations and on three important elements of the argumentative essay: thesis, main points, and organization. Since there appears to be an intimate though unspecified connection between reading and writing, we will consider each element from the viewpoint of both audience and author. This chapter, then, is designed to improve your analytical ability to read and write argumentative essays. Before we begin, however, a few preliminary remarks are in order about the functions of two closely related kinds of essay: argumentative and persuasive.

ARGUMENT AND PERSUASION

As you know, there are many kinds of writing: fiction, biography, poetry, textbooks, news reports, letters, and so forth. Though writing takes many forms, classical rhetoricians grouped writing and speech into only four forms of discourse, or the expression of ideas. The first is narrative, or storytelling— either fictional or factual. The second is description, which is writing that tells how something looks, sounds, feels, tastes, or smells. Description is used mostly in narration to provide a setting and help establish characterization. The third form of discourse is exposition, which is an informative usage designed to express or clarify facts and ideas. The fourth form of discourse is persuasion, which is intended to induce readers to accept the opinion of the writer. Sometimes this form is referred to as persuasion *and* argument, because it is difficult to distinguish them from each other in practice. In fact, most arguments carry persuasive elements, and most persuasion is grounded in the same rational approach that defines argument. But there are theoretical differences between these forms of discourse that are useful to pinpoint.

In theory, argument and persuasion can be distinguished by purpose and technique. The purpose of an argument is to establish the truth of a contention wholly on the basis of a supporting body of logically related statements that are true. Ordinarily, then, *the purpose of the argumentative essay is to win assent—that is, acceptance of a contention.* In her argumentative essay, for example, Jackie Watson is trying to convince the reader that voluntary euthanasia should not be permitted. Her technique for achieving this purpose is to assemble a number of reasons that, taken together, constitute a rational appeal to the audience's understanding.

In contrast, persuasion tries to make an audience think or act in accordance with the writer's will. Thus, *the purpose of a persuasive essay is to move an audience to action—to win consent as well as assent.* For example, Jackie might have tried to persuade members of her audience to write their legislators opposing any nonrestrictive euthanasia legislation. Also, she might have relied mostly on emotional techniques to win audience consent, as persuasive writing usually does.

But the fact is that many argumentative essays, including the best, carry a persuasive function: They do, indeed, aim at the audience's will as well as its intelligence. Keying on an audience's will requires that writers be especially mindful of how their audience views them, for audience consent to follow a particular course depends largely on how it perceives the writer. The writer must appear to be someone of good sense and good will and someone with whom the audience can readily identify. When arguing to persuade, therefore, writers must solidify their relationship with the audience.

Similarly, most argumentative essays are not merely bloodless exercises in preparing syllogisms. Although they are based on a rational foundation and use induction and deduction in development, they also make judicious use of emotional techniques. Jackie's personal example might fall into this category. Part of the job of intelligent reading, then, is to sort out the legitimate emotional appeal from the illegitimate one; part of the job of effective argumentative writing is to know how to use emotional appeals legitimately.

In conclusion, although there are theoretical differences between persuasion and argumentation, these distinctions blur in extended argument; they most certainly do in argumentative essays. Indeed, the argumentative essay typically enlists several forms of discourse. Thus, Jackie uses narrative to recall her aunt's dilemma and exposition to report that mistaken terminal diagnoses are rare. The point is that it is impossible to draw a sharp line between argument and persuasion in an essay. For this reason I will use the term *argumentative essay* to refer to persuasion as well.

In order to better read and write argumentative essays, we must inspect some of their features. We will concentrate on three: thesis, main points, and organization. But before discussing these, we must examine a most important ingredient in writing argumentative essays—indeed in any communication process—audience.

AUDIENCE

Have you ever wondered what makes a comic like George Carlin or Richard Pryor so funny? Certainly, mannerisms, temperament, delivery, time, and sense of the tragic and absurd all contribute. But ultimately what makes any comic funny is the audience: Without audience response, laughter, a comic "dies."

This is why comics spend much time studying their audiences—learning their age, social and educational backgrounds, sexual and racial make-up, biases, inhibitions, fears, and basic outlook on life. Indeed, audience characteristics influence the comic's choice of words, dialect, and points of reference. Such considerations help the comic draw and walk that thin line between "funny" and "offensive," between good humor and bad taste. When comics overstep the line, chances are it's because they have ignored or misjudged the characteristics of their audience.

There is a lesson in this for you, the would-be argumentative writer. While you are not trying to entertain or amuse your readers, you are trying to win them over. For the comic, winning over the audience means getting them to laugh often. For the writer, it means getting the audience to agree with you. Whether or not either succeeds depends largely on how well each has shaped the material to suit the audience.

Shaping an argument to suit your audience requires the same kind of audience study that the comic makes. You must keep in mind the values, prejudices, and basic assumptions of the people you want to influence. You must also be aware of their educational, economic, and social backgrounds; their ages; their occupations; and their feelings about current issues. Here is an audience inventory of key areas to think about when analyzing your audience, before putting pen to paper:

1. *Age*: How old are the members of my audience? What effect, if any, will their ages have on what I'm trying to say?

2. *Values*: What is important to my audience—family, job, school, neighborhood, religion, country? What are their fundamental ideals—being successful, getting married, realizing their potential, ensuring law and order, guaranteeing civil liberties, establishing international harmony?

3. *Economics*: Is my audience wealthy, middle-class, poor? Are they currently employed, unemployed, training for employment?

4. *Social status*: From which social group does my audience come? What's important to this group? What references will they identify with?

5. *Intellectual background*: What does my audience know about my subject? What can I take for granted that they will know? Which words can I expect them to understand; which ones should I make sure to explain?

6. *Expectations*: What will my audience be expecting of my essay? Why will they be reading it? What will they be looking for?

7. *Attitude*: What can I assume will be my audience's attitude toward my topic? Will they likely be sympathetic, hostile, or indifferent?

Taking an audience inventory makes your writing job simpler than it otherwise would be. To see why, let's suppose that you're interested in lining up George Carlin for a show that your college club is sponsoring. You approach Mr. Carlin and find him receptive. In short order, you work out arrangements and set a performance date. Now, you would certainly think it odd if, at some point, Mr. Carlin didn't ask you: "Who's the audience? Tell me something about them." Indeed, if Mr. Carlin didn't ask, you'd undoubtedly volunteer the information to ensure that his material will be appropriate. Once Mr. Carlin knows who his audience will be, then he can start shaping his material accordingly; he can start creating material that a group of college students will likely find amusing.

The same applies to writing argument. Without knowing your audience, you lack any sound basis for selecting material; choosing vocabulary; employing persuasive devices; and, most important, knowing how to strike just the right pose that will win your audience's respect, sympathy, and approval. So, in saying that knowing your audience will help you write better, I mean that audience considerations assist you in deciding what to include, how to express it, and what image to project. Before I say more about image, let me develop an example that will further show how important it is to be aware of your audience.

Suppose that you are a member of a student group that has been selected to meet with a board of professors and administrators to consider giving students academic credit for work experience. You have been chosen to argue the case in favor of such a policy.

In preparing your case, you should identify the characteristics of the members of your audience. First, they will be mostly middle aged, from thirty-five to fifty-five. Second, they probably never received any such credit when in school, and just as likely have never been associated with any institution that gave such credit. Third, they will be intelligent, educated people who see themselves as open-minded, reasonable, and flexible. Fourth, they will be concerned about the institution's academic integrity. Fifth, they will be troubled about the "nuts and bolts" of implementing the policy. (Will any kind of work experience count for credit? If not, what conditions should be met to warrant credit?) Sixth, they will be sensitive to the opinions of alumni, the board of trustees, and parents, all of whose financial and moral support the school needs. Now, armed with this kind of common sense information about your audience, you can give your argument form and character.

Before leaving this matter of audience, I should make one more point. Earlier I indicated that taking an audience inventory can help you decide which image or role to project as writer. In fact, deciding the role that you as writer will play for your audience follows and is related to audience analysis.

Persona

Rhetoricians use the term "persona" to refer to the role or identity assumed by a writer or speaker.[1] The person that you select depends largely on audience considerations. For example, in arguing your case before the group of professors and administrators, you will want to appear thoughtful, intelligent, serious, and mature. On the other hand, suppose you were addressing a student audience. While your argumentative purpose remains the same—to win assent—you would probably be more effective if you struck the pose of an angry young person who sees elitism and fundamental injustice in a traditional policy of giving academic credit only for course work. You might heighten this image by projecting yourself as a youthful progressive locked in combat with academic traditionalists out of step with the times.

Before writing a single word, then, you must learn about your audience. Although the purpose of the argumentative essay always is to win assent (as well as consent, when the essay tries to persuade), how and whether it will do this depends largely on audience considerations. These same considerations greatly influence the choice of persona. With these important observations behind us, we may now turn to three essential ingredients of the argumentative essay: thesis, main points, and organization.

Exercises

2.1 Pretend that you are writing a letter to the editor of your local paper protesting the city council's decision to impose a 10 P.M. to 7 A.M. curfew in all city parks. What particularly rankles you is that the curfew will prevent you from jogging between 6 and 7 A.M. in a neighborhood park, as is your custom. Identify your audience and persona, that is, list the specific characteristics of the audience you must keep in mind and the important characteristics that you must convey to your audience.

2.2 You are asked to write an argumentative essay for some course you are currently taking. Presumably, the paper will be read only by your instructor. What specific characteristics of this person must you keep in mind? What important characteristics must you convey to this person? Suppose that the paper was intended more for a student audience, an audience of your peers. In what ways would the audience and persona characteristics be different?

---

[1]"Persona" comes from the Latin word for the masks worn by actors in ancient classical drama to immediately classify their roles for the audience. Accordingly, a smiling mask signaled a comic character, a sorrowful mask a tragic character.

2.3 Using the preceding exercises as models, create two situations that call for you to argue some case. Then identify audience and persona characteristics. In replying, follow this scheme:

Situation:_____

Specific characteristics of the audience I must keep in mind:

1. _____

2. _____

3. _____

4. _____

Others:_____

Important characteristics to convey to the audience:

1. _____

2. _____

3. _____

4. _____

THESIS

In Chapter 1 we saw that every argument makes a contention. For example, in the short argument "Because of environmental hazards, off-shore drilling for oil should not be permitted," the arguer contends that off-shore drilling for oil should not be permitted. Extended arguments also make such assertions, and the primary one is termed the thesis.

The thesis is an argumentative essay's contention, or main idea. It is what the argument is all about, the main point the arguer is advocating. The thesis, which is typically a generalization, is very important: Without it the writer will flounder and fail for lack of a controlling purpose, and the essay will present little more than a tangle of sentences and paragraphs.

The thesis is critical in both evaluating and constructing arguments. Its importance in evaluation lies in one simple fact: Support material can only be assessed according to whether it advances the thesis. As for essay construction, the thesis provides the writer a focus and basis for selecting material and suggests an organization. Because of the thesis's centrality in the argumentative essay, the critical reader must be able to identify the thesis, and the argumentative writer must be able to formulate it.

Identification

There is no sure way to identify the thesis of an argumentative essay. Sometimes it appears early in an essay, and at other times, late. Sometimes writers express it directly; they actually provide a *thesis proposition—that is, a statement of the argument's main idea.* At other times they merely imply a thesis proposition, which readers are left to express. But even when writers don't make a thesis proposition explicit, attentive readers can infer it, because an argumentative essay always concerns some topic about which the writer has an attitude. Taken together, topic and attitude produce thesis, a statement of which is the thesis proposition.

The topic is the central subject the argument deals with. Determining the topic of an essay calls for a careful reading of the paragraphs, which, of course, are always about somebody or something. That somebody or something is the topic of the argument. Accordingly, if you want to discover the topic of an essay, determine the common concern of its paragraphs.

Attitude refers to the writer's feelings or viewpoint toward the topic—in other words, to what the writer is interested in telling the audience about the topic. Again, a careful reading of an essay reveals attitude. With topic and attitude in hand, the reader has the thesis. These relationships can be diagrammed as shown on page 53, top.

Again, identifying the thesis is vital for evaluating arguments, because support material can only be assessed according to whether it advances the thesis. Thus, failing to determine an essay's thesis, you cannot intelligently evaluate the essay. Reason enough, then, to take seriously the task of thesis identification.

Exercise

2.4 A good way to practice identifying theses is by noting the main idea of a paragraph. Remembering that a thesis proposition is a statement of the main idea (that is, author attitude toward topic), write the thesis proposition for each of the following paragraphs.

1. "Contrary to popular assumption, volcanoes are anything but rare. The Smithsonian Scientific Event Alert Network often reports several dozen per quarter. America's slice of the volcanic 'ring of fire' includes the Cascades, a mountain range that arcs across the Pacific Northwest. When peaceful, shimmering Mt. St. Helens exploded this past spring, blasting 1.3 billion cubic yards of rock into powder, the people of Washington state received a rude lesson about nature's penchant for change. Bathed in ash

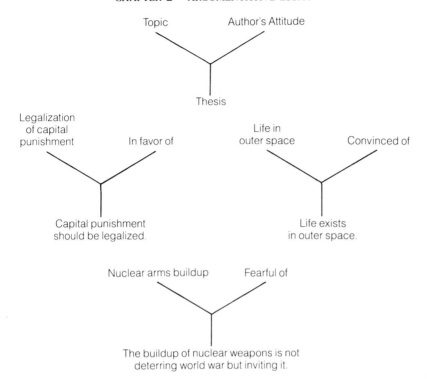

every few weeks over the summer, the Washingtonians queasily came to the realization that the mountain might stay belligerent for years, that they had, in a sense, been living on borrowed time between inevitable eruptions. 'There are potential volcanoes all over the Cascade Range where Mt. St. Helens stands,' says geologist Alfred Anderson of the University of Chicago. 'There's still a lot of change, a lot of formations, going on in that area of the world.'" (Edward M. Hart. "The Shape of Things to Come." Next: A Look into the Future, December 1980, pp. 69–70.)

2. "The building itself is part of the fun of attending the IRT [Indiana Repertory Theatre], which has just marked the opening of its ninth season by moving into a brand-new house. Unlike the plush new cultural Xanadus that have expanded the options, problems, and egos of some regional companies, the IRT's new house is an old house that's undergone an admirable job of restoration. For the measly sum of 5.2 million 1980-inflated dollars, architect Evans Woolen has taken a 53-year-old 3,300-seat movie-and-vaudeville palace and turned it into one of the most efficient, intelligent and appealing theatres in the country, with a main playing space where none of the 600 seats is more than 39 feet from the stage, and a soon-to-open 250-seat upper stage that has the probing intimacy of an operating room theatre." (Jack Kroll. "Hoagy, Bix and Wolfgang." Newsweek, November 17, 1980, p. 114.)

3. *"After thirteen years in universities, trying to teach writing and literature, I am convinced it is impossible to teach anyone to write, compose, paint, sculpture, or innovate creatively. With luck, you might get across minor techniques, or perhaps elementary craftsmanship suitable for low skill level commercial production. And, of course, you can teach about art and creativity and perhaps inspire self-confidence in individuals who already possess innate creative abilities. You can also teach individuals to recognize and appreciate perceptual innovation and significance. And, of course, you can teach about the importance of creativity in our cultural heritage. But no one can be taught to create a significant human experience in any media form."* (Wilson Bryan Key. The Clam-Plate Orgy and Other Subliminal Techniques for Manipulating Your Behavior. *New York: New American Library (Signet), 1980, p. 69.)*

Formulation

Much of what I just said about identifying theses applies to writing thesis propositions. Before we see how to write them, let's consider the need to construct theses that embody arguable assertions that can be developed in an extended essay.

Arguable Assertions To begin, not every contention is so arguable that it can or should be developed in an essay format. For example, some contentions are easily verified. "Millions of Americans smoke cigarettes," "Nearly half the households in the United States are supported primarily by working women," and "A spirochete causes syphilis" are assertions that can be easily confirmed or disconfirmed. The ease with which these statements can be evaluated precludes the need—and certainly the wisdom—of constructing extended arguments to demonstrate their truth.

In contrast are contentions so disputable, controversial, or opinionated that they lend themselves to elaboration. "Life exists outside our solar system," "Coffee is bad for one's health," "Many of today's films subtly attempt to justify violence directed against women," and "Television network news departments practice racism in hiring on-camera personnel" are examples. These are statements that need to and might be supported by appropriate documentation and so would constitute arguable assertions for development in essays.

In addition to easily verified assertions are those that defy objective verification. Objective verification means confirmation outside the self, in the real world. All the preceding propositions are at least objectively verifiable, although some are not arguable in essays. In other words, we can go outside ourselves into the world, collect data and evidence about these contentions, and thereby confirm or disconfirm them. But what about statements such as "I am nervous," "I feel that something dreadful is about to happen," or "Drinks with sugar taste better than the sugar-free kind"? Confirmation of these statements lies within the persons expressing them. Personal experience, if honestly reported, is enough to verify such statements. Since what is needed to confirm these statements is available only to the persons making them, there is no point in constructing arguments to prove them. Yes, I might *explain why* I feel something dreadful is about to happen, but I wouldn't attempt to *demonstrate* to you *that* I feel this way, certainly not in an argumentative essay.

So, assertions that can be easily verified or ones that defy objective verification should never be theses of argumentative essays. Of course, they can and do appear in extended arguments as support materials. For example, in attempting to demonstrate—that is, form the deduction—that female workers deserve the same pay as their male counterparts, I might point out that half the households in the United States are supported primarily by working women. Or to demonstrate how effective a suspense film is, you might report that throughout the film you were filled with presentiment. In such cases these facts would serve to support the arguable contentions that we were advancing.

So much for assertions that are not appropriate for essay development. What about assertions that are? Assertions worthy of essay development generally fall into five categories: assertions about meaning, value, consequences, policy, and fact.

1. *Assertions about meaning.* Assertions about meaning are generalizations that focus on how we define or interpret something. For example, what we mean by concepts and terms such as *pornography, equal opportunity, the just state, person, death,* and *mental incompetence* are often the concerns of lengthy essays, even books. In Chapter 6 we will examine essays that are developed primarily by definition.

2. *Assertions about value.* Assertions about value are generalizations that express an assessment of worth. Some examples are "Abortion is never right," "*Godfather II* is a *better* film than *Godfather I*," and "The two-party system is the *most effective* way of structuring our political system." Although value assertions can rarely be argued conclusively and always present unique problems in argument, they do constitute a large part of what people argue about. For this reason, we will take a special look at value arguments in the next chapter of this book.

3. *Assertions about consequences.* Assertions about consequences are generalizations about the causal patterns involved in certain ideas and actions. Such arguments usually constitute responses to hypothetical, "what if," questions. Accordingly, they often take the form of "If X, then Y": "If the Equal Rights Amendment were passed, then women would be subject to the draft"; "If passive euthanasia were permitted, then active euthanasia would be bound to follow"; or "If government cut back support to the arts, then many local cultural activities would dry up." Since contentions based on causal patterns figure prominently in argumentative essays, I will say considerably more about this developmental pattern later, in Chapter 5.

4. *Assertions about policy.* Assertions about policy are generalizations dealing with policies. Such contentions are usually expressed in the form of a proposal using the words *ought* or *should* (which, incidentally, often signal value assertions as well). Examples are "Capital punishment should be reinstated," "College professors ought to take attendance in their classes," "Prisoners should be allowed to exercise cohabitation rights," and "Terminally ill patients ought to be informed of their condition."

5. *Assertions about facts.* Assertions about facts are generalizations dealing with alleged descriptions of actual states of affairs. "The universe will continue to expand," "China is tooling up for a war with Russia," "People can communicate with one another over great distances without using any of the conventional means of communication," "An earthquake registering at least 7 on the Richter scale will probably rock California within the year," and "Shakespeare wrote all the plays and poems attributed to him," are statements that purport to describe things as they actually are, were, or likely will be.

In formulating a thesis, writers generally focus on one of these five types of assertion. Of course, in developing the essay they often call on a variety of these types. Thus, you might draw up an argument whose thesis is "Gun control should be mandatory in every state" (a policy assertion). In supporting your position you might stipulate what you mean by "gun" and "gun control" (meaning), point out that certain states with gun control have lower rates of crimes involving handguns than states without gun control (fact), discuss the social merits of gun control (consequences), and conclude that failure to enact such legislation is immoral (value).

With these preliminary considerations behind us, let's now see what's involved in actually writing the thesis.

Writing the Thesis As indicated earlier, writing the thesis is vital because it helps the writer focus, limit, and organize the topic. Although there is no one way to write a thesis, the following steps do provide a logical and useful approach. You have probably encountered a similar sequential strategy elsewhere in your composition studies, but reconsidering the steps will reinforce your learning and skill.

Step one—decide on a subject. The *subject* is the area of concern or interest. "Education in the United States," "The Electoral Process," "Drugs," "Feminism," "The Penal System," "Religion," and "Conflict between the Generations" all represent subjects or areas that are ripe for argumentative exploration. The first job of the argumentative writer, then, is to decide on a subject. Often, instructors do this for students. "Write a 500-word essay on advertising," your English professor might tell you. Faced with such an assignment, you could be confused. "What *about* advertising?" you wonder. Your instincts rightly tell you that advertising is far too broad and unwieldy a subject to be handled in a mere 500 words. Before making any progress, then, you must identify some aspect of advertising that is manageable within the prescribed format.

Step two—identify possible topics. The "what about" question you asked when faced with the assignment can be viewed as a groping for a topic. The topic is an aspect of the subject. Obviously, subjects can spawn countless topics. For example:

Subject	*Possible Topics*
Baseball	Salaries of players
	The strike of 1981
	A uniquely American pastime
Education in the United States	The high costs of college education

	Shortcomings in public secondary education
	Misplaced priorities
Religion	The Moral Majority
	The decline of institutional religion
	The increasing interest in Eastern religion
Advertising	Relationship to the law
	Deceptive practices
	Impact on the economy

In this step of thesis writing, the writer must list the possible topics for development in the essay. Accordingly, this stage can be viewed as a brainstorming session in which you identify as many possible aspects of a subject as you can. From this list will come the topic you will write about.

Step three—select and limit the topic. Having composed a list of possible topics, you should then select one you want to write about and limit it. Note that this step consists of two operations: selection and limitation. The second operation is very important, for failing to limit your topic may mean that you later find it unmanageable. The proper limits of the topic are usually determined by the length of the proposed essay. The possible topics we've listed could be, and have been, the subjects of books. So, to tackle any of them in a 500- to 1,000-word essay would prove unwise. They must be narrowed to allow development within 500 words. Here are some possibilities for the subject "Advertising":

Possible Topics	*Limited Topic*
Relationship to the law	The impact on big business of three landmark decisions in consumer law
Deceptive practices	The use of ambiguity to sell aspirin, toothpaste, and mouthwash
Impact on the economy	Effects on the retail prices of alcoholic and nonalcoholic beverages

It is worth noting that the suggested limited topics contain a most common and effective method of controlling an essay—dividing it into parts. Thus, the first limited topic refers to *three* landmark decisions; the second refers to *aspirin, toothpaste,* and *mouthwash;* the third to *alcoholic* and *nonalcoholic* beverages. From the writer's viewpoint, these divisions tell precisely what the essay must discuss, even the order it will follow (for example, aspirin, then toothpaste, then mouthwash). Similarly, from the reader's viewpoint, these divisions focus the topic and suggest the order of consideration: The reader knows what you will discuss and roughly when. So using such division devices is enormously helpful, because they maximize the chances of effective communication.

Step four—determine your attitude toward the topic. Earlier we saw that the thesis consists of a topic and the author's attitude toward it. Determining your attitude will help you hone in on what it is you're trying to demonstrate. For example, you may be *fearful* of the impact of the three landmark decisions; *critical* of the use of ambiguity to sell aspirin, toothpaste, and mouthwash; or *convinced* of the significant effects of advertising costs on the retail prices of alcoholic and nonalcoholic beverages. In identifying your attitude, be mindful of the categories of assertion that arguments ordinarily make; this will simplify your task of composing the thesis statement. Thus, your fear about the three legal decisions springs from a concern about *consequences;* your criticism of ambiguity probably relates to *value* or *policy;* and your conviction about the impact of advertising costs reflects some ultimate assertion of *fact* and perhaps of *value* ("significant" implies a value assertion).

Step five—write the thesis statement. The next step consists of wedding the topic and your attitude toward it in a single proposition, which is typically a generalization. Again, in writing the thesis statement, it is most helpful to be clear about the type of contention you want to make; this will ensure a sharp focus. As for the topics under discussion here, you might write a thesis statement such as the ones in the diagrams below and on page 60.

Step six—test the thesis proposition. After writing the thesis statement, it's a good idea to check it for focus. After all, you want to make sure that your topic and viewpoint are crystal clear. A good way to check your statement is to have somebody else read it. Ask the person to answer this question: "What do you think I'm trying to demonstrate in my essay?" If the reply corresponds

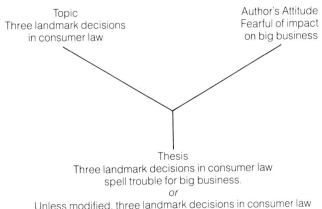

Topic
Three landmark decisions
in consumer law

Author's Attitude
Fearful of impact
on big business

Thesis
Three landmark decisions in consumer law
spell trouble for big business.
or
Unless modified, three landmark decisions in consumer law
could seriously undercut big business.

with your purpose, you have a well-focused thesis proposition. If it doesn't, then back to the drawing board!

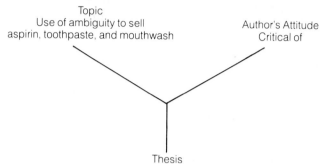

Topic
Use of ambiguity to sell
aspirin, toothpaste, and mouthwash

Author's Attitude
Critical of

Thesis
Stricter regulations are needed to restrict the widespread
use of ambiguity to sell aspirin, toothpaste, and mouthwash
or
Employing ambiguity to sell aspirin, toothpaste, and
mouthwash is reprehensible.

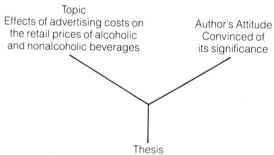

Topic
Effects of advertising costs on
the retail prices of alcoholic
and nonalcoholic beverages

Author's Attitude
Convinced of
its significance

Thesis
Even a cursory look at the pricing structure of
alcoholic and nonalcoholic beverages reveals
the significant effects of advertising costs.
or
Make no mistake about it: Consumers pay dearly for the
costs of advertising alcoholic and nonalcoholic beverages.

Exercise

2.5 By using the six steps just discussed, write a thesis proposition for each of the following subjects:

1. Job Opportunities for Women
2. Freedom of the Press
3. The Judicial System in the United States
4. Drug Usage among Minors
5. The State of Marriage Twenty Years from Now

6. Restoring Cities
7. Gun Control
8. Premarital Sex
9. College Curricula
10. Defense Spending
11. The Plight of the Handicapped
12. Extracurricular Activities in College
13. Junk Foods
14. Changing Sex Roles
15. Contemporary Music

MAIN POINTS

The second component of the argumentative essay is main points. Every argumentative essay has *main points, or principal support assertions offered to advance the thesis.* In the jargon of argument, the main points constitute the premises of the claim. The points offered are a crucial part of any extended argument, for they underpin the thesis.

Since evaluating an argument consists chiefly of inspecting support material, readers must closely study the main points of an essay. Are they relevant, clear, and logical? Is each point sufficiently made? Does it actually advance the thesis? These are just some of the questions that intelligent, critical readers ask of support material.

It is usually not difficult to identify the main points of an argument, especially of a tightly organized one. But even when the essay is loosely ordered, a close reading of the paragraphs and awareness of the connection between them usually reveals the main points.

As an example, consider Jackie Watson's essay on the topic of voluntary euthanasia. The thesis proposition of this essay appears in the italicized portion of the last sentence of the opening paragraph: "Although the young man's motives were probably noble, and although the plight of countless terminally ill patients needs no documentation, *there are good reasons to resist the legalization of voluntary euthanasia, no matter what its form.*" The writer is making a *policy* assertion; her purpose is to show why voluntary euthanasia should not be legalized. To advance her thesis, she offers four points:

1. Our culture has traditionally prohibited euthanasia (paragraph 2).
2. Terminal patients are not capable of a rational and voluntary choice (paragraph 3).

3. Allowing a death choice puts a terrible burden on patients and families (paragraphs 4 and 5).

4. Mistaken diagnoses are possible (paragraph 6).

If we had to evaluate this argument, we would have to assess the merits of each point, or premise. This requires an inspection of the support offered. To repeat, in the chapters ahead you will develop skills for doing this assessment, skills that will enable you to say more about an extended argument than simply, "I don't agree" or "I agree." These skills will equip you to examine the support material objectively and judge it by criteria for good argumentation.

Just as critical reading requires the identification of main points, good argumentative writing involves developing main points. What sources do writers use in selecting and developing main points? Where do they get the material to support their theses?

Sources and Development

Since any argumentative essay must demonstrate its assertion, writers must ask of their theses: "Why?" or "How?" *Why* should voluntary euthanasia not be legalized? *Why* are stricter regulations needed to restrict the widespread use of ambiguity to sell aspirin, toothpaste, and mouthwash? *How* does even a cursory look at the pricing structure of alcoholic and nonalcoholic beverages reveal the enormous effect of advertising costs? The writer's job, then, is to marshal reasons that answer the *why* or *how* question. In the jargon of argument, the writer must assemble the premises that entail the claim advanced.

In assembling reasons (premises) and the support material for them, writers call on several sources. One is *observation*. Observation can be considered awareness of what occurs outside the writer. Usually observations are close, first-hand studies of scenes, people, objects, and events. In composing her essay, Jackie Watson calls on observation to make judgments about the effect of drugs and pain on free, rational choice (point 2) and to indicate the possibility of mistaken diagnoses (point 4). She also uses it to report the details of the shooting (first paragraph).

Personal experience is a second source of reasons. Personal experience, as distinguished from observation, refers to what goes on *inside* the writer. It is one's consciousness of thoughts, ideas, and involvement with incidents, persons, places, and things.[2] Jackie effectively uses personal experience in recounting her family's ordeal, which serves as support material for point 3.

Informed opinion is a third rich source for developing reasons and support material. Informed opinion is the views of others who have studied the same subject. Jackie invokes this source in references to the Bible and society (point 1) and to doctors and nurses (point 3).

---

[2]Morton A. Miller. *Reading and Writing Short Essays*. New York: Random House, 1980, p. 106.

Finally, *organized research* is a fourth source of material. Organized research is the systematic sifting of evidence from records, reports, and other printed sources. Jackie doesn't call on this source, but she could have. For example, some material is available on alternative approaches to the treatment of the dying. One approach advocates giving such patients whatever drugs—and in whatever doses—are necessary to kill their pain. Considerable evidence indicates that this treatment can be given without addicting the patient. Jackie could have enlisted some of this research to make the point that there may be no need for voluntary euthanasia legislation, because there is an effective alternative to the conventional way of treating the dying.

In short, writers generally call on one or more of these four sources when assembling their main points and support material. A useful approach to developing main points, then, is to brainstorm in terms of these sources. Make a list of observations, personal experiences, informed opinion, and organized research relevant to the contention you wish to make. From this list, select the most effective points, and then shore them up with support material by again relying on these sources.

Exercise

2.6 *In complete sentences, identify the main points in the following excerpt from an essay. Then indicate where the author obtained his material for each point—from observation, personal experience, informed opinion, or organized research.*

Four Things That Threaten Our Schools

By Felix Morley

In four separate areas one may now observe conditions which suppress individual distinction in our public schooling. Each is making a contribution to the present demoralization.

That most strongly emphasized in Dr. Hansen's book[3] is the planned retardation of ability, illustrated both by the automatic promotion of incompetent pupils and by the refusal to give any meaningful reports on individual performance. A big issue, in the case of the Washington superintendent, was his insistence on the "track system." This in general grouped students in accordance with demonstrated ability, though without denial of passage from the "basic" track to one of the three higher divisions. In a court decision, in June, 1967, a federal judge labeled this ability grouping discriminatory and therefore unconstitutional.

---

[3]Editor's Note: The reference is to *Danger in Washington*, by Carl F. Hansen, former superintendent of schools in Washington, D.C., Council for Better Education, 1968.

Since the local board of education made no appeal, the verdict stands; which makes it seemingly illegal for any public school in the country to classify pupils by ability, at least openly. Of course competent and courageous teachers will continue to give special consideration to able students. Without such stimulative direction the process of education would be unworthy of that name. But this *cause célèbre* in the nation's capital has been an encouragement to mediocre performance in every public school. It sanctifies the already strong position of those who think there should be no competition except in athletics.

This helps to emphasize that the teaching profession itself is the second educational field in which initiative is now actively discouraged. Here, too, Dr. Hansen's observations are timely, especially in regard to the unionization of teachers. As he aptly observes, this development inevitably discredits the teacher who puts the training of his or her pupils first. From the union viewpoint featherbedding is preferable to speed-up and any instructor who opposes a strike call is a potential scab.

Moreover, unionization builds a wall between the teaching and the administrative divisions in the public schools, even though close relations between these functions are essential.

Dr. Hansen wrote *Danger in Washington* with special reference to that city, and before the protracted teacher strike which paralyzed the New York city schools for a large portion of the current academic year. Otherwise his comments on "the growing unproductiveness of the teacher" might well have been stronger. Regardless of the rights and wrongs in the New York or any other particular issue it is clearly demoralizing for the pupils when teachers strike. The psychological effect goes far beyond the loss of study time.

When teachers play hooky en masse, why should pupils feel any obligation to take their studies seriously? What arguments can a dropout teacher use to influence a pupil who would like to do the same? And why not have truant officers for defecting teachers as well as for the defecting taught?

Ill-judged intervention by the federal government has in many instances proved itself a third demoralizing factor in public education. Here Dr. Hansen has certainly been close to the source of the difficulty. In the Washington "showcase" he has witnessed the development of an enforcement machinery that "has reached an incomprehensible complexity, and promises to grow in this respect . . . until it becomes unmanageable."

Interference with the administration of the schools is justified by the federal funds made available to them. But these are channeled through many uncoordinated agencies with divergent and often rapidly shifting programs. Probably every school superintendent in the country could give illustrations of this confusion but one seems especially pronounced in

Washington. This is the practice of governmental agencies in luring good teachers from their work to give them "advisory" or "consultative" jobs at higher salaries.

Sometimes, Dr. Hansen charges, the real purpose of this poaching is to develop parental "militancy" towards public school administration.

Even without such intolerable activity the general morale of pupils in the big city schools is bad enough to define it as a fourth area where education, in any true sense of the word, is moving backwards. Senseless vandalism shows a repugnance to the public school system as such and has reached a stage where the mere repair of wantonly damaged property is often a sizable budgetary item. Most disastrous for educational standards is the sexual promiscuity now apparent in city high schools. This seems to be extremely serious in the District of Columbia, where Dr. Hansen estimates a "one-out-of-10 chance that the Washington schoolgirl will bear a child out of wedlock."

On the other hand there are signs that in working down into the high schools the college demand for "student power" has constructive aspects. This can be seen in uncensored publications which question the alleged right of public school teachers to strike, and ask why competition for grades is not as desirable as competition for the football team. If questions like this are being planted in juvenile minds by anxious parents, so much the better.

Dr. Hansen's rather angry reply to those who forced him from superintendence of the Washington public schools is sometimes, as he himself admits, "abrasive." It will stir controversy. That is all to the good for most of the points made by this pugnacious Nebraskan are applicable in some degree to the public schools in every large American city.

Most of his points will be difficult to ignore, and even more so to brush off. It cannot be charge, for instance, that this superintendent was ever opposed to integration, which he worked resolutely to forward. Anyway this can scarcely be called an issue any longer in the District of Columbia, where only 6.5 percent of the total public school attendance is now white.

The Supreme Court has certainly compounded the problems of the public schools, but many of them were germinating before the historic decision of 1954. The roots run deep, to curious and eventually self-destructive educational theories that were making headway even before the First World War. One of these is that a democratic system demands indulgence for the incompetent. Its twin maintains that discipline of any kind restricts the development of personality.

If these wholly permissive ideas are to control in our public schools, neither Khrushchev nor any of his successors in the Kremlin will need to worry about burying us. We'll do the interment job for them. As Dr. Hansen asks poignantly, at the close of his important study:

"How can America become great—or even survive as it is—without intellectual excellence? How long can this nation continue to disdain the academically gifted among its young?"[4]

Exercise

2.7 *Assume that you have become interested in five of the theses you developed in Exercise 2.5. Based on your own experience and observations, write down everything you can think of that is relevant to each thesis. Then select three points from each list that you think are the most important for supporting the thesis.*

ORGANIZATION

*Organization, a third component of the argumentative essay, is the framework that ties together the reasons we assemble to support our asser-*tion. In general, argumentative essays can be structured in one of two organizational patterns: (1) We can structure our argument on a series of independent reasons—*series structure*, for short; or (2) We can structure it on a closely linked chain of interdependent reasons—*chain structure*, for short. The structure ordinarily depends on how the main points relate to one another.[5]

In her essay about voluntary euthanasia, Jackie Watson made a series of four main points to show that voluntary euthanasia should not be legalized. Although these reasons were carefully related to the thesis, of course, they were not dependent on one another. Each supported Jackie's thesis with separate reasons for opposing the legalization of voluntary euthanasia. In presenting independent reasons such as these, writers need not be concerned with tight linkage between the points, since one point need not logically entail another. Rather, writers have two main tasks. They must arrange the main points in the most effective argumentative order. (Usually, the strongest reason comes first, followed by the weaker reasons, and ending with a strong summarizing reason to conclude the argument forcefully.) And they must reassert the connection between each reason and the thesis, so that the assertion is reinforced throughout the essay. This reinforcement can usually be done through signal words and phrases.

---

[4]From *Nation's Business*, December 1968. Copyright © 1968, *Nation's Business*—The Chamber of Commerce of the United States. Reprinted by permission of the publisher.
[5]See Donald McQuade and Robert Atwan. *Thinking in Writing: Structures for Composition.* New York: Knopf, 1980, pp. 410–412.

The other organizational method, the chain structure, is used when we are making a series of interdependent points. For example, suppose that Jackie is arguing that a voluntary euthanasia decision is impossible in the case of most terminally ill patients. She may then argue through a set of closely linked reasons that voluntary decisions, by definition, presuppose freedom of choice; that freedom of choice entails the absence of freedom-limiting constraints; that such constraints almost always limit terminally ill patients, for they are either in excruciating pain or delirious from powerful drugs; that, since they are constrained, most terminally ill patients are not free; that, since they are not free, most terminally ill patients cannot make a voluntary choice; that, since most terminally ill patients cannot make a voluntary choice, therefore voluntary euthanasia is impossible in most cases of the terminally ill. Here the strength of the argument depends on the strength of the chain of reasons, the conclusion of one main point becoming the premise of the next. Clearly, the organization of the chain-structured argument depends less on an arrangement of points according to their relative importance than it does on an arrangement of points according to their logical sequence.

Beyond these general structures, argumentative essays can be organized to follow one or more specific patterns. Among the most common of these are (1) the inductive essay, (2) the pro-and-con essay, (3) the cause-and-effect essay, and (4) the analysis-of-alternatives essay. The choice of specific pattern depends largely on considerations of purpose and audience.

Inductive Essay

As we saw in the preceding chapter, an inductive argument is one that usually moves from the specific to the general, from bits and pieces of evidence to probable conclusions. Accordingly, in an inductive essay examples, illustrations, facts, opinion, and other forms of evidence are used to draw a general, probable conclusion.

The inductive order is especially useful when your purpose is to convince the audience of a rather controversial assertion—for example, "The use of saccharin should be prohibited," "The United States should have a national health insurance program that guarantees all citizens health care and services despite their ability to pay," or "Public schools are not giving young people what they need to survive in a highly technological society." Audiences often greet such controversial assertions of value, policy, or fact with prejudice and distrust. As a result, they can tune you out very early in your essay. If you're to overcome audience skepticism, you must win them over slowly, point by point. The inductive order helps you do this by turning audience attention to the evidence, which is allowed to speak for itself. Thus, the support material is usually presented first; then, in the final paragraph or two, the assertion is made. Ideally, having seen the evidence, members of the audience will change their minds or at least be receptive to your controversial conclusion.

For example, suppose your purpose is to convince a skeptical audience that Americans are not as well fed as they think they are. Using the inductive order, you might structure your essay as follows:

FACT 1: *According to the most recent information, 20 percent to 50 percent of Americans run some risk of not meeting the U.S. recommended daily allowance for at least one or more of the vitamins C, A, B$_1$ (thiamine), B$_2$ (riboflavin), and folic acid. . . .*

FACT 2: *Although the diets of most Americans may be richer in minerals than they were fifty years ago, minerals such as iron and calcium are still likely to be insufficient. . . .*

FACT 3: *Many people today, young and old, are dieting and skipping meals. As a result, they may be eliminating foods that contain many vitamins, including C, E, and B-complex vitamins. . . .*

CONCLUSION: *These facts point to an unmistakable conclusion: There are serious gaps in our national diet, most frequently because of poor eating habits.*

Pro-and-Con Essay

Notice that in the preceding example you tried to present a "closed case" for your contention. But you might not have been so one-sided in your presentation. Instead, you might have presented a more balanced approach.

The pro-and-con essay attempts to reach a balanced conclusion by treating an issue as an open question worth thinking about. In a pro-and-con essay, the writer usually begins by discussing the pros and cons. The discussion serves as a basis for a balanced conclusion. This format, then, consists of: (1) confirmation of an idea, (2) objection to the idea, and (3) a balanced conclusion. This format has special audience appeal, because it flatters the members' intelligence and sense of fair play. It also makes the writer appear thoughtful and impartial. Here's an example:

CONFIRMATION: *Undoubtedly the United States enjoys one of the highest standards of living and is the largest producer of food products in the world. Our agricultural and industrial resources understandably make many Americans and non-Americans alike consider us the "best fed" people on earth. . . .*

OBJECTION: *Current evidence suggests that we are far from realizing the nutritional promise of our bountiful resources. For one thing, 20 percent to 50 percent of us runs some risk of not meeting the U.S. recommended daily allowance. . . .*

CONCLUSION: *Calling ourselves the "best fed" people on earth is misleading. Rather, we appear to be potentially the best fed people on earth. Whether we realize our potential depends largely on whether we can close the gaps in our national diet by improving our eating habits. . . .*

Cause-and-Effect Essay

The cause-and-effect essay, which is especially appropriate in advocating consequential assertions, attempts to sort out or trace the conditions that have produced some phenomenon. One way to do this is by presenting the major causes in chronological order, as in treating some historical event; another is to arrange the causes in order of importance. Often writers of a cause-and-effect essay have in mind some remedy, which they present after they have discussed the causal conditions underlying the problem. In that event, the writer's purpose is twofold: (1) to make the audience aware of the causes and (2) to make it accept the proposed solution. The cause-and-effect essay, then, often follows this structure: statement of problem, various causes, proposed solution. Here's an example:

STATEMENT OF PROBLEM: *It is commonly thought that Americans are the "best fed" people on earth. Yet current evidence indicates that there are serious gaps in our national diet. . . .*

FIRST MAJOR CAUSE: *The deficiencies in our national diet are attributable to several factors. Perhaps the most important is poor diet. . . .*

SECOND MAJOR CAUSE: *Lack of education is another reason for the deficiencies in our national diet. Although public school curricula inevitably include a "health" component, very little of it is devoted to the study of proper nutrition. . . .*

THIRD MAJOR CAUSE: *Still another factor that explains our nutritional deficiencies is the medical profession's traditional ignorance of or lack of interest in proper nutrition. Historically, doctors have spent little time impressing on patients the link between poor diet and ill health. . . .*

CONCLUSION PROPOSAL: *Undoubtedly, we Americans have the potential for being the "best fed" people on earth. But until we change our eating habits, schools start instructing students in proper nutrition, and health professionals begin reinforcing this instruction, we stand little chance of realizing our potential.*

Analyzing-Alternatives Essay

Often the writer's purpose in an essay is to make the audience accept one of several alternatives. Writers accomplish this by structuring the essay according to options. The essay that analyzes alternatives, then, tries to make the audience accept one option as preferable by examining and eliminating other less desirable options. This strategy is especially useful in making the audience accept the "lesser of the evils" or an untried approach. For example:

THESIS: *There are many ways of improving the eating habits of elementary school children. . . .*

FIRST ALTERNATIVE: *One way is for the U.S. Department of Health and Human Services to exercise tighter control over the school lunch program. Undoubtedly this approach will invite a full-scale social debate about the proper role of government in relation to business and consumers. . . .*

SECOND ALTERNATIVE: *Another approach is for schools to prohibit the sale of junk food on campus. Where this has been tried, it has met widespread opposition from children, parents, and, of course, the junk-food industry. . . .*

THIRD ALTERNATIVE: *A third alternative is to make nutrition a basic and continuing part of a child's education. This approach has the advantage of being far less controversial than either of the other two. More important, it respects the autonomy of individuals by equipping them to make informed food choices but not restricting their choices. Perhaps most important, this approach stands the best chance of getting students to eat properly outside school and of developing sound, life-long eating habits.*

Exercises

2.8 Which organizational pattern does Jackie Watson use in developing her essay? How would you describe her audience? Her persona?

2.9 Identify the organizational patterns evident in the following essay excerpts.

1. The United States certainly has both the human and material resources to reduce its crime rate. We have enough money and know-how to devise and underwrite innovative ways of dealing with crime and criminals. Indeed,

some communities have done just that. Yet a presidential commission recently reported that, as a whole, the United States is losing its fight against crime.

What we lack, of course, is the will. We Americans value our creature comforts too much to allow our personal incomes to be taxed for ambitious crime-prevention expenditures.

So, to say that as a nation we have a serious crime problem is really to admit that we are unwilling to devote more than a minor fraction of our great wealth and human resources to the enterprise of crime prevention.

2. "There are many different methods of achieving limitation of births.

"Abortion is undoubtedly preferable to infanticide, though we know too little about the physiological and psychological damage which it may cause to recommend it without serious qualms.

"Contraception certainly seems preferable to abortion, and indeed the moral objection to contraception in principle seems to be confined to a single major branch of the Christian church. Even there, the difference in practice between this church and the rest of society is much smaller than the difference in precept. Contraception, however, also has its problems, and it is by no means an automatic solution to the problem of population control.

"The fact that we must recognize is that it is social institutions which are dominant in determining the ability of society to control its population, not the mere physiology of reproduction." (Kenneth E. Boulding. The Meaning of the Twentieth Century. New York: Harper & Row, 1979, p. 79.)

3. "Political pressures in this presidential year have given a militant minority of women powerful leverage for enactment [of the Equal Rights Amendment]. However, the respective state of the Union may come to regret ratification, if the two-thirds majority approves.

" . . . legal scholars from the University of Chicago, Yale, and Harvard [have argued] that while the amendment would have no effect upon discrimination, it would 'nullify every existing federal and state law making any distinction whatever between men and women, no matter how reasonable the distinction may be, and rob Congress and the 50 states of the legislative power to enact any future laws making any distinction between men and women, no matter how reasonable the distinction may be.'

"Like the civil rights movement, Women's Lib is seeking, by using the power of the state, to forbid individual discrimination as opposed to discrimination legally enforced.

"But like some elements of the civil rights movement, militant feminists are not really interested in reform, but rather in revolution and destruction of the existing social fabric of the society." (Jeffrey St. John. "Women's Lib Amendment Not Simple Legal Formula." Columbus Dispatch, May 9, 1972, p. 23.)

4. *"America's young people have found a potent, sometimes addictive, and legal drug. It's called alcohol.*

"Why are youngsters rediscovering booze? One reason is pressure from other kids to be one of the gang. Another is the ever-present urge to act grown up. For some, it eases the burden of problems at home or at school. And it's cheaper. You can buy a couple of six-packs of beer for the price of three joints of pot.

"Perhaps the main reason is that parents don't seem to mind. They tolerate drinking—sometimes almost seem to encourage it.

"The Medical Council on Alcoholism warns: The potential teenage drinking problem should give far more cause for alarm than drug addiction. Many schools have reacted to teenage drinking. They've started alcohol-education programs. But a lot of experts feel that teenagers are not going to stop drinking until parents do." (Carl T. Rowan. "Teenagers and Booze." In Just Between Us Blacks. New York: Random House, 1974, pp. 95–96.)

2.10 Using one of the four organizational patterns, write a 500- to 1,000-word essay supporting one of the theses you chose in answer to Exercise 2.7. (Use the main points you developed in answering the same exercise.) Before beginning, identify your audience and persona.

SUMMARY

Argument and persuasion can be theoretically distinguished by purpose and technique. The argumentative essay's purpose is to win assent through rational appeal; the persuasive essay's purpose is to win consent through emotional appeal. In practice, however, the two cannot be easily separated: Argumentative essays often try to win consent and use emotional techniques legitimately. For our purposes, the term *argumentative essay* will include persuasive essays.

Argumentative essays are multiparagraph arguments. They generally consist of a series of subordinate arguments used as support for some main contention. As such, argumentative essays exhibit all the facets of a short argument: premise and conclusion, signal words, unexpressed premises, premise support, and generalizations that are drawn and applied.

To write effective argumentative essays, writers must know their audience. This calls for an audience inventory that isolates key audience characteristics. Armed with this information, the writer can then give an argument shape and character. Just as important, writers must decide on the appropriate persona or role they will play, that is, the characteristics that must be conveyed to the audience to gain their respect and win their approval.

Three key parts of an argumentative essay are the thesis, main points, and organization. The thesis, which typically is a generalization, is the essay's assertion or main idea. Identifying the thesis of an essay calls for a recognition of the topic and author's attitude toward it. In formulating theses, writers must make sure that they construct arguable assertions—that is, assertions that are disputable, controversial, or opinionated enough to allow development in an essay format (for example, "Life exists outside our solar system" or "Coffee is bad for one's health"). Assertions worthy of development generally fall into five categories: assertions about meaning, values, consequences, policy, and fact.

In writing a thesis, follow these six steps: (1) decide on a subject, (2) identify possible topics, (3) select and limit the topic, (4) determine your attitude toward the topic, (5) write the thesis statement, and (6) test the thesis proposition.

The second component of the argumentative essay is main points—that is, principal support assertions offered to advance a thesis. Observations, personal experience, informed opinion, and organized research are common sources of support material.

The third component is the framework that ties together the main points assembled to support the assertion. In general, an argumentative essay can be organized according to a series structure or a chain structure. More specifically, it can be structured according to an inductive, a pro-and-con, a cause-and-effect, or an analysis-of-alternatives format.

READING FOR ANALYSIS

The following argumentative essay deals with the handicapped. State the thesis and the kind of assertion it is. In complete sentences express the main points and the sources of each. Identify the organizational pattern. Does the essay try to persuade? Explain why you think it does or does not. Finally, describe the kind of audience the author seemingly has in mind, as well as her persona. Ruth Lauer is a former chief psychologist of the New York City school system.

Handicapped: According to Whom?
Public Law 94-142 May Be Dangerous to Your Child.
By Rachel M. Lauer

Half of the children in New York City will be labeled *handicapped* in less than five years. Any child can be called emotionally or mentally handicapped if he or she has failed or misbehaved beyond the teacher's coping powers. This past year, about four thousand children per month were referred by teachers for examination; 97 percent of these children were called handicapped and then placed in special education facilities. According to Public Law 94-142, there are no restraints on how many children teachers can refer for examination and special placement. The rate of referral is increasing.

The law affecting New York City is the same for the entire nation. Its original, benign intent was to spur school districts into providing equal educational benefits for all handicapped children capable of learning. But what are some of the side effects?

Lawyers and public hearing officers are being hired in large numbers to handle huge case loads of protests from parents. Lawyers argue for parents that their children were wrongly diagnosed, wrongly placed, and that they were placed too fast or too slowly, or shouldn't have been placed at all. No one has counted the millions spent on second-guessing the clinicians who do the labeling. One case alone of a child whom the court decided had been misdiagnosed as retarded resulted in an award of $750,000.

School psychologists are being hired in increasing numbers nationwide, because the law requires them to do the evaluations. However, in New York City, as in most other large cities, psychologists have been pressed into an assembly-line process of testing and more testing; they must "turn out" two or three major decisions on children each day. They are not allowed the time to work with the child in his or her classroom, to help the teacher make adjustments, or even to find out what the teacher has or has not done to help the child. This past summer, ten thousand children were diagnosed as handicapped while their teachers were away on vacation!

Since state and federal reimbursements for providing children with special education do not cover the costs, local education monies are being shifted from regular class budgets to special education budgets. Regular teachers protest against increased class size. Monies are "saved" by firing guidance counselors and teachers of music, art, physical education, and so forth. Parents of normal and handicapped children are thrown into competition for the dollar.

To make matters worse, a recent New York City school board ruling proclaimed there was no longer any money for "preventive work" in the schools. That is, psychologists and social workers cannot work with families and teachers *before* the children have failed in their work or provoked the teachers beyond endurance. Thus, the concept of closing the barn doors after the horses have escaped has become an institutional policy. Why? Because the law requires that all children referred must be examined and placed within sixty days to prevent more court actions, and the waiting lists grow faster than clinicians can be hired to reduce them.

Long-Term Effects

Thus far, there has been no money to evaluate whether children placed in special education facilities are getting anything special for all the money spent on them. In New York City, special classes were created so fast that ordinary, inexperienced teachers were hired "off the street" to cover them. Emotionally disturbed children are thrown together in room after room as if togetherness had some curative value. Hundreds of untrained resource room teachers are handed fifteen children to tutor each hour, each child with a different prescription to follow.

The effect upon a child labeled emotionally disturbed or retarded can be devastating. Who knows what long-term effects there will be upon the child whose records, maintained on public file for years, label them emotionally disturbed, learning disabled, or retarded. Will they be able to graduate? Get jobs? Enter the armed services? Qualify for college? At present, there are extremely limited funds for getting children out of special education categories once they are in. Although the law requires reexamination of each child every three years, New York City is not yet able to keep up with the requirements to get the children into their placements.

Such chaos occurred in New York City as a result of Public Law 94-142 that the federal courts have taken over the running of the special education division; that is, a judge is now the official "master" of the gigantic program. Thus, we have a situation in which the judicial branch of the government has taken over executive functions. As a result of class-action suits, lawyers are writing extensive documents detailing exactly how clinicians and educators should function.

What Can Be Done?

Undoubtedly, in different sections of the country, Public Law 94-142 is being executed in different ways despite its extreme specificity. In some places, its value may exceed its defects. But I believe it behooves us as citizens to find out, for humanitarian as well as fiscal and professional reasons, what is happening in our local districts. Getting unbiased information may be impossible. Public officials, who owe us detailed and accurate reports, often give in to their fear of incessant questioning and potential law suits. They may become experts at covering, rationalizing, minimizing, and denying what is going on. Many clinicians are afraid of losing their jobs, such as they are. Teachers may seek relief from difficult children no matter what the cost. Parents seem to see the whole scene from the sole viewpoint of their particular child. But, if a citizens' group (parents association, advocacy group, or neighborhood association) invited a variety of persons to speak out on the issue, I believe a pattern of "truth" would emerge.

To change the law, or make this one work sanely, will require the efforts of many different kinds of people working together; single groups of lawyers, parents, or educators cannot do it alone. School psychologists who have canvassed many people in New York State as a whole have come up with the following recommendations:

1. Federal and state funding be rearranged so that monies flow to special services rather than to diagnostic labels.

2. Handicaps be defined not in terms of a child's defects alone but in terms of a mismatch between the child's needs and the school's resources.

3. Psychological evaluations be redefined to include analyses of the school's practices as well as the child's defects.

4. The object of evaluation be redefined as not the child alone but the social units in which the child functions: the classroom, peer group, and family.

5. The psychologist should ask not only, "What is wrong with this child?" but "What resources or coping skills would enable this social unit to help its own members more effectively?"

6. The psychologist should not do all the diagnostic work, but should help members of each social unit learn how to observe their own transactions, plan for changes, and implement these changes themselves.

These recommendations are significant not only for educators but also in a broader sense for all those concerned with the effects of language and labeling. The recommendations move attention from individuals to social interaction, from static labeling and categorization to the processes taking place in school situations. The thrust is toward helpful changes for pupils, teachers, and parents.[6]

THEME TOPICS

1. A chairman of the Federal Communications Commission once described television as "a vast wasteland." What he meant was that most network (CBS, NBC, ABC) programming wasn't fit for an adult. Would you agree? Use detailed evidence from shows that you have watched to write an essay (500 to 1,000 words) arguing your case. Present your material inductively.[7]

2. Write a pro-and-con paper in answer to one of the following questions:
   Should the draft be reinstated?
   Should college students be required to take English composition?

---

[6]This article first appeared in the Humanist, November/December 1980 and is reprinted by permission.
[7]Unless otherwise indicated in text or by your instructor, assume for all "theme topics" exercises in this book that the audience is your class.

Should the United States limit future immigration?
Should the sale of marijuana be legalized?
Should federal employees, such as postal workers and air traffic control-
lers, be permitted to strike?

3. Write an essay in which you analyze that *major causes* of one of the
   following: marital problems and divorce, cheating on exams, illiteracy
   among high school graduates, or the epidemic proportions of venereal
   disease among people under twenty-five.

4. Write a paper in which you analyze *major alternatives* for achieving one of
   the following goals: a reduction in violent crimes, a more integrated public
   school system, equal job opportunities for women, avoidance of nuclear
   war, a more favorable U.S. image abroad, a fair allocation of the costs of
   environmental cleanup, energy independence, or a more equitable distribution of the world's wealth and resources.

Patterns and Pitfalls

3. Facts and Opinions

The great Russian novelist Fyodor Dostoyevsky (1821–1881) once observed, "Freedom and bread enough for all are inconceivable together." What he meant was that liberty with economic development for everyone is impossible. Either only some are fed and all are free; or all are fed and only some are free.

If the dilemma posed by Dostoyevsky is a genuine one, then individually and collectively we face a dreadful choice: food or freedom? In our international relations, ought we try to feed bodies or minds and spirits? Influencing our choice, of course, will be all sorts of assumptions about human nature and human relations and about the kind of world we want. At the same time, these assumptions will be further shaped by our choice.

But perhaps Dostoyevsky was wrong, or at least overstating the issue. Maybe the dilemma he posed is a false one. It may be that food and freedom are possible for all. Theologian Michael Novak, for one, has written passionately to this effect, as the following essay well illustrates.

READING FOR ANALYSIS

Novak is a resident scholar in religion and public policy at the American Enterprise Institute and is the author of ten philosophical works and two novels.

"Human Rights: No More Small Men"
by Michael Novak

*"A state which dwarfs its men, in order that they may
be more docile instruments in its hands . . . will find
that with small men no great thing can really be
accomplished."*
                              John Stuart Mill, 1859

1   In 1948, most of the world lay gripped in poverty and much of it lay under the rubble of the most devastating war in human history. That year, when the United Nations ratified the Universal Declaration of Human Rights, there were only 49 independent nations in the world. The triumph of Allied armies in Asia, North Africa and Europe had carried Western civilization, particularly the United States, to its highest point of historical prestige.
2   It was quite natural, in those days, that the formulations of the Universal Declaration of Human Rights should have been modelled on the Bill of Rights of the United States, and on the concepts, institutional experiments, and ideals about which Abraham Lincoln spoke at Gettysburg. He observed that the Civil War was, "testing whether that nation, or any nation, so conceived and so dedicated, can long endure."

Can Nations Based on Human Rights Endure?
3   The foundation of human rights is the limited state.
4   Neither the Thousand Year Reich contemplated by Hitler nor Stalin's

state was conceived to be limited. At Auschwitz alone, Hitler killed four million persons of almost every European nationality and, in all the death camps, he killed at least twelve million. According to Aleksandr Solzhenitsyn, Lenin and Stalin between them killed 65 million of their fellow citizens in a terror that began in 1923 and continued during and after the war in a vast, dark and sprawling Gulag.

5   That is why Pope John Paul II as one of his first acts visited Auschwitz and later, at the United Nations, recalled that the Declaration of Human Rights owes its origin to so much bloodshed, so much anguish, already endured in our century of unlimited states.

6   Imagine what the Universal Declaration of Human Rights would have been had Hitler won the war or if Stalinism had everywhere prevailed. Words about human rights would have had no more substance than the paper on which they were inscribed.

What Is a Limited State?

7   In the first place, a limited state is one which does not impose a philosophy, does not hack humans to the mold of the "new man," does not forbid liberty of conscience. A limited state is a state "under God"—in operational terms, a state separated from, and under the judgment of, the transcendent claims of the free individual conscience.

8   Second, a limited state is prevented, as if by a moat, from intruding into the homes of its citizens. They have rights against the state. Law itself is conceived to be not solely an expression of the will of the state, but a set of limitations upon the will of the state. The law regards individuals as the source of inalienable rights.

9   This is a magnificent conception. It stands as a defense against all forms of collectivism. No matter how sweeping or how total the claims of states may be, these claims crash into impenetrable walls at the boundary of individual conscience.

10   Yet of all forms of political economy, none so thoroughly limits the state, and none so thoroughly respects the right of individuals, as democratic capitalism—that is, those two dozen or so nations which are democratic in polity, at least partly capitalist in economy, and liberal and pluralistic in ethos.

The Greatest Social Power in the World

11   Democratic captialism is not the Kingdom of God. It is not without sin. It is a system much in need of improvement, and subject at all times to continuous lawful revolution.

12   Still, by limiting the state, democratic captialism liberates the energies of individuals and whole communities. By respecting the unpredictable potential of the individual, it unleashes the greatest social power in the world, a power which in 200 short years has transformed the world.

13   For when the system of democratic capitalism first appeared in history, about 1800, the population of the world was not quite 900 million. Today, through creative inventions, advances in medicine, and economic development pioneered by democratic capitalistic societies, living human beings number 4.4 billion.

For Even the Poorest Nations

14   Still, the task of feeding, clothing, and housing these new millions demands immense new productive skills. Vast new wealth must be created. Great mountains of goods are needed for schools, clinics, homes. Simple things, like clean running water, are in many places still not available. Refrigeration and electric lights, basic sanitation and reliable sources of food, are inexcusably absent.

15   Thus, the economic development first imagined by Adam Smith in his *Inquiry into the Nature and the Causes of the Wealth of Nations* (1776) is a still unfinished task. Perhaps in one more century, by the year 2076, all the poorest nations will have experienced decisive economic growth. But that hasn't happened yet.

16   Lincoln said this nation could not endure, half-slave and half-free. Neither can the world long endure, half-slave and half-free—or half-starved and half-fed.

Human Rights and Economic Development

17   For the future, two points are crucial. Adam Smith did not write about the wealth of *Individuals*, or even the wealth of *Scotland*, but about the wealth of *Nations*. The fundamental intention of democratic capitalism is to raise the material base of all nations, of every part of humankind.

18   Second, human rights and liberty are not merely the goal for which wealth is to be created. They are the means of creating it.

19   The world needs to know that human rights work, that liberty is effective, that the practical choice is not "first bread, then liberty." Systems which deny liberty in the name of bread usually produce neither bread nor liberty.

20   The experiment with human rights which is conceived in liberty, and dedicated to the proposition that all men are created equal, is also an experiment in economic development. If all humans are equal, each must be free to make significant economic decisions—and if they are so free, the greatest social energy within the universe will be released.

21   It is wrong to pit human rights against economic development, to deny the former in the name of the latter. It is not only morally wrong, or politically wrong. It is also economically wrong. Free persons dream. Free persons invent. Free persons create. Freedom enriches, for wealth is not fixed but created.

22   The dream of democratic capitalism, which gave rise to the Bill of Rights, is not solely a moral dream or a political dream; it is also an economic dream.

With Due Respect

23   Respect for human rights inspires moral dynamism. Respect for human rights generates political vitality. Respect for human rights releases economic energies. It does all three of these at once.

24   Economic development is fundamentally an achievement of the human spirit. The imprisonment of that spirit in so many places, in so many ways, not only denies inalienable rights, but causes starvation and misery. Without respect for human rights, technical assistance is hollow, outside aid merely hides decay, and proven technologies fail. At the heart of hope lies the wit of individuals choosing for themselves.

25   The experiment of human rights works.[1]

Although the subject of Novak's essay is profoundly important, our primary interest in it is as an extended argument. This section of our study deals with patterns that are typically used in developing argumentative essays. Novak's essay illustrates one of the most common patterns: the development of an opinion.

Opinion relates to the argumentative essay in two distinct, though related, ways. On the one hand, any kind of argumentative essay may, and typically does, rely on opinions for development. In this sense, opinions function as sources of premises and support material and ways of expressing them. On the other hand, an argumentative essay may be one whose presentation relies primarily on the development of some overriding opinion. Novak's is such an essay. He is of the opinion that democratic capitalism delivers freedom with economic development. His essay, then, can be viewed as an extended argument whose presentation relies largely on the development of this opinion.

In order to evaluate and write the argumentative essay of opinion, you must know something about the nature of opinions and the problems associated with forming and appealing to them. This chapter deals with these and related issues. Specifically, it highlights the following subjects: (1) the difference between fact and opinion; (2) the relationship between observation and opinion; (3) fallacies associated with improper observation; (4) the use of the opinions of others—that is, of authority; (5) the use of statistics, studies, polls, and surveys; (6) fallacies associated with the improper use of authority and statistics; and (7) the value judgment, a special kind of opinion assertion. Finally, and most importantly, this chapter will consider two strategies for developing the argumentative essay of opinion.

---

[1]From *The SmithKline Forum for a Healthier American Society*, September 1981. © 1981 SmithKline Corporation. Reprinted by permission of the publisher's agency.

FACT AND OPINION

Ideally, a fact is what is actually the case. It is something that can be verified by close observation or measurement. That water freezes at thirty-two degrees Fahrenheit, that Washington is the nation's capital, that most professional basketball players are over six feet tall—all are facts. Anyone can confirm these assertions. Understandably, relevant facts are strong support for a thesis.

In contrast to facts, opinions are *what is believed* to be the case. That vitamin C can prevent the common cold, that life exists in outer space, that Robert E. Lee was a greater general than Ulysses S. Grant—all are opinions, not facts. Although such assertions cannot be verified, the evidence on which they are based can be. Thus, if a ballistics expert reports that two bullets were fired from the same gun, that's an opinion based on observations that the expert has made. This opinion cannot be confirmed, but the observations on which it is based can be. It is the expert's task, therefore, to reassure skeptics that the opinion is founded on observations that they themselves could share or verify. If the expert sufficiently reassures the audience—that is, convinces it of the legitimacy of the observations—then the opinion has the weight of fact.

Writers who offer opinions face the same job as the ballistics expert— convincing the audience that their opinions are erected on a solid factual base. Although this is no mean task, a couple of tactics are helpful: (1) keeping opinions close to the facts and (2) being wary of offering unsupported opinions on unresolved questions.

1. *Keep opinions close to the facts.* Remember that your task in advancing a thesis is to give solid substance to one point at a time. If you accomplish this, by the end of the paper you will have won the audience's assent or consent. But the more you editorialize, the more difficult you make your task. For one thing, you may drive off your audience, which may take offense at the cavalier way you gloss over controversial points. Or you may so distract the audience that your main point is obscured. Indeed, sometimes just a word or phrasing in a sentence so dislodges the opinion from fact that the statement becomes highly questionable. For example, suppose you were dealing with the fact that Ronald Reagan won the 1980 presidential election. Here are two ways you might interpret that fact: (1) "The voters expressed their resentment of liberal policy in sending Ronald Reagan to the White House in the 1980 election" and (2) "The voters expressed their desire for a change in sending Ronald Reagan to the White House in the 1980 election." Both sentences report a fact and offer an opinion on it. The problem with the first version is that it puts a far greater burden of justification on the writer than does the second. It's much easier to establish that the vote signaled a desire for change than that it expressed resentment of liberal policy. Thus, the audience is far more likely to accept the second opinion than the first.

Again, suppose the fact is that 50,000 illegal aliens are living in Los

Angeles. Here are two ways that this fact might be interpreted: (1) "Fifty thousand illegal aliens are holed up in the warrens along the back alleys of lower Los Angeles" and (2) "Unable to afford other accommodations, fifty thousand aliens are living in deserted buildings in Los Angeles." The first version is packed with opinion as a result of the use of emotive language. It calls up a rodentlike image by using "holed up" and "warrens." "Back alley" reinforces this picture of the aliens. As a result, readers might easily infer that the illegal aliens are unclean and diseased, even a menace. Far less debatable is the second version, which merely opines that the aliens are living as they are because they cannot afford other accommodations. We have, then, two interpretations of the same fact. One interpretation strays dangerously far from the facts, unless the writer intends to justify the implied opinions. The other interpretation hugs the facts, thereby presenting the writer as a level-headed commentator and precluding the need for exhaustive justification.

2. *Be wary of offering unsupported opinions on unresolved questions.* Often an important issue has not been settled. Does vitamin C help prevent the common cold? Does constant exposure to mass-media violence make a person violent? Do pornographic materials make people more or less likely to commit sex-related crimes? Does capital punishment deter crime? Does premarital sex make for better or worse marriages? Though intriguing, such questions yield no certain answers.

This doesn't mean that you should avoid such issues. On the contrary, I indicated in Chapter 1 that highly controversial issues make ideal topics for argumentative essays. By the same token, because of their debatable nature you cannot expect your audience to accept your viewpoint on mere say-so. Precisely because these questions are unresolved, taking a stand on them requires considerable support. Highly opinionated people often forget this and offer viewpoints but not support. In short, if you want to argue that excessive watching of television undermines a child's reading ability—fine. But recognize that this is a highly controversial and unresolved issue, which means that you must make a strong case for your opinion. Opinion support is especially vital when the opinion itself functions as support material. For example, suppose that in supporting the thesis that parents should not allow their children to watch television more than an hour a day, you assert the opinion that watching television undermines a child's reading ability. Because this reason is an opinion on an unsettled question, you cannot leave it unsupported. If you do, the audience is justified in rejecting it as doubtful, and with it your thesis.

Exercises

3.1   Below are five topics. For each, write a sentence that expresses a fact, one that expresses an opinion, and one that expresses both a fact and an opinion.

SAMPLE: *abortion*

FACT: Some doctors perform abortions.

OPINION: Doctors should not perform abortions.

FACT/OPINION: Even though doctors perform abortions, they should not because abortion is murder.

SAMPLE: the film Raiders of the Lost Ark

FACT: Raiders of the Lost Ark was a box office hit.

OPINION: The special effects used in Raiders of the Lost Ark excelled those used in any other fantasy film.

FACT/OPINION: Raiders of the Lost Ark was that rare fantasy film which, while dazzling us with brilliantly conceived and executed special effects, was also a box-office hit.

—health foods

—sex and violence in films

—the 55 MPH speed limit

—prenuptial agreements, in which partners decide ahead of time how property will be divided should the marriage end in divorce

—soap operas

3.2 Repeat the preceding exercise with five topics of your own.

3.3 Both passages in the following sample offer an interpretation of available facts. The first is less factual than the second. After reading this sample, write five such pairs of your own.

LESS FACTUAL: Without provocation, the police attacked the gang members, beating boys and girls alike.

MORE FACTUAL: After a fight broke out, the police moved in to disperse the rival gangs. In the ensuing melee, four youths were injured. A girl and two boys were treated at the emergency room of General Hospital for cuts and bruises.

FORMING OPINIONS

In approaching argumentative papers to be developed through opinion, writers often put the cart before the horse: They form an opinion before gathering or organizing material. Although it is impossible to approach many subjects with pure objectivity, the opinion should ideally grow out of the investigation. The danger of approaching a subject with preconceived notions is that you may select only material that supports your position. The result is overlooked evidence. So, rather than ferreting out facts to fit a preconceived opinion, you should develop an opinion to fit the facts that you have found.

If we were talking science, we'd say: Use the scientific method in forming opinions. *The scientific method is a way of investigating a phenomenon that is based on the collection, analysis, and interpretation of evidence to determine the most probable inference.* Briefly, evidence yields opinion.

Essential to evidence are observations. Whenever scientists weigh something, measure it, or take its temperature and then record their findings, they are making observations. In forming an opinion, you should perform similar activities: interviewing people, reading up on a subject, reflecting on your own experience, examining the alternatives, and so on. The resulting observations form the basis for the evidence that supports your opinion.

Obviously, then, observation is crucial to informed opinions. Just as obviously, not all observations are correct. This is why, contrary to popular opinion, not all opinions are created equal. What distinguishes the informed opinion from the uninformed one is the quality of the observations on which it is based. Evaluating opinions—ours and those of others—calls for an inspection of the supporting observations. If the observations are reliable, the opinions are informed.

Reliable Observations

Reliable observations should meet certain criteria concerning the conditions under which they were made and the abilities of the people who made them. Specifically, there are five key factors to consider in evaluating observations: (1) the physical conditions under which the observations were made, (2) the sensory acuity of the observer, (3) the background knowledge of the observer, (4) the objectivity of the observer, and (5) the supporting testimony of other observers.

1. *Physical conditions.* Physical conditions are the circumstances under which the observations were made. For example, if a dentist diagnoses your condition solely on the basis of a telephone conversation with you, then the diagnosis is highly suspect. Contrast that diagnosis with one made in the dentist's office after a thorough examination that includes X rays of the troublesome molar. In this case, the conditions under which the observations

are made are far more conducive to forming a correct medical opinion. The point is that, before you accept any observation, you should ensure that the physical conditions under which it was made were favorable.

2. *Sensory acuity.* Sensory acuity refers to the quality of the observer's senses. Some people see and hear better than others; some have more sharply developed senses of smell and taste, even touch. Observations must always be evaluated in the light of the observer's ability to have made them.

In science, where precise measurements are crucial, instruments heighten the observer's sensory acuity. As a result, in evaluating the reliability of scientific investigations where exact measurements of height, weight, volume, and temperature are crucial, it's necessary to evaluate the accuracy of the instruments as well as the sensory acuity of the person making the observations.

The technological extension of the human senses can be decisive in providing evidence to support an opinion. A classic example is found in the invention of the telescope, which allowed so many of the assertions of the so-called Copernican revolution to be confirmed. In our own times, we have had mechanical marvels such as the Pioneer 11 spacecraft, which journeyed far from home and, with the aid of elegantly sophisticated cameras, elevated to a fact our *opinion* that Saturn is girdled with radiation.

3. *Necessary background knowledge.* Necessary background knowledge is what an observer must already know to make a reliable observation. Although we can know we have a toothache, we are not qualified to diagnose the ache as resulting from a cavity, nerve deterioration, or gum disease. That's the job of the dentist, who is qualified by background knowledge to offer an opinion.

We needn't look far to see how often this criterion is abused. For example, celebrities are paid handsomely to endorse everything from mouthwash to presidential candidates. More often than not, these super-salespeople lack the necessary background to make their pitches anything more than uninformed opinions, albeit lucrative ones.

4. *Objectivity.* Objectivity is the quality of viewing ourselves and the world without distortion. Although it is true that we can never be completely impartial, we can be aware of our biases and try to minimize their impact on our observations. The same applies to how we evaluate the observations that support the opinions of others. Especially noteworthy is an awareness of the observer's assumptions—that is, what the person takes for granted. For example, the observations that the American Medical Association (AMA) makes in arguing against national health insurance must be viewed in the light of the association's historical assumption that fee-for-service, or free-enterprise, medicine is best and that anything else is socialistic. Don't misunderstand. This does not mean that we should summarily dismiss the AMA opinion, but, on the other hand, we should not automatically accept the AMA view without seeking the considered opinion of a more disinterested party. In short, we

must consider how the loyalties, or built-in biases, of observers may be coloring their observations, thereby warping the evidence to fit a predetermined conclusion. Always challenging, this task is most formidable when we ourselves happen to be the observers. Failing to introspect, to compensate for the universal tendency toward selective editing, we can cook up all sorts of indigestible evidence to support opinions.

5. *Supporting testimony*. Supporting testimony is the observations of other observers that tend to back up the evidence presented. Supporting testimony is one of the most important criteria in establishing the credibility of our opinions. In investigating a matter, if you find that the collective weight of other people's well-considered views supports a position, then that position is greatly strengthened. This is not the same as subjecting an issue to a head count or popularity contest. Rather, it's invoking the experience of others who, having met the other four criteria, corroborate one's own observations about the evidence presented.

These five principles are most useful in evaluating our own opinions and those of others. Although it's possible that an opinion based on observations that pass these tests may ultimately prove wrong headed, these criteria do provide a generally reliable way of determining whether we have enough of the right kind of evidence to qualify an opinion as "informed." Further, they keep us from falling victim to certain fallacies associated with unreliable observations.

Unreliable Observations: Two Common Fallacies

Because the argumentative essay that is developed through opinion inevitably serves up factually based inferences, we must first ensure that the facts are accurate, representative of the whole picture, and complete. What is untrue is not a fact; what is not known for sure should not be passed off as fact. Support material should not suppress significant facts or introduce extraneous information. Judgments should be based only on sufficient evidence. But beyond this there are two fallacies associated with forming doubtful opinions: questionable evaluation and provincialism.

Questionable Evaluation One of the most common fallacies associated with opinion papers is the questionable evaluation. *The fallacy of questionable evaluation consists in making a controversial assertion without support or making a controversial assertion that cannot stand up under investigation because of its breadth.* For example, consider again the opinion that excessive watching of television undermines a child's ability to read. We would naturally expect support for this assertion. In the absence of support, it is a questionable evaluation. Even if the person does offer some support, if most of the evidence impugns the assertion, then the claim is a questionable evaluation.

Questionable evaluations run rampant in advertising. The aspirin industry is a choice illustration. Various manufacturers of aspirin hawk their
products as "extra-strength pain relief," the tablet that is "50 percent stronger
than aspirin," or the "pain reliever that doctors recommend most." Presumably these assertions are to entail the conclusion "You, the consumer, should
buy this product."

The sinister thing about such assertions is that they *appear* to be facts,
especially when mouthed by some distinguished-looking figure dressed in a
white smock and armed with the "findings of the latest research." But don't be
duped: The alleged facts are the opinions of the manufacturer. As soon as you
recognize the assertions as opinions, you will rightly ask for the observations
on which they are based. But don't hold your breath waiting for them: The
Federal Trade Commission (FTC) has found that all analgesic products are
effective to about the same degree.[2] Why believe the FTC rather than the
aspirin manufacturers? With respect to the tests for reliable observations, the
FTC's observations pass muster; the aspirin manufacturers' do not. Thus,
we'd be wise to consider the assertions of superiority by aspirin manufacturers questionable evaluations. Here's another example of a questionable
evaluation, with comment:

EXAMPLE: *"With the addition of television to the many other tools the
press corps employs, the Vietnam War was the best-reported
war in history." (Robert Taylor, president of CBS, Inc.
Speech to the Los Angeles World Affairs Council, October
24, 1973.)*

COMMENT: *It is true that, given the technological resources of the
media, the Vietnam War potentially might have been the
best-reported war in history. But was it? Perhaps not.
According to many journalists, much reporting of the war
amounted to regurgitating of data spoon-fed to reporters by
military press officers. Also, if we assume that Taylor was
referring to the American press, then his opinion is questionable, because many important war stories were first
filed by the foreign press corps. Indeed, in some instances,
editors of U.S. newspapers engaged in self-censorship. For
example, a Washington Post reporter learned that two army
intelligence officers had said that the Central Intelligence
Agency and army intelligence were training personnel in
torture and assassination techniques to be used against
members of the National Liberation Front in Vietnam.[3] Yet
the story never appeared in the Washington Post. At the very
least, then, "best reported" is sorely in need of definition,*

---

[2]The editors of Consumer Reports. *The Medicine Show.* Mt. Vernon, N.Y.: Consumers Union,
1972, pp. 9–13.

and the entire statement requires justification. Until those are forthcoming, the opinion is best regarded as a questionable evaluation.

Provincialism When opinion in an argument lacks objectivity, the fallacy called provincialism often results. *The fallacy of provincialism consists of viewing things exclusively in terms of group loyalty.* People who appeal to provincialism insist on seeing the world through the eyes of the group with which they identify. Thus, the salesperson who argues that you should buy a domestic car rather than an import because "it's only the American thing to do" is appealing to provincialism.

During the heated debate in 1980 over the treaty that would cede maintenance of the Panama Canal from the United States to Panama, provincialism was much in evidence. Indeed, most of the arguments against the treaty seemed to assume that (1) the United States had some kind of proprietary claim over the canal or (2) Americans were uniquely qualified to run the canal. Both assumptions, of course, were rooted in provincialism.

But the fallacy of provincialism need not be confined to examples of national loyalty. Sometimes the group identified with is considerably smaller, perhaps a profession or occupation. Thus, an economist might argue, "The present administration deserves very low marks, because it's quite clear that it knows nothing about basic economics." Here an opinion is formed about competence exclusively in terms of economics, the author's field. Similarly, an educator might favor the reinstitution of the military draft because it would help sagging college enrollments, or police officers might favor a relaxation of search-and-seizure regulations because it would simplify their jobs.

Exercises

3.4 *Identify the fallacies of questionable evaluation or provincialism in each of the following opinions.*

1. *"We submit that Congress should allow a tax-free savings certificate, as proposed in the All Savers Act (H.R. 3456 and S. 1279). This would be one of the most significant economic moves of the last 50 years.*

    "It would be free from federal income tax.

    "It would be offered in affordable denominations.

    "It would be insured by a federal agency.

    "And it would pay a rewarding net return.

    "Free from tax. Affordable. Insured. Rewarding.

    "That spells fair. That's what we call it. And that's what it is." (Advertisement sponsored by the Savings and Loan Foundation.)

---

[3] See George Wilson. "The Fourth Estate as the Fourth Branch." *Village Voice,* January 1, 1970.

2. *"Dial is the most effective deodorant soap you can buy."* (Advertisement.)

3. *"The great Declaration of Independence begins: 'When in the course of human events.' . . . and for the first time in man's history announce[s] that all rights come from a sovereign, not from a government but from God."* (Henry J. Taylor. Topeka Daily Capital, July 1970. Quoted in Howard Kahane. Logic and Contemporary Rhetoric. Belmont, Calif.: Wadsworth, 1980, p. 28.)

4. *"It is the government's inherent right to lie if necessary to save itself when faced with nuclear disaster. This is basic."* (Arthur Sylvester, former assistant secretary of defense for public affairs.)

5. *"By permitting our highest elected officials and those they appoint to administrative posts to classify information as confidential, and by placing no constraints on those public servants, we deny the public information necessary for proper decision making in the democratic process."* (Robert C. Jeffry. "Ethics in Public Disclosure." Speech delivered at the 59th annual meeting of the Speech Communication Associates, New York, November 11, 1973.)

6. *"Totalitarian regimes imposed on free peoples, by direct aggression, undermine the foundations of international peace, and hence the security of the United States."* (President Harry S. Truman. "The Truman Doctrine." March 12, 1947.)

7. *"In his opinion [Supreme Court Justice William H.] Rehnquist said Congress [was] completely justified in excluding women from the draft and from draft registration because they are unable to serve as well as men in combat positions."* (Jim Mann. "Court Upholds All Male Draft." Los Angeles Times, June 26, 1981, part I, p. 7.)

8. *"For police department officials to talk to reporters, people from the CAO [City Administrative Office], the board of police commissioners, people in the mayor's offices, council members—that is serious. There is a theme of disloyalty about that kind of thing."* (Los Angeles Police Chief Daryl F. Gates, reacting to criticisms leveled against his department by a retiring deputy police chief. David Johnston. "LAPD's Problems Serious, Retiring Top Officer Says." Los Angeles Times, June 29, 1981, part I, p. 3.)

9. *"'I know that with my father's leadership at the White House, this countries [sic] armed services are going to be rebuilt and strengthened. We at Dana Ingalls Profile want to be involved in that process."* (Michael Reagan, in a letter to the Small and Disadvantaged Business Utilization Office at Tinker Air Force Base, seeking to have his firm placed on bid lists as a supplier of machine parts and small assemblies. George Skelton. "Son to Quit Jobs Over Use of Reagan's Name in Letter," Los Angeles Times, May 15, 1981, part 1, p. 1.)

10. "The Kennedys are the greatest exploiters of women since plantation days." (Nancy Gager Clinch, Los Angeles Times, July 22, 1973, p. 2.)

3.5 Assume that you are the individual identified below. In a sentence or two express an opinion that is based on an appeal to provincialism.

Police officer: Fortunately, all signs indicate that crime will continue to increase for the forseeable future.

College student:

A physician:

A life insurance salesperson:

A member of a terrorist organization:

A male reporter to a female weight lifter:

Girlfriend to boyfriend:

Boss to worker:

College athletic recruiter to high school prospect:

OPINIONS OF OTHERS: LEGITIMATE AND ILLEGITIMATE APPEALS TO AUTHORITY

Clearly, we do not form our opinions in a vacuum. Neither do other people. Often as not we merely rely on the viewpoints of others or call on them to lend credibility to our opinions. In brief, we invoke authority.

Authority is an expert source outside ourselves on whom we base our opinion. For example, someone declares, "Cigarette smoking is hazardous to health, because the surgeon general says so." The person is basing a viewpoint about cigarette smoking on authoritative testimony, the word of the U.S. surgeon general. In this instance, the person's opinion is well founded, because (1) the authority invoked is indeed an expert in the area and (2) there is general agreement among the experts in support of the view. When these two criteria are present—expertise and general agreement among experts—then the appeal to authority is a legitimate one and provides solid support for opinions. But not all appeals to authority are legitimate.

False Authority

The fallacy of false authority consists of violating either of the two criteria for a justifiable appeal to authority. Most endorsements of products by celebrities are examples of appeals to false authority, because the endorsers lack relevant expertise. Athletes who endorse milk, for example, probably aren't nutritionists or in any other way qualified to speak about the benefits of drinking milk. What's more, there isn't even agreement among the experts about the value of drinking milk. In fact, milk is not good for everyone. So the implied claim that the sponsor makes—that you should drink milk because so-and-so does or thinks it's a good idea—is an appeal to false authority. So are the following:

> EXAMPLE: *The United States should sell sophisticated radar planes to Saudi Arabia, because the president thinks it's a good idea.*

> COMMENT: *For many Americans there isn't any more potent authority figure than the president. Nevertheless, even granting the president's expertise, the president isn't the only expert on the sale of sophisticated radar planes to the Saudis. Nor is the military. Such a transaction is fraught with geopolitical considerations that make the viewpoints of others admissible and desirable. In brief, because there is no general agreement on the proposition, the appeal to the president constitutes a use of false authority.*

> EXAMPLE: *There is no doubt in my mind that humans are inherently aggressive. After all, Darwin thought so, and so do social scientists such as Konrad Lorenz and Robert Ardrey.*

> COMMENT: *Whether humans are inherently aggressive continues to puzzle social scientists. Although the authorities cited do support an aggressionist view, others do not: Gordon Allport, Carl Rogers, and most recently Ashley Montagu. Given the lack of consensus about this aspect of human nature, the assertion constitutes a false appeal to authority.*

In addition to this kind of fallacious appeal, illegitimate appeals to authority are frequently made to two additional sources: popularity and tradition.

Popularity

The fallacy of popularity (democracy or public opinion) consists of relying exclusively on numbers to support a contention. "Five million people have already seen this film! Isn't it about time you did?" "Why do I think the president's program is sound? Because the polls indicate than an overwhelming number of the public support it." "More people choose Brand X than any of the leading competitors. Reason enough for you to buy Brand X." Each of these passages touts something by giving to sheer numbers the force of authority. But numbers alone don't make truth or substantiate an opinion. The appeals are fallacious.

Tradition

The fallacy of tradition consists of appealing to feelings of reverence or respect for some custom that supports the view being advanced. For example, Jane's friend tells her: "I don't think you should keep your maiden name after marrying. In this culture the woman always takes her husband's name. That's what distinguishes a married woman from a single one." Although there may be good reasons for a woman's keeping her maiden name after marrying, this certainly isn't one of them. The appeal is strictly to tradition. But why should custom necessarily dictate present behavior? It needn't, and that's the point.

Again, George Miller insists that his son Bob go to a certain college. "My father and his father before him went to State U.," he tells Bob. "Why, it's a family tradition!" Maybe so, but State U. may not be the best choice for Bob.

Beware of certain phrases in your own writing and that of others that often signal appeals to tradition. Among these phrases are *the Founding Fathers, the earliest settlers, from time immemorial, tried and true, the lessons of history, it says so in, look at the record, in the past, customarily, traditionally, historically,* and the like. This is not meant to imply that tradition has no place in formulating opinion. On the contrary, when tradition is backed up by other facts and reason, then it's a respectable and effective opinion source. When appealing to tradition, therefore, provide evidence that will convince the audience that the tradition is worth preserving.

Exercises

3.6 *Which of the following assertions would you take on authority? Explain.*

1. *Light travels at 186,000 miles per second.*

2. *A body probably can't accelerate to the speed of light.*

3. *Men have a stronger sex drive than women.*

4. *Marijuana can cause a loss of sexual desire.*

5. *Fluoridated water is a health hazard.*

6. *The earth follows an elliptical orbit.*

7. *Sugar contributes to tooth decay.*

8. *The earth was once visited by astronaut gods.*

9. Democracy is the best form of government.

10. Smoking contributes to heart disease.

11. Women are not suited for military combat.

12. On the average, college graduates make more money in their lifetime than nongraduates.

3.7 Identify the fallacies of authority in the following opinions: false authority, popularity, tradition.

1. The golden rule is a sound moral principle because it is a part of every system of ethics ever devised.

2. "Avis features cars designed by Chrysler." (Advertisement.)

3. **Frank:** I think I'd prefer something more nutritious to drink than Tang.
   Anne: More nutritious? Don't you realize that NASA chose Tang for its astronauts?
   Frank: Really? OK, let me have a glass.

4. "A football Saturday in New Haven, 1934. This was it. The last game of the season. Harvard-Yale!
   "Chanting 'Boola, Boola!' they spill out of fraternity houses and run for the stadium.
   "It was at such a moment that a coach had told his team, 'Gentlemen, you are about to play football for Yale against Harvard. Never in your lives will you do anything so important.'
   "Now, there is no stopping them. These are Saturday's children on a winning streak. And at university clubs throughout the world, old Blues profoundly wish them well.
   "Ballantine's Scotch was there. Like those classic days, the classic scotch. With a taste to be celebrated again and again. Taste is why you buy it." (Advertisement.)

5. Owner of a San Francisco restaurant, reacting against a proposed truth-in-advertising ordinance to require restaurant owners to identify food prepared off the premises and then frozen: "Three-quarters or seven-eighths of the people who come into my place . . . don't give a good goddamn." (Los Angeles Times, July 4, 1974, part 1, p. 11.)

6. Clint Eastwood, justifying the film roles he does: "A guy sits alone in a theatre. He's young and he's scared. He doesn't know what he's going to do with his life. He wishes he could be self-sufficient, like the man he sees up there on the screen, somebody who can look out for himself, solve his own problems. I do the kind of roles I'd like to see if I were still digging swimming pools and wanted to escape my problems." (Time, January 9, 1978, p. 48.)

7. The late U.S. Representative William M. Ketchum, speaking against transferring the maintenance of the Panama Canal to Panama: "Our forefathers at the turn of the century built that waterway through hazardous and hard work for the security and well-being of future generations. I refuse to stand on the sidelines and watch this resolve be destroyed. Consequently you can be assured that I will do everything possible to see that the Congress defeats any bill which seeks to relinquish U.S. rights to the Canal." (Form letter in response to a constituent's letter expressing support of the transfer.)

8. "Drink Irish Mist. Ireland's legendary Liqueur." (Advertisement.)

9. "Home: San Francisco
   Age: 30
   Profession: produces rock-music specials
   Last book read: Sybil
   Favorite quotation: "There's only one thing worse than losing—death."
   Female preference: bright, witty, unclinging
   Scotch: Dewar's, what else?" (Advertisement.)

10. The old saying "A man's home is his castle" paraphrases the U.S. Constitution's guarantee that each person's property and right to privacy are sacrosanct. That's why labor unions should not be allowed access to private property without the owner's permission.

11. "Mr. Skotheim's criticisms raise the general problem, which Professor David M. Potter so cogently discussed not long ago in a review in the Journal of Southern History, of 'how far it is possible to proceed in judging historian interpretations without grounding these judgments in an understanding of the history which is being interpreted.' Perhaps the teaching profession is at fault in encouraging young scholars like Mr. Skotheim to undertake studies in methodology and historiography before he has demonstrated his competence in research." (David M. Donald, Journal of Southern History, vol. 26, 1960, pp. 156–157. The author of this letter is responding to criticism of his assertion that most abolitionists were descended from old and socially dominant northeastern families. Skotheim had criticized Donald's thesis on the grounds of imprecise data, the absence of a control in the research, and a false extrapolation from abolitionist leadership to all abolitionists. Cited in David Hackett Fischer. Historians' Fallacies. New York: Harper & Row, 1970, pp. 283–284.)

12. "In that melancholy book, The Future of an Illusion, Dr. Freud, himself one of the last great theorists of the European capitalist class, has stated with simple clarity the impossibility of religious belief for the educated man today." (John Strachey. The Coming Struggle for Power. New York: Random House (Modern Library), 1935, p. 170.)

13. "The elegant Lord Shaftesbury somewhere objects to telling too much

truth: by which it may be fairly inferred that, in some cases, to lie is not only inexcusable, but commendable." (Henry Fielding. Tom Jones. New York: Random House, 1950, p. 645.)

14. "But can you doubt that air has weight when you have the clear testimony of Aristotle affirming that all elements have weight, including air and excepting only fire?" (Galileo Galilei. Dialogues Concerning Two New Sciences. Trans. Henry Crew and Alfonso De Salvio. New York: Macmillan, 1914, p. 77.)

15. "England's King George III was the symbol against which our founders made a revolution now considered bright and glorious. We must realize that today's Establishment is the new George III. Whether it will continue to adhere to his tactics, we do not know. If it does, the redress, honored in tradition, is also revolution." (William O. Douglas. Points of Rebellion. New York: Random House, 1970, p. 95.)

3.8 You are trying to convince a group of preadolescents of the health hazards of smoking. Make your case in one well-developed paragraph that relies primarily on legitimate appeals to authority.

3.9 You are an advertising executive who has been asked to write a short piece (no more than 100 words) extolling the virtues of a new toothpaste your company is about to market. You decide to rely on authoritative appeals in the ad. Write the copy for the ad, keeping in mind that your purpose is to sell the product.

STATISTICS

Writers sometimes use statistics to shore up opinions. Although statistics are not themselves authorities, they can carry an authoritative clout. In my limited space, I can't mention everything that could or should be asked when using or confronting statistics. But three questions stand out: Does the statistic make any difference? Is it complete? Is it knowable?

First, statistics are useful when they tell us something worth knowing, and they tell us something worth knowing when they make a difference. For example, suppose that the U.S. Department of Health and Human Services released figures showing that diabetes was the nation's third most common disease, behind cancer and heart disease, and that its incidence among people under twenty-five had risen 5 percent in the last ten years. Such figures would certainly alert government, the medical community, and the general public to an alarming health problem and to the need for corrective measures. Thus, the figures would make a difference to anyone concerned about disease control.

But statistics are often bandied about that, in fact, make no difference at all, although they may appear to. For example, for several years the U.S. Postal Service has been selling its used delivery vehicles to the general public. Posted on the dashboards is a sticker that reads: "This vehicle has met all applicable safety standards." Although such an assertion seems meaningful, it isn't, because so few safety standards apply to this government vehicle to begin with. As a result, it has a very high center of gravity, which makes it easy to roll over, an upholstered dashboard with protruding knobs and switches, and a steering column that has been likened to an iron pipe pointed at the chest of the driver. The abnormally high number of single-vehicle accidents involving the vehicle belie the safety reassurances of the sticker. Indeed, many in transportation safety have called it the most dangerous vehicle on the highway today. In a word, a sticker indicating that such a vehicle has met 100 percent of the applicable safety standards is meaningless.

As another example, consider diet-control products. Some diet aids are said to depress appetite. Thus, if we eat a candy before meals, it is asserted, our blood-sugar level will rise enough to stifle appetite. But candies don't bring about a great rise in blood sugar. Even more important, there is no clinical evidence to show that an increase in blood sugar inhibits appetite. But even if something were inhibited, it would be hunger, not appetite. But obesity is caused by appetite, not hunger; and an appetite is a learned way of behaving, associated with a complex network of pleasurable physical and psychological feelings. So again, such assertions make no difference.

A second thing to look for with statistics is completeness. Statistics that are incomplete are as meaningless as statistics that make no difference. For example, suppose that, in justifying an increase in its premium rates, an insurance company argued that it had paid out $3 billion more in claims than it collected in premiums over the past eight years. Although these figures might be accurate, the profit picture of an insurance company is hardly drawn by subtracting claims from premiums. What must also be considered is the money that was made by investing premiums.

Third, in handling statistics we should ask whether they are knowable. For example, not too long ago it was reported that more than half the money spent on birth control worldwide was for abortions. But such a statistic is highly questionable in the light of two facts. First, there are widespread taboos about birth control and abortion in many parts of the world. Second, socialist and Third World countries have very different economies from the United States and often from each other. Given these realities, one author concluded that "the figure can have been no more than only the wildest guess."[4]

Thus, we should find out of any statistic whether it makes a difference, is

---

[4]Perry Weddle. *Argument: A Guide to Critical Thinking.* New York: McGraw-Hill, 1978, p. 90.

complete, and is knowable. But there are some statistics that require additional scrutiny, in terms of how they were arrived at. Perhaps the most common sources of statistics that we use and confront daily are studies, surveys, and polls. Since these sources can have the force of authority and since they produce blizzards of statistics, we should have a look at them.

STUDIES, SURVEYS, AND POLLS

Among the most common sources of authority or informed opinion are studies, surveys, and polls. For example, "Two out of three doctors recommend Bayer"; "By the end of this decade, more women will be working than men"; "Eighty-four percent of Golden Lights smokers switch from higher-tar brands and stay"; "Studies conducted at a leading university prove that Excedrin gives you faster headache relief"; and "By the year 2000 the average price of a house will be $200,000." It seems that we are bombarded everywhere by statistics that are often the results of studies, surveys, and polls. This kind of statistical generalization is often invoked to support an opinion. The central question for the writer and reader of argument is: Under what conditions can studies, surveys, and polls be used as legitimate sources of authority?

Studies

It is impossible to consider all the many aspects of research studies. So, I will restrict myself to providing some basic guidelines for the intelligent use and evaluation of studies in argument when they function authoritatively. These guidelines can be boiled down to the following six:

1. *Determine the subjects involved.* It is important to know as much as possible about the subjects involved in a study in order to make sure that subtle individual differences haven't biased the results. The age, general health, emotional state, diet, and possibly even the sex of the subjects are just some of the things that might have a bearing on the effects of a drug, for example. Just as important is information about side effects that subjects may have reported, including the stages at which these side effects were reported. Further, it is important to know whether the subjects reported cures or relief from the product and whether their reactions differed from those of patients using conventional treatment or products. For example, not long ago Galaxo, Incorporated, an American subsidiary of a large international drug company, touted the "remarkable therapeutic effects of Ventolin" for asthma sufferers. Perhaps the subjects tested did experience relief when they used the drug. But in reporting the test results and in promoting the drug, Galaxo didn't mention that the Food and Drug Administration (FDA) had said that Ventolin had little more or no more therapeutic value than the asthma drugs already available.[5]

---

[5]See Allan Parachini. "The Medical Community Ponders 'a Touchy Subject.'" *Los Angeles Times,* July 9, 1981, part 5, p. 1.

2. *Determine for how long the search was conducted.* Sometimes a product that shows great early promise proves disappointing later. Research done hastily encourages hasty generalizations, which, in the case of drugs, can be dangerous.

3. *Determine who conducted the testing.* In general, the research of impartial parties is more reliable than the research of those with a vested interest. Thus, research on a brand of aspirin or antihistamine done by some independent agency (for example, the National Institutes of Health, the FDA, or the FTC) would ordinarily be more objective than research done by the company developing the product for sale. Although objectivity does not guarantee reliability, it is nevertheless a fundamental part of the scientific method. Also relevant is information about the individuals conducting the tests; personal, as well as institutional, bias can compromise objectivity, thereby shaping results.

4. *Determine to which stage of research the assertion refers.* This guideline speaks especially to drugs, which are usually subjected to three stages of research: test-tube, animal, and human. Not knowing which stage the research is based on, we cannot intelligently assess it. Also significant is information about follow-up studies.

5. *Determine how the study was conducted.* This most important guideline addresses the method of research. Specifically, it points up the need to control variables—that is, factors that, left uncontrolled, can invalidate the research. As a simple illustration, suppose that the manufacturer of a dishwashing detergent wanted to find out about the effects of the product on the hands of users. One obvious thing researchers would have to do is ensure that the subjects were not using hand creams or lotions during the testing. Of course, sometimes even such an obvious control as this can be flouted, perhaps unintentionally. One company actually boasted the beneficient effects of its detergent while failing to mention that the subjects involved in its tests had worn rubber gloves while washing dishes!

6. *Determine how extensive the testing was.* This guideline refers to sample size and representativeness. As we saw in studying the generalization, small and nonrepresentative samples can lead to faulty generalizations.

Although these six guidelines do not address all the issues that could be raised, they do provide a useful distillation of the major ones. In reading and writing about the results of studies, you would be wise to follow these directives in order to detect and avoid illegitimate appeals to authority through the use of statistics.

Polls and Surveys

Polls and surveys are an even more popular source of supposedly authoritative statistics than are studies. Like studies, polls and surveys invite caution and scrutiny. The following guidelines are offered with that in mind.[6]

1. *Determine the sponsor's and survey's name.* Just as we should determine who conducted a study, we should identify the sponsor and survey in order to assess objectivity. Of course, simply because the sponsor has an interest in the results of a poll or survey does not of itself discredit the results. But it does alert us to a potential conflict of interest and should warn us to check some other, less partial source before accepting the results. Similarly, that a survey is anonymous or is not done by one of the better-known polling firms (for example, Gallup, Roper, Harris) does not invalidate the results. On the other hand, in the case of an obscure pollster we cannot assume that its research method is reliable, as we can with Gallup, Roper, and Harris, whose techniques are widely known and demonstrably reliable.

2. *Determine the date of contact.* The date of contact refers to when the poll or survey was conducted, which is important to know because it can lead to a whole different interpretation of the results. For example, a poll may report that the president is enjoying unprecedented popularity. But this finding doesn't mean much if the poll was taken just before some major international or domestic blunder.

3. *Determine the method of contact.* The method of contact is the procedure used to take the sample. A poll or survey must approximate the ideal of *randomness*, which means that each member of the population to be sampled has an equal chance of being sampled.

To illustrate, suppose that you wanted to find out what students in your college thought of the school newspaper. In the next issue you included a questionnaire asking readers to respond. The sample you arrived at would *not* be random, because only readers of that issue of the paper had a chance of being sampled. Remember, you wanted to find out what the students *as a whole* thought. One way to ensure randomness in this instance would have been to place the names of *all* students in a drum and then select names, one at a time, until you had a sufficient sample.

In dealing with large groups, ensuring randomness is no easy or inexpensive matter. As a result, pollsters modify the process by using what is termed a stratified random sample. In a stratified random sample, relevant strata within the group are identified, and a random sample from each stratum is selected in proportion to the number of members in each stratum. Suppose, for example, that a television station wanted to determine the popularity of its programs. It could establish relevant strata on the basis of characteristics that could influence viewer preferences: age, sex, educational level, geographic area, and so on. Having established these strata, it would then *randomly* select respondents from each stratum in direct proportion to the numbers within it.

---

[6]See Perry Weddle. *Argument: A Guide to Critical Thinking.* New York: McGraw-Hill, 1978, pp. 130–132.

In short, the stratified random sample, which is a reliable technique for taking a sample, calls for three steps: (1) identification of the strata within the population, (2) determination of the number of instances in each stratum, and (3) random selection of the same proportion for each stratum.

4. *Determine the sample size.* Before accepting or using a poll's or survey's results, find out how large the sample was. The importance of this guideline lies in the connection between sample size and margin of error. The following chart expresses this connection in a typical public opinion poll that might be conducted by Gallup, Harris, or Roper.[7]

Sample Size and Sampling Error

Number of Interviews	Margin of Error (%)
4,000	± 2
1,500	± 3
1,000	± 4
750	± 4
600	± 4
400	± 5
200	± 6
100	±11

Here is how these relationships of size and sampling error might operate in a typical situation. Suppose a properly conducted poll of 1,500 people indicates that presidential candidate A will receive 51 percent of the vote and candidate B will receive 49 percent. Since the margin of error is 3 percent, A could receive as much as 54 percent of the vote or as little as 48 percent; B could receive as much as 52 percent or as little as 46 percent. Thus, candidate B could actually win the election, and the pollster would be justified in maintaining his accuracy—providing, of course, that the percentages fell within the prescribed limits. In short, this race would be too close to call.

5. *Determine as much as possible about the questions.* Often it isn't the way that the sample is taken that undermines a poll or survey but the questions that are asked. Like any other form of discourse, questions can be ambiguous (for example, "Do you think it's a *good practice* for employers to seek out minority members and women for jobs?") or biased (for example, "*Given that the future of the free world depends on U.S. strength,* do you think that we should increase defense spending?"). Where questions are ambiguous or biased, the answers they elicit are questionable.

---

[7]Charles W. Roll, Jr., and Albert H. Cantril. *Polls: Their Use and Misuse in Politics.* Copyright © 1972 by Basic Books, Inc. Reprinted by permission of the publisher.

Used properly, studies, polls, and surveys can be reliable sources of authority. Used improperly, they have an appeal that is not logical but strictly psychological. Before leaving this subject, it would be valuable to pinpoint some fallacies associated with their use.

Exercises

3.10 *From your television viewing and from reading, compile a list of advertisements that appeal to studies. How many satisfy the guidelines discussed? Write to an advertiser requesting the specifics of a study. Ask for some of the items suggested in the guidelines.*

3.11 *Report to your class the particulars of a public opinion poll that you've come across in a newspaper or magazine. Evaluate the poll or survey in light of the preceding guidelines.*

Fallacies

We saw earlier that useful statistics must be complete, must make a difference, and must be knowable. In general, the same applies to studies, polls, and surveys. Beyond this, four fallacies so often accompany the use of studies, polls, and surveys that they bear special mention. They are the biased sample, semantical ambiguity, biased question, and false dilemma.

Biased Sample *The fallacy of biased sample consists of using a sample that is not representative of the population being studied.* For example, the makers of Zest soap wanted to find out what consumers thought of their product. Predictably enough, they found that consumers thought highly of the soap. But the survey was biased, because those interviewed already were Zest loyalists. Again, in 1936 the *Literary Digest* predicted victory by Alf Landon over President Franklin D. Roosevelt. The problem with the survey was that ballots were sent mainly to people listed in telephone books and city directories, which meant that only the relatively well-to-do were sampled. Again, a house-to-house survey was once made to determine what magazines people read. The replies indicated that a large percentage of households read *Harper's* but not many read *True Story*. This was odd, because publishers' figures clearly indicated that *True Story* sold millions of magazines, while *Harper's* sold hundreds of thousands. When pollsters eliminated all other possible explanations, they faced the unmistakable conclusion that many of the re-

106

spondents had lied. Indeed, on personal subjects respondents often confuse, intentionally or otherwise, their ideal and actual selves. This can lead to survey results that are faulty generalizations.

Semantical Ambiguity The *fallacy of semantical ambiguity consists in using a word or phrase that can easily be interpreted in two or more ways.* A good example of semantical ambiguity in polls and surveys can be seen in the use of the word *average.* How many times have you read about the *average* American, student, or household or the *average* cost of a house, college tuition, or an automobile? But *average* can carry one of three meanings: mean, median, and mode. *Mean* is an arithmetic average, derived by adding up the value of items and dividing by the number of items. *Median* is the figure right in the middle of all the items, or the figure above which 50 percent of the items fall and below which 50 percent fall. *Mode* is the figure in a distribution that occurs most frequently. To show how ambiguous *average* can be, consider the prices of just five houses:

$200,000

$ 95,000

$ 65,000

$ 45,000

$ 45,000

By this account the average price may be $90,000 (mean), $65,000 (median), or $45,000 (mode). Used shrewdly, then, *average* could lead to various and opposed judgments about the relative affluence of a neighborhood (for example, "This is a rather well-off neighborhood, because the average house costs $90,000").

Semantical ambiguity also crops up when superlatives are used in reporting research, as in "Dial is the *most* effective deodorant soap you can buy." This statement appears to mean that Dial is a better deodorant soap than any other soap. Curiously, what the company meant by "most effective" was *as effective as* any other soap. More will be said about ambiguity generally in Chapter 7.

"Weasels," words used to evade or retreat from a direct or forthright statement or position, are another source of semantical ambiguity. Weasels allow somebody to say something without really saying it. *Help* is a good example. We are told that products variously help prevent cavities, help keep our homes germ free, help fight old age, help make us feel young, and so on. *Help*, of course, means simply to aid or assist, and nothing else.[8] So, reports of research that show that a product can "help" really shouldn't count for much, although admittedly they carry an authoritative wallop. There are other

---

[8]See Paul Stevens. "Weasel Words: God's Little Helpers." In *Language Awareness*, ed. Paul A. Eeschol, Alfred A. Rosa, and Virginia P. Clark. New York: St. Martin's Press, 1978, p. 75.

weasels: *up to* (as in "provides relief up to eight hours"), *as much as* (as in "saves as much as one gallon of gas"), and *virtually* (as in "virtually no tar"). These words and phrases function to say what cannot be said; for, in most cases, statistical studies necessary to back up the specific assertion just aren't available. If the support data were available, rest assured that the advertiser would happily summon them.

Biased Question *The fallacy of biased question consists of asking a question that is worded to draw a predetermined reply.* For example, a pollster asks a respondent this question: "*Given the thousands of handgun-related deaths that occur annually in this United States,* do you think that some kind of gun-control legislation is needed?" Given its introduction, this question clearly predisposes the respondent to answer in the affirmative.

Sometimes the bias can result from the substitution of just one word for another. For example, here are several questions that the maker of Alamo Brand pet food asked respondents in a "pet owner's opinion study." Observe how the word *that* biases the questions, when really *whether* or *if* should have been used.

1. Did you notice that Alamo Brand looks meatier than the dry dog food you have been using?
2. Did you notice that Alamo Brand has a meatier feel than the dry dog food you have been using?
3. Did you notice that your dog preferred and enjoyed Alamo Brand more than his usual dry dog food?
4. Did you notice that your dog appeared more contented and satisfied after eating Alamo Brand?

False Dilemma *The fallacy of false dilemma consists of erroneously reducing the number of possible choices on an issue.* Poll questions are notorious for setting up false dilemmas. For example: "Are you for or against the women's liberation movement?" Maybe the respondent is indifferent to the movement. "Do you think the United States should support the Israelis or the Arabs in the Middle East?" Perhaps the respondent thinks that the United States should support both sides equally. "Should or should not handguns be outlawed?" Possibly the respondent believes that handguns should be stringently controlled. By reducing the range of choices to two, when there is a middle ground for moderate views, pollsters introduce bias into their questions and thus into their findings.

Exercises

3.12 *The following exercises make use of statistics, studies, polls, and surveys. Where statistics are used, determine if they are complete, make a* difference, and are knowable. Examine the studies, polls, and surveys for the same qualities and also for the fallacies of biased sample, semantical ambiguity, biased question, and false dilemma.

1. **Norm:** May I use your phone?

   Ned: You could if I had one.

   Norm: No phone?

   Ned: I've got one on order.

   Norm: Well, good luck! Did you know that on the average it takes anywhere from 90 to 180 days to get a phone installed in this area?

2. A poll is being conducted to determine whether the students at a college are for or against the semester system. A sample is taken in the library on a Tuesday between 9 A.M. and noon. Every tenth person passing through the turnstile at the main entrance is asked for an opinion. The results indicate that 58 percent of the students oppose the semester system, 42 percent favor it, and 10 percent don't care one way or the other. The student government decides to use these findings to pressure the administration to drop the semester system and adopt the quarter system.

3. To predict the next election, candidate Jensen's forces take a sample. They phone at random 2 million registered voters and find out that well over half intend to vote for their candidate. About 30 million are expected to turn out for the election. Based on their poll, Jensen enthusiasts anticipate an easy victory.

4. **Wife:** Well, you're running true to form—having a drink before dinner.

   Husband: What's that supposed to mean?

   Wife: According to a study just released, more middle-aged men have at least one drink before dinner than any other age group of males or females.

5. Poll question: Do you think the United States should accept Soviet influence in Egypt?

6. Poll question: Do you favor or oppose an increase in military spending?

7. **Ruth:** Well, the evidence is in. Business leaders continue to discriminate against women on the job.

   Rick: Why do you say that?

   Ruth: Because the results of a study prove it. A thousand business leaders were picked at random and asked: "If you had to choose between a male and a female for a job with your firm and the two happened to be equally qualified, which would you choose—the male or the female?" And guess what. Sixty-eight percent said they'd pick the male.

8. Poll question: Should the United States continue to spend billions of dollars annually on defense while neglecting needed domestic problems?

9. **Joyce:** I don't know why so many people are criticizing the president for giving tax breaks to big business.

Justin: Are you kidding? Business needs tax breaks the way Bedouins need sand.

Joyce: That's how much you know.

Justin: What are you talking about?

Joyce: Here, read this. It reports that one of the biggest companies in the United States made exactly one cent in profits out of every sales dollar last year.

10. "The average American child by age eighteen has watched 22,000 hours of television. This same average viewer has watched thousands of hours of inane situation comedy, fantasy, and soap opera and an average of 4,286 separate acts of violence." (Quoted by Howard Kahane. Logic and Contemporary Rhetoric. Belmont, Calif.: Wadsworth, 1980, p. 100.)

11. A number of years ago a report revealed that the number of deaths chargeable to steam railroads in one year was 4,712. On the basis of this statistic, some people probably inferred that train travel was extremely dangerous.

12. In the past 5,000 years young men have fought in 14,523 wars. One of four persons living during this time has been a war casualty. A nuclear war would add 1,245,000 new victims to this tragic list.

13. **Stan:** You know, it's really outrageous the way people's political freedoms are flouted.

Anne: Where?

Stan: Worldwide. Did you know that in the past year the political liberties of 823.3 million people were violated?

14. Drivers in their twenties pay a very high premium because they have more accidents than drivers in any other age group.

15. Only 63 of an estimated 950 rape cases that occurred in Kern County last year were reported.

16. "Yes, sir, I'd be delighted to give you a special deal on this new van—$500 off the sticker price!"

17. "The extra-strength non-aspirin in Datril-500 worked better than two leading prescription pain relievers." (Advertisement.)

18. **Wyatt:** I think it'd be outrageous to allow oil companies to drill off the California coast, and plenty of Americans would agree.

Ellen: How do you know how many Americans would agree?

Wyatt: Because a survey just conducted proves it.

Ellen: Who conducted it?

Wyatt: The Sierra Club.

110

19. Administrators at Hudson State College are interested in determining why its graduates attended Hudson and what factors contributed to their successful completion. So they devise a questionnaire, which they send to graduates. Among the questions asked is this one: "How important does each of the following items appear to you now that you have graduated? (Please answer each item that applies.)" The respondents are asked to react to the items as follows: not important, important, very important, no opinion/not applicable. Here are some of the items: writing emphasis, logic course, math course, science courses, behavioral sciences courses, humanities courses.

20. "Fact: Ready-to-eat cereals do not increase tooth decay in children.

    Fact: Ready-sweetened cereals are highly nutritious.

    Fact: There is no more sugar in a one-ounce serving of a ready-sweetened cereal than in an apple or banana or in a serving of orange juice.

    Fact: The per capita sugar consumption in the United States has remained practically unchanged for the last fifty years." (Part of a two-page advertisement entitled "A Statement from Kellogg Company on the Nutritional Value of Ready-Sweetened Cereals.")

21. "The phrase 'average person' means a hypothetical human being whose attitude represents a synthesis and composite of all the various attitudes of all individuals, irrespective of age, in Tennessee society at large, which attitude is the result of human experience, understanding, development, cultivation, and socialization in Tennessee, taking into account relevant factors which affect and contribute to that attitude, limited to that which is personally acceptable, as opposed to that which might merely be tolerated." (From "The Tennessee Obscenity Act" of 1978.)

22. Scores on scholastic aptitude tests are declining. So, students must not be as bright today as they once were.

3.13

1. You are a politician who feels very strongly about an issue. Wanting to generate some "statistical" support for your position, you draft a questionnaire to be sent to your constituents. Choose the issue and write five questions in such a way that they will elicit responses that support your position.

2. In a previous exercise you were asked to write advertising copy for a new toothpaste your company was about to market. This time, rather than relying on appeals to authority, write the copy making use of weasels. Then go back and delete all weasels. Can any of your weasel-free claims be supported?

OPINIONS AND VALUES

Some of the opinions we hold take the form of generalizations (most often pseudoinductive and noninductive) that express values—that is, assessments of worth. "Abortion is wrong," "The Who are a sensational rock group," "*Moby Dick* is a superb novel," "Democracy is the best form of government," and "The sale of handguns should be prohibited" are examples. Each of these statements reports the worth that the speaker attaches to something.

Ordinarily we think of value assertions as expressing assessments of worth in morality, art, politics, and social affairs. Thus, in the realm of morality, someone may hold the following value opinions: "People shouldn't lie," "Deceptive advertising is wrong," and "Abortion is sometimes good." In art: "Picasso is a great painter," "Beethoven's Fifth Symphony is his best," and "*Moby Dick* is a superb novel." In politics: "Capitalism allows the greatest amount of individual initiative," "Socialism destroys individual incentive," and "Democracy is the best form of government." And in social affairs: "Euthanasia should be legalized"; "Despite one's ability to pay, everyone is entitled to medical care"; and "The sale of handguns should be prohibited." There are two things to keep in mind in dealing with opinions that express values: the need to clarify meaning and the need to provide factual support.

Clarity

One key requirement in evaluating and formulating value opinions is to clarify their language. Words that imply value judgments, such as *good, bad, should, ought, great,* and *best,* encourage many interpretations. Thus, they invite *semantical ambiguity* in argument. Ambiguity can be avoided only if the value terms are defined.

In defining value terms keep in mind that they can carry several meanings. Consider, for example, the value opinion "Deceptive advertising is wrong." Those making this assertion may mean "wrong" in the sense that they *personally* disapprove of it. Or they may mean "wrong" in the sense that *society* disapproves of deceptive advertising. Thus, rather than expressing a personal preference they are expressing a social preference. Or by "wrong" they may mean that deceptive advertising does not conform with some *principle* of fairness that they have in mind or that deceptive advertising violates the *law.* Here the value opinion is not based on personal or social preference but on conformity with some principle, standard, or law. They may even mean "wrong" in more than just one of these senses.

The same observations apply to artistic judgments. In "*Moby Dick* is a superb novel" one may mean "superb" in the sense of *personal approval, social approval, conformity with some artistic standard,* or any combination of these meanings. So, in order to ensure common understanding with your audience, define the value words you use. By the same token, as a reader you

112

have a right to expect such definitions in the value opinions you read. When the terms are not defined and the context does not clarify their meanings, then at the very least semantical ambiguity is present.

Factual Support

It is as important to provide factual support for value opinions as for any others. There are a number of ways to provide this support, but two bear highlighting: appealing to principle and appealing to consequences.

Appeal to Principle Value opinions often involve evaluations of individual action or practices in terms of some general principle. It is then necessary to express the general principle and show why the specific subject is covered by the principle.

For example, suppose you were writing a paper that argued that it was wrong to disconnect a particular person from a life-support system. In providing support, you could indicate a principle on which you were basing your opinion, such as: "It's always wrong to kill someone intentionally" or "Only voluntary acts of euthanasia are permissible." You would then have to show that the case being considered was of the type covered by the principle. In order to do this, you might show, in the case of the first principle, that the person was, in fact, not dead before being removed from the machine or, in the case of the second principle, that neither the consent of the person nor the person's surrogates had been obtained. Additionally, you might want to spend time supporting the principles themselves, explaining why you thought they were worth endorsing.

You can take the same approach to a social policy question. Suppose you were writing a paper in support of the Equal Rights Amendment (ERA). You could appeal to some principle of equality, such as: "Women deserve to be treated equally" or "All people should be treated equally." Having established the principle, you could then show that women in fact are not treated equally.

Applied to an artistic judgment, the approach works the same way. Thus, in arguing that Oedipus Rex is a good play, you might apply the classical ideal of unity and catharsis and then show how the play is covered by this ideal.

Appeal to Consequences Another good way to provide factual support for value opinions is by appealing to purported consequences and providing data to justify the forecasts. For example, were you arguing the generalization that handguns should be prohibited, you might try to show that the rates of violent crimes would decline in the wake of appropriate legislation. Of course, you'd have to provide information to back up your prediction. Again, if you were arguing that married couples should be required to undergo genetic counseling before having a child, you might show that fewer defective babies would be born if that were the case. Again, you'd have to provide data to back up your contention.

So, providing factual support is as important in expressing value opinions as in expressing nonvalue opinions (for example, "Life exists in outer space," "Cancer is caused by a virus," "I am going to make my first million before I'm forty"). Two good ways to provide this support are (1) the establishment of some general principle and the fact that some specific individual, action, or practice is the type covered by the principle; and (2) a prediction of consequences and provision of data to support the forecasts. In the best value opinion essays these techniques are integrated. For example, arguing against the sale of handguns, you could express a principle (for example, "Society has an obligation to protect the lives of its citizens"). Then, by predicting the consequences of handgun control, you could show how the prohibition is covered by the principle. Similarly, in arguing for genetic counseling, you might appeal to the principle that parents have a right to know as much about the health of their unborn as possible. Then, by showing the kind of information prospective parents can get from genetic counseling and the range of alternatives that thereby opens to them, you could show how genetic counseling is covered by your principle.

Although relying on principle and consequences goes far to substantiate opinions, it is not enough. Even if we employ principle and consequences in providing factual support for a value opinion, we can leave the opinion unsupported. The reason is that the factual support may not really be providing justification for our opinion but rather pseudojustification.

JUSTIFICATION AND PSEUDOJUSTIFICATION

Justification can be defined roughly as reasons that would convince unbiased, informed, and rational people that the value opinions are correct. Ordinarily these reasons are facts. But not all of the facts that writers offer for opinions are necessarily justification for the opinions. As we have seen, facts can be unknown by the writer, irrelevant, or based on false authority; or they may in some other way prove illegitimate. Beyond this, there are several things that appear to be justification for value opinions but are really pseudojustification.[9] You should be aware of these in order (1) to avoid confusion as you attempt to support your own views and (2) to understand and evaluate the support that others offer for their views.

First, justification is not the same as giving one's motivations. Nonetheless, in trying to justify a value opinion people sometimes confuse motivation with justification and thereby end up offering pseudojustification in the form of motivation. For example, asked to justify having cheated on an exam, a student replies: "I had to pass the test in order to complete the course. I guess I panicked when I didn't know the answers." Similarly, trying to justify having

---

[9]See Peter A. Facione, Donald Scherer, and Thomas Attig. *Values and Society: An Introduction to Ethics and Social Philosophy.* New York: Prentice-Hall, 1978, pp. 26–32.

left the scene of an accident, a motorist argues: "I had to. You see, I don't have any insurance, and I knew I couldn't cover the costs of the damage I caused." In fact, the student and motorist are providing pseudojustifications for their actions. They have explained what moved them to act as they did, but they have not offered reasons that should convince anyone that their judgments and actions were correct.

Second, justification is not the same as rationalization. Rationalization consists of giving reasons for a choice *after the fact*, after we have already decided what to do. To rationalize is to choose first and look for reasons later. When we rationalize, we endorse or reject reasons because they support or weaken a predetermined choice.

For example, you may be familiar with Edgar Allan Poe's most famous poem, "The Raven," which is about the death of a beautiful woman. After he wrote this poem, Poe published a theory of poetry in which he enumerated all the qualities that he thought a good poem should have. All of them happened to be evident in "The Raven." Poe said that he wrote "The Raven" to conform with his poetic principles. Not everyone agreed. Some have insisted that the poem preceded Poe's formulation of the principles—that Poe, in fact, gave reasons for constructing "The Raven" as he did *after* he had written it. If this is true, then Poe was rationalizing, not justifying.

Politicians are prone to pseudojustifications in the form of rationalizations. Thus, it's a rare Washington politician who will publicly premise a vote on anything other than "the national interest." But in many cases far less noble reasons explain the vote: reelection worries, political debts, lobbyist pressure, even invincible stupidity.

Third, excuses, although relevant in assigning blame or praise, are irrelevant for justification purposes. Generally speaking, we don't hold people accountable for their actions when circumstances are beyond their control, when they have no alternative, or when their freedom to choose is so constrained that they cannot choose freely. A good excuse provides a reason for not blaming, punishing, or holding someone accountable. But it does not alter what they did.

To illustrate, suppose that a firm doesn't meet the air pollution standards of the Environmental Protection Agency (EPA) within the time prescribed. There is no altering the fact that the firm didn't comply with the standard. But there may be good reasons to exonerate the company: Maybe the cost of the antipollution devices was more than the business could bear; maybe the time allotted was simply insufficient to complete the job; or maybe the company had other reasons. But none of these facts, taken alone or together, can be considered justification; they are excuses. Indeed, when the EPA chooses not to prosecute or fine the firm but to extend the deadline for it, it in no way condones what the firm did. It simply recognizes that extenuating circumstances argue to excuse the firm from blame.

Likewise, when President Gerald Ford pardoned Richard Nixon, he wasn't approving of what Nixon had done. In fact, judging from what Ford said during and after the Watergate scandal, we can infer that Ford disapproved of Nixon's behavior. So, Ford's pardon was an excusing of Nixon from prosecution. Maybe there were good reasons for the pardon; maybe there were not. But that's an issue distinct from whether or not Nixon was *justified* in doing what he apparently did. So, the pardon could in no way be viewed as justification for Nixon's behavior, although, given the climate of the time, it's not hard to understand why it was viewed that way. Missing the distinction, others in power might take the pardon to justify similar behavior of their own.

A good illustration of the confusion that can arise when justification is not distinguished from excuse can be seen in the September 27, 1981, telecast of *60 Minutes*. The program was wholly devoted to a round-table discussion of the propriety of the tactics that the show's reporters sometimes use in getting stories—for example, misrepresenting their identities or "ambushing" subjects with embarrassing questions when the cameras are rolling. Some panel members defended such tactics by appealing to the public's right to know about serious fraud and corruption. At the same time, they insisted that they were not condoning such unprofessional behavior. But other panel members said that this was inconsistent, a case of "having it both ways." The apparent inconsistency resulted from a failure to distinguish excuses from justifications. It seems that in supporting the tactics by appeal to the public's right to know the defenders were really offering an excuse for not holding the reporters accountable for their conduct. At the same time, they seemed to recognize that a person's not being blameworthy doesn't justify what the person did. Thus, they criticized the tactics as unprofessional and said they should be avoided. Had a distinction been drawn between excuses and justification, the confusion, and subsequent charge of inconsistency, might have been avoided.

In supporting opinions, then, make sure that you are providing justification, not pseudojustification in the form of motivation, rationalization, or excuse. In reading opinions, guard against being taken in by these temptations to confusion, which arise in part from the common tendencies toward provincialism and evasion of responsibility.

Exercises

3.14 Identify the value words in each of the following statements and indicate what possible interpretations can be put on these words.

1. William Shakespeare is the world's greatest playwright.
2. Infanticide is wrong.
3. The United States should have a national health insurance program.
4. Lying is sometimes moral.
5. President Reagan's firing of the nation's air traffic controllers was a reprehensible act.

6. *The air controllers should not have struck.*

7. *War is never morally justifiable.*

8. *It's all right to kill in self-defense.*

9. *There ought to be stricter laws concerning child abuse.*

10. *A woman should never have an abortion merely on the grounds of convenience.*

11. *The women's liberation movement threatens the survival of the family as we know it.*

12. *Communism is godless.*

13. *No invention has had a greater social impact on the United States in the twentieth century than the automobile.*

14. *The Iranian seizure of the American embassy in Tehran was an act of political desperation inspired by religious fanaticism.*

15. *Poetry is the highest artistic form.*

3.15 Below are ten situations. For each, give an example of (1) giving motivation, (2) rationalizing, and (3) offering an excuse.

1. A motorist is stopped for running a traffic signal.

2. A hairdresser raises his prices for a wave.

3. A television network refuses to allow an obscure political candidate air time.

4. A friend breaks a date.

5. The personnel director of an insurance company asks female applicants about their marital status.

6. A politician abruptly shifts her position on school prayer.

7. A teenager badgers his parents for a car.

8. A state government requires its residents to carry an identification card at all times.

9. A student fails an exam.

10. A professor misses a class.

THE OPINION ESSAY

I have spoken so far of how opinions can be used in developing an argument. Sometimes, of course, an essay is directed to developing an opinion. Indeed, the stating and supporting of an opinion is a popular way to develop an essay. Thus, a writer composes an essay telling what he or she thinks about the younger generation, college costs, the Moral Majority, supply-side economics, or some other subject. In such essays writers may simply be interested in telling the audience how they feel about something: "These are my opinions about this subject, and here are my reasons for holding them."

But sometimes an argument is embedded in an opinion essay. You may be telling the members of an audience not only that you don't like the increase in college costs but also that they shouldn't either; in fact, they should do something about it. Or your purpose may be not only to express your fear of the Moral Majority but also to convince your audience that it should fear the movement as well, even oppose it. In fact, argumentative essays can be effectively developed by stating and supporting an opinion. Of course, when developing the opinion, keep in mind the preceding discussion.

There are two common strategies for writing argumentative essays in which presentation relies primarily on the development of an opinion. These are (1) defending the opinion and (2) adjusting the opinion.

Defending the Opinion

In defending an opinion, the writer states it early in the essay and devotes the rest of the essay to defending it. The defense typically is arranged inductively; that is, examples, illustrations, fact, authority, and other forms of evidence are used to justify the assertion. The strength of this approach is that from the beginning the paper rivets the writer's and reader's attention on the central point. As a result, the writer is protected from straying and thereby introducing irrelevant material; the reader is protected from confusion and drawing erroneous inferences.

In writing this kind of paper, then, you would typically present your opinion as the thesis at the end of a short opening paragraph. You would then support this thesis with main points made through example, cases, facts, and, perhaps, principle and consequences. Here are excerpts from two essays developed by defending an opinion; the opinion theses are not italicized.

SCHOOL ATHLETICS

OPENING PARAGRAPH (OPINION THESIS): *Probably for as long as interscholastic sports have been around, people have wondered about their merit. As school funds dry up, the debate grows hot. The upshot is that today many athletic programs are in jeopardy.* But if school districts are wise, they will resist the impulse to discontinue athletic programs.

FACTS: *Athletic programs serve vital functions in a school. First, they provide students an outlet for pent-up energy. Second, they teach students how to compete. . . .*

118

CONSEQUENCES: *Athletic programs also help finance many extracurricular activities, such as dramatics, music, forensics, and various clubs. . . .*

AUTHORITY: *If skeptics are not convinced by these considerations of the merits of school athletics, they should ponder the recommendations of the National Education Association and the President's Council on Physical Fitness. . . .*

PUNISHING JUVENILE OFFENDERS

OPENING PARAGRAPH (OPINION THESIS): *In recent years, the United States has experienced an alarming increase in juvenile crime—that is, crime committed by individuals under the age of majority. Whether the category is murder or robbery, mugging or rape, vandalism or arson, the story is the same: Juvenile crime is on the rise. The only way to combat this trend is to start treating juveniles no differently from adult offenders.*

PRINCIPLE: *For those offended by the prospect of sentencing a twelve-year-old to life in prison, let them consider what justice means. If anything, justice implies that people should get what they deserve and that all people should be treated equally. Is it "just," then, to put a twenty-two-year-old murderer away for twenty years, but not a twelve-year-old murderer? . . .*

CONSEQUENCE: *Besides the question of justice, there are the sinister social effects of pampering juvenile offenders. . . .*

CASE: *As an example, take the case of a seventeen-year-old Memphis youth. When he was twelve, this young man was arrested for malicious mischief. . . .*

Adjusting the Opinion

Another way to develop an argument through opinion is to withhold the opinion until the end of the essay. In this strategy the writer establishes common ground with the audience by first presenting a generally accepted opinion. The writer then takes a close look at this opinion and eventually modifies, or adjusts, it.

The pro-and-con format is a most appropriate way for structuring this kind of essay. Recall that the pro-and-con essay attempts to reach a balanced conclusion by treating an issue as an open question worth thinking about. In the case of opinions, the pro-and-con discussion serves as a basis for adjusting the generally accepted opinion. Also, it involves both writer and reader in the kind of process by which opinions are actually formed.

Here are two examples of the adjusted-opinion essay, based on the same topics as before—school athletics and juvenile crime. Notice how the writer makes the same support material conform with this strategy and that the thesis comes toward the end.

SCHOOL ATHLETICS

OPENING PARAGRAPH (COMMON VIEW): *Probably for as long as interscholastic sports have been around, people have wondered about their merits. Do they really accomplish what they are supposed to? Do they put too much emphasis on winning? Are they overly exclusionary? Today, cutbacks in school funds have sharpened the point of these questions and have given credence to the view that school sports are a frill that many school districts can no longer afford.*

OBJECTION 1: *Before jettisoning organized athletics, however, school districts should realize that school sports provide vital functions. First, they give students an outlet for pent-up energy. Second, they teach students how to compete.*

OBJECTION 2: *Athletic programs also help finance many extracurricular activities, such as dramatics, music, forensics, and various clubs. . . .*

OBJECTION 3: *In addition, there are to be considered the recommendations of the National Education Association and the President's Council on Physical Fitness. . . .*

ADJUSTED VIEW: *Although the inclination to discontinue school sports is understandable, several factors argue for their retention. These factors deserve careful consideration in any debate about the worth of school sports.*

PUNISHING JUVENILE OFFENDERS

OPENING PARAGRAPH (COMMON VIEW): *In recent years, the United States has experienced an alarming increase in juvenile crime—that is, crime committed by individuals under the age of majority. Whether the category is murder or robbery, mugging or rape, vandalism or arson, the story is the same: Juvenile crime is on the rise. Our society has traditionally treated the juvenile as a special kind of offender, one who warrants punishment different from that given an adult, even though the crime may be the same. It is safe to say that a great portion of the population probably still holds this attitude.*

OBJECTION 1: *Although the inclination to protect children is understandable, even laudable, one may still wonder whether different treatment is fair treatment. If anything, justice implies that*

120

people should get what they deserve and that all people should be treated equally. Is it "just," then, to imprison a twenty-two-year-old murderer for twenty years but not a twelve-year-old murderer? . . .

OBJECTION 2: *Besides the question of justice, there are the sinister social effects of pampering juvenile offenders. . . .*

ADJUSTED VIEW: *No one questions that the desire to protect children springs from the noblest of human instincts. Yet several pressing reasons point to the need to reassess our traditional attitudes toward the juvenile offender. Surely, these reasons are worth considering in any discussion about the disposition of children who commit crimes.*

SUMMARY

Opinion bears on argumentative essays in two distinct, though related, ways. On the one hand, any kind of argumentative essay may rely on opinion for development. In this sense, opinions are a way that main points or premises are presented. On the other hand, an argumentative essay may be one whose presentation relies primarily on the development of an opinion. In this sense, the opinion is the thesis. Either way, the argumentative writer must be schooled in the proper use of opinion.

An opinion is what is believed to be the case. It is distinguished from a fact, which, ideally, is what is actually the case. Writers must erect their opinions on a solid factual base. This means that they should (1) keep opinions close to facts and (2) be wary of offering unsupported opinions on unresolved questions.

Observations are crucial in forming sound opinions. If observations are reliable, the opinions based on them are informed. There are five key factors to consider in evaluating observations: (1) the physical conditions under which the observations were made, (2) the sensory acuity of the observer, (3) the background knowledge of the observer, (4) the objectivity of the observer, and (5) the supporting testimony of other observers.

In offering facts to support opinions, writers must ensure accuracy, representativeness, and completeness. There are two fallacies associated with doubtful opinions: questionable evaluation and provincialism.

QUESTIONABLE EVALUATION: *making controversial assertions without support, or ones that cannot stand up under investigation because of their breadth*

EXAMPLE: *"The Vietnam War was the best-reported war in history."*

PROVINCIALISM: *viewing things exclusively in terms of group loyalty*

121

EXAMPLE: *"The present administration deserves low marks, because it's quite clear that it knows nothing about basic economics"* (asserted by an economist).

In forming and justifying opinions, writers often turn to the informed views of others—that is, to authority. Authority is an expert source outside ourselves. Appeals to authority are legitimate when (1) the authority is, in fact, an expert in the field and (2) there is a general agreement among the experts in support of the view. Illegitimate appeals to authority take three forms: false authority, popularity, and tradition.

FALSE AUTHORITY: *violating either of the two criteria for a legitimate appeal to authority*

EXAMPLE: *"Humans are undoubtedly aggressive animals, because Darwin said they were."*

POPULARITY: *relying exclusively on numbers to support an assertion*

EXAMPLE: *"Five million people have already seen this film. Isn't it about time you did?"*

TRADITION: *appealing to feelings of reverence or respect for some custom that supports the view being advanced*

EXAMPLE: *"Jane shouldn't keep her maiden name after marrying. After all, in this culture a woman always takes her husband's name."*

Statistics often have the force of authority. In using and confronting statistics, we should ask at least three questions: Do the statistics make a difference? Are they complete? Are they knowable?

Studies, polls, and surveys are rich sources of statistics and themselves can be authoritative. In using and evaluating studies always determine (1) the subjects involved, (2) for how long the research was conducted, (3) who conducted the testing, (4) to which stage of research the assertion refers, (5) how the study was conducted, and (6) how extensive the testing was. Respecting polls and surveys, always determine (1) the sponsor's and survey's name, (2) the date of contact, (3) the method of contact, (4) the sample size, and (5) as much as possible about the questions. The following fallacies are commonly associated with improper use of studies, polls, and surveys:

BIASED SAMPLE: *using a sample that is not representative of the population being studied*

EXAMPLE: *using Zest soap loyalists in a suvey to study consumer feelings about Zest*

SEMANTICAL *using a word or phrase that easily can be interpreted in two*
AMBIGUITY: *or more ways*

EXAMPLE: *the use of* average *or* "weasels" *such as* help, up to, *or as*
much as

BIASED *asking a question that is worded to draw a predetermined*
QUESTION: *reply*

EXAMPLE: *"Given that thousands of handgun-related deaths occur*
annually in the United States, do you think that some kind
of gun-control legislation is needed?"

FALSE DILEMMA: *erroneously reducing the number of possible choices on an*
issue

EXAMPLE: *"Do you think the United States should support the Israelis*
or the Arabs in the Middle East?"

Many opinions take the form of generalizations that express values—that is, assessments of worth. In expressing value opinions, writers must ensure clarity and factual support. Two common ways to provide factual support are appealing to principle or appealing to consequences. In providing factual support, writers must be especially careful to offer justification and not pseudojustification.

Justification is reasons that would convince unbiased, informed, and rational people that the value opinions are correct. In contrast, pseudojustification refers to motivations, rationalizations, and excuses.

Finally, an argumentative essay may rely for its presentation primarily on the development of an opinion. When writing such an essay, writers should keep the aforementioned points clearly in mind. Further, they should call on two useful strategies for developing this kind of essay: (1) defending the opinion or (2) adjusting the opinion.

Questions for Analysis

These questions pertain to Michael Novak's article, "Human Rights: No More Small Men" on pp. 82–85.

1. State Novak's thesis and list his main points.
2. What kind of assertion is Novak's thesis: meaning, value, policy, consequences, or fact?
3. List the various sources Novak relies on for support material.
4. Which strategy for developing the argumentative essay of opinion does he employ?

5. Does the opening quote by the nineteenth-century English philosopher John Stuart Mill function as an appeal to authority?

6. Identify three fact statements, six opinion statements, and six opinion/fact statements. Rewrite all the opinion/fact statements to rid them of opinion.

7. Is any provincialism evident in paragraph 2?

8. Is the reference to the Gettysburg Address (paragraph 2) relevant?

9. In paragraph 3 the author writes, "The foundation of human rights is the limited state." Is this statement a fact or an opinion? If an opinion, is it a value opinion?

10. Throughout the essay, Novak refers to "human rights." Is the meaning of "human rights" clear?

11. Does Novak make use of authority in paragraph 4? If so, is the appeal legitimate?

12. Prepare a syllogism for paragraph 4.

13. Is the reference to Pope John Paul II (paragraph 5) an appeal to authority? If so, is it legitimate?

14. Is the difference between a limited state and an unlimited state clear?

15. Why do you think the author places "under God" in quotation marks (paragraph 7)? What does he mean by "under God"?

16. Paragraph 12 states a value opinion, and paragraph 13 seems to provide a fact in an attempt to support the opinion. Taken together, the two paragraphs form an argument. Several assumptions underlie this argument. Identify them. Are any of the assumptions questionable evaluations? Are the assumptions provincial?

17. Is the reference to Adam Smith (paragraph 15) an appeal to authority? If so, is it legitimate? What about the reference to Lincoln (paragraph 16)?

18. Is Novak's observation that "systems which deny liberty in the name of bread usually produce neither bread nor liberty" (paragraph 19) a qualified or an unqualified generalization? Is it a fact or an opinion? If it is an opinion, do you think it can be supported? Dostoyevsky once said, "Freedom and bread enough for all are inconceivable together." What do you think he meant? Is this a false dilemma? Are you inclined to agree more with Novak or Dostoyevsky?

19. In paragraph 21 the author says, "It is wrong to pit human rights against economic development, to deny the former in the name of the latter." Does he base this value opinion on a consideration of principle or consequences?

READING FOR ANALYSIS

Birch Bayh is a Democrat who represented Indiana in the U.S. Senate for eighteen years. In 1980 he was defeated. Some think that Bayh's defeat, and the defeat of other like-minded politicians, was caused in part by the rise of the New Right and its active opposition to candidates expressing liberal political and social philosophies. In the following essay Bayh states his opinion about the emergence of the New Right.

Morality and Manipulation: Which Will Wither First, the New Right or the Bill of Rights?

By Birch Bayh

1   Ever since the defeat in 1978 of two "targeted" Democratic U.S. senators, there has been a cacophony of debate about the import of the simplistic, venomous brand of politics practiced by assorted self-appointed apostles who euphemistically christen themselves "the New Right." As one of their "targets" in 1980, I can testify that this movement is not a harmless political curiosity. It should be taken seriously. Only then will it be appreciated for what it is—the antithesis of true American beliefs—and be stripped of its pretense of power and rejected.

2   The New Right specializes in "single-issue" politics, the exaggeration of a given issue to the exclusion of all others. When applied to the so-called New Right, single-issue politics refers not to one issue but to a whole category that includes any perceived threat against the American family and national fiber. This includes, but is not limited to, the equal rights amendment, "kicking God out of the public schools," the "give-away" of the Panama Canal and abortion "on demand." Against these devilish intrusions stand the "conservative" leaders of the New Right—Terry Dolan, Howard Phillips, Paul Weyrich and Richard Viguerie, and their religious compadre, the Rev. Jerry Falwell and associates.

3   They are less interested in the outcome of any of those singularly important issues than in using them to achieve a political goal: destruction of the progressive tradition that has characterized 20th-Century American politics. Plainly put, the idea is to rub people's emotions so raw that a small percentage will vote its bigotries and frustrations, neglecting to ask how the New Right stands on other issues of more importance to family and national well-being. In these days of low voter turnouts, a group that can change a few thousand votes can control an election.

4   Now these self-proclaimed messiahs are readying for the 1982 election. Already they have spotted the mark of Cain on a couple dozen congressional foreheads, and, with their direct-mail fund-raising mills buzzing, are cranking up the true believers for another computerized assault. Once again, their targets are those unwitting souls who support equal opportunity for women and minorities, or who express grave concern about violence in the home, or who want to reduce federal spending but not at the expense of legal services for the poor, or who

believe that the nation's legitimate need for a strong defense is met not one whit by billion-dollar outlays for ineffective, antique weaponry such as the B-1 bomber.

5   My reflections on the New Right derive from experience. As chairman of the Senate judiciary subcommittee on the Constitution, I was an appalled witness to New Right schemes to alter and circumvent the Constitution of the United States. For instance, having failed in their attempts to amend the Constitution to prohibit abortion, to require prayer in schools and to ban court-mandated busing, the extreme right sought to strip the federal courts, including the Supreme Court, of their jurisdiction over these complex matters. Such proposals are assaults on our system of government and deserve to be rejected outright.

6   In the last week, the New Right has come up with another worrisome attempt to impose politics on the judiciary, demanding the rejection of Sandra Day O'Connor's nomination to the Supreme Court. In typical fashion, the opposition ignores her reputation as a moderate conservative and her experience as an Arizona state legislator and judge. Instead, the New Right is focusing solely on her support for the equal rights amendment and freedom of choice in abortion.

7   When I sought reelection in 1980, the New Right did its best to associate my name with the phrase "baby killer." I respect those good people who in conscience favor the prohibition of abortion by every available legislative means. However, I repudiate the right-wingers whose exploitation of the issue has little to do with conscience. Rep. Henry Hyde Jr. of Illinois, once a defender of anti-abortion hit lists, did a turnaround when those groups decided to target Republicans in 1982. It was a clear case of choosing politics over principle.

8   I also was attacked by a "religious" arm of the New Right, the Moral Majority (the name itself suggests self-righteous pretensions). On the Sunday before the election, the Rev. Greg Dixon, the head of the Indiana Moral Majority and a member of Jerry Falwell's national executive committee, used his church sanctuaty to distribute pamphlets implying that I promote homosexuality. The pamphlets were from my oponent's campaign committee. Other literature suggested that I favor experimentation on live, aborted fetuses. Dixon characterized my 18 years in the Senate as anti-God—but of course, he wasn't talking about my record on legislation aimed at healing the sick, feeding the hungry or clothing the poor, all part of God's mandate as I understand it.

9   There is nothing particularly new about any of this. Indeed, there is nothing new about the New Right. It is a public-relations fiction created by right-wing extremists of long standing who understand our penchant for convenient labels and the media's obsession with anything purporting to be new. "The New Right" is a tag, a phrase without substance; "the Repressive Right" is a more apt description.

10   And there is nothing new about the New Right's leadership, tactics or

temperament. Richard Viguerie labored in the Young Americans for Freedom vineyard 20 years ago and eventually migrated to George Wallace's presidential campaigns. Paul Weyrich and Joseph Coors, a walking charitable trust for extreme right-wing causes, go way back. And Howard Phillips is an old hand, the fellow Richard Nixon assigned to dismantle Lyndon Johnson's programs to help the underprivileged. Terry Dolan, the young director of the National Conservative Political Action Committee, is the only neophyte within the inner circle.

11   Nor is there anything new about the politics of emotional intimidation and moral coercion. This brand of single-issue politics reaches at least as far back as the Anti-Saloon League and probably to the first witch hunt. When the president of the Southern Baptist Convention says that "God does not hear the prayers of a Jew," I don't think ill of my Baptists friends; I remember, instead, how old a cancer anti-Semitism is. When preacher Dixon of Indianapolis says that Jews will go to hell, I remember how he campaigned against John F. Kennedy, saying that America would go to hell if a Catholic occupied the White House.

12   The Repressive Right holds pluralism, diversity and tolerance in complete disdain. It practices a politics of alienation by which neighbors are pitted against neighbors. It nurtures a mean-spiritedness designed to suppress open political debate, intimidate potential opposition and force conformity. Indeed, it seems hell-bent on punishing people who value individual rights and civil liberties.

13   Again, there is nothing new—or conservative, in the best sense of the word—about any of this; but it is utterly serious.

14   There are important issues to be debated before the 1982 election; the passage of the equal rights amendment, the renewal of the Voting Rights Act, the nuclear-arms race and the survival of the Social Security system, to name a few. The human-life amendment also deserves careful scrutiny; what would it mean to extend legal rights to the union of cells at conception? I don't know the answer, but the Repressive Right does not even want the question asked.

15   That is why I offer this free and unsolicited advice to the candidates of 1982, Republican or Democrat: It is axiomatic in politics that power is not what you have but what people think you have. The Repressive Right claims powers that it does not have. Those claims must not go unchallenged. For instance, it claims credit for defeating Sen. John C. Culver of Iowa, Sen. Frank Church of Idaho, me and others last year. I can't speak for my colleagues, but the Repressive Right had less to do with my defeat than 18% unemployment among Indiana autoworkers and outrageous interest rates.

16   On the other hand, candidates shouldn't underestimate the tactics of the Repressive Right. They owe it to the electorate to take clear-headed, affirmative stands on difficult issues—so clear that no amount of right-wing newspeak and electronic claptrap will obscure the debate.

17   During my years in public service, I have developed a profound respect for the American people and our form of government. Liberal or conservative, whatever their age, race or sex, Americans are more practical than ideological, more altruistic than cynical. They respect the dignity of the individual, cherish their liberty and yearn for a productive and a public-spirited consensus. And for that reason, if no other, they will reject the straw men of the "New Right" in the same way they have always rejected the politics of fear and repression which is perennially searching for a new home.[10]

Questions for Analysis

1. State Bayh's thesis and list his main points.
2. What kind of assertion is Bayh's thesis: meaning, value, policy, consequence, or fact?
3. What strategy for developing an argumentative essay of opinion does the author use?
4. Do you think his essay is argumentative, persuasive, or both?
5. Is the title of the essay a false dilemma?
6. Cite five fact statements, five opinion statements, and five fact/opinion statements. Rewrite the opinion/fact statements to rid them of opinion.
7. Prepare a syllogism or chain of syllogisms for any two paragraphs.
8. Does the opening paragraph rely on provincialism?
9. In the first paragraph, Bayh says that "this movement is not a harmless political curiosity." Is this a value assertion? If so, is Bayh's basis for the opinion principle or consequence?
10. Do you think Bayh is objective? He insists (in paragraphs 1 and 5) that he knows what he's talking about. Do you think he's in a position to?
11. Does Bayh ever define the New Right? If not, do you think a definition is in order? If you do, why?
12. Prepare two syllogisms for the last two sentences of paragraph 3.
13. Do you think the opening sentence of paragraph 3 is a questionable evaluation?
14. Does paragraph 3 rely on an appeal to tradition to discredit the New Right?
15. Is there an appeal to tradition in paragraph 5?
16. In paragraph 6 the author characterizes the New Right's focus on O'Connor's "support for the equal rights amendment and freedom of choice in

---

[10]From the *Los Angeles Times*, July 19, 1981. Reprinted by permission of the author and publisher.

abortion" as an "attempt to impose politics on the judiciary." Does the rest of this paragraph demonstrate this claim, or is it irrelevant to the claim?

17. Paragraph 11 is full of value assertions. Do you think any (or all) of them is questionable?

18. About halfway through his essay, Bayh substitutes the term *Repressive Right* for *New Right*. Do you think there is some provincialism behind the switch?

19. Do you think paragraph 15 is consistent with what has preceded it?

READING   FOR   ANALYSIS

The following fact/opinion essay by journalist Richard Reeves is offered without follow-up questions. But for your own analysis you may want to (1) identify Reeve's thesis, main points, and organizational structure; (2) identify the kind of assertion the author is advancing; (3) list the sources he uses in developing support material; and (4) separate all facts from opinions and identify related fallacies, if any.

Abscam's Ominous Legacy:
Videotapes Can Convict As Surely As a Jury
By Richard Reeves

1   *Security World* is not a place. It is a magazine. More precisely, it is "The magazine of professional security administration and practice"—and it has almost 42,000 subscribers.
2   Looking through recent issues, a scary exercise, you find articles with

titles like: "Three Missions for Closed-Circuit Television in Physical Security, Detection, Surveillance, Access Control." The subtitle is: "Human factors important consideration in tactical deployment."

3   Tactical deployment of what? Television cameras, of course. Little eyes are everywhere. One of the biggest advertisers is Panasonic, which pays for a two-page color spread that begins: "Nobody lets you keep an eye on people, places and things more ways than Panasonic."

4   Little Brother is watching. Television cameras—like Panasonic's Newvicon—are hidden in corners, behind walls, behind pictures. Sometimes they're out in the open if the person paying for the electricity believes that their very visibility is a deterrent to what he wants to deter—outsiders, thievery, free speech. The company, and many others, will also provide "dummy" cameras complete with little red lights to make you believe that you're being observed even when there's nothing behind the little eye but styrofoam.

5   We now know, of course, that the Government, the Federal Bureau of Investigation, is a major customer of the advertisers in *Security World*. Equipment like this was what the FBI used to trap congressmen talking about bribes with agents posing as Arabs—Abscam. The places where the meetings were held were "eyed"—or whatever the equivalent visual term is for bugging. Big Brother is watching, too.

6   In fact, on Tuesday, Oct. 14, 1980—a date I think will prove historic—almost all of us were watching. On that day, the United States Supreme Court ruled, in effect, that video surveillance (videotapes) introduced in evidence during trials was public information. The tapes could be released to network television. That night, the network news broadcasts did show the Abscam tapes from the case of Pennsylvania representative Michael Myers—first editing them, of course, to highlight the most dramatic moment, the congressman taking the envelope with the cash inside.

7   American justice was set back, by my disgusted reckoning, about 300 years. Showing the tapes to the Nation, with narration by Walter Cronkite and friends, was the modern equivalent of pillory. Myers was put in the stocks in the town square so people could come by and spit on him.

8   But whatever justice suffered, television made another leap forward. The networks got what they wanted—three minutes of very good film. The industry got further proof of the value of its product and technology—and a license to sell more little "eyes" for discreetly applied surveillance.

9   So, television technology is now available for detection and apprehension (cameras), trial and conviction (the first run of the tapes in court) and massive public humiliation (nationwide distribution of the tapes).

10   The Supreme Court's effective backing, perhaps unintentional, gives the security business, both governmental and private, more respectability

than I would like to see it have. The people who go to security-industry trade shows seem different from me and you. When I went to a show at the Los Angeles Convention Center, I asked the demonstrator of a $1995 voice stress analyzer—a "lie detector" for your telephone—whether the gadget was illegal. "Sure," he said. "In California it's against the law to tape another person without his permission. But, hey, everybody's doing it, and no one is ever going to be convicted. The police could break in while you're taping and they couldn't do anything. A tape is inadmissible as evidence if you don't identify yourself at the beginning—and you're not going to do that, right?"

11   But "evidence" does not have to be used in court to be effective. Showing it on television could be enough. Now that the networks have seen how popular Abscam-like tapes can be, they might start commissioning them for themselves. Why wait for the next big trial that involves videotapes? Hell, why not plant cameras and mircrophones anyplace they can't be found? Why not use tapes done by outsiders with an ax to grind, maybe a clerk somewhere who thinks his boss is on the take? Why not set up your own Abscam operations? Why not hire a couple of actors and ruin the reputation of someone you don't like? A third party mentioned in a tape has no defense, no recourse.

12   The legal answer to those questions would be that tapes like those fantasized would not be admissible in court. Big deal! If I were Ozzie Myers, I would rather be convicted in court than on network television.

13   That's the point. Television has great power both as prosecutor—Mike Wallace for the people—and as the society's communicator of shared information. Gossip and unproved allegation can convict as surely as a jury, and videotapes shared by a hundred million people are a little more effective than gossip.

14   The danger—and I think it is very great—is that the technology of television can provide a crude alternative to the procedures of justice established over hundreds of years. If we work at it and if the courts don't think about the implications of what they're doing, we could institutionalize 1940s' movie blackmail with its bedroom and motel photographs. You follow me around with your Sony and I'll be after you with my Panasonic. We'll see who gets enough to go to court . . . or to a network.[11]

THEME   TOPICS

Write a 500- to 1,000-word argumentative essay. Develop your paper either by defending an opinion or by adjusting it.

---

[11]From *Panorama Magazine*, January 1981. Reprinted by permission of the author.

1. Some students criticize instructors for lecturing all the time. Do you think that the lecture method is the best way for a professor to conduct a college class in, say, history? Assume your audience is one of your professors.

2. Even though the Supreme Court has ruled that making only males register for the draft is not discriminatory against females, some people believe that it is. Do you?

3. One of the more curious offshoots of the interest in self-help literature and strategies is a program designed to help people marry for money. Among other things, workshop participants are instructed on how to snag a rich spouse. What is your opinion of such programs? Pretend that you are writing to a friend who has read an advertisement for such a workshop and is thinking about taking it.

4. Sex education continues to be a controversial issue. Suppose that you could decide whether to start a sex-education program at the junior-high level. Would you support or oppose such a program?

5. Students sometimes complain that, although teachers say that they want students to participate in class, they really don't. When students do speak up, so the charges go, the instructor usually "shoots them down." The fear of being embarrassed has led many students to "clam up" or to say only what they believe the instructor wants to hear. Do you think that it's the better part of wisdom for students to say what they really think or to tell teachers what they want to hear?

6. Advances in medical science have made the possibility of surrogate parenthood a reality. Today it is possible for a couple to have "its own child" even though one of them lacks the capacity to produce a child. For example, suppose a husband is sterile. It is possible for his wife to be inseminated with a donor's sperm. In the case of a wife who can't conceive, it's possible for her husband's sperm to be used to inseminate another woman, who carries the child to term in place of the wife. In both cases the newborn is then turned over to the couple. What's your opinion of such procedures?

7. Some people argue that a person's sexual preference should never be a ground for excluding the person from employment. Others contend that it should be, as, for example, in the case of an admitted homosexual elementary school teacher, member of the military, or intelligence agent. Do you think that a person's sexual preference should ever be a relevant employment criterion? Pretend that you are a personnel director who has been asked by your employer to draft a position paper to be submitted to the firm's board of directors.

4. Comparison and Analogy

A young job applicant is pondering a question on a psychological test administered by a large company: "Which of the following magazines do you read regularly?" Among the magazines listed are *People, Mother Jones, Business Week, Playboy, Fortune, Time, Harper's* and *Sports Illustrated*. As it happens, the candidate reads *Mother Jones, Playboy,* and *Sports Illustrated* regularly. But if he lists *Mother Jones,* he fears he will be considered too liberal for the job, perhaps even a "radical." If he lists *Playboy,* he feels he might be judged a bounder, or worse. And if he lists *Sports Illustrated,* he suspects he might be viewed as a "jock." So, he decides to put down *Time, Business Week,* and *Fortune*.

Owing to a merger, a woman who solicits magazine advertisements suddenly finds herself out of a job. The woman is fifty-seven and, despite a good record, stands little chance of landing a job in her field because of its bias in favor of youth. She is vigorous and healthy, and only a considerable amount of

133

gray in her hair suggests her age. So, before beginning her job hunt she touches up her hair with black dye. She realizes that the truth about her age may well come out in time, but she figures that she can deal with that situation when it arises. Indeed, she and her husband decide that she can easily pass for forty-five, and she so states her age on her résumé.

What do you think of such behavior? Better yet, suppose that you wished to *defend* this behavior in an essay. How would you proceed?

READING FOR ANALYSIS

A few years ago, Albert Carr, who is a professor of business administration at Harvard University, wrote an essay in which he attempted to defend such behavior as acceptable lying. Here's an excerpt from that essay:

"Is Business Bluffing Ethical?"
By Albert Z. Carr

1   Most executives from time to time are almost compelled, in the interests of their companies or themselves, to practice some form of deception when negotiating with customers, dealers, labor unions, government officials, or even other departments of their companies. By conscious misstatements, concealment of pertinent facts, or exaggeration—in short, by bluffing—they seek to persuade others to agree with them. I think it is fair to say that if the individual executive refuses to bluff from time to time—if he feels obligated to tell the truth, the whole truth, and nothing but the truth—he is ignoring opportunities permitted under the rules and is at a heavy disadvantage in his business dealings.

2   We can learn a good deal about the nature of business by comparing it with poker. While both have a large element of chance, in the long run the winner is the man who plays with steady skill. In both games ultimate victory requires intimate knowledge of the rules, insight into the psychology of the other players, a bold front, a considerable amount of self-discipline, and the ability to respond swiftly and effectively to opportunities provided by chance.

3   No one expects poker to be played on the ethical principles preached in churches. In poker it is right and proper to bluff a friend out of the rewards of being dealt a good hand. A player feels no more than a slight twinge of sympathy, if that, when—with nothing better than a single ace in his hand—he strips a heavy loser, who holds a pair, of the rest of his chips. It was up to the other fellow to protect himself. In the words of an excellent poker player, former President Harry Truman, "If you can't stand the heat, stay out of the kitchen." If one shows mercy to a loser in poker, it is a personal gesture, divorced from the rules of the game.

4   Poker has its special ethics, and here I am not referring to rules against cheating. The man who keeps an ace up his sleeve or who marks the cards is more than unethical; he is a crook, and can be punished as such—kicked out of the game or, in the Old West, shot.

5   In contrast to the cheat, the unethical poker player is one who, while abiding by the letter of the rules, finds ways to put the other players at an unfair disadvantage. Perhaps he unnerves them with loud talk. Or he tries to get them drunk. Or he plays in cahoots with someone else at the table. Ethical poker players frown on such tactics.

6   Poker's own brand of ethics is different from the ethical ideals of civilized human relationships. The game calls for distrust of the other fellow. It ignores the claim of friendship. Cunning deception and concealment of one's strength and intentions, not kindness and openheartedness, are vital in poker. No one thinks any the worse of poker on that account. And no one should think any the worse of the game of business because its standards of right and wrong differ from the prevailing traditions of morality in our society.[1]

You'd probably agree that the position asserted here is indeed provocative. Later you'll have ample opportunity to evaluate it. But what particularly interests us now is the way the argument is developed. Carr's argumentative essay is one whose presentation relies primarily on the development of a comparison. The comparison being made is between business and poker. In essence, the author argues that, given all the other similarities between poker and business, unethical behavior should be accepted in business, just as it is in poker. Comparing two or more things, as Carr does, is still another way to develop an argumentative essay.

This chapter examines the nature and structure of comparisons, including faulty comparisons. It also considers an important type of comparison called the analogy. Actually, the preceding essay involves an analogy. In order to evaluate this or any other analogy, it's important to apply specific criteria. We will cover these criteria and also meet another fallacy, the false analogy. Finally, we will learn how to set up and write an argumentative essay whose presentation relies primarily on the development of a comparison or analogy.

COMPARISON AND CONTRAST

Comparison reflects a basic arrangement of ideas—a pattern of thinking translated into writing. The term *comparison* also refers to contrast, and an essay developed by comparison typically employs contrast. Technically speaking, comparison focuses on likenesses, usually between things we view as different (for example, living at home and living on campus while attending college). Contrast points up differences, mainly between things usually considered similar, such as male and female brain structure. In practice, however, comparison and contrast usually function together, and so I will use *comparison* to refer to contrast as well.

We needn't go far to spot everyday decisions that involve comparisons. The food we eat, clothes we wear, television programs we watch, books we read, friends we choose, and recreation we enjoy all involve comparisons, although perhaps on an unconscious level. Sometimes the comparisons we make to chart a course become explicit. Thus, we seriously weigh the choice of a major or wonder whether to experiment with drugs or casual sex. Or we think about where we'd like to live. In little and big ways, subtle and overt, our decisions reflect the centrality of comparative thought in our lives.

Regarded as a way of thinking and writing, a comparison establishes similarities between things from the same class. For example, you might compare rock with country, two kinds of music. Or you might compare electronic (television and radio) news with print news, two kinds of journalism. Comparisons involve two operations: (1) isolating two categories of the same subject and (2) isolating common features of the two categories. The relationship can be charted as follows:[2]

$$A \text{ is like } B \text{ with respect to } S.$$

	S	
A	S_1	B
A	S_2	B
A	S_3	B
A	S_4	B

In this scheme, A represents the first category in the comparison and B, the second. S represents the subject under which the categories fall. $S_1, S_2, S_3,$ and S_4 represent the bases for establishing similarities (and differences).

To illustrate the process involved in comparison, suppose you were interested in comparing living at home and living on campus. You might employ the sort of arrangement shown on page 137 (top).

Although this is an example of a very simple comparison, it does illustrate some important aspects of the logic of comparisons. First, the things to be compared must come from roughly similar areas of experience or levels of abstraction. It would be appropriate, for example, to compare one science-fiction film, extracurricular activity, politician, form of birth control, economic system, or energy source with another. But it would not be appropriate

---

[2]See Donald McQuade and Robert Atwan. *Thinking in Writing: Structures for Composition.* New York: Knopf, 1980, p. 188.

S
Living location while
at college

At home   On campus

S_1
_____   Costs   _____

S_2
_____   Convenience   _____

S_3
_____   Freedom   _____

to compare, say, an automobile with a forest or a political system with a baseball game. Second, the subjects must share at least several characteristics; otherwise there is no basis for the comparison.

When used as the primary means of developing an essay, comparisons ordinarily have a point to make. When the writer's purpose is to win audience assent or consent, then the comparison is used to advance an argument or help persuade. For example, one writer may underscore the similarities between athletic competition and business competition or war in order to convince the audience that football is more than just a game. Another writer might contrast the brain structures of the male and female in order to convince the audience of the possibility that behavioral differences between the sexes are best explained biologically, not environmentally.

Exercise

4.1   Using the scheme just presented, set up a comparison between the following pairs. Indicate at least three points of comparison.

1. Two politicians
2. Two kinds of automobile
3. Two cities
4. The sexual attitudes of the present generation of young people and the attitudes of their parents' generation
5. Solar and nuclear energy
6. Capital punishment and life in prison
7. College education and noncollege education
8. Living in an apartment and living in a house
9. Having children and not having children

FAULTY COMPARISONS

Comparisons used in argument can go awry in many ways. Three of the more common ways involve incompleteness, selectivity, and false dilemma.

Incomplete Comparison

The fallacy of incomplete comparison consists of making a comparison on too few points. As indicated, a good comparison must include at least several significant, common points. If it doesn't, then any conclusion based on the comparison will probably be a hasty one. For example, it would be hasty to conclude that living at home is better than living on campus on the basis of just one point of comparison: costs. Similarly, it would be premature to infer that solar energy is preferable to nuclear energy simply because the former may be safer. Although it is one's prerogative to weigh safety more heavily in any comparison of the two, it is not good form to disregard other points of comparison. In not broadening the base of comparison to include at least several significant points, the writer lacks sufficient evidence for drawing a conclusion.

Selective Comparison

The fallacy of selective comparison consists of selecting only those points of comparison that advance one's claim, while ignoring or suppressing other significant points. Overzealous to make a point, writers may select only points of comparison that establish the assertion, while ignoring or suppressing points that detract from it. When they do this, they render the comparison faulty by concealing evidence. For example, suppose you were comparing the relative merits of two automobiles, A and B. You compare them in terms of safety, style, price, and power. By these criteria, car A excels. But missing from your bases of comparison are such significant categories as fuel efficiency, maintenance costs, performance, and engineering. Should comparison on these points weaken your conclusion, you are arguing erroneously. In fact, since these factors are so significant in assessing a car, any conclusion drawn without considering them would be incorrect.

We can also make selective comparisons and argue erroneously when we introduce a point of comparison but then ignore relevant information about it. For example, suppose that car A is cheaper than car B because its basic price does not include a radio and air conditioner, whereas B's basic price does include these items. Omitting this fact in the comparison is calculated to mislead the audience.

False Dilemma

Potentially the most devastating fallacy associated with comparisons is the false dilemma, which we met in Chapter 3. This results when the writer assumes that two or more categories exhaust all the options available and then proceeds with a comparison that, in effect, argues for one of the categories. Advertisers particularly exploit this technique. Thus, an ad for a bank begins: "A logical alternative to the stock market: Madison Savings and Loan." Although a comparison involving the relative merits of investing in the stock market and in a bank is certainly permissible, it is not legitimate to use that comparison to conclude that one or the other is the best investment of *all* the alternatives. Again, manufacturers of modestly priced cars like to compare their products with luxury cars (for example, Volvo or Subaru with Mercedes or BMW). Based on the points considered (usually price and fuel efficiency), the modestly priced car inevitably comes out the better choice. Not only do such ads usually omit relevant points of comparison on which their product might not fare as well (for example, engineering and maneuverability), they imply that there are only two alternatives: their modestly priced car and the competition's very expensive car. Of course, there is considerable middle ground in the choice of a new car. In drawing comparisons that do not exhaust all the alternatives, then, the fair-minded writer is careful to point this out. Failing to do this, one can write a rather lengthy and otherwise acceptable essay that is predicated on a false assumption.

Here's an example of an ad that capitalizes on both the false dilemma and selectivity in making a comparison:

EXAMPLE: *"Arthritics: Arthritis Strength Bufferin provides more com-plete help than Anacin, Bayer, and Tylenol. Greater amount of pain reliever than Bayer or even Anacin for hours of relief from minor arthritis pain. Stomach protection ingredients Bayer and other aspirin do not have. More anti-inflammatory and anti-swelling ingredients than Anacin. Tylenol has none." (Advertisement.)*

COMMENT: *The analgesic effect of any of these products comes from its aspirin content. To the degree that aspirin in this "arthritic product" happens to meet the requirements of the arthritic's condition, it may bring a measure of relief. But the price of relief is rather expensive, compared with plain aspirin, which costs much less and does the job. The typical patient suffering from rheumatoid arthritis who can tolerate aspirin may be maintained on as many as twenty five-grain tablets of aspirin a day. Arthritis Strength Bufferin contains 7.5 grains, or 50 percent more than the typical patient would need. So why pay the extra money? And why choose any of these name brands when plain aspirin may prove just as effective? In making the comparison, then, this ad excludes a plain aspirin from consideration and conceals that, on the basis of cost and effect, plain aspirin may be the best choice.*

ANALOGY

Comparisons can show similarities between like things, or things drawn from the same general category. Sometimes, however, we don't compare like but unlike things, as in "Football is war," "The human brain resembles a computer," or "Business is like poker." Such comparisons are generally termed analogies.

Analogy is a special kind of comparison, involving two basically unlike things, which is made in order to focus on properties in one that are already obvious in the other. Usually, one of the subjects in an analogy is familiar and the other is unfamiliar. When both subjects are familiar, then it is their properties that are joined in the pattern of familiar and unfamiliar, as when the eye is compared with a camera in regard to both having a lens.

An analogy can be likened to a simile or metaphor, to which it is closely related. A simile is a comparison between basically unlike things, and it uses a comparative word such as *like* or *as*. "My love is like a red, red rose" is an example of a simile. A metaphor is a comparison between unlike things in which one thing is directly identified with another without the use of a comparative word. For example,

> "Life's but a walking shadow, a poor player
> That struts and frets his hour upon the stage,
> And then is heard no more."
> —Shakespeare

Thus, when the poet writes, "I wandered lonely as a cloud," he compares the properties he finds in his experience with what we all find in the cloud: isolation, drift, fragility, evanescence. He uses a simile to make some suggestion implicitly. An analogy, then, is simply a more explicit kind of reasoning than a simile or metaphor, but is a natural cousin of both.

Uses

Sometimes analogies are used in description to help produce a picture in the reader's mind, as in "The human tongue is like a cracked cauldron that beats out tunes to set a bear dancing when it would make the heavens weep with its melodies." At other times analogies are used to help in explanation, making

140

the unfamiliar understandable by comparison to the familiar. Illustrative of this use is a scientist's observation about the joys of doing science:

One of the pleasures of science is to see two distinct and apparently unrelated pieces of information suddenly come together. In a flash what one knows doubles or triples in size. It is like working on two large but separate sections of a jigsaw puzzle and almost without realizing it until the moment it happens, finding that they fit into one.[3]

In this passage a comparison is drawn between doing science and doing a jigsaw puzzle, in order to enlighten the audience about the pleasures of science. Both the descriptive and explanatory forms are nonargumentative uses of the analogy.

Analogy is also used in argument. *When used in argument, analogy is a method of reasoning whereby we infer possible similarities between two things on the basis of established similarities.* For example, Fred infers that he will do well on the next math test because he did well on the last one. The two things said to be similar are the two tests. There are three respects in which the two entities are said to resemble each other: in being math tests, in being given in the same class, and in Fred's doing well on them. But the three points of the analogy don't play identical roles in the argument. The first two occur in the premises and the third in both the premises and conclusion. Broadly speaking, then, Fred's argument can be described as having premises that assert, first, that two things are similar in two respects and, second, that one of those things has a further characteristic from which the conclusion is drawn that the other thing also has that characteristic.

Of course, not every analogical argument need cover exactly two things or three characteristics. For example, Fred happens to believe that life probably exists on other planets in our solar system. His opinion is based on the similarities between earth, which supports life, and the other planets: Pluto, Neptune, Uranus, Saturn, Jupiter, Mars, Venus, and Mercury. First, Fred observes that all these other planets revolve around the sun, as earth does. Also, they borrow light from the sun, as earth does. In addition, several are known to revolve on their axes and are subject to the same laws of gravitation as earth. In contrast to the simple argument about the math test, this one draws analogies across nine things (the known planets) in five respects: (1) in revolving around the sun, (2) in borrowing light from the sun, (3) in revolving on an axis, (4) in being subject to the same laws of gravitation, and (5) in supporting life. The fifth point of analogy occurs in both Fred's premises and conclusion.

Despite their numerical differences, however, all analogical arguments have the same general structure, or pattern. Accordingly, each analogical argument proceeds from the observation that two or more things are similar in one or more respects to the conclusion that the things are similar in some

---

[3]John Tyler Bonner. "Hormones in Social Amoebae and Mammals." *Scientific American*, vol. 221, no. 5, November 1968, p. 81.

other respect. Schematically, where a, b, c, and d are any entities and P, Q, and R are any properties or respects, an analogical argument can be represented as having the following form:

> *a, b, c, and d all have the properties P and Q.*
>
> *a, b, and c all have the property R.*
>
> *Therefore, d has the property R.*

As is true of all inductions, the conclusion drawn analogically is never certain, only probable. Thus, there's no guarantee that Fred will do well in the next math test or that life exists on some other planet.

Exercises

4.2 Indicate whether the following are argumentative or nonargumentative uses of the analogy. Explain.

1. *"How like a winter hath my absence been*
   From thee."—Shakespeare

2. *"Thou [west wind] from whose unseen presence the leaves dead*
   Are driven, like ghosts from an enchanter fleeing."—Shelley

3. Television programs shouldn't be interrupted by commercials. After all, movies in theaters aren't.

4. Plenty of important people, including elected officials, cheat on their taxes. Why shouldn't I?

5. You're sure to get a bad grade in Professor Bronson's class, Anne. He doesn't like to have girls in his science classes.

6. **Ted:** Why do you think you're going to sleep well tonight?
   Liz: Because I've just had a glass of sherry.
   Ted: I don't get it.
   Liz: Well, last night I had some sherry and slept like a log.
   Ted: I see.

7. It's so hot today you could fry an egg on the sidewalk.

8. Sin, like a barn fowl, comes home to roost.

9. **Lance:** Have you seen Woody Allen's latest movie?
   Lois: I don't have to to know I'll like it. Woody's never made a film I haven't liked.

10. *"We have waited for more than 340 years for our constitutional and God-given rights. The nations of Asia and Africa are moving with jet-like speed toward gaining political independence, but we still creep at horse-*

and-buggy pace toward gaining a cup of coffee at a lunch counter." (The Rev. Dr. Martin Luther King, Jr. "Letter from Birmingham Jail." In Why We Can't Wait. New York: Harper & Row, 1963, p. 51.)

11. "The objections which have been brought against a standing army, and they are many and weighty, and deserve to prevail, may also at last be brought against a standing government. The government itself, which is only the mode which the people have chosen to execute their will, is equally liable to be abused and perverted before the people can act through it." (Henry David Thoreau. "Resistance to Civil Government." In The Writings of Henry David Thoreau, ed. Wendell Glick. Princeton, N.J.: Princeton University Press, 1973, p. 79.)

12. "One of the most popular [explanations for student revolt is that] too many students still live in an adolescent stage of parent rejection, and if a university insists on maintaining its role of parental substitute, it must be prepared to face rebellious offspring." (Bill Ward. "Why Students Revolt. The Nation, January 25, 1966, p. 29.)

13. "Father was always a bit skeptical of this story, and of the new flying machines, otherwise he believed everything he read. Until 1909 no one in lower Binfield believed that human beings would ever learn to fly. The official doctrine was that if God had meant us to fly He'd have given us wings. Uncle Ezekiel couldn't help retorting that if God had meant us to ride He'd given us wheels, but even He didn't believe in the new flying machines." (George Orwell. Coming Up for Air. New York: Harcourt Brace Jovanovich, 1950, pp. 52–53.)

14. "Perhaps the most startling discovery made in astronomy this century is that the universe is populated by billions of galaxies and that they are systematically receding from one another, like raisins in an expanding pudding." (Martin J. Rees and Joseph Silk, "The Origin of Galaxies," Scientific American, vol. 22, August 1969, p. 81.)

4.3 Construct five passages which illustrate argumentative use of the analogy.

EVALUATING ANALOGICAL ARGUMENTS

In evaluating analogical arguments, it's necessary to determine the strength of the connection between the things compared. The stronger the connection, the more likely the conclusion; the weaker the connection, the less likely the conclusion. When the conclusion is very likely, then the argument is a good one; when the conclusion is unlikely, the argument is a poor one. Five criteria can be applied to analogical arguments in order to assess them: (1) the number of entities involved in the comparison, (2) the number of relevant likenesses among the entities, (3) the number of disanalogies, (4) the number of dissimilarities, and (5) the strength of the conclusion relative to the premises.

1. *Number of entities.* Ordinarily, the more entities lying at the base of the analogy, the stronger the conclusion. Thus, if Fred had done well in two or three other tests, he would be more justified in expecting to do well on the next one. The reason is that ordinarily, the larger the sample, the more representative of the class it is.

2. *Number of likenesses.* The more likenesses among the entities, the stronger the analogical argument and the more likely its conclusion. In his original argument Fred had two likenesses in his premises: (1) the entities were both math tests and (2) they were both given in the same class. Suppose Fred could point out additional likenesses, such as that both were the same kind of test and both were given by the same instructor. These additional likenesses would strengthen his analogy.

3. *Number of disanalogies.* Disanalogies are points of difference between the instances mentioned. Disanalogies weaken analogical arguments. For example, if Fred studied much less for the upcoming test than he had for the last, he couldn't expect to do as well. Or, in the case of his other argument, the fact that not all the planets revolve around the sun at the same distance from it that earth does is a disanalogy in his comparison; a difference in distance could produce a difference in temperature that would make life impossible.

4. *Number of dissimilarities.* Naturally, the larger the number of instances appealed to in the premises, the less likely that they will all be disanalogous to the instances mentioned in the conclusion. To manage disanalogies between instances, it is not necessary to increase their number. The same result can be achieved by taking instances in the premises that are dissimilar to one another. The less similar the instances of the premises are to one another, the less likely it will be that all of them are disanalogous to the conclusion's instance.

For example, suppose that Fred had done exceedingly well on all the tests in his other courses. That the other tests and the conditions under which they were taken varied would say much for Fred's scholarship and test-taking ability. This, in turn, would make it more likely that he would do well on the next math test.

5. *Strength of conclusion.* A final criterion in assessing analogical arguments deals with the strength of their conclusions. The more conservative the conclusion relative to the premises, the more likely it is. For example, suppose Fred had got a grade of ninety on his last math test. Ninety percent, then, would be the outer limit that he could reasonably predict for his score on the next test. The more under that limit he predicted, the more likely would be his conclusion. Thus, if he concluded that he would get at least an eighty, that

would be a stronger conclusion than if he expected to get a ninety; if he inferred that he would get seventy-five, that would be an even stronger inference.

Exercises

4.4 *Each of the following two analogical arguments is followed by several additional premises. Indicate where the additional premise would strengthen, weaken, or have no effect on the conclusion. In all cases, use the criteria for evaluating analogies. Finally, create two additional premises for each argument, one that strengthens and one that weakens the argument.*

1. On two separate occasions, you have bought a new car from the same dealership. Each car performed well for two years. Now that you're again in the market for a car, you conclude that you'll get another good car at the same dealership.

   A. Suppose that you had bought three new cars rather than two, with the same happy results.
   B. Suppose that the other cars you had bought had standard transmissions, but the new one would have an automatic transmission.
   C. Suppose that you had used the other cars almost exclusively for city driving but intended to drive the new one mainly on the highway in your new job as a sales representative.
   D. Suppose that the dealership had recently come under new ownership and management.
   E. Suppose that you expected to get 30 months of good performance. What about 18 months?

2. Connie has taken two literature courses and found both interesting and rewarding. She earned and received an "A" in each. So she fully expects that the next literature course she takes will prove equally as interesting and rewarding.

   A. Suppose that the previous courses had been in American literature and the next one would be in English literature.
   B. Suppose that the previous courses had been in American and English literature.
   C. Suppose that Connie would have the same professor whom she had had in the previous courses.
   D. Suppose that in each instance Connie had had a different professor and that now she would have still another professor.
   E. Suppose that Connie expected to get at least a "B" in the new course. What about an "A"?

4.5 *Both of your friend Jim's parents died in their early fifties of lung cancer. Jim is convinced that he too will develop the disease and, as a result, die young. You, however, disagree, for you can think of three disanalogies that Jim is overlooking. State them.*

4.6 *Salesman Willie Loman has stayed at the Grand Illusion Inn every spring for the past five years on his annual swing through Connecticut, and has been quite satisfied with the accommodations. On his visit to New England this spring, he fully expects to enjoy his stay at the Grand Illusion. But you have just returned from a weekend there and think that Willie will be disappointed. Cite three disanalogies between the inn as Willie remembers it and what you experienced during your stay.*

4.7 *Analyze the structure of the following analogical arguments and evaluate them in terms of the criteria previously explained.*

1. Children are very much like puppies. They have to be trained and taught how to behave. Otherwise, like dogs, they will grow up to be wild and troublesome.

2. It makes no sense to be in favor of some instances of abortion but opposed to all instances of mercy killing. After all, if preventing a person from being born is all right under certain conditions, it must be all right under certain conditions to stop someone from living.

3. Most women have a penchant for child care. Since the sick and infirm resemble children in many ways, women are also well qualified to care for the ill.

4. "It is urged that motion pictures do not fall within the First Amendment's aegis because their production, distribution, and exhibition is a large-scale business conducted for private profit. We cannot agree. That books, newspapers, and magazines are published and sold for profit does not prevent them from being a form of expression whose liberty is safeguarded by the First Amendment. We fail to see why operation for profit should have any different effect in the case of motion pictures." (Justice Tom C. Clark. Burstyn v. Wilson, 343 U.S. 495 [1952].)

5. "A married woman in her late twenties says she has been going topless for the last four years when the weather is pleasant, when she is working in her yard, driving her car, or riding a motorcycle with her husband. . . . A state highway patrolman, T. L. Hooks, stopped her Sunday while she was riding topless on a motorcycle with her husband. . . . Hooks said he later let

her go because there is no law prohibiting her from being topless in public. 'I guess it's not legally indecent to do that,' he said, 'but I still believe it's improper. It could cause accidents.' The woman's husband supports her action. 'You can't have two sets of moral values, one for men and the other for women,' he said. And she said: 'If a man can go without a shirt, then so can I. There's not much difference between the chest of a man and the chest of a woman. A little more fat on the woman, a little more hair on the man. . . .' " ("If a Man Can Go Without a Shirt, Then So Can I." Miami News, July 25, 1974. Reported in Howard Pospesel and David Marans. Argument: Deductive Logic Exercises, 2nd ed. Englewood Cliffs, N.J.: Prentice-Hall, 1978, p. 48.)

6. " *'Looky here, Jim; does a cat talk like we do?'*
   'No, a cat don't.'
   'Well, does a cow?'
   'No, a cow don't, nuther.'
   'Does a cat talk like a cow, or a cow talk like a cat?'
   'No, they don't.'
   'It's natural and right for 'em to talk different from each other, ain't it?'
   'Course.'
   'And ain't it natural and right for a cat and a cow to talk different from us?'
   'Why, mos' sholy it is.'
   'Well, then, why ain't it natural and right for a Frenchman to talk different from us? You answer me that.'
   'Is a cat a man, Huck?'
   'No.'
   'Well, den, dey ain't no sense in a cat talkin' like a man. Is a cow a man?—or is a cow a cat?'
   'No, she ain't either of them.'
   'Well, den, dey ain't got no business to talk like either one er the yuther of 'em. Is a Frenchman a man?'
   'Yes.'
   'Well, den! Dad blame it, why doan he talk like a man? You answer me dat!' " (Samuel Langhorne Clemens [Mark Twain]. The Adventures of Huckleberry Finn. New York: Harper & Row, 1951, pp. 86–87.)

7. "*Now if we survey the universe, so far as it falls under our knowledge, it bears a great resemblance to an animal or organized body, and seems actuated with a like principle of life and motion. A continual circulation of matter in it produces no disorder; a continual waste in every part is incessantly repaired; the closest sympathy is perceived throughout the entire system; and each part or member, in performing its proper offices, operates both to its own preservation and to that of the whole. The world, therefore, I infer, is an animal, and the Deity is the soul of the world, actuating it, and actuated by it.*" (David Hume. Dialogues Concerning

147

Natural Religion, ed. L. A. Selby-Bigge. Oxford, England: Clarendon Press, 1850, p. 103.)

FALSE ANALOGY

The fallacy of false analogy consists of overlooking significant differences in a comparison and assuming that, because two things are alike in one or more respects, they must be alike in some other respect. For example, a student argues that students should be allowed to use their texts during examinations, since lawyers can use their law books in preparing a case and doctors can check their medical books in making a diagnosis. Although there is a similarity in the cases compared—each is seeking information—the similarity is trivial compared with the outstanding difference: Doctors and lawyers are not taking tests to see what they have learned, but students are.

Again, someone argues analogically that people shouldn't allow pornographic material into their homes any more than they should serve their families contaminated foods. Presumably the reason for not serving contaminated food is that it makes people physically ill. But there's no solid evidence that reading or viewing pornographic material makes a person ill, physically or mentally. Here's an additional example of the false analogy, with comment.

> EXAMPLE: *Iran's Ayatollah Khomeini, defending state executions of those convicted of adultery, prostitution, or homosexuality: "If your finger suffers from gangrene, what do you do? Let the whole hand and then the body become filled with gangrene, or cut the finger off? . . . Corruption, corruption. We have to eliminate corruption." (Time, October 22, 1979, p. 57.)*

> COMMENT: *The analogy is this: Physical disease is to an individual body as moral corruption is to the state. Since the diseased parts of the body must sometimes be removed in order to preserve the life of the body, so moral corruption must sometimes be rooted out in order to preserve the integrity of the state. But Khomeini overlooks many points of difference that make the analogy false. First, physical disease and moral corruption differ in nature and form. Whereas people can easily agree that a hand is gangrenous and must be removed, they can rarely agree as easily about what constitutes moral corruption. Moreover, with a few isolated exceptions, people today don't agree that moral corruption*

148

> *warrants execution. Khomeini also overlooks that an indi-*
> *vidual is not part of the state in the same way that a member*
> *of the body is a part of that body. The fundamental differ-*
> *ence is that a body member has no life or integrity, not even*
> *meaning, except in reference to the whole body. In contrast,*
> *an individual has meaning and substance independently of*
> *any relationship with the state.*

It should be clear from this discussion of analogies that we must approach their use cautiously in writing, for analogies frequently suppress significant differences between the things compared. Used carefully, though, analogies can be enormously helpful in organizing and expressing our ideas. They can also stimulate creative thinking. By detecting relationships between things, we may start to see new implications and connections that lead to a new understanding of a subject.

Exercise

4.8 *Identify the analogies in the following passages and determine whether they are sound or false. Explain.*

1. *Colleges should start paying students for getting high grades. After all, business handsomely rewards its top people with bonuses and commissions, and everybody can see the beneficial effect of that practice on worker productivity.*

2. *Charging students tuition in public colleges is as objectionable as charging people for withdrawing books from a public library.*

3. The best reason for avoiding saccharine is that the chemical has produced cancer in experimental rats.

4. Venus has roughly the same diameter as earth and has approximately the same mass. So, it's likely that, since life exists on earth, it exists on Venus.

5. The federal "bail-out" of big companies such as Chrysler and Pan American World Airways is wrong, because the government makes no effort to rescue small businesses that are failing.

6. Because the Panama Canal is as much a part of the United States as any one of the fifty states, the Senate should never have approved the treaty that will turn it over to Panama.

7. "There is absolutely no reason for any presidential candidate to apologize for raising the matter of Chappaquiddick vis-à-vis Senator Kennedy. To the contrary Chappaquiddick is as much a part of Senator Kennedy's background as is the date of his birth. Considering its implications it merits serious discussion and consideration." (Letter to Time, November 5, 1979, p. 5.)

8. Apartment tenant, commenting on landlords' policy of prohibiting children: "When I first moved into this complex, the ages of the tenants varied from twenty-one to thirty-five. Then the older generation moved in and most of my friends said how the place was going to pot. Well, today do you know that the place is a better one because of them? That's why I think it would not be bad to allow children here. I think it would be a better place because of them." (60 Minutes, January 22, 1978.)

9. "The Congress extended the time in which the Equal Rights Amendment can be passed—it decided to send the struggle, the game, into extra innings—a 40-month extension to June 1982. To anyone in the stands this would be like an umpire on the field saying to a team with a 7-to-0 lead at the end of the last inning: 'I am now changing the rules of the game to give the losers another chance to win.' How many more chances, oh, umpire? Until the loser becomes the winner?" (Jerry Cederblom and David W. Paulsen. Critical Reasoning. Belmont, Calif.: Wadsworth, 1982, p. 140.)

10. "Are interior decorators really necessary? Yes. But not for the accepted reasons. Since one cannot set one's own broken leg one relies on a doctor. Without a formidable knowledge of legal intricacies one depends on a barrister. Likewise, unless the individual is well versed in the home furnishing field the services of an interior decorator are a distinct advantage." (Helen-Janet Bonellie. The Status Merchants: The Trade of Interior Decoration. Cranbury, N.J.: Barnes, 1972, p. 36.)

11. President Ronald Reagan, suggesting a way to pacify those who object to the sight of oil rigs off their beaches: "Maybe we ought to take some of those liberty ships out of mothballs and anchor one at each one of the oil

platforms between that and onshore, because people never objected to seeing a ship at sea." ("Reagan Supports Watt Stand." Santa Barbara Evening News Press, August 5, 1981, p. A-4.)

12. "In Sweatt v. Painter . . . in finding that a segregated law school for Negroes could not provide them equal educational opportunities, the Court relied in large part on 'those qualities which are incapable of objective measurement but which make for greatness in a law school.' In McLaurin v. Oklahoma State Regents, 339 U.S. 637 . . . the Court, in requiring that a Negro admitted to a white graduate school be treated like all other students, again resorted to intangible consideration: 'his ability to study, to engage in discussions and exchange views with other students and, in general, to learn his profession.' Such considerations apply with added force to children in grade and high schools. To separate them from others of similar age and qualifications solely because of their race generates a feeling of inferiority as to their status in the community that may affect their hearts and minds in a way unlikely ever to be undone." (U.S. Supreme Court. Brown v. Board of Education of Topeka, 1954.)

13. "Suppose that someone tells me that he has had a tooth extracted without an anesthetic, and I express my sympathy, and suppose that I am then asked, 'How do you know that it hurt him?' I might reasonably reply, "Well, I know that it would hurt me. I have been to the dentist and know how painful it is to have a tooth stopped without an anesthetic, let alone taken out. And he has the same sort of nervous system as I have. I infer, therefore, that in these conditions he felt considerable pain, just as I should myself.' " (Alfred J. Ayer. "One's Knowledge of Other Minds. In Theoria, vol. 19. Oxford, England: Oxford University Press, 1953, p. 51.)

14. "By what conceivable standard can the policy of price-fixing be a crime, when practiced by business men, but a public benefit, when practiced by the government? There are many industries in peacetime—trucking, for instance—whose prices are fixed by the government. If price-fixing is harmful to competition, to industry, to production, to consumers, to the whole economy, and to the 'public interest'—as the advocates of the antitrust laws have claimed—then how can that same harmful policy become beneficial in the hands of the government? Since there is no rational answer to this question, I suggest that you question the economic knowledge, the purpose and the motives of the champions of antitrust." (Ayn Rand. Capitalism: The Unknown Idea. New York: New American Library, 1966, p. 52.)

15. "One ought to be able to hold in one's head simultaneously the two facts that [artist Salvador] Dali is a good draughtsman and a disgusting human being. The one does not invalidate or, in a sense, affect the other. The first thing that we demand of a wall is that it shall stand up. If it stands up, it is a good wall, and the question of what purpose it serves is separable from that. And yet even the best wall in the world deserves to

be pulled down if it surrounds a concentration camp. In the same way it should be possible to say, 'This is a good book or a good picture, and it ought to be burned by the public hangman.' " (George Orwell. "Benefit of Clergy." The Collected Essays, Journalism, and Letters of George Orwell, vol. 3. New York: Harcourt Brace Jovanovich, 1979, p. 71.)

THE ESSAY OF COMPARISON OR ANALOGY

An argumentative essay's presentation often relies primarily on the development of a comparison or analogy. In developing such an essay, it is crucial to be clear about what is being compared. It is just as important to be clear about the basis for the comparison—that is, about the points being compared. Beyond this, writers must make sure that they have included all significant points of comparison and have not been unfair in selecting the points to be compared. Finally, if the development is based on the assumption that the subjects being compared are the only alternatives on which a choice rests, writers must ensure that the entities do, in fact, exhaust all the options.

Regarding analogies, we can always expect to find differences in the ones we construct. As a result, there will always be a tension between the logical limits and rhetorical utility of a constructive analogy. The writer's job is to determine just how far a comparison by analogy can be pushed. In determining the limits of an analogy, it is useful to list beforehand all the relational correspondences. This will help define the limits of the comparison and indicate how many points of similarity an essay requires.

There are two basic ways for developing the argumentative essay by comparison or analogy: subject by subject or point by point. Both are refinements of the structure that calls for analyzing alternatives, and in both cases the argumentative thesis is best stated early.

Subject-by-Subject Method

In the subject-by-subject format, one of the two or more subjects of comparison or contrast is dealt with fully, point by point, and then the other is presented. This approach is best used when the comparison is to be brief and the points are not so elusive that readers forget what was said in the first half of the essay. Writers using this format must take care that both subjects are being compared according to the same points of comparison. A subject-by-subject arrangement for an essay comparing television news with print news could be arranged as follows:

1. Introduction, including thesis that makes an argumentative assertion
2. Television journalism
   A. Nature

B. Format
C. Coverage
3. Print journalism
   A. Nature
   B. Format
   C. Coverage
4. Summary

Here's how such an essay might evolve:

INTRODUCTION/
        THESIS: *For most of us today television is our main source of news. This is unfortunate, because the print media, especially newspapers, are a better source. A look at the nature of television and newspapers, as well as the news format and coverage of each, leads to this assessment.*

FIRST SUBJECT
      POINT 1: *Television is essentially a passive medium. All we have to do is sit in front of the tube and "let it happen." This has sinister implications when it comes to news. . . .*

      POINT 2: *The most noteworthy thing about the format of television news is time. Regardless of the complexity or significance of an event, it somehow must be fitted into a prescribed number of minutes. The problem with such an approach is that. . . .*

      POINT 3: *Regarding coverage, television news excels in bringing into our living rooms dramatic events of singular importance: presidential inaugurations, space launchings, natural disasters, and so on. But because of its time limitations, television news cannot cover important stories in the depth they may deserve. Even more important, it cannot devote much attention to investigative reporting, which as often as not is left to such fine shows as 60 Minutes and 20/20. . . .*

SECOND SUBJECT
       POINT 1: *In contrast to television, the print media encourage active involvement in what's being reported. Not only must we make some effort to acquire a newspaper, we must then read it. Reading requires mental involvement, often at a rather high level. It also accommodates individual differences in our capacity to follow and absorb what is being reported. . . .*

       POINT 2: *With respect to format, print news is not restricted by considerations of time. A newspaper can devote as much space to a story as it sees fit and can afford. . . .*

POINT 3: *Of course newspapers cannot give the visual coverage to stories that television does. Admittedly this is a distinct disadvantage, for the significance of some events, such as a war, is best communicated by pictures, not words. But newspapers can cover a war, or other stories, in far greater detail. . . .*

SUMMARY: *What, then, does a consideration of television versus print journalism on the basis of nature, format, and coverage reveal? . . .*

Point-by-Point Method

In the point-by-point method, the bases for comparison are discussed one by one within paragraphs of the essay that present each of the points in relation to each subject. Each of the points of comparison could be developed in either a single paragraph or a series of paragraphs, with a roughly equal amount of space given to each of the sides. The advantages of the point-by-point method are that it allows the writer to draw fine connections between subjects and eliminates the possibility that the reader will forget what was said earlier. Here's how the essay just discussed might be set up point-by-point:

1. Introduction, including a thesis that makes an argumentative assertion
2. Nature
   A. Television journalism
   B. Print journalism
3. Format
   A. Television journalism
   B. Print journalism
4. Coverage
   A. Television journalism
   B. Print journalism
5. Summary

Here's how the essay might develop:

INTRODUCTION/
THESIS: *Same as in subject-by-subject method*

FIRST POINT: *By nature, television is a passive medium. All we have to do is sit in front of the tube and "let it happen." This has sinister implications when it comes to news. . . .*

In contrast, the print media encourage active involvement in what's being reported. Not only must we make some effort to acquire a newspaper, for example, but then we must read it. Reading requires mental involvement. . . .

154

SECOND POINT: *With respect to format, television news is severely restricted by considerations of time. Regardless of the complexity or significance of an event, . . .*

No such time limitation is imposed on print journalism. A newspaper can devote as much space to a story as it sees fit and can afford. . . .

THIRD POINT: *Regarding coverage, television news excels in bringing into our living rooms dramatic events of singular importance. But because of time limitations, television news cannot cover important stories in the depth they may deserve. . . .*

While print journalism cannot compete with television visually, it is superior to television news in fleshing out stories, in providing detail and depth. . . .

SUMMARY: *Same as in subject-by-subject method*

SUMMARY

Writers frequently use comparison and analogy to advance arguments. A comparison reflects a basic arrangement of ideas—a pattern translated into writing. The term *comparison* also refers to contrast, and the essay developed through comparison typically employs contrast as well. Technically, though, comparison focuses on likenesses, usually between things we view as different (for example, living at home and living on campus while at college); contrast points up differences, mainly between things usually considered similar (for example, male and female brain structure).

Any comparison involves two operations: (1) isolating the categories of the same subject and (2) isolating common features of the two categories. Three errors are particularly noteworthy in connection with faulty comparisons:

INCOMPLETE
COMPARISON: *making a comparison on too few points*

EXAMPLE: *concluding that living at home is better than living on campus, on the basis of just one point of comparison: costs*

SELECTIVE
COMPARISON: *selecting only those points of comparison that advance one's claim, while ignoring or suppressing other significant points*

EXAMPLE: *concluding that one car is better than another on the basis of a comparison that overlooks significant points of comparison, such as maintenance costs and engineering*

FALSE DILEMMA: *assuming that two or more categories exhaust all the options*

> EXAMPLE: *asserting that investments in stocks are better than investments in savings accounts, on the basis of a comparison that assumes that these are the only investment alternatives*

Analogy is a special kind of comparison, involving two basically unlike things, which is made in order to focus on properties in one that are already obvious in the other. Analogies can be used nonargumentatively, as in descriptions (for example, "The human tongue is like a cracked cauldron. . . .") or explanations (for example, comparing science to a jigsaw puzzle in order to show the joys of doing science). When used in argument, analogy is a method of reasoning whereby we infer possible similarities between two things on the basis of established similarities. Schematically, where a, b, c, and d represent any entity and P, Q, and R are any properties or respects, an analogical argument can be represented as having the following structure:

> *a, b, c, and d all have properties P and Q.*
>
> *a, b, and c all have properties R.*
>
> *Therefore, d has the property R.*

Analogical arguments, which at best produce probable inductions, are evaluated in terms of (1) the number of entities involved in the comparison, (2) the number of relevant likenesses among the entities, (3) the number of disanalogies, (4) the number of dissimilarities, and (5) the strength of the conclusion relative to the premises.

Poor analogical arguments overlook significant, relevant differences between the things compared, and they result in the fallacy of false analogy.

FALSE ANALOGY: *overlooking significant differences in a comparison and assuming that, because two things are alike in one or more respects, they are alike in some other respect*

> EXAMPLE: *asserting that students should be allowed to use their texts during exams, because doctors can use their medical books in making a diagnosis*

Often an argumentative essay's presentation relies primarily on the development of a comparison or analogy. In making a comparison in an essay, writers must be clear about what they are comparing and about the basis of the comparison. Also, they must make sure that they have included all significant points of comparison and have not been unfair in selecting the points to be compared. In addition, if the essay is based on the assumption that the things being compared are the only alternatives on which a choice rests, writers must ensure that the entities do, in fact, exhaust all the options. In drawing analogies writers must determine just how far a comparison by analogy can be pushed. To determine this, it helps to list beforehand all the relational correspondences between the entities.

Two formats are especially useful in writing argumentative essays whose presentation relies primarily on the development of a comparison or analogy. One is the subject-by-subject format; the other is the point-by-point method.

Questions for Analysis

These questions refer to Albert Carr's article, "Is Business Bluffing Ethical?" on pp. 134–135.

1. State Carr's thesis, and list his main points.
2. What kind of assertion is Carr's thesis: meaning, value, policy, consequences, or fact?
3. Which is the primary source of his material: personal experience, observation, informal opinion, or organized research?
4. Carr believes that individual executives who refuse to bluff from time to time ignore opportunities permitted under the rules (paragraph 1). As a result, they penalize themselves. Presumably, Carr regards such self-sacrificial acts as, at the very least, foolish. His analysis here and elsewhere seems to originate in and be restricted to a business purview. Is his appeal provincial?
5. How does Carr qualify his opening-sentence generalization? Do you agree with his observation?
6. Do you agree with the generalization expressed in the last sentence of paragraph 1?
7. Prepare a syllogism for paragraph 3, beginning with sentence 4.
8. According to Carr, what likenesses do business and poker have?
9. Given these similarities that poker and business have, what is their additional similarity, according to the author?
10. In what ways, if any, are business and poker disanalagous? Do you think that these disanalogies seriously weaken Carr's analogy? Do you think the analogy is a false one?
11. Do you think that the reference to Harry Truman is an appeal to authority? If so, is it a sound one?
12. In paragraph 3 Carr says: "No one expects poker to be played on the ethical principles preached in churches." What principles do you think he has in mind?
13. In paragraphs 4 and 5 he distinguishes between the special ethics of poker and rules against cheating. What is the difference between the two?

14. Recall the example that began the chapter, that of a middle-aged woman who deliberately misrepresents her age on a job application. According to the author, this action would fall under "bluffing"; that is, it would be within the accepted rules of the business game. In other words, it would be like a poker player's betting a whopping sum on a worthless hand, with the hope, of course, that the other players would take the bluff and fold. What disanalogies, if any, are there between these two kinds of behavior?

READING FOR ANALYSIS

In the past decade or so we have become particularly sensitive to the depletion of the world's bounty and, of course, the potential catastrophe that would result from overtaxing the supply of natural resources. Compounding the problem of increasing demands for limited resources is the fact that the gap between the world's "haves" and "have nots" is ever widening. As a result, some are calling for a redistribution of the world's wealth. For example, at an international conference in Cancun, Mexico, in October 1981, Third World countries and some Western nations suggested that the rich countries must share their wealth with the poor ones. Should they? Do the affluent nations have a moral obligation to share their wealth with the poorer ones? Some think not.

In 1974 biologist Garrett Hardin wrote this essay, which has since become a classic of environmental literature. Hardin not only rejects the contention that the affluent nations have an obligation to help the needy ones but argues further that they have the duty *not* to help. In the short excerpt that follows, Hardin uses a graphic analogy to make his point.

Lifeboat Ethics: The Case against Helping the Poor
By Garrett Hardin

1   Environmentalists use the metaphor of the earth as a "spaceship" in trying to persuade countries, industries and people to stop wasting and polluting our natural resources. Since we all share life on this planet, they argue, no single person or institution has the right to destroy, waste, or use more than a fair share of its resources.

2   But does everyone on earth have an equal right to an equal share of its resources? The spaceship metaphor can be dangerous when used by misguided idealists to justify suicidal policies for sharing our resources through uncontrolled immigration and foreign aid. In their enthusiastic but unrealistic generosity, they confuse the ethics of a spaceship with those of a lifeboat.

3   A true spaceship would have to be under the control of a captain, since no ship could possibly survive if its course were determined by

committee. Spaceship Earth certainly has no captain; the United Nations is merely a toothless tiger, with little power to enforce any policy upon its bickering members.

4   If we divide the world crudely into rich nations and poor nations, two thirds of them are desperately poor, and only one third comparatively rich, with the United States the wealthiest of all. Metaphorically each rich nation can be seen as a lifeboat full of comparatively rich people. In the ocean outside each lifeboat swim the poor of the world, who would like to get in, or at least to share some of the wealth. What should the lifeboat passengers do?

5   First, we must recognize the limited capacity of any lifeboat. For example, a nation's land has a limited capacity to support a population and as the current energy crisis has shown us, in some ways we have already exceeded the carrying capacity of our land.

6   So here we sit, say fifty people in our lifeboat. To be generous, let us assume it has room for ten more, making a total capacity of sixty. Suppose the fifty of us in the lifeboat see 100 others swimming in the water outside, begging for admission to our boat or for handouts. We have several options: We may be tempted to try to live by the Christian ideal of being "our brother's keeper," or by the Marxist ideal of "to each according to his needs." Since the needs of all in the water are the same, and since they can all be seen as "our brothers," we could take them all into our boat, making a total of 150 in a boat designed for sixty. The boat swamps, everyone drowns. Complete justice, complete catastrophe.

7   Since the boat has an unused excess capacity of ten more passengers, we could admit just ten more to it. But which ten do we let in? How do we choose? Do we pick the best ten, the neediest ten, "first come, first served"? And what do we say to the ninety we exclude? If we do let an extra ten into our lifeboat, we will have lost our "safety factor," an engineering principle of critical importance. For example, if we don't leave room for excess capacity as a safety factor in our country's agriculture, a new plant disease or a bad change in the weather could have disastrous consequences.

8   Suppose we decide to preserve our small safety factor and admit no more to the lifeboat. Our survival is then possible, although we shall have to be constantly on guard against boarding parties.

9   While this last solution clearly offers the only means of our survival, it is morally abhorrent to many people. Some say they feel guilty about their good luck. My reply is simple: "Get out and yield your place to others." This may solve the problem of the guilt-ridden person's conscience, but it does not change the ethics of the lifeboat. The needy person to whom the guilt-ridden person yields his place will not himself feel guilty about his good luck. If he did, he would not climb aboard. The net result of conscience-stricken people giving up their unjustly held seats is the elimination of that sort of conscience from the lifeboat.

10   This is the basic metaphor within which we must work out our solutions.[4]

Questions for Analysis

1. State Hardin's thesis, and list his main points.
2. What kind of assertion is Hardin's thesis: meaning, value, policy, consequence, or fact?
3. What is the author's primary source of material: personal experience, observation, informed opinion, or organized research?
4. What strategy does he use for developing an essay by comparison or analogy?
5. Prepare a syllogism for the environmentalists' argument as paraphrased by Hardin in the second sentence of paragraph 1. What is the unexpressed premise?
6. The author opens paragraph 2 with a question. Do the next two sentences of the paragraph answer the question, or do they evade it?
7. What disanalogies does Hardin cite between a spaceship and earth? Do you agree that these differences significantly weaken the comparison?
8. In paragraph 3 the author says that the United Nations has "little power to enforce any policy upon its bickering members." Is this a qualified or unqualified generalization? Do you agree with it?
9. According to Hardin, what likenesses do a lifeboat and a rich nation share?
10. Are you prepared to accept Hardin's analogy between a lifeboat and a rich nation? Or do you find significant disanalogies between them?
11. Suppose someone said, "One major difference between a lifeboat and a nation is that, in the case of the lifeboat we know precisely what its carrying capacity is, but in the case of a nation we do not know that for sure." Do you think that this point does, in fact, raise an important disanalogy between a lifeboat and a nation?
12. In the preceding chapter you learned that writers provide support for their value opinions by appealing to principle and consequences. What principle and consequences does Hardin appeal to in determining that a rich nation should not help a poor one?

READING   FOR   ANALYSIS

The following essay is offered, without follow-up questions, for your own careful analysis. In the essay Isaac Asimov, in effect, argues that applying

---

[4]Excerpt from *Psychology Today Magazine.* Copyright © 1974 Ziff-Davis Publishing Company. Reprinted by permission of the publisher.

economic pressure on advertisers to reevaluate the television programs they sponsor is censorship and thus will lead to widespread repression of thought and work. The strength of the essay, therefore, depends on the soundness of the implied analogy between applying economic pressure and censorship. You might: (1) identify the author's thesis, main points, and organizational structure; (2) indicate the kind of assertion the author is advancing; (3) list the sources the author uses in developing support material; and (4) evaluate the implied analogy. Also, inasmuch as this essay was written for the world's best-selling magazine *(TV Guide)*, think about Asimov's audience and the persona he chooses.

Censorship: It's 'A Choking Grip'

By Isaac Asimov

1   There is a move now to clamp down on the sexy aspects of television and return it to the purity of *Ozzie and Harriet*.

2   Lift those necklines! Thicken those brassieres and rivet them firmly in place! Unleer those lips! Unwiggle those hips!—And watch what you say!

3   The penalty? The New Puritans will reckon up the sex-points, watching narrowly for every hint of cleavage, for every parting of kissing lips, and will then lower the boom on all advertisers who fail the test. By striking at the pocket-nerve, the Puritans hope to produce a new kind of television that will be as clean, as pink, as smooth and as plump as eunuchs usually are.

4   In a way, I sympathize with the purity brigade. The emphasis on top-front and bottom-rear gets wearisome after a while and blunts their very real values through overfamiliarity. Sniggering isn't the most amusing form of laughter, and eyebrow-lifting-cum-leer doesn't make for the pleasantest countenance.

5   Nevertheless, there is nothing that salaciousness can do that, in the long run, will do as much harm as the choking grip of orthodoxy. If you set up a standard of purity and right-thinking and begin to demand that this be the standard for all; if you take to watching your neighbor lest he disagree with your conception of right, and punish him if he does so; if you make certain we all think alike or, if necessary, don't think at all; then there surely will be a general crushing of intellectual liveliness and growth.

6   In a healthy society, dissent is free and can be endured. If you think that a sex-ridden society, or a permissive society, or a think-as-you-please society is *not* healthy, you have but to try the kind of society in which unbridled repression sees to it that you think, write, say and do only what some dominating force says you may, and you will then find out what an unhealthy society really is.

7   It has happened before, many times, and there's no mistaking the results.

8   In the 16th century, the Protestant movement split the Church in Western Europe. In some regions, the result was a move, to a greater or lesser degree, in the direction of a religiously permissive society. In other regions, orthodoxy gathered its forces and clamped down, determined that opposition views would be excluded totally.

9   Nowhere had the drive for orthodoxy made as much headway as in Spain, which was then the most powerful nation in Europe. But that power faded as the grip of orthodoxy closed about the national throat. There were many reasons for this decline, but surely one of them was the fear of thinking that permeated the land. Spain did not share in the fermenting growth of commerce, manufacturing, science and technology that boiled and bubbled in France, Great Britain and the Netherlands.

10   Italy was a divided country in early modern times and had no political or military power to speak of; but it had a vigorous intellectual life throughout the Middle Ages; and art, science and literature reached a glittering peak between 1300 and 1600.

11   The greatest of all Italian scientists was Galileo, who, in his old age, was brought before the Inquisition in 1632 for espousing too effectively a variety of heretical opinions. He himself was not actually tortured, and he lived out his last years in peace. It was Italy that suffered, for the cold water dashed in the name of orthodoxy on intellectual venturesomeness played its part in that nation's scientific decline. Italian science never sank to the almost-zero level of Spain's, but its leadership passed to the northern nations.

12   In 1685, the powerful French king Louis XIV put an end to a century-old toleration of his country's Protestant citizens, the Huguenots, thousands of whom were driven out so that France might become solidly orthodox. They fled to Great Britain, the Netherlands and Prussia, subtracting their intellectual and technological strengths from France and adding them to France's enemies. That was surely a contributing factor to France's slow decline thereafter.

13   Nineteenth-century Germany saw the greatest flowering of science up to that point. Germany, as a whole, was not remarkable for its liberty, but, like Italy, it was split into numerous states. Unlike Italy, there was no religious uniformity among those states, and what one did not allow, another would. In the competition among them, dozens of great universities flourished.

14   However, in Austria, Germany's largest state and therefore the most effectively orthodox, science and technology advanced least, and progress of all sorts languished.

15   The most madly repressive regime modern Europe had seen was established by Hitler in 1933. In the space of a few years, he clamped a ferocious Nazi orthodoxy first upon Germany and then upon much of Europe. Jewish scientists and, indeed, scientists of any kind who were

insufficiently Nazi were harried and driven out. These refugees subtr[e]
their strength from Germany and added it to Great Britain and the Un[i]
States, thus contributing to Germany's defeat.

16   Soviet and Chinese insistence on Communist orthodoxy has undou[b]
edly weakened both nations. How can it have helped but do so? Any
national practice that deadens the spirit and suppresses variety and
activity of thought surely will produce a national coma.

17   Are there examples of the opposite? The one most frequently cited is
the sexual abandon of the Roman Empire, as shown in I, Claudius, which
supposedly led to the fall of Rome.

18   Not so. That sexual abandon was confined to a small aristocracy and
was greatly exaggerated by the scandalmongers of the age for political
reasons. In any case, under those wicked early emperors the Roman
Empire was at the height of its power. It was in later centuries, when the
empire lay under the power of a religious orthodoxy that condemned all
dissent, that Rome fell.

19   So perhaps we had better endure the naughtiness of television and
hope that good taste among viewers will eventually prevail, rather than
set foot on the path of censorship and suppression. For that path, if
followed, will surely lead to destruction.[5]

THEME TOPICS

Comparison and Contrast

Each topic below consists of a pair of related items. Choose one pair and, using
either a subject-by-subject or point-by-point order, write an argumentative
essay (500 to 1,000 words) that relies for its presentation primarily on the
development of a comparison (or contrast).

1. Living together before marriage/not living together before marriage

2. Capital punishment/life in prison

3. Living on campus/living at home while attending college

4. Nuclear/solar energy

5. Having one's own child/adopting

6. Going to a public college/going to a private college

7. Going steady while in high school/"playing the field"

---

[5]From TV Guide Magazine, July 18, 1981. Copyright © 1981 by Triangle Publications, Inc.,
Radnor, Pennsylvania. Reprinted by permission of the author and publisher.

Analogy

1. It is sometimes said that the best training ground for war is the athletic field. Write an argumentative essay (500 to 1,000 words) in which you either (1) argue by analogy that sports are indeed good preparation for soldiering, or (2) argue that sports are not a good preparation for soldiering because of major disanalogies between athletic contests and war.

2. In part children learn to do arithmetic because they are well motivated at school and at home. Write an argumentative essay (500 to 1,000 words) in which you either (1) argue by analogy that children could be motivated and trained to use their mental skill to solve emotional problems, as they are taught to use their mental skills to do arithmetic, or (2) argue that children could not be so motivated and trained because of outstanding disanalogies between learning to do arithmetic and learning to solve one's emotional problems.

3. The police are looking for a sixteen-year-old young woman who, they suspect, is implicated in a crime. They come to her home and ask her father if he knows the whereabouts of his daughter. The father admits that he does but refuses to tell on the ground of legal privilege. He reasons that, if the husband/wife relationship is guarded against legal intrusions, then the parent/child relationship should be as well, even though technically it is not. Write an argumentative essay intended to be read by the father, in which you either support or reject his analogy.

4. Under the "fairness doctrine," a television station that broadcasts, say, a political viewpoint must make time available for opposing viewpoints. Newspapers, however, don't fall under the fairness doctrine. For example, if a newspaper lambastes the oil industry for "price gouging," it is not obliged to provide rebuttal space. Some people think that the fairness doctrine should be extended to cover newspapers. Write an argumentative essay (500 to 1,000 words) in which you either (1) argue by analogy that newspapers should fall under the fairness doctrine or (2) argue that newspapers should be exempt from the fairness doctrine because of significant disanalogies between newspapers and television. Pretend that you are writing the essay for your local newspaper.

5. Cause

READING FOR ANALYSIS

News is big business, perhaps the biggest in television these days. Advertising time on a popular news program such as *60 Minutes* costs more than it does on most other television programs. At first glance this seems a healthful sign. After all, since advertising costs are determined by audience size, tens of millions of Americans must be tuning in to news programs. Doesn't this mean that as a society we are becoming better informed than ever before? Perhaps. But one media monitor has expressed his doubts.

Robert MacKenzie writes a column for *TV Guide*. Not too long ago he wrote the following essay about the public's quickening appetite for news.

The News Junkies

By Robert MacKenzie

1   When did we all become news junkies? Within the past four or five years a whole nation has gotten hooked on news. I have numerous friends and relatives who suck up a network newscast with their morning coffee, keep an ear to all-news radio on the way to work, catch an hour of local TV news and a half-hour network report when they get home, then get a final fix of late-evening news before calling it a day.

2   Demand creates supply. Local stations across the country are adding an extra hour or half hour to their evening newscasts. At the network level, news is gobbling up the available scraps of nonprime time. *Morning with Charles Kuralt* is expanding to 90 minutes on CBS, squeezing *Captain Kangaroo* back to a half hour, ABC's *Nightline* keeps its fans up until midnight.

3   News was once a money-losing proposition for television, a required public service that stations and networks supported more or less grudgingly. Now news is hot, a big chip in the ratings game. But why?

4   Obviously, news has more fascination when it directly affects us, and in the past few years news events have hopped right into our laps. The oil crisis was not a distant nuisance happening to someone else, but a maddening mess that had all of us fuming in gas-pump lines. Economic news becomes riveting when you watch your dollar shriveling at the grocery store. Crime news gets compelling when your car has been cracked open and the house next door has been burgled. You could explain our obsession with news as a byproduct of anxiety.

5   But all of this jumpiness, if it exists, hasn't inspired us to read more newspapers. The main beneficiary of news junkiedom is television. The reasons, maybe, can be found in the technological gearing-up of television news and its adaptation of show-biz techniques.

6   Minicams, helicopters and live-on-location reports have been used to boost ratings in local news, even though there may be no good reason to be "live from the city-hall steps," and though you may not be able to see much from the helicopter. The feeling of "being there" has a power of its own. ABC's evening newscast has lifted some of NBC's audience by such catchy devices as occasionally going live to Peter Jennings in London, though Peter may be the only man in London who is awake at that time.

7   Television news has learned how to hook us and hold our eye, but are we better informed? We know the price of a barrel of oil, but do we know how the Saudi government works? We know what the steps of the city hall look like, but do we really know what goes on inside? Are we being updated when we need to be backdated?

8   A memo from a local news director to his crew set forth some principles: Grab 'em in the first 10 seconds. Hold stories under two minutes, but when you have action, let it run. Cover talking heads with film of action. When nothing is moving on camera, move the camera.

9   All this preoccupation with packaging seems to pay off at the box office. TV techniques have made news exciting and interesting. And a junkie doesn't ask himself fundamental questions about addiction or about the chemical composition of his dope. He's too busy shooting up, or thinking about his next fix.[1]

You should recognize that MacKenzie is doing more than making some idle observations about news. He is advancing the contention that the very techniques that make news exciting and interesting also make its coverage superficial, thereby leaving us no better informed. In a word, he is arguing.

Although the author does use a graphic analogy (drug addiction) to dramatize his point, he seems to rely primarily on a cause-and-effect analysis in order to establish his thesis. He offers two causes to account for the burgeoning popularity of news: (1) the direct impact that news happenings have on us and (2) the show business techniques used to present news. He then suggests that, although the second cause may be the prime reason for the news's popularity, it is detrimental to good news coverage.

This essay, then, can be viewed as one whose presentation relies primarily on the development of a cause-and-effect relationship, which is still another way to construct an argumentative essay. The present chapter considers this pattern of development. Specifically, it examines the concept of cause, fallacies associated with faulty causation, and, of course, the cause-and-effect essay itself. Consistent with the dual function of our study, this chapter attempts to make you both a better reader and a better writer, with respect to causal arguments.

CAUSAL CONCEPTS

"Is vitamin E good for the heart?" "What will be the results of President Reagan's 'New Federalism'?" "Did Lee Harvey Oswald act alone in assassinating President Kennedy?" "Can laughter actually help cure disease?" How we answer such questions depends largely on what we understand by "cause," for in all instances the questions imply that something is the cause of something else.

The word *cause* has many "cousins" that convey the idea of causation. For example, *produce* means "to cause something to be or happen"; *prevent* means "to cause not to happen"; *kill* means "to cause to die"; and *vaporize* means "to cause a thing to change into vapor." Such terms—and there are thousands of them—become parts of causal statements.

A causal statement is one that asserts a relationship between two things such that one is said to bring about the other. A simpler way to say this is that a

---

[1]From *TV Guide* Magazine, May 16, 1981. Copyright © 1981 by Triangle Publications, Inc., Radnor, Pennsylvania. Reprinted by permission of the publisher.

causal statement reduces to the assertion "A causes B." Thus: "Cigarettes cause cancer and heart disease," "Vitamin B_1 prevents beriberi," and "Capital punishment deters crime."

When causal statements are supported, causal argument results. A causal argument is one that attempts to support a causal statement. You needn't look far for numerous examples of causal arguments. Just examine the many commercial and public-service messages you come across daily. There you'll find causal arguments ranging from ones about toothpaste ("People who use a fluoride toothpaste have fewer cavities than those who do not") to ones about rent control ("If rent control is enacted, landlords will let their buildings fall into disrepair") and ones about nuclear energy ("Establishing commercial nuclear power plants will make us less energy dependent"). Similarly, in your reading and studies, you come across, even formulate, causal arguments that relate to economics, politics, education, the arts, and other fields.

But the idea of cause is a tricky one. "Cause" may mean different things for different people. As a simple example, suppose that you suddenly awake one morning to discover that your alarm clock didn't go off, thereby putting you half an hour behind schedule. As you are trying to wake up, the thought of the English composition exam crowds into your mind. It dawns on you: You will only have one hour to write an essay from scratch! You bolt out of bed, brush your teeth, splash some cold water on your face, and race for the car. You're only minutes from school when you're stopped for speeding. You plead with the officer to be quick about it, but he decides a lecture is in order. So there you sit for fifteen minutes while the policeman dresses you down. When you finally get to class you have only a fraction of the allotted time left to write your essay. You do the best you can, but as you leave class, you know you "bombed out."

Clearly there is a sequence of events that led up to your failing the English exam. This sequence could be stated in the form of conditions, as follows: "If the clock had gone off, . . ." "If I hadn't been stopped for a ticket, . . ." "If I hadn't been late, . . ." "If I'd had more time, . . ." All of these can be considered events that contributed to the eventual effect: your failure.

Where there is a causal sequence of several events—say, A causing B, B causing C, C causing D, and, finally, D causing E—E can be regarded as the effect of any or all of the preceding events. The nearest of the events, D, is ordinarily considered the proximate cause; others are considered more and more remote.

Thus, how you respond to a question about why you failed the exam depends in part on your interests and perspective. From your standpoint, the "cause" may be the proximate event—that is, the lack of time. But from the instructor's viewpoint, the "true" cause probably would be the more remote event, your tardiness. Furthermore, when reminded of your tardiness, you might fall back on still a more remote cause, the speeding ticket or the clock. So, one consideration in the meaning of cause relates to where an event stands in a causal sequence of several events.

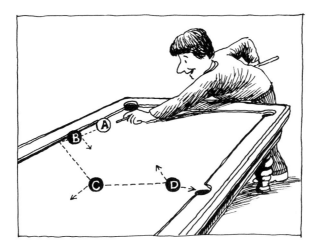

But the sequential aspect of cause is not the only consideration. Another factor is the exact cause-and-effect relationship between two events or entities. There are four possible relationships, termed necessary, sufficient, necessary and sufficient, and contributory. Although in some ways similar, these four relationships are different enough to be considered separate causal concepts.

Necessary

A necessary cause is a condition that must be present if the effect is to occur. Thus, if in "A causes B" the term *"causes"* implies a necessary condition, then A must be present for B to occur. In other words, in the absence of A, B cannot occur; or simply, "If no A, then no B." In this sense electricity is a cause for light in a bulb: If no electricity, then no light. Similarly, oxygen can ordinarily be considered a necessary condition for fire: If no oxygen, then no fire.

Sufficient

A sufficient cause is a condition that by itself will bring about the effect. Thus, if in "A causes B" the term *"causes"* implies a sufficient condition, then when A is present, B will always occur. In other words, the presence of A is always enough to bring about B; or simply, "If A, then B." In this sense, a blown fuse is a sufficient condition for a light to go out. If the fuse blows, the light will go out; no other condition is necessary. But, of course, a blown fuse is not a necessary condition for the light to go out; for, should the fuse not blow, the light could still go out, perhaps because the power company turned off the current when you failed to pay the electric bill.

169

Necessary and Sufficient

A necessary and sufficient cause is a condition that must be present for the effect to occur and one that will bring about the effect alone and of itself. Thus, if in "A causes B" the term "*causes*" implies a necessary and sufficient condition, then B will occur *when and only when* A occurs. A and only A is enough to bring about B. Or simply: "If and only if A, then B."

Instances of a single necessary and sufficient condition are understandably rare, but they do occur. For example, the spirochete is a necessary and sufficient condition for syphilis. Far more common are instances of several necessary conditions that, taken together, constitute a sufficient condition and sometimes a necessary *and* sufficient condition. For example, taken together, current, a bulb in working order, correct current for the bulb, and satisfactory wiring constitute a necessary and sufficient condition for an electric light to burn.

Contributory

A contributory cause is a factor that helps create the total set of conditions, necessary or sufficient, for an effect. Thus, a violent storm can be a contributory cause to your room's suddenly being pitched into darkness. The violent storm can help create the conditions that cause the lights to go off. But obviously the light may go off without a storm; and the light may remain on in the presence of a storm. So, to say that A is a contributory cause of B is to say that B is more likely to occur when A occurs than when A does not occur. The lights in your room are more likely to go off in the presence of a violent storm than in its absence.

Usually we speak of contributory causes when we wish to emphasize the complexity of a problem. For example, in discussing the cause of the fall of the Roman Empire, historians generally cite a number of contributory causes: the rise of Christianity, moral decay, economic chaos, weak leadership, and so on. Of course, speaking of contributory causes doesn't rule out the possibility of focusing on one chief or sole cause. Thus, while mentioning the nexus of contributory causes to explain the fall of the Roman Empire, some historians focus on the rise of Christianity, others on economic disorder. Once again, as with proximate and remote causes, one's interests and viewpoints are influential in the attribution of cause. With these distinctions behind us, we can now turn to some common problems in causal reasoning.

Exercises

5.1   *Sometimes we feel that people are too limited in their perception of the causes that have contributed to a problem. We think that they have not* been resourceful enough in considering the full range of options or alternatives open to them in solving a problem. Choose a topic where this limited view seems to you especially common or obvious. Make a list of possible causes or alternatives.

5.2 Cite a cause of each of the following occurrences and indicate which kind of cause it is.

> fatigue
>
> weight loss
>
> fever
>
> increase in adrenaline
>
> inflation
>
> earning potential
>
> eye color
>
> an effective argumentative essay

5.3 A business major friend can't see why she has to take a course in argumentative writing and analysis. "Such a course isn't going to make me a better business person," she tells you. But you aren't convinced. Prepare a brief rebuttal to her position in which you try to establish a causal connection between taking such a course and success in business.

FAULTY CAUSATION

Before isolating some fallacies connected with faulty causation, we should mention three main sources of confusion that are related to cause-and-effect reasoning. One consists of confusing a cause with an effect. In causal analysis it is important to distinguish between causes and effects. Failure to do so muddles the presentation and results in erroneous reasoning. Thus, if you were writing a paper about the relationship between poverty and health, you would have to determine whether poverty was a cause of poor health, whether poor health was a cause of poverty, or whether the relationship could operate either way. (Indeed, you would have to determine whether any causal connection existed to begin with.) We have already noted a classic example of this confusion. Anthropologists studying a South Seas tribe found its members believing that body lice advanced good health. In fact, every healthy person had some lice. In contrast, most sick people didn't. The natives assumed that being healthy was an effect of having the lice, when in fact it was the cause for having the lice: Lice prefer healthy bodies.

Another source of confusion consists of confusing cause with a sign or symptom. A runny nose, headache, and scratchy throat are symptoms of a cold, not the causes of it. Heavy drinking may be a symptom of an emotional problem, not necessarily a cause of it. International terrorism may be a sign of social and political instability, not necessarily a cause of it. Because signs and symptoms are clearly associated with causal sequences, it is easy to mistake them for causes.

The third source of confusion involves correlations. A correlation is a connection between properties that members of a group have. For example, a study may indicate that users of a particular toothpaste have far fewer cavities than nonusers. It is tempting to infer from this—indeed, advertisers would have us do precisely that—that the particular toothpaste prevents cavities. But such statistical correlations of themselves are insufficient for establishing causal connection. The difference in the number of cavities may be better accounted for in terms of overall dental hygiene and diet.

Of course, it is true that a high degree of correlation between two sets of data may strongly suggest a causal connection. But the correlation is not enough to establish such a connection. For example, medical scientists knew for some time that a statistical correlation existed between cigarette smoking and lung cancer—that the incidence of lung cancer in the smoking population was higher than in the nonsmoking population. Although this suggested a causal connection, researchers had to investigate the smoking process, with special attention to its impact on the lungs. Carefully controlled studies involving animals and humans revealed that smoking not only injures lung tissue but produces malignant lesions. Based on this kind of hard evidence, researchers could demonstrate a causal (contributory) connection between smoking and lung cancer and had a basis for accepting the statistical correlation as a causal one. But the point remains: Statistical correlations are not necessarily causal correlations.

FALLACIES OF CAUSATION

There are a number of fallacies associated with faulty causation. We'll consider five: questionable cause, causal oversimplification, neglect of a common cause, post hoc, and slippery slope.

Questionable Cause

The fallacy of questionable cause consists of asserting a causal relationship when there is no evidence for one. For example, when the Borana tribe in

Kenya witnessed the solar eclipse of June 30, 1973, it contended that it had been caused by the white men who, having landed on the moon, learned the secrets of the heavenly bodies and were now tampering with them. Similarly, in Nigeria Islamic emirs have waged *jihad*, or holy war, on single women, because they believe that the women bring on drought in western Africa. Again, after a tornado ripped through sections of Louisville, Kentucky, in 1973, an evangelist marched through town warning passersby to mend their evil ways or expect another devastating storm. As these examples illustrate, the fallacy of questionable clause is so obvious that it rarely turns up in serious argument. But the next four fallacies, which are decidedly more subtle, sometimes infect the otherwise well-considered argument.

Causal Oversimplification

The fallacy of causal oversimplification consists of assuming that a necessary or contributory cause for an event is the sufficient cause. As its definition indicates, causal oversimplification stems from a fundamental failure to distinguish among the various kinds of cause. As a result, a person may assume that a necessary condition is a sufficient one. For example, intense debates are waged over the wisdom of increased defense spending. Very often proponents of more military spending assume that such expenditures ensure security. Although defense expenditures may be a necessary condition for a nation's security, they certainly aren't a sufficient condition. After all, the money may be misdirected; or a nation may simply lack the will to defend itself.

A similar problem can arise when contributory causes are assumed to be sufficient causes. For example, a person may argue that, if there were less violence in movies and on television, fewer crimes of violence would be committed. At most, violence portrayed on television or in movies is a contributory cause to real-life violence. But to contend that reducing cinematic violence will reduce real-life violence is to treat the relationship as a sufficient one.

Neglect of a Common Cause

The fallacy of neglect of a common cause consists of failing to recognize that two seemingly related events may not be causally related at all but rather effects of a common cause. For example, suppose a person suffers from both depression and alcoholism. It's tempting to infer that one is causing the other—the depression causing the drinking, or the drinking causing the depression. But both may be the effects of some underlying cause, such as a profound emotional disturbance.

A classic example of neglecting a common cause can be seen in a humorous remark attributed to Abraham Lincoln. It seems that, while General

Ulysses S. Grant was handily winning battles in the West, President Lincoln received lots of complaints about the general's drinking. One day a delegation told him, "Mr. President, the general is hopelessly addicted to whiskey." To which Lincoln reportedly replied, "I wish General Grant would send a barrel of his whiskey to each of my other generals."

In a more serious vein, a counselor to President Ronald Reagan, Edwin Meese III, seemed to neglect the common cause in explaining why the United States was considering hiding 200 MX missiles among 4,600 shelters scattered across the Utah and Nevada desert. Meese called the system "a bad idea . . . dictated only because the Carter administration's slavish adherence to SALT II [an arms-limitation treaty], and that was the only reason for 4,600 holes in the ground." But the primary reason, which Meese omitted, was to give the Soviet Union an uncertain target to shoot at in any surprise attack. Presumably, this was important because of the vulnerability of existing U.S. Minuteman missile silos to increasingly accurate Soviet weapons.

Post Hoc

The post hoc fallacy consists of asserting that one event is the cause of another merely because the first preceded the second. For example, someone observes that crime among youth has increased in the United States since the arrival of punk rock from England. The person concludes, therefore, that punk rock is causing an increase in juvenile crime. Again, someone observes that every war in this century followed the election of a Democratic president. Therefore, the person concludes, the Democrats are the war party. In each case a person assumes that one event caused another simply because it immediately preceded it.

Why we make post hoc fallacies is easy to understand. Since causes precede effects, it's tempting to causally associate events occurring near one another in time. But neither immediate nor remote temporal succession is enough for establishing a causal relationship. Simply because the Roman Empire declined after the appearance of Christianity does not in itself prove that Christianity caused its decline. By the same token, simply because murders may decline after the enactment of the death penalty does not demonstrate that the death penalty caused the decline. Although it's true that the nearness of events in time may suggest an association that should be further investigated, it is insufficient for establishing causal relationships, much the same as statistical correlations alone are not enough to establish causation.

Here's one final example of the post hoc fallacy, with comment:

> EXAMPLE: " 'Before he took B_{15} he [her husband] could barely get up for his meals [because of a severe heart condition],' said Jayne Link, a 51-year-old Glen Cove, New York, widow.

'Two weeks after he started taking the vitamin pill he was completely changed.' Then Bill stopped taking the vitamins. Three months later he was dead—victim of a fifth heart attack. . . . Now Mrs. Link takes B_{15} herself for arthritis. 'I take it constantly, three 50 milligram tablets a day,' she said. 'I have a slipped disc in addition to the arthritis. I tried everything under the sun to relieve the pain. But nothing else has worked.' " (Globe, September 11, 1979, p. 22.)

COMMENT: *A number of factors could account for the husband's recovery and the wife's relief from pain. Perhaps B_{15} is beneficial for the heart and combats various maladies. But simply because a person's condition appears to improve after taking a vitamin doesn't establish that the vitamin produced the effect.*

Slippery Slope

The slippery slope fallacy consists of objecting to a particular action because it supposedly will lead inevitably to a similar but less desirable action, which in turn will lead to an even less desirable action and so on down the "slippery slope" to some ultimate horror. Thus, "Don't touch the first drink, my boy," a father tells his son. "You'll end up a drunk." Will taking the first drink lead inevitably to alcoholism? Not necessarily. Indeed, for most people it never does, although it's true that every alcoholic had to take that first drink. Again, someone says, "I'm opposed to a national health insurance program, because, if it's enacted, it won't be long before the government will take over other aspects of our lives, and pretty soon we'll be living in a socialistic state." Notice how the speaker uses a chain of events, on the basis of whose final, undesirable link she rejects the first link. But if the ultimate horrid consequence is not inevitable, then the appeal is fallacious. In other words, if the chain can be broken at any point between first and objectionable last event, then the appeal is a slippery slope. In this example, a socialistic state certainly is not the inevitable consequence of a national health insurance program. Granted, such a program might make us more disposed toward other similar programs. But each of those is a separate and distinct issue that could, should, and probably would be debated on its own merits.

Exercise

5.4 Do the following passages commit fallacies? If so, are they fallacies of questionable causation, causal oversimplification, neglect of a common cause, post hoc, or slippery slope? Explain.

1. "Impeach the Press!" (Bumper sticker popular during a time of intense social and political turmoil.)

2. Since more suicides occur during the Christmas season than at any other time during the year, there must be a causal connection between Christmas and suicide.

3. **John:** I've decided to get married.
   Jim: Really? I thought you were a confirmed bachelor.
   John: I was until I read an article that reported married men live longer than bachelors.
   Jim: No kidding!

4. **Sandy:** I don't think it's wise to permit any form of euthanasia.
   Sam: Oh, I don't know. In cases of terminal illness, I think it might be okay to allow the patient to decide.
   Sandy: Oh, sure, and before you know it people will be terminated without their consent. In fact, it won't be long before so-called undesirables such as prisoners and derelicts will be put to death.

5. Right after Egyptian President Anwar Sadat started his crackdown on political dissidents, he was assassinated. That's clear evidence that one of those dissident groups must have been behind Sadat's murder.

6. **Student:** How come I failed this course?
   Professor: You didn't perform.
   Student: Not perform! At the beginning of the semester you said that in order to pass we had to attend class regularly, read the assignments, participate in class discussion, take all the tests, and do a term paper.
   Professor: Correct.
   Student: Well, I did all that and still failed.

7. It's no wonder kids can't read today. In the old days they spent a good part of their leisure reading. But today they spend it watching television. Excessive television viewing explains why kids can't read.

8. Many people who are good at math also have musical talent. So, there must be a connection between math and music, such that ability in math helps people develop their musical talent.

9. **Student:** Professor, why don't you allow questions in class?
   Professor: It's simple. If I let one person ask a question, then someone else will want to ask one. Pretty soon I'll be spending the entire session answering your questions, and we'll never get anything done.
   Student: I see.
   Professor: Good. Any more questions?

10. **Wife:** Honey, your car is making a funny sound.
    Husband: Funny sound? I've never heard it.
    Wife: Well, it was doing it all day today.
    Husband: I knew I shouldn't have let you drive my car.

11. "Going nude to the graveyard was where Eva Ronna drew the line. She willingly took five baths a day, placed an egg under her bed for five days and burned a lock of her hair. But when a 'spiritual healer' in East St. Louis, Ill., told Ronna to go to a local cemetery 'just like I came into the world' to break a voodoo spell, Ronna replied: 'Honey, it's too cold for that.'

    "But Ronna said the healer went in her stead and, believe it or not, the spell, which she said had made her 'act crazy' and drink excessively, was broken.

    "Ronna is one of thousands of persons in all parts of the country who stand ready to do almost anything to break a hex, including paying sizable sums of money. Ronna's cure cost her $300." (Lee May. "Voodoo Casts Its Spell on Many in U.S." Los Angeles Times, August 13, 1981, part 3, p. 1.)

12. Ed Davis, a former Los Angeles police chief, commenting on the possible connection between sex crimes and pornography: "I don't know. I'm trying to find out. I had a meeting with a bunch of policemen recently and I asked them how many had arrested rape suspects, and all of them had. How many of them had found any unusual quantity of pornographic literature in the rape suspects' homes? All of them had. Pornography gets into the hands of socially inadequate people who can't express themselves normally and be attractive, in love, or go through the courting routine and all that sort of thing." New West, December 19, 1979.)

13. "Looke but uppon the common playes of London, and see the multitude that flocketh to them and followeth them: beholde the sumptuous Theater houses, a continuall monument of London prodigalitie and folly. But I understande they are now forbidden bycause of the plague. I like the pollicye well if it hold still, for a disease is bud bodged or patched up that is not cured in the cause, and the cause of plagues is sinne, if you looke to it well: and the cause of sinne are players: therefore the cause of plagues are playes." (Quoted in the preface of Hardin Craig. Shakespeare: The Complete Works. Glenview, Ill.: Scott, Foresman, 1961, p. 27.)

14. "Your boss has a bigger vocabulary than you have. That's one good reason why he's your boss." (W. Funk and L. Lewis. Thirty Days to a More Powerful Vocabulary. New York: Funk & Wagnalls, 1970, p. 3.)

15. "Adolf Hitler slipped three cents to a Viennese whore in 1910 and she slipped him a few million bacilli of syphilis. Ironically, that one case of syphilis besmirched a cultured and civilized nation with depravity and sadism previously unknown in the history of the world." (David Reuben. How to Get More Out of Sex. New York: McKay, 1975, p. 222.)

16. A story is told about a female passenger on the Italian liner Andrea Doria. On the fatal night of the Doria's collision with the Swedish ship Gripsholm off Nantucket in 1956, the passenger returned to her cabin and

turned on a light switch. Suddenly there was a great crash. Then all that could be heard were the sounds of grinding metal and the shouts and screams of panicked passengers and crew. Convinced that she had done something terrible, the woman burst from her cabin and explained to the first person in sight that she must have set the ship's emergency brake.

17. *Since 1840 every U.S. president elected in a year ending in zero has died in office. On the basis of this, one concludes that President Reagan, elected in 1980, will die in office.*

18. *For want of a nail, the shoe was lost; for want of a shoe, the horse was lost; for want of a horse; the rider was lost; for want of a rider, the message was lost; for want of a message, the regiment was lost; and for want of a regiment, the battle was lost. Therefore, it can be said that for want of a horseshoe nail alone, the battle was lost.*

19. *"Two ads were prepared, set in editorial style with no pictures, two columns, 100 editorial lines. The last paragraph a phone number. Ad number 1 differed from ad number 2 only in headline. Number 1's read, 'It's not the heat it's the humidity. New room cooler dries the air.' Number 2's headline read, 'How to have a cool home. Even on hot nights.' Number 1 was run one Friday in May in the local daily (circ. 400,000) and number 2 was run the following Friday. Number 1 produced 75 calls, number 2 produced 160 calls. Obviously number 2 was more effective at generating response."* (Perry Weddle. Arguments: A Guide to Critical Thinking. New York: McGraw-Hill, 1978, p. 187.)

20. *A survey indicates that more than half of all college students with below-average grades smoke pot. In contrast, only 20 percent of non-smokers have below-average grades. On the basis of this, one person concludes that pot smoking causes students to get lower grades. Another person concludes that getting lower grades causes one to smoke pot.*

21. *"Everybody I talked to there [in Vietnam] wants to know why they can't go in and finish it, and don't let anybody kid you about why we're there. If we weren't, those Commies would have the whole thing, and it wouldn't be long until we'd be looking off the coast of Santa Monica [at them]."* (Bob Hope, quoted in Anthony J. Lukas. "This Is Bob (Politician-Patriot-Publicist) Hope." New York Times Magazine, October 4, 1970, p. 86.)

22. *The women's liberation movement is partly responsible for the energy crisis, because it encourages more women to enter the job market. This means more people are consuming energy on highways and at jobs than there used to be. (A paraphrase of a statement by General Electric's energy systems manager, John C. Fisher, in a speech to the National Academy of Science, January 29, 1973.)*

23. *"Perhaps intimidated by flak from Capitol Hill, the Social Security Advisory Council has backed away from a proposal to increase the maximum pay subject to Soc-Sec taxation from $14,000 to $24,000 to*

keep the plan on a pay-as-you-go basis. Instead, it has recommended shifting the cost of medicare to the general fund. The proposal, if adopted, would begin the process of transforming Social Security into an out-and-out welfare program. Once we start in that direction, where do we stop?" ("A Quick About-Face." New York Daily News, January 21, 1975, p. 37.)

24. *"Ninety percent of our breakfast cereal comes from Kellogg, General Mills, Quaker Oats, or General Foods; it is they who have decided that breakfast cereal and sugar are almost inseparable."* (Jeffrey Schrank. Snap, Crackle, and Popular. New York: Delacorte, 1977, p. 77.)

25. *In 1920, King Alexander of Greece died of blood poisoning, the result of a bite by a pet monkey. The king's death was followed by a plebescite, a new king, and a bloody war with the Turks. In reaction, Winston Churchill observed: "A quarter of a million persons died of that monkey's bite."* (Winston Churchill. The World Crisis: The Aftermath. Oxford, England: Oxford University Press, 1929, p. 386.

THE CAUSE-AND-EFFECT ESSAY

The preceding observations should be kept in mind when employing any causal argument in writing. They are just as important to remember when writing an argumentative essay whose presentation relies primarily on the development of a cause-and-effect relationship (for example, "Capital punishment deters crime," "Light sentences are contributing to the increase in crime," or "The Pill has revolutionized sexual mores"). Indeed, our discussion suggests several guidelines in approaching this kind of argumentative essay.

First, always review all the available data and support evidence. Failing to do this, you can easily make faulty connections between events, overlook the real causes, or leave a true causal relationship unestablished. Analyzing data is especially necessary when arguing social policies or issues. Examples: "Sex education is needed to reduce the incidence of venereal disease among adolescents," "Poverty must be conquered if we are to reduce the urban crime rate," or "Children are not learning how to read and write because elementary schools devote too much time to frivolous matter."

Second, reexamine your argument to see whether there are other possible causes and effects. Again, this is especially important when developing theses such as the aforementioned. Even when there is a strong evidence for a causal connection, be sure to indicate the kind of connection it is: necessary, sufficient, necessary and sufficient, or contributory. Where appropriate, also say whether the cause is proximate or remote. In any event, never leave the interpretation of cause up to the readers; otherwise, confusion will result.

Third, always offer support for your causal assertion. As in any other argumentative essay, support can take the form of examples, fact, and informed opinions. Statistics and legitimate authority can also effectively shore up causal arguments. No matter the kind of evidence, controversial causal assertions should never be left unsupported.

Fourth, avoid fallacies of faulty causation. Even one causal fallacy in an extended causal argument is enough to undercut the whole paper. The reason is that the writer shows a flagrant ignorance of the concept of cause. Insofar as the paper is developed by cause, it is suspect.

So much for these guidelines. Let's now see how a cause-and-effect essay can be developed.

Writers use causal analysis both as a means of explaining and as a way of structuring material. In examining essay structure in Chapter 2, we saw that the cause-and-effect format is especially useful in advancing claims about consequences—that is, in attempts to sort out or trace the conditions that have produced some phenomenon. Recall that in organizing such an essay, a statement of the problem is followed by the major causes, which, in turn, are followed by a summary or conclusion. In general, an extended causal argument can be developed in the same way. More specifically, it can arrange causes chronologically or in their order of importance.

Chronological Order

One way to develop the cause-and-effect essay is by presenting the major causes in chronological order, as when treating some historical event. Typically, the thesis is stated in the form of some problem, the major causes are served up in chronological order, and a summary is made. Of course, since we're speaking of an argumentative essay, the thesis must assert an arguable contention and not just make some causal observation. Here's an example of how a causal argumentative essay might be developed following a chronological order:

THESIS
STATEMENT
OF PROBLEM: *It is commonly acknowledged that, on the whole, Americans are no longer as gullible about their government as they once were. We are less accepting and more skeptical, less trusting and more suspicious. If we are less gullible, it's little wonder; in recent years we have been lied to with what seems like metronomic regularity.*

MAJOR CAUSE
EVENT 1: *Perhaps the immediate roots of our disillusionment with government can be traced to the U-2 incident of 1960,*

180

which was shrouded in governmental lies. Recall that the U-2 was a highly sophisticated surveillance plane that was shot down over Russia. . . .

MAJOR CAUSE
EVENT 2:   But the U-2 was just a sign of things to come. Ahead of us lay Vietnam, which turned out to be a quagmire of governmental lies, half-truths, and distortions. . . .

MINOR CAUSE
EVENT 3:   No sooner did the Vietnam War end than Americans again faced the specter of deceit at the highest levels of government: the Watergate scandal. . . .

SUMMARY: Certainly these events don't in themselves account for the pervasive skepticism with which we currently greet governmental proclamations. Numerous other social, political, and cultural events also figure in the calculation. But who can deny that the U-2, Vietnam, and Watergate were watersheds in the making of a nation of skeptics?

Order of Importance

A second way to develop a causal argumentative essay is to present the causes in their order of importance, typically leaving the most important for last. This pattern proceeds much as the former does: thesis statement of problem, major causes, and summary. Additionally, in this kind of essay the writer often tacks on some remedy for the problem. Here's an example of an essay developed by arranging causes in their order of importance:

THESIS
STATEMENT
OF PROBLEM: College professors often complain that today's students can't follow a lecture, indeed not even a monologue that goes beyond ten or fifteen minutes. Why can't they?

MAJOR CAUSE 1:   For one thing, many lectures and professors are simply boring. Although it may be possible to feign interest in the face of a bore, it's difficult to say tuned in. . . .

MAJOR CAUSE 2:   In addition, students easily get distracted. Many young people lack the self-discipline required to sit still and follow the meanderings of a lecture. Students are also beset by other pressing concerns, some academic, some social. . . .

MAJOR CAUSE 3:   But the biggest factor in the equation is television. Whether we like it or not, this generation has been raised on a steady diet of TV, which has equipped it more to receive visual messages than auditory ones. Just as important, television

*viewing has accustomed young people to receive informa-
tion in nice, digestible chunks—no longer than ten minutes
before a commercial break for a snack. . . .*

CONCLUSION
WITH REMEDY: *No doubt, maintaining student attention and interest will
continue to challenge the classroom lecturer. One way for
professors to meet this challenge is to brighten the lectures
with anecdotes and entertaining asides—that is, comic relief. Another way is to integrate visuals into classroom activities. Still another way is to punctuate the lectures with
class discussion.*

In each of these models the argument proceeds from *effect to cause.* But
many essays move from cause to effect. The cause-to-effect essay can be
patterned in much the same way as those we have just outlined. Here's an
example, following the order-of-importance format.

THESIS
STATEMENT
OF PROBLEM: *Given how easy it is to get a divorce today and how many of
us get divorced, it is easy to overlook the personal and social
impact of divorce. Indeed, the potential effects of divorce
are so pernicious that we should do everything possible to
make a marriage work.*

MAJOR
EFFECT 1: *Divorce most obviously affects the partners themselves. The
often-seen gallant posturing notwithstanding, divorced
people do feel a profound sense of loss and disappointment,
even failure. In fact, studies indicate. . . .*

MAJOR
EFFECT 2: *When a family is involved, divorce can send emotional
shock waves through every child, regardless of age, sex, and
emotional stability. Again, studies of children from broken
homes indicate. . . .*

MAJOR
EFFECT 3: *But, given that more than half of the marriages in the United
States end in divorce, perhaps the most serious potential
effect of divorce is that it undermines social stability. . . .*

CONCLUSION
WITH REMEDY: *There is no easy solution to the problem of divorce and its
sinister personal and social effects. Making marriage
counseling more accessible to couples might help. Also,
courses in marriage and family at the high school level seem
warranted.*

SUMMARY

A causal statement asserts a relationship between two things such that one is said to bring about the other. Causal statements reduce to the form "A causes B," as in "Cigarettes cause cancer." A causal argument is one that attempts to support a causal statement.

The term *cause* can carry many meanings. For example, we can speak of a proximate cause—that is, an event near the effect—or a remote cause—an event further away from the effect. Also, the exact cause-and-effect relationship between two entities can be specified as necessary, sufficient, necessary and sufficient, or contributory.

NECESSARY
CAUSE: *a condition that must be present if the effect is to occur*

EXAMPLE: *electricity as a necessary condition of light in a bulb*

SUFFICIENT
CAUSE: *a condition that by itself will bring about the effect*

EXAMPLE: *a blown fuse as a sufficient cause for a light to go out*

NECESSARY AND
SUFFICIENT: *a condition that must be present for the effect to occur and one that will bring about the effect alone and of itself*

EXAMPLE: *the spirochete as a necessary and sufficient cause for syphilis*

CONTRIBUTORY
CAUSE: *a factor that helps create the total set of conditions, necessary and sufficient, for an effect*

EXAMPLE: *a violent storm as a contributory cause of your room's suddenly being pitched into darkness*

Faulty causation arises when causes are confused with effects, symptoms, or statistical correlations. Specifically, there are five fallacies associated with faulty causation: questionable cause, causal oversimplification, neglect of a common cause, post hoc, and slippery slope.

QUESTIONABLE
CAUSE: *asserting a causal relationship when there is no evidence for one*

EXAMPLE: *contending that a people's evil ways brought on a tornado*

CAUSAL OVERSIM-
PLIFICATION: *assuming that a necessary or contributory cause is a sufficient one*

EXAMPLE: *assuming that increasing defense spending will ensure national security; assuming that reducing cinematic violence will reduce the rate of violent crimes*

NEGLECT OF A
COMMON CAUSE: *failing to recognize that two seemingly related events may not be causally related at all but rather effects of a common cause*

EXAMPLE: *contending that depression causes alcoholism or alcoholism causes depression, when both may be the effects of a profound emotional disturbance*

POST HOC: *asserting that one event is the cause of another merely because the first preceded the second*

EXAMPLE: *contending that, because juvenile crime increased immediately after punk rock arrived in the United States, punk rock must have caused the increase*

SLIPPERY
SLOPE: *objecting to an action because it supposedly will lead inevitably to a similar but less desirable action, which in turn will lead to an even less desirable action, and so on down the "slippery slope" to some ultimate horror*

EXAMPLE: *objecting to a national health insurance program because it supposedly will lead to a socialistic state*

An argumentative essay's presentation often relies primarily on the development of a cause-and-effect relationship. When writing this kind of essay, writers must keep in mind the aforementioned points about cause. Specifically, they should review all the available data and support evidence, reexamine their arguments for other possible causes and effects, support all causal assertions, and avoid fallacies of faulty causation. Two appropriate formats for developing the cause-and-effect argumentative essay involve arranging causes in chronological order or in their order of importance.

Questions for Analysis

Refer to Robert MacKenzie's article "The News Junkies" and consider the following questions.

1. State MacKenzie's thesis, and list his main points.
2. What kind of assertion is MacKenzie's thesis: meaning, value, policy, consequence, or fact?

3. List the various sources that the author relies on for his support material.

4. Which strategy for developing a cause-and-effect essay does he use?

5. Is he arguing from cause to effect, effect to cause, or both?

6. Prepare a syllogism each for paragraphs 2 and 4.

7. In paragraph 2 what is the cause and what is the effect? What kind of cause would you say this is—necessary, sufficient, necessary and sufficient, or contributory?

8. In paragraph 4 what is the cause and what is the effect? Is the cause necessary, sufficient, necessary and sufficient, or contributory?

9. In paragraph 5 MacKenzie says that "all of this jumpiness, if it exists, hasn't inspired us to read more newspapers." Assuming this is true, how would you account for it?

10. Do you think the phrase "if it exists," cited in the preceding question, is a weasel? Is this conditional phrase consistent with the statements made in paragraph 4?

11. MacKenzie says in paragraph 6 that "ABC's evening newscast has lifted some of NBC's audience by such catchy devices as occasionally going live to Peter Jennings in London." What two facts is MacKenzie asserting in this sentence? How would you characterize the implied causal connection?

12. Do you agree that "minicams, helicopters and live-on-location reports have been used to boost ratings in local news" (paragraph 6)? Or do you think this is a questionable evaluation?

13. Evaluate the analogy between news watching and drug addiction (viewers as junkies) according to the criteria developed in Chapter 4. Determine whether the analogy is a good one.

14. Identify as many generalizations as you can. Distinguish between qualified and unqualified generalizations.

15. Which of the generalizations, if any, do you think the author has adequately supported? Which, if any, do you think lack adequate support?

16. Does the author rely on provincialism in the first paragraph?

17. Assuming that there is a popular demand for more news, what do you think is causing it?

18. Do you think that the author has overlooked any other causes that might be contributing to the popular appeal for television news? Do you think he is guilty of causal oversimplification?

19. Can you think of news programs that do not support—or even contradict—MacKenzie's observations?

20. The author implies that the "preoccupation with packaging" (last paragraph) is incompatible with solid news reporting. Expressed causally, the

contention seems to be that preoccupation with packaging is a sufficient condition for inadequate news coverage. Would you agree?

READING FOR ANALYSIS

In recent years we have been shocked and sickened by the spate of bombings, skyjackings, executions, assassinations, and other terrorist acts. Various explanations and remedies have followed in the wake of these atrocities. Yet terrorism persists and even shows signs of being intractable. What to do? The following essay by a *Newsweek* general editor, Douglas Davis, addresses the problem of terrorism, its causes and solution.

Living with Terrorism

By Douglas Davis

1   Terrorism is yet another of the new and bitter truths we must learn to face, constantly. Like political corruption and high-priced oil, it is here to stay, day in, day out, in your life and in mine. Nobody in public life is ready to admit this fact. Terrorist incidents like the explosion at La Guardia Airport in 1975 that killed eleven and the recurrent attempts to kill or kidnap politicians are being blamed on the "sick," the "irresponsible," "extremists of right and left," or "madmen," plain and simple. But these are not explanations. They are either lies or tragic mistakes, and we should be ready now—after being misled so often by official analyses in the past—to unravel the truth for ourselves. It doesn't require expensive teams of psychologists or reams of statistical tables. All it takes is indignant common sense, freed from the myths and illusions with which we have collectively been supplied throughout this century.

2   The grandest myth of all is that we live in an advanced state of civilization, in which the brute passions of men and women have been exorcised by education and material well-being. We complacently watch movies depicting terrorism in the Old West, violent revolutions in the eighteenth century, and sadistic executions in the Roman Empire, assuming that this was the lot of pre-industrial man. But our own newspapers are filled each day with reports as savage as anything fiction or history can supply. The streets of cities all over the world are a theater of urban violence that can apparently be repressed only by police methods that exceed the violence of terrorism itself.

Our Violent Culture

3   Argument One, then, is this: the Old West Is Now. Man is as brutal as he ever was, therefore we should not be surprised by these incidents or

consoled that adjustments in police patrols, the minimum wage, or prime-time TV schedules will help. There is in fact every reason to suspect that man has escalated brutality to a new pitch, because his capacity to maim is greater, whether he acts in the mass on an airborne bombing mission or alone, as a terrorist. The instant carnage in Irish streets and Israeli villages is peculiar to our time, not only in swiftness and scale but in effectiveness as propaganda: terror always delivers a market, scoring in media of all kinds—and it is you and I who make up that market, whatever our protestations to the contrary. Arafat's remark to the U.N.—"Who among you has not been a terrorist?"—was chillingly correct. In our time, terror is a conventional tool of politics.

4   But let us not think that the fault lies in the weaponry alone—the new technology of destruction, another fashionable scapegoat—because it is always a man who is behind the trigger or the timer. Unless we can demonstrate that the terrorists are largely insane, then we must ask, what is it about societies throughout the world that provokes men to extremist violence? What is the provocative ingredient in twentieth-century life? Again I suggest that the answer is obvious and hardly requires the high-priced advice of panel- and seminar-bound experts.

From Despair to Rage

5   The single quality of modern society that distinguishes it absolutely from the past is this: massive, overwhelming numbers. More people, more cities, more books, more cars, more everything. In self-defense, nation after nation has erected vast bureaucracies—a tidal wave of administrators—to control those numbers. There is no equivalent time in history, an age when mechanized, computerized bureaucracy straddles the globe, from Moscow to Peking to New York, all of it impossible to move or reform. Hannah Arendt called it "rule by Nobody."

6   Half of our serious literature—since Kafka's "The Castle"—has dealt with the despair provoked by this desperate condition, in which men feel helpless before a blind, inhuman, uncommunicative force. It is a small step from despair to rage and violent self-assertion, based on the conviction that nothing else counts. Has anyone noticed that we no longer produce a literature of utopia? Secular perfection—the idea of rational progress—was deserted by men of literary genius early in this century, long before the rise of street terrorism. Instead of "Erewhon" or "Utopia," we now write "Nineteen Eighty-four," which is simply the best-known example of the large anti-utopian movement. Some of the keenest intellects of our time have in fact counseled violence as the last hope of change: Sartre, Frantz Fanon, Tom Hayden. Their ancestor was Bakunin, the Russian nineteenth-century anarchist who quarreled with Marx on this very issue. "We will become ourselves," he wrote, "when the whole world is engulfed in fire."

The Only Answer

7   Argument Two, then, is this: there is no easy, logical, or orderly Way Out. Do not believe that another psychoanalytic study or a new method of negotiating with terrorists—or even a solution to the crises in Ireland or the Middle East—will render our lives immune from threat. Both the cause and the effect—rigid Rule by Nobody ending in desperation and rage—are locked into the organizational structure of our time. It is in fact a trap of our own devising, a catch-22 of the soul. On the one hand we have taught ourselves to believe in the possibility of utopia—that is, secular progress—and on the other hand denied its realization, even its hope.

8   Where does this leave us? Not at a point where world-saving crusades against violence or unbalanced budgets can save us. The only answer—hardly dramatic—is the nourishment of values counter to those that have brought us to this state. Nobody can say precisely what those values are, but their direction is clear enough: toward private and sensate goals, leaner living, smaller cycles of achievement, and decentralized thinking. In the other direction lies what is apparently impossible: quantitative expansion that succeeds only in psychic despair. The bigger and stronger we get, the more vulnerable we become to lone and fugitive assault. We can hold empires at bay with megaton weapons but cannot make the corner drugstore safe. It is a cruel, unerring and permanent paradox.[2]

Questions For Analysis

1. State Davis's thesis, and list his main points.

2. What kind of assertion is his thesis: meaning, value, policy, consequence, or fact?

3. List the various sources that he relies on for his support material.

4. Which strategy for developing the cause-and-effect essay does Davis use?

5. In paragraph 1 Davis writes that "nobody in public life is ready to admit" that terrorism is here to stay. Is terrorism, in fact, here to stay? Should this assertion be treated as a questionable evaluation? Do you think the contention that nobody in public life will admit that terrorism is here to stay is a generalization that needs to be qualified? If so, how would you do it? Does Davis offer any evidence for this generalization?

6. Would it be fair to say that, although the characterization of terrorists as "sick," "irresponsible," "extremists of right and left," and "madmen" (paragraph 1) may point to the immediate or proximate causes of terrorist acts, they do not speak to the remote, though foundational, causes?

---

[2]From *Newsweek*, June 14, 1976. Copyright © 1976 by Newsweek, Inc. All rights reserved. Reprinted by permission.

7. Davis serves up a mix of fact and opinion. Give half a dozen examples of each that you find in the essay.

8. The author contends that the conventional "explanations" for terrorism really are either "lies or tragic mistakes" (paragraph 1). Is this a false dilemma?

9. In paragraph 1 Davis says that all it takes to unravel for ourselves the truth about terrorism is "indignant common sense." What does he mean? Stated causally, indignant common sense is the cause of the effect "unravel[ing] the truth about ourselves." What kind of cause is this: necessary, sufficient, necessary and sufficient, or contributory?

10. At the end of paragraph 1 Davis says that myths and illusions have caused us to misunderstand terrorism. Do you think that he establishes this point? Is there any question in your mind about what he means by "myths and illusions"?

11. Do you agree that people generally believe "that we live in an advanced state of civilization, in which the brute passions of men and women have been exorcised by education and material well-being" (paragraph 2)? Do you agree that we watch the movies cited "assuming that this was the lot of pre-industrial man"? Can you think of examples of films that speak directly to terrorism, violence, and sadism in contemporary society?

12. Do you agree that "man is as brutal as he ever was" (paragraph 3)? Has the author provided enough support for this opinion?

13. Do you agree that "the single quality of modern society that distinguishes it absolutely from the past is this: massive, overwhelming numbers" (paragraph 5)?

14. Has Davis committed causal oversimplification in stressing the significance of numbers but overlooking things such as economics and the concentration of people in cities?

15. Assume that numbers are at the root of violence and that numbers, which distinguish modern society from the past, help explain contemporary acts of brutality. But if numbers were much smaller in the past, how is brutality in the past to be explained? Has the author overlooked additional factors that contribute to brutality?

16. Does Davis ever rely on authority to make his points? If so, are the appeals legitimate?

17. Does the author provide enough support for the contention that computerized bureaucracies are impossible to move or reform (paragraph 5)?

18. In paragraphs 5 and 6 the author establishes causal links among numbers, bureaucracies, despair, and rage: numbers produce bureaucracies, bureaucracies produce despair, and despair produces rage. Prepare a chain of three syllogisms that expresses these causal relationships. What is the nature of the cause in each case: necessary, sufficient, necessary and sufficient, or contributory?

19. Davis is pessimistic about the chances of successfully combating terrorism. Why? Do you agree?

20. What solution does the author propose in the last paragraph? Do you
think that the meanings of the following phrases are clear: "private and
sensate goals," "leaner living," "smaller cycles of achievement," and
"decentralized thinking"?

21. Underlying the entire essay is the assumption that terrorism is a bad
thing. Even if it is, it does not necessarily follow that no act of terrorism is
ever justifiable. Do you think that an act of terrorism could ever be
justified? Perhaps you'd like to write an essay in which you argue your
point.

READING   FOR   ANALYSIS

The following cause-and-effect essay is offered without follow-up questions
for your own careful analysis. You might: (1) Identify the author's thesis, main
points, and organizational structure. (2) Indicate the kind of assertion the
author is advancing. (3) List the sources the author uses in developing support
material. (4) Evaluate all causal assertions and identify related fallacies, if
any. Caryl Rivers is a coauthor of *Beyond Sugar and Spice: How Women
Grow, Learn, and Thrive.*

Teen Pregnancies Involve More Than Sex
By Caryl Rivers

1   A virtual epidemic of pregnancies is under way in this nation's
teen-age population; in 1979 alone, 262,700 babies were born to unwed
teens. Predictably, educators, parent groups and editorial writers have
responded to this news with a clamor for more and better sex education.
Indeed, that is urgently necessary, but sex education alone is not the
answer. We need to take a clear-eyed look at how we are bringing up
young girls in this culture; otherwise, we won't come anywhere near
understanding the psychological dynamics that lead little girls into unwed
teen-age motherhood.

2   We tend to see teen-age pregnancy in terms of sexuality, which we
start worrying about when girls reach puberty. In fact, that is a dozen
years too late. The lessons that little girls learn when they are 2 or 5 or 7
have a direct bearing on the issues they will confront when they reach
adolescence. The girl who receives early training in independence and
assertiveness has a good chance of not falling into the trap of premature
motherhood.

3   Why is this so? If you examine the sexual behavior of teen-agers, you
find that, for girls, the driving force is not libido but the need for love and

acceptance. When you read the letters that teen-agers send to advice columnists, one theme emerges with great frequency: "I don't want to have sex, but I'm afraid I'll lose my boyfriend."

4   It is very hard for a teen, at an age when peer pressure and the desire for male attention is intense, to insist that she will set her own timetable for when she will engage in sex. And, if she decides that she is ready for sex, she probably has to take the initiative in insisting on contraception. To do this requires a sense that she can and must control her own destiny. The ability to make demands, handle conflict, plan ahead—these are not qualities that a girl can develop overnight at puberty. Yet too often we do not train our girls early in these traits.

5   When psychologists Grace Baruch and Rosalind Barnett of the Wellesley Center for Research on Women and I surveyed the scientific literature on women and young girls, we found a number of troublesome currents. We found that girls tend to underestimate their own ability, and that they do so in pre-school and when they are seniors in college. We also found that the closer girls got to adulthood, the less they valued their own sex.

6   Psychologist Lois Hoffman of the University of Michigan, a specialist in this field, says that girls' undeveloped self-confidence causes them to cling to an infantile fear of abandonment and a belief that their safety lies only in their dependence on others.

7   I saw a demonstration of this when I was a chaperone on a Girl Scout camping trip. The girls, age 9 to 12, repeatedly ran to the troop leader, seeking her approval before deciding where to put a sleeping bag or whether to put on bug spray. They needed far more help and approval in making even simple decisions than would a group of boys the same age—even though many girls of that age are bigger and stronger than boys.

8   One reason for this behavior is that girls get more approval when they ask for help than boys do. When psychologist Beverly Fagot studied parents of 2-year-olds, she found more expressions of approval given to girls seeking help than to boys. This was true even when the parents said they believed in treating both sexes alike.

9   Girls receiving such messages are less likely to take risks, to test their own abilities. Instead, they try to figure out what it is that adults want from them and concentrate on being "good little girls." They never learn to handle conflict or even temporary lack of approval.

10   At adolescence, too often they transfer this dependency from parents to boyfriends. They get pregnant "by accident," not really understanding that they have any responsibility for or control over what happens in their lives.

11   If we care, not only about teen-age pregnancy but also about the psychological health of girls, we must be on guard against the viruses of self-devaluation and dependence. We must be sure that girls are not given permission to fail because of "those little eyes so helpless and appealing."

ιfortunately, many of the school programs designed to enhance the
ϸment of girls' skills—encouraging them to try science and math,
ιing their athletic abilities—are falling by the wayside in an era of
cutting. It may not be easy to see how a girl's ability to do calculus
or sink a free throw relates to the pregnancy statistics, but the link is
there. If we help girls develop confidence and self-esteem, then perhaps
they can deal with issues of sexuality as strong individuals, not merely as
victims.

13   All the sex education in the world will not put a real dent in the
pregnancy rate if we can't persuade young girls that they can—and
must—control their future, not merely collide with it.[3]

THEME   TOPICS

Choose one of the following topics, and write an argumentative essay whose
presentation relies primarily on the development of a cause-and-effect relationship. Follow either the chronological order or the order of importance.

1. Road accidents

2. Marital problems and divorce

3. Poor student performance in school work

4. The alarming increase in juvenile crimes of violence

5. The widespread increase of youth gangs

6. Dislike of the United States abroad

7. Poor voter turnout

8. Decline in institutionalized religion

9. Interest in evangelism

10. The rise of the Moral Majority

11. Chronic failure to pass gun-control legislation

12. The swing to conservatism in the United States in the 1980s

13. The increase in the number of working women

14. The increase in teenage alcoholism

15. The decline in the number of students majoring in the liberal arts (literature, philosophy, history, foreign languages, and so on)

---

[3]From the Los Angeles Times, December 15, 1981. Reprinted by permission of the author and publisher.

6. Definition

READING FOR ANALYSIS

What do off-track betting, smoking rooms, and coeducational dormitories have in common? In the following essay, Norman Cousins, editor emeritus of *Saturday Review*, claims that each is an example of how individuals and institutions avoid responsibility. According to Cousins, such examples are signs of an increasing social tendency to ignore, even deny, the realities of human experience.

Cop-Out Realism

By Norman Cousins

1   On all sides, one sees evidence today of cop-out realism—ostensible efforts to be sensible in dealing with things as they are but that turn out to be a shucking of responsibility.

193

2   Example: Until fairly recently, off-track betting was illegal in New York State. Gambling on horses was regarded as a disguised form of stealing, run by professional gamblers who preyed upon people who could least afford to lose. Also outlawed was the numbers game, in which people could bet small amounts of money on numbers drawn from the outcome of the day's horse races.

3   Attempts by government to drive out the gambling syndicates had only indifferent results. Finally, state officials decided that, since people were going to throw their money away despite anything the law might do to protect them, the state ought to take over off-track betting and the numbers racket.

4   It is now possible to assess the effect of that legalization. The first thing that is obvious is that New York State itself has become a predator in a way that the Mafia could never hope to match. What was intended as a plan to control gambling has become a high-powered device to promote it. The people who can least afford to take chances with their money are not only not dissuaded from gambling but are actually being cajoled into it by the state. Millions of dollars are being spent by New York State on lavish advertising on television, on radio, in buses, and on billboards. At least the Mafia was never able publicly to glorify and extol gambling with taxpayer money. And the number of poor people who were hurt by gambling under the Mafia is minuscule compared to the number who now lose money on horses with the urgent blessings of New York State.

5   A second example of cop-out realism is the way some communities are dealing with cigarette-smoking by teenagers and pre-teenagers. Special rooms are now being set aside for students who want to smoke. No age restrictions are set; freshmen have the same lighting-up privileges as seniors.

6   The thinking behind the new school policy is similar to the "realism" behind New York's decision to legalize off-track betting and the numbers game. It is felt that since the youngsters are going to smoke anyway, the school might just as well make it possible for them to do it in the open rather than feel compelled to do it furtively in back corridors and washrooms.

7   Parents and teachers may pride themselves on their "realism" in such approaches. What they are actually doing is finding a convenient rationalization for failing to uphold their responsibility. The effect of their supposedly "realistic" policy is to convert a ban into a benediction. By sanctioning that which they deplore, they become part of the problem they had the obligation to meet. What they regard as common sense turns out to be capitulation.

8   Pursuing the same reasoning, why not set aside a corner for a bar where students can buy alcoholic beverages? After all, teenage drinking is a national problem, and it is far better to have the youngsters drink out in the open than to have them feel guilty about stealing drinks from the cupboard at home or contriving to snatch their liquor outside the home.

Moreover, surveillance can be exercised. Just as most public bars will not serve liquor to people who are hopelessly drunk, so the school bartender could withhold alcohol from students who can hardly stand on their feet.
9   It is not far-fetched to extend the same "reasoning" to marijuana. If the youngsters are going to be able to put their hands on the stuff anyway, why shouldn't they be able to buy it legally and smoke it openly, perhaps in the same schoolroom that has been converted into a smoking den?
10   We are not reducing the argument to an absurdity; we are asking that parents and teachers face up to the implications of what they are doing.
11   The school has no right to jettison standards just because of difficulties in enforcing them. The school's proper response is not to abdicate but to extend its efforts in other directions. It ought to require regular lung examinations for its youngsters. It ought to schedule regular sessions with parents and youngsters at which reports on these examinations can be considered. It ought to bring in cancer researchers who can run films for students showing the difference between the brackish, pulpy lungs caused by cigarette smoking and the smooth pink tissue of healthy lungs. The schools should schedule visits to hospital wards for lung cancer patients. In short, educators should take the U.S. Surgeon-General's report on cigarettes seriously.
12   In all the discussion and debate over cigarette smoking by children, one important fact is generally overlooked. That fact is that a great many children *do not* smoke. The school cannot ignore its obligation to these youngsters just because it cannot persuade the others not to smoke. It must not give the nonsmokers the impression that their needs are secondary or that the school has placed a seal of approval on a practice that is condemning millions of human beings to a fatal disease.
13   Still another example of cop-out realism is the policy of many colleges and universities of providing common dormitories and common washrooms for both sexes. The general idea seems to be that it is unrealistic to expect young people not to sleep together. Besides, it is probably reasoned, if people are old enough to vote they are old enough to superintend their own sex habits. So, the thinking goes, the school might just as well allow them to share the same sleeping and toilet facilities.
14   The trouble with such policies is that they put the school in the position of lending itself to the breakdown of that which is most important in healthy relations between the sexes—a respect for privacy and dignity. No one ever need feel ashamed of the human body. But that doesn't mean that the human body is to be displayed or handled like a slab of raw meat. Sex is one of the higher manifestations of human sensitivity and response, not an impersonal sport devoid of genuine feeling. The divorce courts are filled to overflowing with cases in which casual, mechanistic attitudes toward sex have figured in marital collapses. For the school to foster that casualness is for it to become an agent of de-sensitization in a monstrous default.

195

15   The function of standards is not to serve as the basis for mindless repressive measures but to give emphasis to the realities of human experience. Such experience helps to identify the causes of unnecessary pain and disintegration. Any society that ignores the lessons of that experience may be in a bad way.[1]

Certainly, this article is an example of an argumentative essay. The author advances the value assertion that "cop-out realism" is bad and the policy assertion that society ought to enforce behavioral standards. The essay might also be considered persuasive, insofar as Cousins presumably wants our consent as well as assent: He wants us to do something about reversing what he views as a dangerous trend and not merely to sit on our hands saying, "Yes, Norman, you're absolutely right." In order to convince us, he has assembled support materials that serve as premises for his conclusions. But there is a feature of "Cop-Out Realism" that places it in a special category of argumentative essay. That feature is the use of definition.

Cousins's examples function to clarify the meaning of the term *cop-out realism*, which he briefly defines in the opening sentence as "ostensible efforts to be sensible in dealing with things as they are but that turn out to be a shucking of responsibility." Since this short definition isn't very enlightening, Cousins takes time to flesh out its meaning through examples. Indeed, by the time he has finished, we have a pretty good idea of what he means by *cop-out realism*. But Cousins is not just interested in providing a definition of a term. He is concerned, even anxious, about a societal trend that he notices. He thinks that it is bad and that society ought to stop it. He wants us to agree and perhaps take some corrective action. In a word, Cousins is arguing.

Developing an argumentative essay by definition is still another pattern that writers use in advancing a thesis. A definition is an explanation of the meaning of a term. It can take a number of short forms, common among which are denotative, logical, stipulative, and persuasive definitions. Or a definition can be much longer, what is termed an extended definition, as in "Cop-Out Realism." We will inspect each of these definitional forms and also the fallacies associated with their misuse. Most important, we will consider ways of developing argumentative essays through extended definition.

DENOTATIVE DEFINITION

In one sense, the meaning of a term consists of the class of objects that the term can be applied to. This sense of *meaning* is ordinarily termed the denotative, or extensional, meaning.

The denotation, or extension, of a term is the collection, or class, of

---

[1]From *Saturday Review*, September 2, 1978. Reprinted by permission of the author.

objects to which the term can be correctly applied. For example, the denotation of *skyscraper* would be any example of a skyscraper, such as the Pan American building. A denotation of *bridge* would be the Golden Gate Bridge or the Brooklyn Bridge. A denotation of *robin* would be that bird perched on the telephone line outside your window. In brief, defining denotatively is defining through example, and a term is said to denote the objects it can be applied to. Although denotation seems straightforward enough, we can commit faulty denotation by applying a term to an object to which it cannot be applied or to which its application is questionable. For example, to denote *Republican* by giving the example of Senator Edward Kennedy, a Democrat, would be a faulty denotation. Similarly, to denote *radical* with the example of President Ronald Reagan would be highly questionable and, therefore, a faulty denotation. It is very important, then, for writers to be sensitive to the examples they choose to denote terms. If, in arguing, writers use examples from collections of objects that are not denoted by a term, they are guilty of faulty denotation.

Sometimes a denotative issue takes on great moment. Today, for example, a body of law is developing that deals with surrogate parents, as in the case of a woman who bears a child for an infertile couple. Who is to be considered the child's mother—the surrogate or the adopter? The law has always tried to preserve the "family unit," which has traditionally been defined in reference to the biological parents, ultimately the mother. But where surrogates are involved, whom are the terms *mother* and *family unit* to denote? Unless the meanings of these terms are specified, the legal problems could be staggering.

Exercise

6.1 *Define the following terms by giving three denotations for each:* athlete, inventor, musician, national hero, novelist, dramatist, *and* poet.

LOGICAL DEFINITION

Understanding what a term means involves knowing how to use it correctly. But to know how to use a term correctly doesn't require you to know everything that it can be applied to—that is, its complete denotation. You needn't know every object denoted by *skyscraper* to know that a skyscraper consists of the properties common and unique to all buildings over a certain height. To understand what *skyscraper* means, you need only a criterion for deciding what objects fall within the extension of the term *skyscraper*—that is, a *logical* definition.

The logical definition of a term is the collection of properties shared by all and only those objects in a term's extension. Accordingly, the logical definition of *spoon* is "a utensil consisting of a small shallow bowl with a handle, used in eating or stirring." Notice that, like any other logical definition, this one is constructed by using two procedures: (1) placing the term being defined in a class of similar terms and (2) showing how it differs from the other terms in the class. Thus:

Term	Class	Distinguishing Characteristics
A spoon	is a utensil	consisting of a small, shallow bowl with a handle, used in eating and stirring.
A watch	is a mechanical device	for telling time and is usually carried or worn.
Ethics	is the branch of philosophy	concerned with right and wrong actions and with the good and bad of such actions.

A logical definition is a precise, economical way of identifying something. You will have many occasions to use it in writing. For example, if you are using an obscure term such as *tsunami,* you should briefly describe it: an unusually large sea wave produced by an undersea earthquake or volcanic eruption. Leaving obscure terms undefined impedes communication, thereby inviting misunderstanding and fallacies of ambiguity. Over the years a number of rules have been developed for formulating logical definitions.

Rules

There is nothing sacred or immutable about the following rules for logical definitions. In fact, blind reliance on them may on occasion hamper the defining process. But if they are viewed as guidelines and not imperatives, these rules do help writers to avoid—and readers to detect—vagueness and ambiguity in argument.

Rule 1: A good logical definition states the essential characteristics of the term being defined. "Essential characteristics" refers to those properties that are generally considered the criteria for whether an object is denoted by a term. For example, people have agreed to use the property of being a closed, plane figure having three sides and three angles as the conventional criterion for whether something is to be called a triangle. So, defining *triangle* logically requires a listing of these essential characteristics.

Rule 2: A good logical definition should not be circular. A definition is circular if it defines a word in terms of itself. To define *inertial* as "of or pertaining to inertia" is a circular definition. Better: "pertaining to the property of matter by which it retains its state of rest or its velocity along a straight line so long as it is not acted on by an external force." Again, to say that a bequest is something that has been bequeathed is to offer a circular definition. A better rendering would be: "a disposition by will of property."

The trouble with circular definitions is that they are ordinarily understandable only to those who already understand a term's meaning. But for those ignorant of the meaning, such a definition is worthless. In effect, then, writers who use circular definitions assume that their audience already knows the meaning of a term. If the assumption is false, they are not likely to win audience agreement.

Rule 3: *A good logical definition is neither too broad nor too narrow.* This rule means that a logical definition should not denote more or fewer things than are denoted by the term itself. On the one hand, to define *pungent* as "pertaining to any taste or smell" is far too broad. Some tastes or smells are mild, whereas *pungent* means "sharp or biting" tastes or smells. On the other hand, to define *shoe* as "a leather covering for the human foot" is too narrow, for a shoe can be wooden.

Rule 4: *A good logical definition does not use obscure or figurative language.* Obscure language does nothing to illuminate the meaning of a term; it impedes the flow of ideas and retards, rather than advances, an argument. Of course, *obscurity* is itself a relative term. What is obscure to me may be quite clear to you. A legal definition may be obscure to those not trained in the law but understandable to lawyers. This is why taking stock of your audience is vital to effective argumentative writing. If your audience lacks a technical background, then avoid obscure language. Otherwise, you'll only succeed in explaining the unknown in terms of the unknown.

The same cautions apply to figurative language, which is expressive or highly descriptive language. Thus, to define *bread* as "the staff of life" does little to explain what bread is. Similarly, defining *discretion* as "something that comes to people after they are too old for it to do them any good" is amusing but unenlightening. (Indeed, to be amused one must already have some idea of what *discretion* means.)

Rule 5: *A good logical definition is not negative when it can be affirmative.* The reason behind this rule is that a definition is supposed to explain what a term means, *not* what it doesn't mean. There are countless things that *spoon, skyscraper* and *triangle* are not. Listing all these things, even if possible, would not indicate the meaning of *spoon, skyscraper,* and *triangle.* Of course, some terms defy affirmative definition. *Orphan* means a child whose parents are *not* living; *bald* means the state of *not* having hair on one's head. Barring such terms that must be defined negatively, definitions should be stated in the affirmative.

Exercises

6.2 *Criticize the following definitions in terms of the criteria for good logical definitions.*

1. *A circle is a figure whose radii are equal.*
2. *A virtuous person is a person who does good things.*
3. *A democracy is a government in which everybody can vote.*
4. *A dog is a domesticated animal having four legs.*
5. *Alimony means when two people make a mistake and one of them continues to pay for it. Palimony means when two people knew they would make a mistake and one of them continues to pay for it.*
6. *A horse: "Quadruped. Graminivorous. Forty teeth—namely, twenty-four grinders, four eye teeth, and twelve incisive. Sheds coat in spring; in marshy countries sheds hoofs, too. Hoofs hard, but requiring to be shoed with iron. Age known by marks in mouth." (Charles Dickens. Hard Times.)*
7. *"Faith is the substance of things hoped for, the evidence of things not seen." (Heb. 11:1.)*
8. *"Faith may be defined briefly as an illogical belief in the occurrence of the improbable." (H. L. Mencken.)*
9. *"Economics is the science which treats of the phenomena arising out of the economic activities of men in society." (John Maynard Keynes.* Scope and Methods of Political Economy.)
10. *"Justice is doing one's own business, and not being a busybody." (Plato.* Republic.)

6.3   *Give a logical definition for each of the following terms: bachelor, dish, turtle, snack, television, and wife.*

6.4   *Show by means of an example how the denotation of two words or phrases can be the same even though their logical definitions differ.*

Fallacies

In a general sense, any logical definition that illegitimately violates any of the preceding guidelines can be said to commit the fallacy of faulty definition. Beyond this, two specific fallacies of ambiguity result when arguments make use of improper logical definitions: semantical ambiguity and circular definition.

Semantical Ambiguity   *The fallacy of semantical ambiguity consists of using a word or phrase that can easily be interpreted in two or more ways* *without making clear which meaning is intended.* Semantical ambiguity is especially likely when writers don't heed Rule 4 and define in obscure or figurative language.

For example, an editorial entitled "Radicalism in the Film Colony" begins with these two lines: "The continuing involvement of the Hollywood entertainment industry in radical politics is understandably deplorable to the American people. They are outraged because so many stars who have grown rich on box-office receipts exhibit such fierce hostility to and contempt for traditional American values and traditions." Presumably, "radical politics" means "fierce hostility to and contempt for traditional American values and traditions." But this definition is as obscure as "radical politics." Precisely what are these "traditional American values and traditions" the writer speaks of? By leaving such terms unspecified and open to interpretation, the writer is guilty of semantical ambiguity.

Circular Definition   *The fallacy of circular definition consists of defining a word in terms of itself.* For example, suppose a student argues:

> *Professor Jacobs can't be considered a competent teacher, because he is very biased. He is biased against all forms of modern literature. Probably he doesn't like modern literature because he doesn't read it and lacks the capacity to appreciate it.*

The circularity here lies in the fact that "doesn't read [modern literature] and lacks the capacity to appreciate it" really means the same as "incompetent." When the argument is structured, the circularity is most apparent:

> *Professor Jacobs is not a competent teacher, because he is biased.*
>
> *He is biased because he dislikes modern literature.*
>
> *He doesn't like modern literature because he doesn't read it and lacks the capacity to understand it (that is, because he is incompetent).*

By defining *incompetent* in terms of itself, the student violates Rule 2 of a good logical definition and commits the fallacy of circular definition. In order to establish that Jacobs is incompetent, the student would have to provide a definition of *incompetence* that does not beg the question.

STIPULATIVE DEFINITION

Writers often depart from the standard use of a word and employ it in an unconventional way. There is nothing wrong with such departures, so long as the writers indicate the stipulative nature of the definitions. *A stipulative definition, then, is one that attaches unconventional, perhaps unique, meaning to a term.* Examples include: "Murder is the preventing of a human life from coming into existence"; "A trial by jury is the right that guarantees justice to all citizens by allowing them to be judged by their peers"; "Patriots stand by their country, right or wrong."

Ordinarily in writing we stipulate (1) when we believe that a word in existence is ambiguous or has no clear meaning and we want to express a more precise meaning for it, as with *right* or *democracy*, or (2), when finding no word in existence for some meaning we have in mind, we invent one, as with *glitch* for "a brief, unwanted surge of electrical power." You will rarely have occasion to stipulate for the second purpose. But you will undoubtedly have cause to stipulate in order to make the meaning of a word more precise or to show your audience what meaning you intend by the word. Good writers are sensitive to the ambiguity of language, especially to the fuzziness of abstract terms and concepts such as *war, loyalty, justice, culture, education,* and so on. So they see the need to clarify through stipulation. By the same token, pitfalls await writers who fail to indicate the stipulative nature of their definitions. The chief one is semantical ambiguity.

A humorous example of the confusion that can result when writers fail to indicate the stipulative nature of their definitions is provided by the Victorian lady who complained that she did not like a house because it was "very romantic." "I don't understand why you should wish it not to be *very romantic,*" replied a friend. To which the lady responded, "When I said romantic I meant damp."[2] In argument, failure to indicate the nature of a stipulative definition or failure to stipulate results in the fallacy of semantical ambiguity.

PERSUASIVE DEFINITION

Sometimes a word carries positive (or negative) overtones. When a word has acquired a favorable meaning, people sometimes try to use the term to carry a literal meaning different from its ordinary one, in order to take advantage of the word's favorable meaning. For example, let's assume that the word *sophisticated* has a literal meaning equivalent to "having or showing worldly knowledge or experience." Assume further that it is a mark of esteem to have such worldly knowledge or experience. Gradually, the word *sophisticated* acquires a favorable or positive meaning in addition to its literal meaning. Once this has occurred, writers and speakers may try to redefine *sophisticated* in order to exploit its positive charge.

Thus, someone may say, "True sophistication is not worldly knowledge or experience but expedience in the cause of self-interest," or "If Madge were really sophisticated, she wouldn't be caught dead shopping at J. C. Penney's." Of course, there is no such thing as the "true" or "real" meaning of a word, only common or uncommon and exact or inexact meanings. But audiences

---

[2]Sir Lewis Namier. "History and Political Culture." In Fritz Stern, ed. *Varieties of History.* New York: Holt, Rinehart and Winston, 1956, p. 386.

seldom make these distinctions. As a result, writers and speakers can success-fully use the favorable meaning of a word such as *sophisticated* in order to make the audience respond favorably to the assertions that (1) to be sophisti-cated is to practice expedience in the cause of self-interest or (2) shopping at J. C. Penney's disqualifies one from being sophisticated.

A *persuasive definition, then, is a definition that attaches a different literal meaning to a word while preserving the old emotional impact.* Persua-sive definitions are sleight-of-hand tricks: Writers and speakers change the literal meaning while the emotive meaning remains constant. With luck, the audience will never spot the switch and will accept the author's assertion.

The same thing can happen with words that carry negative meaning: Persuasive definitions can be used to make an audience take an unfavorable attitude toward something. For example, it's hardly complimentary today to be called a civil servant. At one time *civil servant* simply denoted an em-ployee in some branch of public service concerned with governmental func-tions outside the armed services. But recently the attitude toward civil service has grown negative. In fact, in some quarters *civil service* implies incompe-tence and inefficiency. As a result, the attitude toward civil servants is unfavorable. Given this picture, some people exploit the unfavorable side of *civil servant* to give the term a new and different literal meaning. For example, someone says: "Well, what can you expect of Thomas? He's a real civil servant, you know"; or "It's impossible to deal with Thomas any more. He thinks and acts like a real civil servant." "*Civil servant*" in these statements doesn't mean that Thomas works in some public service job but that he is incompetent, inefficient, and indolent.

Certainly, words with high emotional charge are the ones most subject to persuasive definition. Moreover, these words are most likely to appear in discussions about controversial issues. So, in dealing with divisive subjects be specially alert to the use of persuasive definition. This doesn't mean that persuasive definitions are necessarily objectionable. On the contrary, sometimes they clarify meaning and legitimately advance a contention. So long as we don't insist on the old positive or negative overtones of a term after we have indicated a new meaning, we are using persuasive definition legitimately. But when we change a word's meaning while preserving the old emotive force, then we are reasoning fallaciously.

Exercises

6.5 Which of the following definitions are stipulative; which are persuasive?

1. The only true soldiers are the ones who stand by their comrades and oppose the enemy even in the face of certain defeat and death.
2. The genuine believer may stumble and fall but goes on undaunted.
3. " 'The true,' to put it very briefly, is only the expedient in the way of our thinking, just as 'the right' is only the expedient in the way of our behaving." (William James. Pragmatism. London: Longman, Green, 1907, p. 80.)
4. "By good, I understand that which we certainly know is useful to us." (Baruch Spinoza. Ethics. New York: The Philosophical Library, 1957, p. 81.
5. "Political power, properly so called, is merely the organized power of one class for oppressing another." (Karl Marx and Friedrich Engels. Communist Manifesto. Ed. Harold Laski. New York: Pantheon Books, 1967, p. 161.
6. "Political power, then, I take to be a right of making laws with penalties of death, and consequently all less penalties, for the regulating and preserving of property, and of employing the force of the community in the execution of such laws, and in defense of the commonwealth from foreign injury, and all this only for the public good." (John Locke. Essay Condemning Civil Government.)

6.6 Give a stipulative, then a persuasive definition for each of the following terms: "equality," "equal opportunity," "civil disobedience," "preferential treatment."

6.7 The term "welfare" (as in "welfare programs") has become one of the most emotionally charged words of our time. "Welfare" literally refers to organized efforts to improve living conditions for needy people; and "on welfare" literally means to be receiving public financial aid because of hardship and need. For many millions of Americans, however, these terms *have negative implications. The writer of the following fictitious letter is one of those persons. Notice how the writer attacks farm subsidy programs by associating them with the unfavorable meanings of "welfare."*

> *Most farmers favor federal subsidies for agriculture. This is ironic because such subsidies are nothing but social welfare programs, which most of these same farmers oppose. The farmer who accepts government payment for not producing or "ploughing back" a crop is as much on the government dole as those who pick up their monthly checks at the neighborhood welfare office. Both are taking something for nothing, which is about as un-American as you can get. So, farmers should stop being hypocritical and recognize government subsidies for what they are: welfare payments.*

Think of some issue that you feel strongly enough about to write a letter to the editor of your local newspaper. In arguing your case, make use of persuasive definition as the writer of the preceding letter did.

Fallacy of Persuasive Definition

The fallacy of persuasive definition consists in illegitimately preserving the old emotive force of a word that has been redefined. An argument that commits this fallacy takes a word with a highly emotive charge, stipulates a new meaning for it, and then provides a context that encourages its old emotive force.[3] Here's an example:

> *I don't know why some people get so mad about companies that deceive, even jeopardize, consumers. Such practices are part of the meaning of free enterprise, which everyone knows is the foundation of our political, social, and economic institutions. Free enterprise means that all of us should do what we think is best for ourselves. That's all business is doing—looking out for itself. If consumers are deceived or damaged, then that's their fault. Let them take a page from the book of free enterprise and look out for themselves. So, rather than condemning business for being ambitious, aggressive, shrewd, and resourceful, we should praise it for acting in accordance with the doctrine of free enterprise, which is the American way.*

This argument takes the term *free enterprise*, which has strong emotive force, and identifies it with certain business practices and behavior (deceiv-

---

[3]See Gerald Runkle. *Good Thinking: An Introduction to Logic.* New York: Holt, Rinehart and Winston, 1978, pp. 55–56.

ing and jeopardizing consumers; ambitious, aggressive, shrewd, and resourceful action). It is the writer's prerogative to make such associations. But besides stipulating, this writer provides *a context that encourages the old emotive impact of the term* free enterprise. Thus, *free enterprise* is associated with the foundations of our political, social, and economic system and with the "American way." Briefly, the writer uses *free enterprise* to carry a new meaning but still wants the term to carry its old emotive wallop. In legitimate argument we can't have it both ways: We can't give a term a new meaning and expect it to have the old emotive force. When we do, we commit the fallacy of persuasive definition. And an audience that falls for this sleight-of-hand commits the same fallacy. Here's another example, with comment:

EXAMPLE: *Murder is whatever prevents a life from coming into existence. By this account, abortion is murder. All societies have proscriptions against murder, and rightly so. There is no more heinous act than to take the innocent life of another. A society that does not stand up to murderers cannot call itself truly civilized. It's obvious, then, that if the United States is worthy of the term civilized, it must prohibit abortion and deal harshly with those who have or commit abortions, since these people are murderers.*

COMMENT: *This argument takes a word with intense negative force, murder (and murderer), and stipulates a new meaning for it: Murder is whatever prevents a human life from coming into existence. There is nothing objectionable about this definitional tack. But having stipulated a new meaning, the writer then provides a context that exploits the old, negative force of murder (and murderer). The same chicanery appears in the treatment of civilized. Clearly, civilized has a favorable emotive side, in addition to its literal meaning. By associating civilized with prohibition of abortion and harsh treatment for violators, the writer attempts to redefine civilized in order to exploit its favorable emotive meaning. In short, the writer attaches a different literal meaning to civilized while preserving the old, positive emotive side of it.*

Fallacy of Question-Begging Definition

The fallacy of question-begging definition consists of attempting to establish an irrefutable position in an argument by means of a questionable definition. Although in theory improper use of any definition in argument can result in this fallacy, persuasive definitions are especially dangerous, because they are often used in an effort to settle an allegedly empirical question (that is, one capable of being proved or disproved through observation or experiment) by appeal to definition alone.

For example, suppose a friend uses a persuasive definition to make this controversial assertion: "Genuine patriots support their country, right or wrong." In response you marshal instances of historical figures who on occasion did not support their country but are ordinarily considered patriots. When presented with such examples, your friend replies, "Ah, but they were not *genuine* patriots." The "evidence" your friend gives for that reply is that on at least one occasion those figures did not support their country. But this evidence has credibility only if the persuasive definition is assumed to be true. But it is the very definition that is in dispute.

As indicated earlier, there is nothing in itself objectionable about a persuasive definition. Writers have the prerogative to define terms however they wish. At the same time, they must also recognize that their definitions may (1) depart from ordinary usage and (2) give the appearance of factual statements. In either case, opponents may justifiably question the definition and produce evidence to counter it. When arguers try to settle the issue by definition alone, they commit the fallacy of the question-begging definition. Here's one further example:

EXAMPLE: **Don:** President Reagan isn't a true Republican.

Donna: Why do you say that?

Don: Because he was once a Democrat.

Donna: So what?

Don: Well, a real Republican is one who has never been anything else but a Republican.

Donna: That's absurd. Plenty of Republicans once were Democrats. Strom Thurmond and John Connolly, just to mention two.

Don: That's precisely why they aren't true Republicans either.

COMMENT: The primary "evidence" that Don gives to support his contention that Reagan, Thurmond, and Connolly are not "true" Republicans is that they were once members of another party, that is, Democratic. But why does that disqualify them from being "true" Republicans? Don replies by saying that "a real Republican is one who has never been anything else but a Republican." In so doing, he attempts to establish his contention about Reagan, Thurmond, and Connolly by means of a definition that renders any counterevidence inadmissible.

EXTENDED   DEFINITION

As the preceding kinds of definition indicate, definitions can sometimes be handled simply in a sentence or two. At other times a simple definition is inadequate to reveal a term's meaning. A paragraph or more—even an entire essay—may be needed, as with *cop-out realism*. Such lengthy, well-developed definitions are termed extended definitions.

The extended definition is yet another pattern for developing argumentative and persuasive essays. In general, it is used when the writer's main concern is clarification, or making sure that writer and audience agree on a definition. In some instances, clarification may involve a careful limiting, in a paragraph or two of an essay, of an abstraction or key term. For example, say your purpose is to define the word *Democrat* and break it down into various kinds of Democrats. First, you would have to define *democratic*, which can refer to: (1) a form of government; (2) when capitalized, a political party or its workers; (3) a set of political beliefs, ideals, or values; or (4) a particular social outlook. Clearly, then, before you can talk about various kinds of Democrats (for example, liberal, moderate, conservative), you must pinpoint your definition of *democratic*, sorting out the meanings you intend from the other possible meanings.

In other instances, you may want to or have to devote an entire essay to definition of a single important, controversial, or abstract term. Abstract terms—words that are extremely general—especially need to be defined, because they can be interpreted in so many ways. For example, unless writers ensure understanding with the audience, words such as *honesty, truth, happiness,* and *justice* encourage multiple interpretations and erroneous conclusions.

In developing extended definitions, writers can use any of the other forms of definition. So they must be alert not to commit the fallacies associated with them: semantical ambiguity, faulty denotation, circular definition, persuasive definition, and question-begging definition.

Although many strategies for developing any essay can be used to write an extended definition, four methods predominate: (1) providing historical background, (2) listing specific qualities and characteristics, (3) isolating a common element, and (4) distinguishing a term from a more familiar term.

Before looking at these methods, let's briefly connect the extended definition to what we learned earlier about the principal features of an argumentative essay: thesis, main points, and organization. The thesis of an argumentative essay developed through extended definition is an assertion about meaning. (Of course, in developing the essay the writer may make additional assertions about consequences, value, policy, and fact.) In assembling their main points, writers call on all four sources of support material: personal experience, informed opinion, observation, and organized research. Although the pro-and-con and analyzing-alternatives formats can be effectively used, the inductive structure seems eminently suited for developing extended definition. The cause-and-effect pattern, though occasionally effective, is perhaps the least used structure for organizing the extended definition.

Providing Historical Background

Sometimes the most effective way to clarify the meaning of a term is to trace major stages in its history. Developing an extended definition through historical background, then, is explaining a word by tracing its development.

Let's pretend that you wanted to convince an audience that capitalism no longer existed in the United States (thesis). In order to establish your contention you might trace the meaning of the word *capitalism*, using an inductive format, as follows:

FACT 1: *As classically formulated, capitalism relies primarily on the market system to determine the distribution of goods and services in society. In other words, under classical capitalism the economic factors working in society were considered free to interplay with one another and establish a stability that would provide the best resources in meeting human needs. This theoretical assumption is evident in the works of classical capitalistic economists such as Adam Smith (1723–1790). . . .*

FACT 2: *Although the free market can be said to have operated in the United States in the decades before World War II, since then it has failed. For one thing, high costs, complex machinery, increasing demands, and intense competition have worked against individual productiveness. For another, whereas the earlier economy of the Industrial Revolution was characterized by relatively free and open competition, the hallmark of classical capitalism, the later economy of our time is made up of a relatively few enormous companies that can fix prices, eliminate competition, and monopolize an industry. . . .*

FACT 3: *Modern facts of economic life belie the easy assumption that we are a capitalistic economy. If we are, we certainly are not capitalistic in the sense of people like Adam Smith. . . .*

Keying on One Element

A second way to develop an extended definition in argument is by keying on some element of a subject and then enumerating specific qualities or characteristics to support the focus. For example, suppose you concluded that the key element in the makeup of a cynic was frustrated idealism. In your view, cynics once perceived people and things as they should be, rather than as they are. When things did not square with their lofty expectations, these people's idealism turned to cynicism. You could develop this argumentative essay by listing the special qualities or characteristics that support this key element. Here's how:

EXAMPLE 1: *Perhaps the most obvious illustration can be found in adolescent love. Many adolescents have a highly romantic concept of love and the opposite sex, which they may even carry into adulthood. But too often, when people and relationships turn out less than perfect, these would-be romantics turn sour on love and the opposite sex. For example, how many times have we heard a man say, "You can't trust women" or a woman say, "All men are bums"? . . .*

EXAMPLE 2: *The most striking example of the idealist-turned-cynic is the "nay-sayer," the person who insists that the world is going straight to the dogs and that there is nothing anyone can do to prevent it. Probe a little and you'll probably find that these defeatists once cherished lofty notions about themselves and the world. . . .*

EXAMPLE 3: *Beyond these obvious examples, even a cursory look at contemporary films shows the line between cynicism and failed idealism. The movie Serpico is a good example. . . .*

Finding the Common Element

A variation of the preceding pattern is to take the position of an impartial observer. Thus, rather than advancing some key element at the outset, you approach the subject with an open mind. You invite your audience to participate in the search to find a common denominator in the application of a term. You then offer a series of test cases, each raising an issue relevant to the term or concept under discussion. Here's how a paper about punishment might be developed by searching for the common element. Notice that the thesis is not stated until the end.

STATEMENT OF ISSUE: *Punishment means different things to different people. . . .*

FIRST TEST CASE: *Parents often punish disobedient children. . . .*

SECOND TEST CASE: *People are fined, imprisoned, even executed for breaking laws. . . .*

THIRD
TEST CASE: *Students consider it unfair for a teacher to punish everyone in a class for the behavior of a few. . . .*

COMMON
ELEMENT: *Central to the idea of punishment seems to be some action that is administered for breaking a law or rule. . . .*

Distinguishing Terms

A fourth way to develop an extended definition in argument is by distinguishing a term from a more familiar one to which it is closely related. This procedure involves systematic comparison and contrast with a familiar synonym or near synonym. Setting a term off from a related, familiar term is a useful way to clarify a word that may be fuzzy in the reader's mind. It can also be most effective when your larger purpose is to win audience assent or consent.

For example, say that you want to advance the contention that assertiveness is a good characteristic to have. In order to make your assertion you decide to distinguish assertiveness from aggressiveness. You might proceed as follows:

DEFINITION OF
FIRST TERM: *To be assertive is to state your feelings, beliefs, or values in a way that, although positive, respects the rights of others. . . .*

FIRST EXAMPLE: *If you're assertive, you stand up for your rights. When the waiter brings you a steak that isn't cooked to your specification, you politely ask that it be taken back and prepared properly. When the boss continually insists that you work overtime without pay, you express your resentment. . . .*

SECOND EXAMPLE: *If you're assertive, you express your emotions in personal relations. When you feel that a friend is taking advantage of you, you say so. When you feel that a boyfriend or girlfriend is treating you indifferently, you speak up. . . .*

THIRD EXAMPLE: *If you're assertive, you are civil. When you know that what you say or do will seriously hurt someone else, you think twice before acting in a trivial matter. . . .*

DEFINITION OF
SECOND TERM: *To be aggressive is to project yourself in a way that is offensive and hostile and is unmindful of the rights of others. . . .*

FIRST EXAMPLE: *If you're aggressive, you try to win through intimidation. For example, in eating out you probably make it clear to the waiter that nothing short of a pound of flesh will placate you, should some dolt foul up your order. . . .*

SECOND EXAMPLE: *If you're aggressive, you try to exploit others. Thus, knowing that your best friend is an easy-going, good-hearted sort, you dump all sorts of problems on the person. . . .*

THIRD EXAMPLE: *To be aggressive is to be reckless and impulsive. Regardless of the feelings and rights of others, no matter how trivial the matter, you tell people exactly what you think and let the chips fall where they may. . . .*

Following one or the other of these four formats provides a handy way to develop an argumentative essay through definition. Keep in mind, of course, that your purpose is to win the audience's assent or consent, not just to define a term. Also, be cautious about the common fallacies associated with definitions.

SUMMARY

A definition is the explanation of the meaning of a term. Denotative, logical, stipulative, and persuasive are four kinds of short definition.

1. **Denotative:** the collection, or class, of objects to which the term can be applied. EXAMPLE: the Pan American building as a denotation of *skyscraper.*

2. **Logical:** the collection of properties shared by all and only those objects in a term's denotation. A good logical definition (1) states the essential characteristics of the term being defined, (2) is not circular, (3) is neither too broad nor too narrow; (4) does not use obscure or figurative language, and (5) is not negative when it can be affirmative.

3. **Stipulative:** attaching unconventional, perhaps unique, meaning to a term. EXAMPLE: defining *murder* as "the preventing of a human life from coming into existence."

4. **Persuasive:** attaching a different literal meaning to a word while preserving the old positive or negative meaning. EXAMPLE: defining *true sophistication* as "expediency in the cause of self-interest."

Certain fallacies are associated with these short forms of definition. Among the more common are:

1. **Faulty denotation:** misapplying a term or applying it in a highly questionable way. EXAMPLE: assuming that *radical politician* denotes Ronald Reagan.

2. **Semantical ambiguity:** using a word or phrase that can easily be interpreted in two or more ways without making clear which meaning is intended. EXAMPLE: defining *radical politics* as "fierce hostility to and contempt for traditional American values and politics."

3. **Circular definition:** defining a word in terms of itself. EXAMPLE: "Professor Jacobs can't be considered a competent teacher, because he is very biased. He is biased against all forms of modern literature. Probably he doesn't like modern literature because he doesn't read it and lacks the capacity to appreciate it."

4. **Fallacy of persuasive definition:** preserving the old emotive force of a word that has been redefined. EXAMPLE: asserting that murder is whatever prevents a life from coming into existence (redefinition of *murder*) and then providing a context that exploits the old negative force of *murder* in order to discredit abortions and impugn those having abortions.

5. **Question-begging definition:** attempting to reestablish an irrefutable position in an argument by means of a questionable definition. EXAMPLE: contending that President Reagan is not a "true Republican," because he was once a Democrat, and then using that defining characteristic (unswerving party membership) of Republicanism to render any counterevidence inadmissible.

In addition to short definitions, writers often use extended definitions, which are lengthy, well-developed explanations of a term's meaning. Four methods for developing an argument by extended definition are especially useful: (1) providing historical background, (2) keying on one element, (3) finding the common element, and (4) distinguishing a term from a more familiar one.

Questions for Analysis

Refer to "Cop-Out Realism" by Norman Cousins, on pp. 193–196.

1. State Cousins's thesis, and list his main points. What kind of assertion is the thesis?

2. What organizational structure does he use?

3. Which strategy for developing extended definitions does Cousins use?

4. What denotations of *cop-out realism* does Cousins provide?

5. It might be said that Cousins's definition of *cop-out realism* is both logical and stipulative. Explain.

6. Evaluate Cousins's logical definition of *cop-out realism* according to the criteria for such definitions.

7. Cousins argues that government-controlled gambling, smoking permission for high school students, and coeducational college dormitories are denoted by *cop-out*. Do you agree, or do you think Cousins commits faulty denotation?

8. On what basis does Cousins determine whether something is "shucking responsibility"?

9. Cousins's definition of *cop-out realism* (opening sentence) implies another kind of realism, which presumably would refer to responsible efforts to be sensible in dealing with things as they are. What do you think would be denoted by *responsible realism*?

10. Is there any reason for assuming that Cousins knows that "the number of poor people who were hurt by gambling under the Mafia is miniscule compared to the number who now lose money on horses with the urgent blessings of New York State" (paragraph 4)? Or should you consider this an unknowable statistical reference? If so, explain.

11. Do you think it follows that, if smoking is permitted, drinking alcohol and smoking pot should be? Or is this a false analogy?

12. In Cousins's view, when school officials permit students to smoke at school, they are ignoring their obligations to nonsmoking youngsters. In other words: Either (1) permit youngsters to smoke and ignore obligations to nonsmokers, or (2) don't permit youngsters to smoke and meet obligations to nonsmokers. Do you think this is a genuine dilemma or a false dilemma?

13. Do you think that Cousins has sufficiently defined "privacy and dignity" (paragraph 14)?

14. Do you think that Cousins's allusion to divorce (paragraph 14) is germane to his argument, or is it irrelevant? Explain.

15. Identify all fact statements, opinion statements, and fact/opinion statements. Rewrite the fact/opinion statements to delete the opinion.

READING FOR ANALYSIS

On January 21, 1981, Americans rejoiced at the release of a group of hostages who had been held for over a year in Iran. It was not uncommon at that time to hear these people proclaimed heroes and welcomed home as such. But were they heroes? Some thought not. Novelist Herbert Gold, for one, thought they were victims and celebrities, but not heroes. Gold explains why in the following essay, published on the eve of the hostages' return. Notice how Gold makes use of three strategies for developing an extended definition: providing historical background, keying on a common element in the meaning of *hero*, and distinguishing *hero* from the familiar *celebrity*. He also makes use of denotative, stipulative, and persuasive definitions.

The Hostages Are Special, but No Heroes—
Let's Not Be Cruel

By Herbert Gold

1   Wonderful; they're coming home. In a world of familiar nightmares, a novel one has perhaps ended. A sovereign state behaved like a terrorist,

and sent its mobs to put hands on the citizens of another state with which it was not at war, and demanded tribute and groveling as its terms for letting free a little group of diplomats, Marine guards, schoolteachers, businessmen.

2   It was an event virtually unprecedented in history. Does this mean that the victims of the melodrama suddenly become heroes?

3   Evidently. Provided that we completely misunderstand, as we have come to misunderstand, the nature of heroes and heroism. The hostages are victims, sufferers, innocents trapped with grieving loved ones. They attracted rage and love because they are symbols of an America that is both mighty and weak. Therefore they will be prodded by press conferences, offered book contracts, examined by psychiatrists, analyzed and, above all, publicized. They are celebrities. They will be media stars. The casting directors of talk shows are panting for them. The ghost writers are warming up their electric typewriters. The data banks are yearning to receive their souls, their personalities, their opinions, their sex lives, their hopes and dreams and their favorite recipes for tuna casserole. They can become almost as famous as the Dionne quintuplets, as Charles Lindbergh. Their use as meat is in the program. The carnivores are waiting. *Soon to Be a Major Motion Picture!*

4   But are these unfortunate people properly to be described as heroes? At present in America we have no heroic leaders, no philosophers or artist heroes, no inspiring military heroes. Of course, we have plenty of actors, rock stars, athletes, talk-show hosts and other celebrities. Because we need heroes we manufacture them. I heard the young man released by the Iranians because of multiple sclerosis applauded on a morning talk show. And I understood why. He was sober, intense, modest, concerned, discreet; I wanted to applaud him, too. But was he a hero?

5   No, he was a victim who bore himself with dignity. He was a victim trapped by history, and he behaved decently. (Then why did he "do" the talk shows? Perhaps because he is an American and they asked him to do his morning talk show duty.)

6   The word "hero" comes from a Greek myth about a lover who drowned for love. Curiously enough, in the original tale Hero was the lady, Leander the lover, but they both ended in the waters of the Hellespont. As the idea developed, heroes came to be seen as great men or women who deserved something like worship for taking a half-step from humanity to divinity. They were sometimes scientists, philosophers, religious visionaries, but, human history being what it is, they most often achieved their status in the killing line—they were fighters. They chose to sacrifice themselves for a cause. Often rituals honored them—slit throats, steaming blood, shameful night-time ceremonies. In any case, whether Galileo or Socrates or Audie Murphy, they *chose* their fate.

7   The superstar celebrity—F. Lee Bailey, Andy Warhol, Rod Stewart—is the fast-food throwaway version of a hero. To be a good goalie or dance a broken-field run with nimble abandon is really a matter of youth,

coordination and television coverage. A sterling character might help, but good knees are essential. The true hero is the man or a woman who changes a place or a world, making it fitter for others. (This eliminates the famous demagogues, the Hitlers and Khomeinis, whom mobs *think* are heroes.)

8   Emerson said that "every hero becomes a bore," but now they sometimes become menaces. The astronaut hero gets religion, hires himself out as a spokesflackperson for aerospace, sells the lint from his pocket as a souvenir of his magic voyage. The power we give our media heroes makes it possible for them to be both bores and menaces, like the once-heroic Charles de Gaulle, who in his dotage led France into massive spending for atomic weaponry and a vain cynicism.

9   Remember when Spiro T. Agnew was a hero to the right? (More recently he was a salesman for the Arabs.)

10   Remember when Rennie Davis, of the Chicago Seven—or is it Ten?—was a hero to the left? (Lately he became a salesman for one of the giggling boy gurus from India; he may be selling life insurance by now.)

11   Do we want to send the accidental victims of Tehran onto this merry-go-round?

12   Of course, not only the need for heroism persists, but also the capacity. All those gawky, burning-eyed lads who pull grandmothers from wreckage, babies from smoke-filled houses, we can agree are authentic heroes. They get their medals, maybe a gold watch. Then back to the gas station. They have achieved something to remember themselves by. They are not charismatic figures, they are not father figures, they are not even Henry Kissinger figures. They are simply people who acted with effective determination in a crisis, who chose to risk their lives when needed.

13   I once knew a classic hero, a college friend who was rejected for officer training on the grounds of psychological unfitness. This judgment set off some atavistic explosion of will in him. He went into battle as a sergeant; he was a natural leader—perhaps also an unnatural one—and a singular murder machine. He feared nothing, he flung himself about like a dervish, heaving steel and explosives. He became a certified, stamped-and-delivered war hero. He returned his medals and gave interviews to the newspapers: "Unfit, was I? Those bastards! Those bastards! Those bastards!"

14   Then he entered civilian life, lost his way after his one bright moment, died an alcoholic. He was a hero, in love with a vision, furious with fate, and doomed.

15   This other thing we have come to call a hero is merely a celebrity. Because he is well-known, he is well-known; the tautology proves itself. And because he is up there in the glare of publicity, he becomes an emissary of our American need. They wouldn't be there, would they?—those basketball players, guitar-rattlers, actors, hostages—if they weren't symbols of the best we can imagine for ourselves?

16   It might be a good idea to question the process that fabricates these answers to our desires. Above all, the celebrity step-hero cannot fulfill his destiny in silence. A ransomed businessman in South America is released after months of captivity when his family or his company pays off the guerrillas or the bandits. Is he a hero? He goes quietly home, shaves, maybe gets a checkup, takes his pension or returns to work in a local office. He had a tough time. But Walter Cronkite did not intone about him, night after night on prime time, "Day Something for the Hostage," so his suffering has no symbolic value. The President did not grow shrill and panicky on his behalf. He is merely a sufferer, of interest to his family and friends; he is unfortunate, not a hero. He passes through the Los Angeles Times on Page 39, and maybe gets a photo in his hometown newspaper.

17   The old notion still clings to the word "hero." The hero is a person of courage and ability, a great doer afflicted with desperate devotion and readiness for sacrifice, a noble soul whom many learn to admire and hope to emulate. Surely it is worth thinking about whether we should still seek to be heroes. But should we risk dreaming of being *hostages*? What a confusion! In an age of catastrophe, this would amount to a catastrophic form of national masochism.

18   It might be untimely to dream of true heroism now—witness the suffering of my college friend—but it is also wrong to confound our decent respect for suffering with brilliant energy and sacrifice. The hostages are not heroes. They are people who have been hurt by others.

19   As they come home, the hostages will try to recover their lives. We are already trying to hand them new lives. What awaits the salesman from Southern California who went to Iran to try to drum up some business? The Marine guards and diplomats and the schoolmaster? Will it now be their fate to tour the noise circuits, be awarded Cadillacs in stadium ceremonies, show their kitchens to People magazine? Should they learn to be shy, lovable and witty for Johnny and Phil and Barbara, and have their hair blow-dried at dawn for the "Today" show?

20   It would be cruel and manipulative to use them as emblems and deny their real humanity. Iran and our own government and the media have already played these games. They were there, making no choices, trying to survive, and were thrust into cruel deceptions and roles. Suddenly home, they are told they can be rewarded with a few months of fame.

21   Anyone must have pity for their sufferings. But did they choose a course that led to sacrifice? Did they fly at some enemy on behalf of their country or to protect their loved ones? Of course not. Stupid hazard and irrational rage selected them to suffer. All of us should now be content with accuracy and not blow hot air over their pains.

22   They could have been martyrs, but fortunately they were not. There is misery and pathos in their months under threat, but neither heroism nor martyrdom correctly names what capricious fate brought their way. The various dignities with which they maintained themselves will be

interesting to explore. As a people, we can ride with the wave of sympathy for their ordeal.

23   But, as we applaud their return, let us not inflate them into this year's astronauts. Let us respect them enough not to use them in the service of our entertainment and anxieties. Let us allow them the dignity of what they really are as human beings. And, in so doing, allow a little for what we really might be ourselves—Americans in a world that may have to make do a while longer without national heroes.[4]

Questions for Analysis

1. State Gold's thesis, list his main points, and indicate which organizational pattern he uses.
2. What kind of assertion is Gold's thesis: meaning, value, policy, consequences, or fact?
3. What historical background does Gold provide to help clarify the meaning of *hero*?
4. What distinctions does Gold draw between a hero and a celebrity?
5. According to Gold, what are the common denominators in the meaning of *hero*? Do you think these are sufficient for writing a logical definition of *hero*, or are there other elements in the makeup of a hero?
6. What denotations does Gold provide for *hero*, *celebrity* and *demagogue*?
7. Cite examples of stipulative and persuasive definitions that Gold uses. Does he use persuasive definition legitimately or fallaciously?
8. Identify all fact, opinion, and fact/opinion statements. Rewrite the fact/opinion statements so that only the fact is expressed.
9. Do you think Gold makes a convincing case for his thesis?
10. Of the two essays, Gold's and Cousins's, which do you think is the more effective argument developed through extended definition? Why?

READING FOR ANALYSIS

The following extended-definition essay is offered without follow-up questions for your own careful analysis. You might: (1) identify the author's thesis, main points, and organizational structure; (2) indicate the kind of assertion he is advancing; (3) list the sources he uses in developing support materials; (4) indicate what kind of definition he provides and identify related fallacies, if any. Essayist Lance Morrow writes regularly for *Time* magazine.

---

[4]From the *Los Angeles Times*, January 20, 1981. Reprinted by permission of the author and publisher.

The Burnout of Almost Everyone

By Lance Morrow

1   Graham Greene's architect Querry had to trek to an African leprosarium to find a metaphor adequate to express his mood; nothing less would be sufficiently wasted, blighted, defunct. Querry was, Greene meant, *A Burnt-Out Case*, like the leper Deo Gratias, his soul far gone. He was a masterpiece of acedia, a skull full of ashes, a rhapsodist of his own desolation.

2   Once, hardly anyone except a Graham Greene character could manage such Gethsemanes of exhaustion. Today, burnout is a syndrome verging on a trend. The smell of psychological wiring on fire is everywhere. The air-traffic controllers left their jobs in part, they said, because the daily tension tended to scorch out their circuits (the primitive "flee-or-fight" reaction to danger squirted charges of adrenaline into bodies that had to remain relatively immobile, tethered by duty to scope and computer).

3   Burnout runs through the teaching profession like Asian flu—possibly because it depresses people to be physically assaulted by those they are trying to civilize. Two years ago, Willard McGuire, president of the National Education Association, said that burnout among teachers "threatens to reach hurricane force if it isn't checked soon." Social workers and nurses burn out from too much association with hopelessness. Police officers burn out. Professional athletes burn out. Students burn out. Executives burn out. Housewives burn out. And, as every parent knows, there usually comes a moment in late afternoon when baby burnout occurs—all of his little circuits overloaded, the child feels too wrought up to fall asleep.

4   One of the biggest difficulties with the concept of burnout is that it has become faddish and indiscriminate, an item of psychobabble, the psychic equivalent, in its ubiquitousness, of jogging. Burnout has no formal psychiatric status. Many psychoanalysts regard the malady as simply that old familiar ache, depression. Even so, plenty of professionals take burnout seriously. Psychological journals are heavy with analyses of burnout.

5   Burnout is progressive, occurring over a period of time. Authors Robert Veninga and James Spradley define five stages that lead from a stressful job to a burnt-out case: 1) The Honeymoon—intense enthusiasm and job satisfaction that, for all but a few dynamos, eventually give way to a time when valuable energy reserves begin to drain off. 2) Fuel Shortage—fatigue, sleep disturbances, possibly some escapist drinking or shopping binges and other early-warning signals. 3) Chronic Symptoms—exhaustion, physical illness, acute anger and depression. 4) Crisis—illness that may become incapacitating, deep pessimism, self-doubt, obsession with one's own problems. 5) Hitting the Wall—career and even life threatened.

6   Burnout may be the late 20th century descendant of neurasthenia and the nervous breakdown—the wonderfully matter-of-fact all-purpose periodic collapse that our parents were fond of. Burnout is pre-eminently the disease of the thwarted; it is a frustration so profound that it exhausts body and morale. Burnout, in advanced states, imposes a fatigue that seems—at the time—a close relative of death. It is the entropy of the other-directed. Even the best worker—especially the best worker—will often, when thwarted, swallow his rage; it then turns into a small private conflagration, the fire in the engine room. A race of urban nomads who have wandered far from family roots tends to turn work into the spiritual hearth, a chief source of warmth and support. When the supervisor proves to be an idiot, when the pay is bad or the job insecure or unrewarding, then the worker experiences a strangely intimate and fundamental sense of betrayal, a wound very close to the core. Or perhaps the wound is his discovery that the core is empty. And with that discovery, he may resort to a pistol, a length of rope or a fistful of pills, leaving behind a note: "Burned out."

7   Despite the psychologists' exertions, the malady is utterly subjective and therefore unpredictable. One policeman will thrive in an assignment that may turn another into an alcoholic. In 1971 a *Wall Street Journal* survey found that the most physically draining and mentally numbing jobs were working at a foundry furnace, selling subway tokens, lifting lids on a steel-mill oven, and removing hair and fat from hog carcasses. Yet one worker took both pride and pleasure in the fact that he could clean a hog carcass in 45 seconds. Incidentally, it is also worth mentioning that being unemployed is a lot more stressful than an unsatisfying job, a fact that some ex-controllers are discovering.

8   Why is burnout, for all its serious implications, somewhat irritating to contemplate? Part of the problem resides in the term itself. It is too apocalyptic (in its private, individual way). Burnout implies a violent process ending in a devastation. The term perfectly captures an American habit of hyperbole and narcissism working in tandem: a hypochondria of the spirit. The idea contains a sneaking self-aggrandizement tied to an elusive self-exoneration. In the concept of burnout, there is no sense of human process, of the ups and downs—even the really awful downs—to which all men and women, in all history, have been subject. It also suggests that too many people become a little too easily thwarted. Most of the world's work, it has often been noted, is done by people who do not feel well.

9   Burnout has a way of turning the sovereign self (as we thought of it once, long ago) into a victim, submissive, but passive-aggressive, as psychologists say; it is like a declaration of bankruptcy—necessary sometimes, but also somewhat irresponsible and undignified. It is a million-dollar wound, an excuse, a ticket out. The era of "grace under pressure" vanished in the early '60s. Burnout is the perfect disorder for an

age that lives to some extent under the Doctrine of Discontinuous Selves. It simply declares one's self to be defunct, out of business; from that pile of ash a new self will arise. In the democracy of neurosis, everyone is entitled to his own apocalypse. Burnout becomes the mechanism by which people can enact their serial selves, in somewhat the way that divorce permits serial marriages. In some cases, the serial selves of burnout are like the marshmallows that Cub Scouts thrust into the campfire flame. They hold them there until they are charred, peel away the blackened outer skin and eat it, then thrust the soft white marshmallow into the flame again, repeating the process until there is nothing left.[5]

THEME   TOPICS

1. Write an argumentative essay by developing an extended definition of one of the following terms: *opportunism, optimism, honor, expediency,* or *respectability.* Try to key on a quality and mention it early in your essay. Support your definition with examples from your own observation, experience, and reading. Be careful that your essay is not just an extended definition but *an extended argument developed through an extended definition.*

2. Write an essay in which you argue that people need to have more sentiment and less sentimentality. Compare and contrast these terms through a series of examples that makes your point.

3. Familiar words are often sources of misunderstanding, as with terms such as *pornography, religion,* and *success.* Choose one of these terms, or some other one, and write an essay in which you and your audience try to find the common denominator.

4. The history of some words reveals curious shifts, even contradictions, in the development of their meanings. Choose one of the following: *conservative, liberal, romantic love,* or *cynic.* Write an argumentative essay in which you demonstrate either that the current meaning of the word differs from its original or that, though different, the current meaning still preserves the essence of the original. Start by looking up the meanings of these words in a college dictionary.

---

[5]From *Time,* September 21, 1981. Copyright 1981 Time Inc. All rights reserved. Reprinted by permission of the publisher.

PART THREE

Troubleshooting for Fallacious Arguments

7. Ambiguity

Alexander M. Haig, Jr., arrived on the State Department scene articulating foreign policy in bewildering language. In his first press conference after becoming secretary of state, the retired general and former commander of the North Atlantic Treaty Organization explored the "risk taking mode of the Soviet Union." He spoke of the State Department as people with "in-place pros" as contrasted with the "augmentees" that he had brought with him to his new assignment. At one point, he wanted to "caveat" a remark with a qualification. Did the new secretary think he would soon travel to the Mideast? one reporter wanted to know. The secretary said he had "no finite" plans. Turning to potential trouble spots, Haig saw a need to "clarify the air" regarding South Korea; and he cautioned that the United States had "a number of watchpots" in Europe, such as Poland. But he saved his most descriptive language for last, when he spoke of international terrorism as not only rampant but "hemorrhaging."

So taken with Haig's enrichment of the language of diplomacy was one London newspaper that it parodied "Haiguition" in an editorial bound to bring tears to the eyes of all lovers of the English language. Here's a snippet:

Gen. Alexander Haig has contexted the Polish watchpot somewhat nuancely. How, though, if the situation decontrols, can he stoppage it mountingly conflagrating? Haig, in congressional hearings before his confirmatory, paradoxed his auditioners by abnormalling this response so that verbs were nounded, nouns verbed and adjectives adverbised. He techniques a new way to vocabulary his thoughts so as to informationally uncertain anybody listening about what he had actually implicationed. At first it seemed that the general was impenetrabling what at basic was clear. This, it was suppositioned, was a new linguistic harbingered by NATO during the time he bellwethered it. But close observers have alternatived that idea. What Haig is doing, they concept, is to decouple the Russians from everything they are moded to. (From *The Guardian,* February 2, 1981. Reported in "Haguition—A Capital Offense." *Los Angeles Times,* February 5, 1981.)

Of course, the editorial exaggerated Haig's style. But sometimes exaggeration is needed to make a point. Clearly, the point is that sloppy use of language produces gibberish. What's more, arguments expressed in such language are fallacious.

In Chapter 1 we learned that informal fallacies are commonplace errors in reasoning that we fall into because of (1) careless use of language or (2) inattention to subject matter. Part 3 of this text is designed to introduce you to the most common informal fallacies, so that you can detect them in your reading and avoid them in your writing. In this chapter we look at fallacies stemming from careless use of language, what are called fallacies of ambiguity. (Chapters 8 and 9 take up fallacies that arise from inattention to subject matter.) But before considering ambiguity, we should examine the emotive use of language, for it is such language that is at the root of Haig's "newspeak" and of much deception.

LITERAL MEANING AND EMOTIVE MEANING

If the purpose of a sentence is to inform or state a fact, then some of its words must refer to objects or events and to their properties or relations. In other words, some of its words must have *literal meaning; that is, they must refer to things, events, or properties.* Sentences that contain terms with literal meanings and that conform to grammatical rules also are said to have literal meaning.

But sometimes the purpose of a sentence is to express attitudes or feelings in addition to or instead of information, as in persuasion. When this happens, some of the sentence's words or phrases may have an emotional suggestiveness or impact besides their literal meanings. In other words, they may have *emotive meaning—that is, positive or negative overtones.*

226

The emotive charges of some words is obvious. *Spade, honky, wetback, kike,* and *wop* are clearly negative. *Love, peace, compassion, courage, patriotism,* and *freedom* are positive. But there are also words that have either neutral or mixed emotive meanings. *Lamp, desk, sky, snow, pen, walk,* and *listen* tend to be neutral words. *Alcohol, businessman, politician, clever,* and *socialism* seem to have mixed emotive meanings.

Of course, it's not always easy to classify terms according to positive or negative charges. What you may consider positive I may consider negative. For example, *pacifism* produces different emotive charges for one who sincerely believes in opposition to war or violence and one who does not. Similar terms are *God, religion, revolution, feminism, open marriage,* and *affirmative action.* Whether such terms are positive or negative, they are nevertheless highly charged.

In addition, some terms that appear to be neutral are actually laden with emotion. For example, *public servant, government official,* and *bureaucrat* refer to the same group of people and thus carry the same literal meaning. But their emotive meanings differ: probably *public servant* is positive, *government official* neutral, and *bureaucrat* negative.

In argument people exploit the emotive aspect of language in various ways in order to advance their assertions. One way is to mask literal meaning by so exciting the audience's emotions that reason gets overlooked. Another way is to mask literal meaning by using unintelligible language. Still another way is to mask what may otherwise be unacceptable by using emotively neutral terms.

Masking by Exciting Emotions

Let's suppose that a group of Hollywood celebrities sponsors a fund-raising event for a presidential candidate. Now, it's possible to report this event in a sentence with strictly literal meaning: "A fund-raiser, sponsored by some Hollywood celebrities for Governor Winston Bryant, took place at the home of film-producer Ty Barton last night." Or the event can be reported in a sentence with emotive meaning: "A sumptuous fund-raising bash was thrown for Governor Winston Bryant by some of Hollywood's most beautiful people last night at the sprawling stone-and-glass home of movie mogul Ty Barton." Although both statements report the same fact, the second gives you a differ- ent impression from the first. In the second, "sumptuous," "bash," "thrown," "beautiful people," "sprawling stone-and-glass home," and "movie mogul," all carry an emotive charge absent in the first statement. Used in a broader context—for example, in an editorial—the second sentence might be part of an effort to mask the literal meaning or implications of an event. If it were, it might appear as follows:

RADICALISM IN THE FILM COLONY

> The continuing involvement of the Hollywood entertainment in- dustry in radical politics is understandably deplorable to the Amer- ican people. Americans are outraged because so many stars who have grown rich on box office receipts exhibit such fierce hostility to and contempt for traditional American values and institutions.
>
> Hollywood's anti-Americanism was on display last night at a fund- raising bash thrown for Governor Winston Bryant by some of Holly- wood's most beautiful people at the sprawling stone-and-glass home of movie mogul Ty Barton. On hand, in addition to movieland types, was a business tycoon known for sidling up to the Russians; a popular actress who regularly presents the Chinese Communists as nice, neat, friendly agrarian reformers; and a director whose anti-American films need no comment.
>
> After several hours of mingling with the movieland moguls over caviar and lobster, the governor, who lusts after his party's nomina- tion for the presidency, was treated to Barton's radical leftist views.

Given the colorful language of this passage, a reader must make a heroic effort to maintain objectivity in evaluating it. In brief, catchwords or labels often mask literal meaning by exciting emotions. One author lists the following labels as among the most common:[1]

Law and order	Alien ideologies
Crime in the streets	Hard-core pornography
Centralized federal bureaucracy	Senseless violence
White power structure	Credibility gap
Fiscal responsibility	Police brutality
Law-abiding citizen	

---

[1]Hans Guth. *Words and Ideas,* 5th ed. Belmont, Calif.: Wadsworth, 1980, p. 97.

Notice that each label carries its own set of ready-made attitudes. In argument, such labels can obscure literal meaning and bias evaluation. The prudent writer, then, uses them only with great care.

Exercise

7.1   *Choose some controversial issue and write an editorial for your school paper that masks by exciting emotions. Then revise the editorial, taking pains to delete all emotive labels and catchwords.*

Masking through Unintelligible Language

Writers often mask literal meaning by using unintelligible or meaningless language, as the aforementioned parody of Haig's language points up. Often such language takes the form of jargon, which is the technical language of a trade, profession, or group. Used enough in and outside a field, technical words turn flaccid, even incomprehensible. For example, here's a sampling of some recent jargon words that the social sciences have spawned: *thrust, nitty-gritty, accountability, commitment, relate to, identify with, sensitive, paranoid, viable, existential, meaningful, awareness, relevant,* and *options.* No doubt, these terms were once vital, and on occasion they remain so. But indiscriminate use has largely reduced them to gobbledygook.

The historian Arthur Schlesinger, Jr., in his book *A Thousand Days,* rails against the U.S. State Department's use of jargon, much of which is contained in the following fictitious memo:[2]

> With respect to your inquiry about our position vis-à-vis the Arabs, we exhort you to zero in on our official stance in response to their oil embargo: to crank in more bargaining leverage, to phase out economic aid and gin up Israel's defensive reaction posture. It's vital that you pinpoint a viable policy and, to keep open our options, a fallback position that we can assume if the flak from the nit-picking opposition intensifies. Once you are seized of the problem in as hard-nosed a manner as possible, which is the objective incumbent on us in future cables, you should review with defense echelons overall objectives, seek breakthroughs, consider crash programs, and staff out policies in meaningful depth until we here are ready to finalize our deliberations and implement our decisions.

[2]Arthur Schlesinger, Jr. *A Thousand Days.* Boston: Houghton Mifflin, 1965, pp. 417–420.

Why do people use such language? Commerce Secretary Malcolm Baldridge surmised: "The only reason I could see for talking that kind of talk [is] a subconscious urge to cover one's self. There is a kind of protection in [such] statements and a recommendation so vague that it can be interpreted two or three ways on a single issue. That's not communicating, that's covering one's flanks."[3] In Baldridge's view, then, people use jargon because it insulates them from responsibility. Regardless of the underlying reasons for its use, jargon masks literal meaning and obscures argument. For this reason, the effective argumentative writer avoids it whenever possible.

Masking the Unacceptable with Neutral Words

A third way to exploit the emotive aspect of language is by masking with emotively neutral words what may otherwise be unacceptable. Such terms are generally called euphemisms, which are polite ways of saying something that is offensive, harsh, or blunt. Thus, instead of *lying* we *fib* or *cover up* (as in the Watergate cover-up). Rather than fighting a war, we engage in a *conflict* (as in the Vietnam conflict) or a *police action* (as in the Korean police action). Rather than *assassinating* people, the Central Intelligence Agency *terminates them with prejudice.* Rather than *surrender,* government officials refer to *crisis resolution* or *conflict termination.* Rather than *firing* an employee, bureaucrats speak of *selecting out;* and instead of *rationing* gasoline, they talk of *end-use allocation.* Rather than speaking of a "tax" some politicians prefer *revenue enhancement.*

Sometimes euphemism is used to gloss over unpleasant realities. Thus, government officials developed a litany of euphemisms to make the harrowing events of Vietnam more palatable. Here are a few examples with "translations":[4]

---

[3]"Commerce Chief Lets the Word Go Forth—Don't." *Los Angeles Times,* July 24, 1981, p. 13.
[4]Howard Kahane. *Logic and Contemporary Rhetoric.* Belmont, Calif.: Wadsworth, 1980, p. 127.

pacification center	concentration camp
incursion	invasion
protective reaction strike	bombing
surgical strike	precision bombing
incontinent ordinance	off-target bombs (usually used when they kill civilians)
friendly fire	shelling friendly villages or troops by mistake
specified strike zone	area where soldiers could fire at anything—replaced *free fire* zone when that became notorious
interdiction	bombing
strategic withdrawal	retreat (when United States and its allies did it)
advisor	military officer (before United States admitted involvement in Vietnam) or CIA agent
termination	killing
infiltrators	enemy troops moving into the battle area
reinforcements	friendly troops moving into the battle area

From the viewpoint of correct argument, the key problem with euphemism and jargon is that both are vague, imprecise uses of language. Their meanings are obscure and blurred, because the connection between the word and referent is uncertain. Nevertheless, masking through jargon or euphemism can be as psychologically persuasive as masking strictly by exciting emotions. The psychological appeal lies in their capacity to win our minds by capturing our hearts.

Because the emotive aspects of language can be used most persuasively in argument, be skeptical of arguments containing emotionally charged words, jargon, and euphemism. By the same token, be cautious about your own use of such language. This doesn't mean that emotive language has no place in communication. Much of our greatest literature, including expository prose, glitters with emotive expression. Indeed, it's doubtful that nonfiction can be written only in emotively neutral terms; at least, *interesting, readable* nonfiction cannot be. But when we are trying to follow or develop an argument, to learn or lay out the truth about something, what distracts us from our goal frustrates us. As a result, when we are trying to reason about facts objectively, referring to them in emotively charged language hinders rather than helps. The point of becoming familiar with the emotive aspects of language, then, is not to dismiss their literary or persuasive value. Rather, it's to prepare to deal with and avoid arguments that would use emotive language to persuade illegitimately.

With these preliminary remarks behind us, let's now turn to fallacies of ambiguity. We will consider the fallacies of semantical ambiguity, equivocation, accent, innuendo, amphiboly, hypostatization, composition, and division.

Exercises

7.2 Translate the following examples of jargon into plain English.

1. It is incumbent on the administration to maximize defense expenditures to ensure a credible U.S. defense posture vis-à-vis our adversaries.
2. I can no longer relate to the viewpoints you hold on domestic phenomena.
3. The various facts of human personality so greatly impinge on behavior that the concept of free will becomes problematic.
4. Many advertisements utilize erroneous appeals to motivate the audience to make a pro-product purchase decision.
5. Our relationship suffers from a fundamental lack of communication, which seems to set up barriers between us in every area of our interpersonal relations.

7.3 How many euphemisms can you identify for the following terms: lying, pregnancy, old age, sexual activity, death, heavy drinking, slums?

7.4 Investigate the use of jargon and euphemism in some major area—for example, the funeral industry, sports, law enforcement, government, education, medicine.

SEMANTICAL AMBIGUITY

The fallacy of semantical ambiguity consists in using a word or phrase that can easily be interpreted in one or more ways without making clear which meaning is intended. For example, a friend says, "I just got a new car." Does she mean a different, possibly used car; or a brand new car? The problem here

232

does not lie in using a word with more than one meaning, for numerous words have more multiple meanings. Rather ambiguity results when the context does not make it clear which of several meanings are intended, thus misleading the reader.

Fallacies of semantical ambiguity often occur with relative terms, that is, words whose meanings depend on some point of reference. Examples include the comparative adjectives *more* and *better* and the personal pronouns *they* and *it*. Words such as *small, big, bright, tasty,* and *smooth* also are relative terms. Their meanings vary according to what they're describing. If we don't know what they are describing, we don't know precisely what the words mean.

Here's an advertisement for Minolta copiers that illustrates semantical ambiguity: "A small business can work a small copier to death in no time at all. . . . Well, you can't blame the copier. Small copiers are only built for small work loads." Imagine the various interpretations readers will impose on "small" in "small copier" and "small work loads." Here's the same problem in another ad: "Dunlop brings you the more affordable steel belted radial." "More affordable" than what? But topping the ambiguity charts must be Kool's assertion "It's the only smoke that's got *it*." There's no telling what the "it" is that Kools supposedly has.

Here are two more examples of semantical ambiguity, with comment:

> EXAMPLE: *Newspaper headline: "President Sees Prospects for Labor"*

> COMMENT: *It's impossible to know precisely what this statement means. Three possibilities are that (1) the president is hopeful about improved labor conditions, (2) the president anticipates work opportunities, or (3) the president will interview candidates for positions in the Labor Department. (We*

can safely assume that the president's wife is not about to have a baby.) Because the statement does not make clear which of the several meanings is intended, readers can arrive at a false conclusion.

EXAMPLE: "It's natural for fresh breath." (Advertisement for Wrigley's Doublemint gum.)
"It's only natural." (Advertisement for Winston cigarettes.)
"Welcome to the pure and natural world of feminine care." (Advertisement for FDS Pure and Natural.)

COMMENT: Each of these ads uses "natural" ambiguously. What is "natural" supposed to mean: that the product contains only natural ingredients? that the use of the product has become commonplace? or that using the product is as natural, say, as eating or sleeping? Natural is one of those words with an intense positive charge for many of us. Consequently, advertisers make hay with it. (But sometimes it boomerangs. For example, in 1976 Tree Sweet Products Company was sued by a consumer for $250,000 in punitive damages and an estimated 75¢ refund for everybody who had purchased the company's grape drink since October 3, 1973. The plaintiff argued that the company had misled her by advertising "natural color," when in fact the product contained "artificial color.") Also, the "it" in the gum and cigarette ads is ambiguous. Does "it" mean "chewing gum," "chewing Wrigley's," or something else? Does "it" mean "smoking," "smoking Winston's," or something else? The "something else," by the way, could be sex, inasmuch as the word is often superimposed visually over a sexually seductive scene.

Exercise

7.5 For each of the following products, write a short advertisement that uses semantical ambiguity: gum, car, mouthwash, beer, perfume.

EQUIVOCATION

The fallacy of equivocation consists of drawing an unwarranted conclusion by using a word or phrase in two different senses in the same argument. Equivocation differs from semantical ambiguity. In equivocation the meaning of a word has actually shifted in an argument, thereby entailing a conclusion. In contrast, semantical ambiguity is present when the meaning of a word or phrase is not at all clear; the term may be taken in several ways. Here's an absurd though illustrative example of equivocation: "John is a weird man, because he does math problems in a weird way." "Weird," as used in the stated premise, refers to an unusual or unorthodox manner of doing arithmetic. But "weird" in the unexpressed premise ("People who do math problems in a weird way are *weird*") refers to an odd or peculiar personality. Thus, we have two different meanings of the same word, used in the same argument, to entail a deduction.

A more serious instance of the equivocation fallacy can be seen in this argument:

> *Certainly, death is the perfection of life. After all, the end of anything is its perfection. And since death is the end of life, death must be the perfection of life.*

The premises of this argument are plausible only when "end" is interpreted differently in each of them: (1) as the goal or purpose of something and (2) as the termination of, or the last event in, a thing's development. These meanings are not logically equivalent. Thus, cleaned up, this argument actually says that (1) the goal of anything is its perfection, and (2) death is the last event of life. Viewed this way, the premises certainly don't warrant the conclusion that death is the perfection of life. Indeed, they entail no conclusion.

Here's another argument that commits the fallacy of equivocation:

> *The laws of gravitation and motion must have a lawmaker for the simple reason that they are laws, and all laws have a lawmaker.*

Here the meanings of "laws" are confused. In the sense that laws are human-made statutes that proscribe certain behavior, all laws do have a lawmaker. But the laws of gravitation and motion are scientific descriptions of how the physical universe operates and as such do not presuppose lawmakers. Therefore, the conclusion is unwarranted. Here is another example, with comment:

EXAMPLE: *People object to sexism and racism on the ground of discrimination. But what is objectionable about disrimination? We discriminate all the time—in the cars we buy, the foods we eat, the books we read, the friends we choose. The fact is that there's nothing wrong with discrimination. So, there's nothing wrong with discriminating against people on the basis of color or sex.*

COMMENT: *When applied to racism and sexism, discrimination means making a distinction in favor of or against a person on the basis of color or sex alone. As such, racial discrimination*

235

and sexual discrimination raise questions of social justice. When people object to racism and sexism on the ground of discrimination, then, discrimination is understood to mean unfair selection. When applied to cars, foods, books, and friends, discrimination simply means to distinguish among items on the basis of some standard. Certainly, in those contexts the term carries no overtones of social justice, and therefore it differs significantly from the use of discrimination in the context of sexism or racism.

ACCENT

The fallacy of accent consists of drawing an unwarranted conclusion, or directing one to it, by the use of improper emphasis. The improper emphasis in the accent fallacy may fall on a word, a phrase, or an aspect of the argument.

For example, everyone is familiar with the famous phrase from the Declaration of Independence "all men are created equal." It's possible to wonder whether Thomas Jefferson meant that "all men are *created* equal" or that "all men are created *equal*." If he meant the former, then we may infer a narrow ideal of equality that focuses on the differences that distinguish, even separate, people after their birth or creation. But if the emphasis belongs on "equal," then we might infer a more extended ideal of equality.

Here's another example of the accent fallacy:

> **Tom:** *I'm not going to contribute any more to your charity.*
>
> **Liz:** *Great! I'll just put you down for the same amount as last year.*
>
> **Tom:** What?

Liz draws the fallacious conclusion that Tom wants to contribute the same as the year before, because she has erroneously accented "more."

Newspapers and advertisements commonly use the accent fallacy to get us to buy their products. "President Declares War," a headline screams in bold print. Concerned that the United States is embroiled in a war somewhere, you buy the paper and anxiously read the article. The "war," you discover, is a "war on inflation." Television uses this tack *ad nauseam.* How many times have you been teased by the promise of "details at eleven?" "Air crash!" a reporter blurts out between programs. "Details at eleven!" Rarely is the eleven o'clock report of the incident as significant as the teaser made it out to be. Indeed, often as not, it isn't even the lead story. In a similar vein, who hasn't been attracted to, or distracted by, the ad that exclaims, "Free!" Then, in print small enough to test the best vision, " . . . with this coupon and a minimum $5.50 purchase." Accent fallacies, all.

The accent fallacy has several variations. One is drawing attention to something in a way that gives the impression that it is special or unique. For example, for years the firm C and H has advertised its sugar as "pure cane granulated from Hawaii!" The manufacturer proudly proclaims:

> *Warm tropical sunshine—gentle tropical rains—rich, fertile soil, born of volcanoes. In Hawaii, there is this happy combination of climate and setting—the perfect place for growing fine sugar cane. We grow it for eighteen months, then harvest and refine it for you to enjoy. C and H—the pure cane sugar from Hawaii!*

Who wouldn't infer that sugar grown under these conditions is better than that which isn't? But the Federal Trade Commission contends that there is no difference in granulated sugars—that sugar from beets or sugar grown elsewhere than Hawaii is not inferior to C and H's.

Another variation of the accent fallacy is the out-of-context quotation that misrepresents the original statement. For example, Professor Johnson says to her class: "Executing murderers is certainly the best form of punishment from a strictly economic view. After all, it's cheaper than housing criminals for the rest of their lives." A student leaves class and tells a friend: "Professor Johnson said today that *executing murderers is certainly the best form of punishment.*" Yes, Johnson did say that; but she also qualified that judgment. There is nothing wrong with quoting out of context, so long as the quote accurately represents what the speaker or writer means. Obviously, the student's quote does not.

In this connection, be alert to the abuse of ellipsis points (. . .), which can be used to indicate that something has been omitted from a quotation. Used fairly, ellipsis helps us write economically. Used unfairly, it results in the accent fallacy. For example, suppose film critic Al Lambaster wrote this about a movie: "Despite its warm, humorous moments, this movie represents the worst piece of filmmaking it has been my misfortune to see all year!" In the hands of the film's promoters, this devastating review might become a complimentary one: " '. . . warm, humorous . . . !' (Lambaster of the *Times*)."

INNUENDO

The accent fallacy often takes the form of innuendo. *The fallacy of innuendo consists of drawing or implying a conclusion, usually derogatory, on the basis of words that suggest but do not assert a conclusion.* "Has Jones been fired?" someone asks you. You may reply directly, "No." Or you may say, "No, as of today." This second response will probably lead the person to believe that Jones's days are numbered. Maybe they are, but without further evidence the person has no logical grounds for inferring that. Just as important, without providing more evidence for your implication, you have no logical grounds for suggesting it through innuendo.

Again, a candidate for county supervisor distributes a brochure in which he promises to restore honesty and integrity to that office. The implication is clear: His opponent is a crook.

In confronting innuendo, always try to make the conclusion explicit. Ask the author to defend the implied conclusion. In the author's absence, never accept an implied assertion without being satisfied that there is enough evidence for it. By the same token, strive to control the emotive side of your own writing, for that's where innuendo takes hold. If you are going to use veiled meanings, ensure that they are properly aligned with your purpose, as well as with reason and evidence. The fallacy of innuendo, like that of accent, does not consist of the use of emphasis but of its unfair or innacurate use.

EXAMPLE: *"Captain L had a first mate who was at times addicted to the use of strong drink, and occasionally, as the slang has it, 'got full.' The ship was lying in port in China, and the mate had been on shore and had there indulged rather freely in some of the vile compounds common in Chinese ports. He came on board, 'drunk as a lord,' and thought he had a mortgage on the whole world. The captain, who rarely ever touched liquor himself, was greatly disturbed by the disgraceful conduct of his officer, particularly as the crew had all observed his condition. One of the duties of the first officer [first mate] is to write up the 'log' each day, but as that worthy was not able to do it, the captain made the proper entry, but added: 'The mate was drunk all day.' The ship left port the next day and the mate got 'sobered off.' He attended to his writing at the proper time, but was appalled when he saw what the captain had done. He went on deck, and soon after the following colloquy took place:*

'Cap'n, why did you write in the log yesterday that I was drunk all day?'

'It was true, wasn't it?'

'Yes, but what will the owners say if they see it? It will hurt me with them.'

But the mate could get nothing more from the captain than 'It was true, wasn't it?'

The next day, when the captain was examining the book, he found at the bottom of the mate's entry of observation, course, winds, and tides: 'The captain was sober all day.' "
(Charles E. Trow. The Old Shipmasters of Salem. New York: Macmillan, 1905, pp. 14–15.)

COMMENT: *This humorous tale nicely illustrates the intentional use of the innuendo fallacy. Clearly, the mate is hoping that the ship's owners will interpret his entry about the captain as*

238

more than the literal truth. Probably, they will infer that the mate recorded the captain's sobriety because it was the exception, not the rule. When they do, the mate will gain his revenge on the captain.

Exercises

7.6 Write a one-paragraph critical review of a movie you have recently seen. Then show how someone might inaccurately quote you out of context.

7.7 Pretend you're a campaign strategist for a congressional candidate trying to unseat the incumbent. Write a pithy advertisement which uses innuendo to discredit your opponent.

AMPHIBOLY

The fallacy of amphiboly consists of making an assertion whose meaning is not clear because of its grammatical construction. Suppose, for example, you come across this item in the college newspaper: "The noted author and lecturer Joe Terhune will talk to graduating seniors about job opportunities in the theater tonight." Will Terhune speak in the theater, or will he speak of job opportunities in the dramatic field? The article is unclear, because the sentence is poorly constructed. Probably the author meant: "Tonight in the theater, the noted author and lecturer Joe Terhune will talk to graduating seniors about job opportunities."

The difference between amphibolous ambiguity and semantical ambiguity is that the former deals with misleading or unclear syntax (that is, sentence structure), and the latter deals with misleading or unclear words or phrases. Accordingly, amphibolies are corrected by reconstructing the sentence; semantical ambiguity is corrected by clarifying the ambiguous words or phrases.

The following are among the typical grammatical errors that make a sentence ambiguous: (1) unclear pronoun reference, as in "Alice would never talk to Pamela when she is on a date"; (2) elliptical construction (that is, the omission of one or more words that are supposed to be understood but must be supplied), as in "Ethel likes bridge better than her husband"; (3) unclear modifiers, as in "I have to take the final exam in two hours"; and (4) missing or misplaced punctuation, as in "Anthropology is the science of man embracing woman."

239

The problem with amphibolies in argument is that they invite the reader to draw an unintended conclusion. Nevertheless, even the best of writers sometimes make amphibolous constructions. This is one reason for proofreading anything you write, preferably a few days after you have written it. Even better, have someone else read your work. A person unfamiliar with a work is far better at detecting amphibolies than the author is.

> EXAMPLE: *"On the face of it the proposal by Duke [University] president Terry Sanford seems innocuous enough. By donating land where an estimated 36 million pages of documents and 880 reels of tape from Nixon's six-year presidency could be housed, university scholars would gain access to a great wealth of research material."* (Barry Jacobs. "Duke Academicians up in Arms over Nixon Library Plans." The Christian Science Monitor, September 4, 1981, p. 5.)

> COMMENT: *The second sentence, which offers support for the assertion of the first, is amphibolous. Who is donating the land? The sentence says that university scholars are. More likely, it's Duke University or some other party.*

HYPOSTATIZATION

The fallacy of hypostatization consists of making a contention or argument that personifies ideas, concepts, or inanimate objects and thereby creates confusion. To personify is to attribute to things and animals qualities that, strictly speaking, are attributable only to human beings. For example, a headline that reads, "Drugs Aim Damaging Blow to American Worker's Productivity" implies that drugs are purposive—that is, that they can have goals and purposes. When we hypostatize, we treat ideas, concepts, or inanimate things in this manner. Examples include "Big business lacks a soul," "The hand of government reaches deep into everyone's pockets," or "Democracy cries out for citizen participation in the electoral process."

Potentially the most dangerous thing about hypostatization is that it can mask responsibility and become pseudojustification for questionable activity. For example, the highly emotive phrase *national security* has been hypostatized to help account for all manner of suspicious conduct. Thus, we have had wiretaps, burglaries, and illicit payoffs that supposedly were conducted because national security "demanded" such actions. Likewise, for several years in the late 1960s and early 1970s, U.S. pilots were bombing Cambodia, although government representatives were telling the people and Congress that no such bombing was occurring. Later, when the truth came out, government officials said that national security had "demanded" the bombing and the secrecy.

240

But government spokespeople are not the only ones who like to employ hypostatization regularly. Madison Avenue advertising executives seem to have elevated hypostatization to a new level of consumer manipulation with the introduction of "brand personality." Brand personality refers to how a brand makes people feel about it, rather than what the qualities or virtues of the brand are. Some agencies and their clients believe that brand personality is what separates exceptional advertising from the ordinary. By their account, Marlboro has brand personality, and Pall Mall does not. Charmin toilet paper does, too; but Scot Tissue doesn't.

Before it can be shaped, we are told, a brand personality must be defined. So, some agencies are trying to describe their products as people. Jell-O, for example, "is that very nice lady who lives next door," says Joseph Plummer, research director at Young & Rubicam, the product's agency. "She's not too old fashioned, loves children and dogs, and has a little streak of creativity, but isn't avant-garde."[5]

Once a personality is defined, it can be used to determine such features as the advertisements' tone, participants, and locales. Thus, in keeping with Oil of Olay's "character," which is described as "a little sophisticated, foreign, mysterious, and slightly exotic," Young & Rubicam executives design exotic settings and focus most skin care products on a model.

In brief, by developing brand personalities, advertisers treat their products as people that consumers can look on as buddies or pals. As one executive puts it, brand personality, when properly developed, results "not just in 'purchase motivation' but in a friendship between product and the consumer.[6]

EXAMPLE: "Our sensitive child. Among all our children the Pinot Chardonnay grapes are perhaps the most delicate. Shy and temperamental, they do poorly in most climates. Yet, here in the Almaden Vineyards in Northern California, warmed by the sun and cooled by the night breezes of the Pacific, they ripen to an abundant perfection. Pinot Chardonnay grapes—we coddle them, nurture them, encourage them along. The result is a most distinguished white wine. Golden in color, full-bodied, fragrant and smooth. A wine reminiscent of the great still champagnes. Yes, we are proud parents." (Advertisement for Almaden Vineyards.)

COMMENT: The image of a helpless child being nurtured by loving parents is hard to resist. The ad makes it sound as if you're adopting a baby, not buying a wine. Don't be conned: By any

[5]Bill Abrams. "Admen Say 'Brand Personality Is As Critical As the Product.' " *The Wall Street Journal*, August 13, 1981, p. 25.
[6]Ibid., p. 25.

other name or description, the fermented juice of grapes is still wine. If you want a child, you'll have to go through conventional channels.

Exercise

7.8 Create a brand personality for some product. Write a paragraph in which you develop the personality as part of an advertising campaign.

COMPOSITION

The fallacy of composition consists of reasoning improperly from a property of a member of a group to a property of the group itself. For example, a man observes that every member of a local club is wealthy and infers that the club itself must be wealthy. But it may not be.

What the man fails to realize is that a whole represents something different from simply the sum or the combination of its parts. The whole either takes on a new character because of its composition or at least does not maintain the particular character of its parts. Thus, each chapter of a book considered individually may be a masterpiece; but the book, considered as a whole, may not be. Each member of an orchestra may be an outstanding musician, but that doesn't imply that the orchestra as a whole is outstanding. People who commit the composition fallacy ignore or forget that integration of the parts often alters the character of the whole.

> EXAMPLE: *"Should we not assume that just as the eye, the hand, the foot, and in general each part of the body clearly has its own proper function, so man too has some function over and above the function of his parts?" (Aristotle. Nicomachean Ethics. Trans. Martin Ostwald. Indianapolis: Bobbs-Merrill, 1962, p. 16.)*

> COMMENT: *No, we shouldn't. That the parts of a human have a function does not necessarily mean that the human being has a function.*

DIVISION

The fallacy of division, the converse of the composition fallacy, consists of reasoning improperly from a quality of the group to a quality of a member of the group. Observing that a club is wealthy, a man infers that each club member must be wealthy or that a particular member must be wealthy. But just as a property of the part does not imply a property of the whole, so a quality of the whole doesn't imply a quality of the part. That a book is a masterpiece does not mean that each chapter is; that an orchestra is outstanding does not imply that each member is an outstanding musician.

EXAMPLE: *"Historian Vernon Parrington often committed this mistake in his great Main Currents of American Thought, where he formed the habit of conceptualizing a problem in group stereotypes and transferring the stereotypes to individual members. Thus,*

> *Most Calvinists were theological determinists. Most New England Puritans were Calvinists. Therefore, most New England Puritans were theological determinists.*
> *The fortunes of the Federalists decayed after 1880. Joseph Dennie was a Federalist.*
> *Therefore, the fortunes of Joseph Dennie decayed after 1800."*

(David Hackett Fischer. Historians' Fallacies. *New York: Harper & Row, 1970, p. 222.)*

CONTENT: *As the author indicates, a good deal of scholarship indicates that the New England Puritans were not determinists or at least were determinists with a difference. Again, simply because the fortunes of the Federalists as a group waned after 1800 doesn't mean that the fortunes of one of the members did. In a sense, stereotyping can indeed be viewed as a variation of the division fallacy.*

SUMMARY

Fallacies of ambiguity are commonplace errors in reasoning that we fall into because of careless use of language. Much ambiguity takes root in the use of emotive language—that is, language with positive or negative overtones. In argument, people exploit the emotive side of language by (1) masking literal meaning by so exciting emotions that reason gets overlooked, (2) masking literal meaning by using unintelligible language such as jargon, and (3) masking what may otherwise be unacceptable by using emotively neutral terms (euphemisms). The point of becoming familiar with the emotive side of language is not to dismiss its literary or persuasive value but to learn how to detect and avoid arguments that would use emotive language to persuade illegitimately.

The following are the more common fallacies of ambiguity:

1. **Semantical ambiguity:** using a word or phrase that can easily be

interpreted in two or more ways without making clear which meaning is intended.   EXAMPLE: "I just got a *new* car."

2. **Equivocation:** drawing an unwarranted conclusion by using a word or phrase in two different senses in the same argument.   EXAMPLE: "The *end* of anything is its perfection. Since death is the *end* of life, death must be the perfection of life."

3. **Accent:** drawing an unwarranted conclusion, or directing one to it, on the basis of improper emphasis.   EXAMPLE: "All men are created equal." Should the emphasis be placed on "created" or "equal"?

4. **Innuendo:** drawing or implying a conclusion, usually derogatory, on the basis of words that suggest but do not assert a conclusion (a form of the accent fallacy).   EXAMPLE: A brochure in which a candidate promises to restore honesty and integrity to an office implies that the opponent is dishonest and lacks integrity.

5. **Amphiboly:** making an assertion whose meaning is not clear because of its grammatical construction.   EXAMPLE: "By donating land where an estimated 36 million pages of documents and 880 reels of tape from Nixon's six-year presidency could be housed, university scholars would gain access to a great wealth of research material."

6. **Hypostatization:** making a claim or argument that personifies ideas, concepts, or inanimate objects and thereby creates confusion. EXAMPLE: "The burglaries and wiretaps are justified because national security demanded them."

7. **Composition:** reasoning improperly from a property of a member of a group to a property of the group itself.   EXAMPLE: "Since every member of this club is wealthy, the club must be wealthy also."

8. **Division:** reasoning improperly from a quality of the group to a quality of a member of the group.   EXAMPLE: "Since this club is wealthy, member Jones must be wealthy also."

There is no simple way to avoid fallacies of ambiguity. Writers must be ever vigilant that the meanings that the audience is likely to attach to words and syntax correspond with the meanings that are intended. One way to ensure this is to define key terms, a subject considered in Chapter 6.

Exercise

7.9 *Identify the emotive language (including jargon and euphemism) and fallacies of ambiguity, if any, in the following assertions and arguments:*

1. *Jeff has a most sophisticated grasp of world affairs. So he must be a very sophisticated person.*

2. **Bill:** *I think I have a very good chance of not getting mugged.*
   Jill: *Why do you say that?*
   Bill: *Because one out of two people in this city can expect to get mugged each year.*
   Jill: *I don't follow.*
   Bill: *Well, I've already been mugged this year.*

3. Notice: The gymnasium will be available to students only between 3 P.M. and 5 P.M.

4. It's absurd to say that poverty is a problem for the United States. Just think: the United States is the wealthiest nation on earth.

5. It's abundantly clear that the human race must someday come to an end, for all humans are mortals.

6. The Bible says to return good for evil. But Connie has never done me any evil. So, it'll be OK to play a dirty trick or two on her.

7. "Can the universe think about itself? We know that at least one part of it can: we ourselves. Is it not reasonable to conclude the whole can?" (Jose Silva. The Silva Mind Control Method. New York: Pocket Books, 1978, p. 116.)

8. "Maker's Mark is the most searched for whiskey in America. . . . If any other whiskey wants to refute our claim, they're going to have to come up with some four thousand letters." (Advertisement for Maker's Mark.)

9. "Givenchy's greatest creation for women. Gentlemen." (Advertisement for Givenchy Gentlemen eau de toilette.)

10. A Labor Department official agreed to an interview on the condition that the newspaper would not print his name. The next day the newspaper printed the interview, with an accompanying photograph that carried a most unusual caption: "Labor official who briefed reporters under the condition that his name not be used."

11. Former Secretary of the Treasury William Simon, commenting on inflation: "This has been here for twenty years and with every year that goes by it's going to take strong medicine to solve it. But it's been turned into a national disgrace by the demagogues who hope it will go away like some magic wand. And a hostile press has convinced the people it was a ripoff by the so-called giant oil companies. . . . It's typical of the neanderthal type of thinking on the hill [that is, in Congress]. Inflation is somebody else's fault. It's not their fault. They're trying to help people. Well, they are putting out the programs that hurt the very people they are trying to help; that hurt the poor and the tired through insidious inflation." ("Simon: Answer 'Free Enterprise'." Bakersfield Californian, September 23, 1976, p. 3.)

12. "Yokohama Steel Radials are tough! . . . This means superior steel radial tires that give you: Better cornering. Better traction. Better control.

Greater protection against road hazards. Longer tread wear. Better gas mileage." (Advertisement for Yokohama tires.)

13. "Great Southern just introduced one of the most exciting life insurance programs the industry has ever seen . . . Lifetime Life. Lifetime Life offers Great Southern's clients total flexibility in deciding on variable amounts of coverage, cash withdrawals, skipping premium payments, while earning interest on policy funds at current market rates—and lots more. . . . Great Southern is an important and exciting part of NLT. A corporation made up of interesting people doing interesting things. And always doing them a little better than they're expected to." (Advertisement for NLT.)

14. "The Minolta EP 520 copier has the capacity to put in a lot of overtime without a lot of trouble. And it takes options to help a growing business handle work overloads. Like a document-feeder and sorter, or a counter to keep track of the copies you've made." (Minolta advertisement.)

15. In order to unify and strengthen China, Chairman Mao used to conduct "purification" campaigns, events that in the last decade of his life became marred by violence and irrationality—especially evidenced in the cataclysmic Cultural Revolution of 1966–1969. These campaigns meant death or imprisonment for many thousands of people. Idi Amin of Uganda also sent thousands to their deaths at the hands of the "Public Safety Unit," the dreaded murder squad during his reign.

16. Newspaper headline: "VD Spread Tops State Efforts."

17. "Well, I condemn the [Watergate] cover-up of virtue. I don't mind if they bring up and reject the cover-up of Watergate. Nixon was wrong to try to help his friends and to cover up for them. But we are wrong to cover up our salvation which we owe to Nixon." (Rabbi Baruch Korff, confidant of former President Richard Nixon, at a speech to the U.S. Citizens Congress in Mission Hills, Kansas, 1976.)

18. "Filthy speech leads to filthy views of humanity. It is a short step from acceptance of brutal speech to participation in brutal treatment of human beings." (Brutalization of Language." Bakersfield Californian, October 19, 1976, p. 20.)

19. **Caroline:** Let's get a Canon copier for the office.
Sandy: Why?
Caroline: Because it gives you better copies than any other copier available.
Sandy: Really? How do you know?
Caroline: Look at this ad. It says: "Twenty-one companies can give you plain paper copiers. Nobody can give you better ones than Canon."
Sandy: Wow! Let's requisition a Canon!
(Quote from an advertisement for Canon copiers.)

20. Bumper sticker: "Stand up to authority!"

21. "The Duke yet lives that Henry shall depose." (Shakespeare. Henry VI, Part II, act 1, sc. 3.)

22. "You might not know it but cigarette smoke is mostly gas—many different kinds. Not just 'tar' and nicotine. And despite what we tobacco people think, some critics of smoking say it's just as important to cut down on some of the gases as it is to lower 'tar' and nicotine." (Advertisement for Fact cigarettes.)

23. Newspaper headline: "Karen Quinlan Critical." The story reports: "Miss Quinlan, who has been in a coma since April 15, 1975, remains in the same condition which has been listed as 'critical' ever since she took a combination of tranquilizers and alcohol."

24. "A foreigner visiting Oxford or Cambridge for the first time is shown a number of colleges, libraries, playing fields, museums, scientific departments and administrative offices. He then asks, 'But where is the University? I have seen where the members of the College live, where the Registrar works, where scientists experiment and the rest. But I have not seen the University in which reside and work the members of your University!" (Gilbert Ryle. The Concept of Mind. New York: Barnes & Noble, 1949, p. 16.)

25. "Nature might stand up
    And say to all the world, 'This was a man!' "
    (Shakespeare. Julius Caesar, act 5, sc. 5.)

26. "The pawnbroker thrives on the irregularities of youth; the merchant on a scarcity of goods; the architect and contractor on the destruction of buildings; lawyers and judges on disputes and illegalities; the military on war; physicians on sickness, and morticians on death. If, then, we have more profligacy, destruction, lawlessness, war, disease, and death, we shall have unparalleled prosperity." (Michel de Montaigne. "That One Man's Profit Is Another's Loss." The Complete Works of Montaigne. Trans. Donald M. Jrame. Stanford, Calif.: Stanford University Press, 1957, pp. 72–77.)

27. "No reason can be given why the general happiness is desirable, except that each person, so far as he believes it to be attainable, desires his own happiness. This, however, being a fact, we have not only all the proof which the case admits of, but all which it is possible to require, that happiness is a good, that each person's happiness is a good and that each person's happiness is a good to that person, and the general happiness, therefore, a good to the aggregate of persons." (John Stuart Mill. Utilitarianism. Ed. Oskar Piest. Indianapolis: Bobbs-Merrill, 1957, pp. 44–45.)

ADDITIONAL EXERCISES
BASED ON READINGS

"Morality and Manipulation: Which Will Wither First, the New Right or the Bill of Rights?" by Birch Bayh (Chapter 3)

1. In paragraph 2 Bayh puts "conservative" in quotation marks. Why? Is the effect an innuendo?
2. Identify all uses of emotive language in the essay.
3. In paragraph 2 Bayh defines "single issue" politics. What kinds of definition does he offer—denotative, logical, stipulative, or persuasive?

"Human Rights: No More Small Men" by Michael Novak (Chapter 3)

1. Do paragraphs 4 and 5 employ innuendo?
2. Does Novak commit the composition fallacy in paragraph 16?
3. Write a one-sentence connotation of "limited state" based on the author's definition expressed in paragraphs 7 and 8. Evaluate Novak's definition in terms of the criteria for a good logical definition.
4. Does the author commit the fallacy of persuasive definition in paragraph 7?
5. What kind of definition does Novak give in paragraph 10? Does the definition sufficiently illuminate the term?

"Abscam's Ominous Legacy: Videotapes Can Convict As Surely As a Jury" by Richard Reeves (Chapter 3)

1. Identify all uses of emotive language.
2. In the first sentence of paragraph 10 Reeves writes: "The people who go to security-industry trade shows seem different from me and you." Could the same thing be said of people who go to aircraft, antique, comic book, or Mary Kay cosmetics shows? If so, is the author exploiting accent, and does the ambiguity of "different" result in innuendo?
3. Do you think that Reeves uses innuendo in reporting his encounter with the demonstrator of the voice stress analyzer (paragraph 10)?
4. The author uses "convict" in paragraphs 12 and 13. Does the term carry the same meaning each time?

"Is Business Bluffing Ethical?"
by Albert Carr (Chapter 4)

1. What does Carr mean by "bluffing" in a business situation? Do you think that *bluffing* carries the same meaning in poker, as Carr suggests; or has he shifted the meaning, thereby equivocating?
2. Carr uses "right" in referring to poker (paragraph 3) and business (paragraph 6). Is the meaning of "right" identical in each case, or has the meaning shifted, thereby producing equivocation?

"Lifeboat Ethics: The Case Against Helping the Poor"
by Garrett Hardin (Chapter 4)

1. Is the phrase "misguided idealists" (paragraph 2) emotive?
2. Is there a division fallacy in paragraph 4?
3. Do you think that "safety factor" (paragraph 7) as applied to a lifeboat carries the same meaning as when applied to a country's agriculture? Or is Hardin guilty of equivocation?
4. In paragraph 7 Hardin raises an important question about distributive justice—that is, who should get what. How do we decide which ten persons to allow into the lifeboat? Hardin suggests possible standards for deciding: merit ("the best ten"), need ("the neediest ten"), and chronological order ("first come, first served"). He expresses these possible standards in the form of questions that themselves are sandwiched between two other questions: "But what ten do we let in?" and "And what do we say to the ninety we exclude?" Is the effect of these two questions to suggest, by innuendo, that a fair determination of who should come aboard is impossible? If so, does it follow that a fair distribution, therefore, poses an insoluble problem or, certainly, one that society should avoid?

"Censorship: It's 'a Choking Grip'"
by Isaac Asimov (Chapter 4)

1. Identify all emotive language.
2. In paragraph 6 Asimov offers a partial description of a "healthy society." What kind of definition is it—stipulative or persuasive?
3. What denotations of an "unhealthy society" does Asimov give?

"The News Junkies" by Robert MacKenzie (Chapter 5)

1. Does MacKenzie rely on innuendo in paragraphs 7 and 8?
2. Identify every instance of emotive language.

"Teen Pregnancies Involve More than Sex"
by Caryl Rivers (Chapter 5)

1. Identify all semantical ambiguity.

"Cop-Out Realism" by Norman Cousins (Chapter 6)

1. Does Cousins use any emotive language?
2. Does he use innuendo in paragraph 11? Explain.

"The Hostages Are Special, but No Heroes—
Let's Not Be Cruel"
by Herbert Gold (Chapter 6)

1. Does Gold use any emotive language?

"The Burnout of Almost Everyone"
by Lance Morrow (Chapter 6)

1. Identify all semantical ambiguity.
2. Identify all uses of figurative language. Do you think the figurative language impedes understanding?

8. Presumption

*I*n the preceding chapter we considered commonplace errors in reasoning that we fall into because of careless use of language. In this chapter and the following one we examine commonplace errors that result from inattention to subject matter.

To begin, suppose you came across the following argument. Would it convince you that the United States should return to the gold standard?

> Thus the real value of gold is something no government can tinker with, proponents of the gold standard say. If the U.S. hooked its money supply to its stores of bullion, the dollar would be firmly anchored. The amount of money in circulation can grow only as the government stockpile grows. No more sudden surges when the Federal Reserve Board loses its grip. No more political pressure to pay for

the national debt by simply starting the printing presses. The money supply will be out of the government's hands, and the dollar will be as good as gold once again.[1]

Sounds pretty good, doesn't it? Before accepting the argument, though, you might want to think about the following objections: (1) It would be difficult pegging the correct price of gold convertibility. For example, when Britain returned to the gold standard after World War I, it picked an unrealistic figure and, consequently, suffered a recession in part caused by the resulting shrinkage in the money supply. (2) Gold is not necessarily stable. Gold prices fluctuate, and the money supply would have to follow along behind. (3) A gold standard might make the United States vulnerable to political pressure from South Africa and the Soviet Union, the world's two principal producers of the metal. (4) If the gold supply didn't grow fast enough, U.S. economic growth could be permanently grounded.

Aware of these objections, you might think twice about the merits of the stated argument. Of course, the passage didn't include these facts. That isn't surprising; in their enthusiasm to advance a contention, arguers sometimes ignore or conceal significant information that weakens their position. An argument that does this commits a fallacy that falls under the heading of *presumption.*

This chapter deals with fallacies of presumption, one group of errors that result from inattention to subject matter. The category of presumption includes fallacies in which facts relevant to an argument have not been represented correctly in the premises; it also includes fallacies in which the premises are based on questionable, although sometimes popular, principles or assumptions. The fallacy of concealed evidence is only one of many common fallacies of presumption that we take up in this chapter. A knowledge of these will help you detect them in your reading and avoid them in your writing.

MISAPPLIED GENERALIZATION

The fallacy of misapplied generalization consists of assuming that what is true under certain conditions must be true under all conditions. Consider this argument: "All citizens in the United States have the right to travel where they want. Therefore, if a convicted murderer wants to leave prison, the authorities have no right to stop him." The first premise in this argument is a general principle that we usually accept. But it doesn't apply to the specific case of a convicted murderer. Applying a generalization to an unusual or atypical specific results in the fallacy of misapplied generalization.

---

[1]Peter Grief. "Panel Poring over Gold with New Monetary Use in Mind." *Christian Science Monitor*, September 4, 1981, p. 14.

Here is a more serious, though similarly flawed, argument advanced by some people who protest the administration of powerful drugs to the terminally ill. "Since narcotics are addictive, they will addict the terminally ill patient. Therefore, they should not be administered." Although narcotics can be habit forming, they need not be. Under carefully supervised conditions, as in a medical context, narcotics can be used effectively with no addictive effect. Indeed, studies conducted in institutions that specialize in the care of the terminally ill indicate that addiction rarely if ever results from the administration of narcotics, even of the most powerful ones.

The fallacy of misapplied generalization should be distinguished from the fallacy of division. As we have just seen, in misapplying a generalization the arguer insists that, since most members of a class have a specific property, any member of the class must also have that property, even though it is an exception. With the misapplied generalization, then, we are always talking about *individual class members*.

By contrast, in the fallacy of division arguers insist that, since the *class itself* has a specific property, any member of the class must also have that property. An example of each fallacy should clarify the difference:

MISAPPLIED   Since most union members are Democrats, union member
GENERALIZATION: Grey must be a Democrat.

DIVISION   Since the union is supporting the Democratic nominee,
FALLACY: union member Grey must be supporting the Democratic
candidate.

In the misapplied generalization, the faulty reasoning moves from a statement about the *members* of a class to a statement about an individual member of it. In the division example, the movement is from a statement about the *class itself* to a statement about one of its members.

Here's a final example of the misapplied generalization, with comment:

EXAMPLE: On a September day in 1980 eight people walked into the Norristown, Pennsylvania munitions plant of the General Electric Company, a major contractor for nuclear weapons. They went to a nose cone for a nuclear missile and, with hammers in hand, began beating it into a plowshare. Then they poured human blood on equipment and classified documents. Initial charges against the group, which included the Reverend Daniel J. Berrigan, included carrying out violence and making terroristic threats; but these were later dropped after some G.E. employees called the group nonviolent and peaceful. In hearing the case Judge Samuel W. Salus said: "The bottom line is that the defendants violated criminal law, and liberty has its bounds." Where-

upon he sentenced Berrigan, his brother, and two other defendants to 3 to 10 years in prison; a fifth defendant to 2 to 5 years; and the remaining three, including a Roman Catholic nun, to 1 1/2 to 5 years. (See Colman McCarthy. "Disobedience Takes Drubbing in Plowshares Eight Case." Los Angeles Times, August 6, 1981, part 2, p. 7.)

COMMENT: *In many quarters the sentences were viewed as harsh because of the special circumstances involved. The defendants' sympathizers pointed out that the eight were no ordinary burglars in intention, appearance, or behavior. But more important, indeed the crux of the defense, was that the defendants were civil disobedients—in this instance, individuals protesting against the manufacturing and spreading of nuclear weapons. In Henry David Thoreau's "Civil Disobedience," citizens of true patriotism are ones who possess the honesty and courage to take action when they believe that their government is acting against the public good. It was in this context, said the apologists of the "Plowshares Eight," that the group had symbolically sought to turn a nuclear weapon into an instrument of peace. In brief, they argued that the special circumstances shrouding the crime warranted a lighter sentence. By contrast, Judge Salus treated this burglary no differently from any other.*

HASTY GENERALIZATION

The fallacy of hasty generalization consists of forming a conclusion based on insufficient evidence or on atypical cases. Sometimes the insufficient evidence in a hasty generalizaion takes the form of an isolated case, which is used to draw the generalization. For example, on the basis of one sour romance, a woman concludes, "No man can be trusted." The sample in question is too small to warrant the generalization.

At other times the insufficient evidence takes the form of several specific cases. Thus, discovering that a few members of the National Organization for Women (NOW) are lesbians, a man concludes, "NOW is made up mostly of lesbians." Again, the sample is far too small to warrant that conclusion.

Just as common is the hasty generalization premised on unusual or atypical cases. This version of the hasty generalization is really the converse of the misapplied generalization. Thus, rather than arguing that prisoners should be allowed unobstructed travel, because all U.S. citizens have the right to go where they want (misapplied generalization), someone argues that the United States is not really committed to the principle of unobstructed travel, because prisoners are not permitted to go where they want. Or, instead of contending that patients under medical supervision will become drug addicts, because narcotics are habit forming (misapplied generalization), someone infers that narcotics aren't really habit forming, because patients taking them under medical supervision rarely become addicted. In the misapplied generalization, arguers try to apply a generalization to an atypical case in order to form a deduction; in the hasty generalization, arguers form an erroneous generalization based on too few atypical cases.

Also, the hasty generalization should be distinguished from the composition fallacy along the same lines that we just distinguished the misapplied generalization from the division fallacy. Thus, in the hasty generalization we argue that, because some members of the group have a specific property, all members of the group do. In the hasty generalization, then, we're speaking about *individual class members.*

By contrast, in the fallacy of composition we argue that, since all members of a class have a specific property, then the *class itself* must have that property. Here's an example of each:

HASTY
GENERALIZATION: *Each of the six union members I met tonight is Democratic. So all the union members must be Democrats.*

COMPOSITION: *Every member of this union supports the Democratic candidate. It follows that this union must be supporting the Democratic candidate.*

Here's an additional example of a hasty generalization:

EXAMPLE: *Sherlock Holmes, forming an impression of Dr. Watson on first meeting: "Here is a gentleman of a medical type, but with the air of a military man. Clearly an army doctor, then. He has just come from the tropics, for his face is dark, and that is not the natural tint of his skin, for his wrists are fair. He has undergone hardship and sickness, as his haggard face says clearly. His left arm has been injured. He holds it in a stiff and unnatural manner. Where in the tropics could an English army doctor have seen much hardship and got his arm wounded? Clearly in Afghanistan." (Arthur Conan Doyle. "A Study in Scarlet." In* The Adventures of Sherlock Holmes. *New York: Berkely Publications, 1963, part 1, ch. 2.)*

COMMENT: *This is Sherlock Holmes at his widely touted, deductive best. Unfortunately, the evidence doesn't warrant any of Holmes's inferences. Certainly Watson could have a military bearing without ever having been in the military, let alone having been a military doctor. And surely old Watson needn't have acquired his tan in the tropics. And un-*

doubtedly a "haggard face" doesn't always mean "hardship and sickness"; nor does holding the arm in a "stiff and unnatural manner" always stem from an injury. Nonetheless, Holmes not only forms these hasty generalizations but also uses them as the basis for his coup de grace—the hasty generalization that Watson was in Afghanistan! Although it is true that the master detective's conclusions were correct, that in no way rescues his generalizations from the realm of the premature.

Exercises

8.1 Write a generalization about each of the following topics. Then show how the generalization could be misapplied: smoking, television, teachers, contemporary movies, early marriage, exercise.

8.2 Examine three beliefs that you hold (e.g., about dating, education, teachers, members of the opposite sex, politicians, etc.) After seriously examining the bases for these beliefs, would you say that they are or are not hasty generalizations?

QUESTIONABLE   CLASSIFICATION

The fallacy of questionable classification consists of categorizing somebody or something on the basis of insufficient evidence. For example, on hearing that his daughter plans to quit school to marry, a father calls her "rebellious." Although she may be rebellious, quitting school to marry is hardly enough evidence to warrant that classification.

Perhaps the most fertile soil for the weed of questionable classification is politics. Just think of the variety of political labels we attach to people: "liberal," "conservative," "moderate," "radical," "reactionary," "progressive," "revisitionist." Frequently these labels are applied thoughtlessly and without warrant.

But questionable labels are not confined to politics. In everyday affairs we classify with dronelike industry. Thus, a woman who supports equal rights for women is called a "women's liberationist." A man who opposes abortion on demand is a "male chauvinist." Anyone for honesty in advertising is considered a "consumer advocate." An athlete is automatically a "jock."

When we lack the evidence for these labels, we commit the fallacy of questionable classification.

The danger of classification generally, and of questionable classification in particular, is that in classifying we tend to view things in just one aspect. Thus, while it's true that Gloria Steinem may be a "women's liberationist," she also is a "voter," "licensed driver," "taxpayer," "consumer," and so on. Seeing her strictly in terms of a single class, we may form an incomplete and inaccurate perception of her.

This doesn't mean that classification should be avoided. On the contrary, as with any generalizing we classify to simplify and order our lives. The psychologist Gordon Allport puts it this way: "Classification brings many grains of sand into a single pail."[2] Without classification, then, our lives would be an empirical sand heap. But Allport also reminds us that classification tends to disregard "the fact that the same grains might have fitted as appropriately in another pail."[3]

Since classification is tricky, writers must be very careful about labeling. Sometimes we have enough evidence for our classifications. At other times, in trying to see simplicity or order in what is complex and disorderly, we classify in a questionable way.

Here are two more examples of questionable classification, with comment:

EXAMPLE: *In sentencing the Plowshares Eight, Judge Salus called them "malcontents."*

COMMENT: *Does acting on grounds of conscience qualify one as a malcontent? If so, the class of malcontent includes such luminaries as Jesus, Socrates, Thoreau, Mahatma Ghandi, the Reverend Dr. Martin Luther King, Jr., and no doubt a galaxy of lesser lights.*

EXAMPLE: *When the Senate Foreign Relations Committee examined William P. Clark, President Reagan's candidate for deputy secretary of state, it was disappointed. Clark didn't seem to know what he should. Indeed, some members found Clark's apparent ignorance shocking. What disturbed them was that Clark couldn't name the prime ministers of South Africa (Pieter W. Botha) or Zimbabwe (Robert Mugabe). Nor did Clark know the names of the European nations reluctant to have tactical nuclear weapons on their soil (Belgium and the Netherlands). Besides, Clark wasn't aware of what was happening in the British Labor Party, which was then split*

[2]Gordon Allport. *The Nature of Prejudice.* Reading, Mass.: Addison-Wesley, 1954, p. 178.
[3]Ibid., p. 178.

by an ideological struggle between left-wing and moderate forces. Despite his lack of knowledge, Clark did have his defenders. One, Senator Nancy L. Kassenbaum, Republican of Kansas, protested, "This is not supposed to be a Foreign Service exam." (See William J. Eaton. "Clark Unqualified for State Department Post, Democrats Say." Los Angeles Times, February 5, 1981, part 1, p. 1.)

COMMENT: *The pejorative categorization of the questions as a "Foreign Service exam" is highly questionable. As some committee members pointed out, Clark at times was to be a stand-in for the secretary of state. This requires an intimate grasp of international affairs, which presupposes a knowledge of basic facts (for example, the names of world leaders or a country's internal problems that could undercut U.S. security). The committee's questions, in fact, might more accurately be termed "soft," insofar as the members seemed to be probing for evidence of a general knowledge and not a profound mastery.*

BEGGING THE QUESTION

The fallacy of begging the question consists of asserting in the premises what is asserted in the conclusion. Sometimes begging the question takes a most transparent form, as when the premise is merely a restatement of the conclusion. For example, Myra asserts that pornographic films are "objectionable," because they are "immoral." But by definition what is immoral is objectionable. Thus, Myra's premise says exactly what her conclusion does. It's as if she had said, "Pornographic films are immoral, because they are immoral."

Again, Ted insists, "User's fees should be tacked onto the purchases of certain goods and services, because that would generate tax revenue." But a user's fee is a tax. So, Ted's premise, like Myra's, is asserting what the conclusion asserts. It's as if he had said, "Taxes should be tacked onto the purchase of certain goods and services, because that would generate tax revenue."

Such arguments, which involve *circular reasoning*, say nothing more than "A is true, because A is true." Although circular arguments may be formally valid (that is, the premises may logically entail the conclusion), such arguments are not sound, because at least one of the premises is as doubtful as the conclusion. That premise cannot logically support the conclusion, although the arguer presumes that it does.

Not all cases of begging the question involve circularity. Often arguers will use evaluative terms or phrases as if they were purely descriptive ones, in order to sway an audience about an issue or situation. For example, in arguing

against abortion someone says, "A baby shouldn't have to suffer and die at the mother's convenience." By calling the fetus a "baby," the arguer implies that it is a human being, an assumption that is hotly contested in abortion debates. Similarly, another person asserts that the student-loan program should be continued, even expanded, because "the right to higher education should not be denied a person for financial reasons." But is the opportunity for higher education a "right"? The speaker, in effect, is asking the audience to accept without proof that higher education is a right. Here are two other examples of begging the question, with comment:

EXAMPLE: **Fred:** God exists.
Fran: How do you know?
Fred: Because it says so in the Bible.
Frank: But maybe the Bible's wrong.
Fred: That's impossible. The Bible is the inspired word of God.
Fran: Hmm, that's a good point.

COMMENT: Logically, it's a bad point. The reasoning is circular. Fred's premise, that the Bible is the inspired word of God, assumes what is to be proved: that God exists.

EXAMPLE: **Tom:** How do you account for the senator's dramatic, come-from-behind victory?
Tish: One big factor is that his campaign was on the rise.
Tom: You mean it had momentum?
Tish: Exactly.

COMMENT: Obviously, a "come-from-behind victory" presupposes a campaign that was "on the rise" and had "momentum." So, to explain such a victory in those terms is to assert what a "come-from-behind victory" itself asserts.

EVADING THE ISSUE

Evading the issue consists of ignoring all or part of an issue. One way to do this is to wander from the point long enough to distract attention from the fact that the issue has been evaded; another way is to seem to address the issue while really skirting it.

For example, a candidate for public office is asked whether she thinks government employees should have the right to strike. Her answer: "The right to strike is not really a political decision. It is something that needs to be thrashed out between labor and management. In the case of public employees, of course, management is the government. So, in answer to your question, I'd say that federal employees, through their representative bodies, need to resolve this issue with government officials." There's no way of knowing where the candidate stands on the issue, for she's evaded the question. Here's another example of evading the issue, with comment:

> EXAMPLE: *Interior Secretary James G. Watt, responding to a question about his possible inability to operate in the face of mounting criticism: "I have one loyalty and that's to the President and to the oath of office and to the American people. The criticism I knew would come with a change of government. We represent a change in philosophy . . . and we recognize that there will be a segment that opposed the President's election, opposed my nomination and will faithfully oppose most of my actions." (Eleanor Randolph. "Watt Rejects Environmentalists' Demand for His Resignation." Los Angeles Times, July 16, 1981, part 1, p. 7.)*

> COMMENT: *Watt has sidestepped the issue, which is whether widespread criticism will hamper his ability to operate. As he*

does, he also wrongly characterizes the sources of the criticism; some of it came from conservative Republicans and organizations such as the National Wildlife Federation, whose members voted two to one for Reagan. In dismissing the criticism by discrediting its sources, Watt also commits the genetic fallacy, which will be considered in the next chapter.

Exercise

8.3 Pretend you are a reporter interviewing a local official about some current issue. Write a short dialogue which illustrates the skill with which the official evades the issue.

IS/OUGHT

The fallacy of is/ought consists of assuming that, because something is the case, it ought to be the case or that, because something is not the case, it ought not to be the case. The is/ought fallacy usually arises with assertions about value or social policy.

For example, a teenager reasons, "It's all right for me to have premarital sex, because all my friends do it." A mother tells her son: "Certainly, there's something wrong with growing marijuana for sale. If there weren't, it wouldn't be illegal." A nurse tells a colleague: "Nurses really shouldn't strike. After all, very few of our profession ever do or even have an interest in that sort of thing." In each case someone fallaciously reasons that the status quo should be maintained simply because it is the status quo or that something is right or proper simply because it is engaged in by many people. In brief, the reasoning moves from what is the case to what ought to be the case.

EXAMPLE: *Philosophy professor Peter A. Bertocci, raising one of the common arguments against sexual control: "And my reader might add: Are you sure that all the fuss you are making about sexual control, yes, even as a means to a fuller love relation, is worth the bother? Since sex is so recurrent in human life would it not be better to remove the bars at this point and let the individuals (and society) use the energy now spent in combating 'sexual license' for other desirable personal and social objectives? If we are actually pitting individuals against a drive that in their ripening years is a*

261

constant thorn in their sides, are we not really flagellating them unnecessarily? Why not make legal and acceptable what so many people are now doing covertly, and at the expense of an artificially created bad conscience?" (Peter A. Bertocci. The Human Venture in Sex, Love and Marriage. Chicago: Association Press/Follett Publishing, 1949, p. 70.)

COMMENT: *The thrust of this argument, which Bertocci objects to, is that, since so many people are having sex for its own sake, then sex for its own sake should receive social and legal approval. But the fact that many people engage in sex for its own sake does not make it right, nor does it mean that society ought to approve of it. Perhaps such behavior is undesirable, both personally and socially. By the same token, simply because society may not approve of having sex for its own sake does not necessarily mean that such behavior is bad or that it should be prohibited.*

WISHFUL THINKING

The fallacy of wishful thinking consists of assuming that, because we want something to be the case, it is or will be the case. For example, suppose that someone argued that there is life after death as follows: "There must be life after death. If not, why would everyone desire it? The historical record is crystal clear on this point: No matter who the people, when or where they lived, they have always thirsted for immortality. What better evidence for believing in life after death?"

Although the wish for immortality may be universal, that in itself does not prove that life exists after death. Our universal desire conceivably could go unsatisfied. Most of us probably desire more wealth and social recognition than we have. But mere wanting does not make us richer or more widely known and admired. That all the nations of the world may desire world peace and international harmony does not ensure such a blissful state.

In a sense wishful thinking is the opposite of the is/ought fallacy. Rather than assuming that what is the case ought to be the case, the wishful thinker assumes that what ought to be the case *is* the case. But the inference from *ought* to *is* is no more valid than that from *is* to *ought*.

Sometimes the fallacy of wishful thinking appeals to the power of the human will to overcome any obstacle. Here's a typical example: "If people really wanted to, they could find jobs." Undoubtedly some people are malingerers. But it seems wishful thinking, even escapism, to presume that any unemployed person could find work if he or she really tried. Again, a father tells his industrious but academically mediocre son, "You could get straight A's if you just applied yourself." Maybe so. But not even heroic application

guarantees superior performance and product. The father so much wants his son to excel that he gives more weight to his own wishful thinking than it may warrant.

EXAMPLE: *President Reagan, urging members of the Future Farmers of America to be optimistic about the nation's future: "Here in Washington, there are a lot of doom-criers, people who think the world is going down. Well, don't you believe it. There's not anything we can't do if we set our minds to it." ("Be Optimistic, Reagan Tells FFA." Los Angeles Times, July 31, 1981, part 1, p. 8.)*

COMMENT: *Although a firm conviction and determined will are needed to solve complex problems, a myriad of things cannot be done by force of will alone. The president assumes that wanting something to be the case will make it so. Of course, such exhortations may inspire creative thinking, new alternatives, and effective action. By the same token, they prime one for deep and bitter disappointment should one's best-laid plans go awry. As the fortune cookie might put it: Skimpy payoff frustrates lofty expectation. Flaky psychology aside, the president's remarks presume that wanting something to be the case will make it so.*

Exercises

8.4 *Construct an is/ought argument for each of the following positions:*

opposed to the legalization of marijuana

263

in favor of the legal right to have an abortion

opposed to handgun control

in favor of the legal right to publish pornographic materials

---

8.5 *Construct a wishful-thinking argument for each of the following issues:*

the existence of extraterrestrial life; the rising crime rate; the increase in divorce; prohibition of hand-guns; increase in political terrorism; increase in teenage pregnancies

---

FALSE DILEMMA

The fallacy of false dilemma consists of erroneously reducing the number of possible positions or alternatives on an issue. For example, not too long ago a sticker adorned the bumpers of many cars: "America—Love It or Leave It!" Underlying this pithy advice was the assumption that one must either support government policy or leave the country. But certainly citizens can love their country enough to be critical of what they see as imprudent policies: Criticism does not logically exclude patriotism. Because a reduction in the number of alternatives often results in only two extreme alternatives, as in this example, the false dilemma is sometimes termed the black-and-white fallacy or false bifurcation. But by any name, the false dilemma remains an erroneous appeal.

Of course, either/or reductions can be legitimate. When two things are genuine contradictories or negatives, they exclude any middle ground. For example, *cold* and *not cold, black* and *not black, conservative* and *nonconservative* are contradictories; they exclude any gradations between their extremes. Accordingly, if the room is cold, it cannot be not cold; if the cloth is black, it cannot be not black; if the politician is a conservative on an issue, the politician cannot be a nonconservative on the same issue.

But contradictories are not to be confused with contraries, which are opposites and thereby allow a number of gradations in between. *Cold* and *hot, black* and *white, conservative* and *liberal* are opposites. There is plenty of middle ground between each term and its opposite. With contradictories (negatives), one of the two extremes must be true and the other false; but with contraries (opposites), both extremes may be false. Thus, the room may be neither hot nor cold, but pleasantly warm. The cloth may be neither black nor white, but green. The politician may be neither conservative nor liberal, but moderate.

False dilemmas result when contraries are treated as contradictories—

264

that is, when opposites are confused with negatives. "If you are not for me," someone says, "you must be against me." Not necessarily. One could be indifferent. *Not for* and *against* are contraries, not contradictories. One may be *not for* and *not against*. But the speaker treats these terms as negatives and thereby commits the fallacy of false dilemma.

Survey questions are notorious for setting up false dilemmas. "Do you think that we should increase or reduce defense spending?" Perhaps the defense budget is just about right. "Should we permit or prohibit the sale of handguns?" Maybe handguns should be sold only under carefully circumscribed conditions—as, for example, when purchasers have a compelling reason to believe that their life is in danger. "Should we support the Israelis or the Arabs in the Middle East? Possibly neither or both equally. So phrased, such questions eliminate the range of alternatives, thereby leading respondents to a predetermined choice of one or the other of the extremes. Just as bad, respondents protesting the questions' illogic are inevitably placed in the *no opinion* category. Since they did have an opinion, such a classification is misrepresentative.

> EXAMPLE: *An examination question: "Write an essay entitled 'Martin Luther King—Idealist or Rebel?' "*
>
> COMMENT: *Defined as "those who conceive of people, things, and conditions as they should be rather than as they are," idealists commonly exhibit rebellious tendencies, such as resistance to authority, control, tradition, and the status quo. Far from being mutually exclusive, then, idealist and rebel may overlap. Indeed, some might say that the active political or social idealist must be rebellious. The question, therefore, poses a false dilemma. So the shrewdest way to respond would be to acknowledge the false dilemma and then demonstrate that King showed both idealistic and rebellious tendencies.*
>
> EXAMPLE: *"At Mercedes Benz, they engineer a great car, without regard to price. Subaru engineers a great car, with regard for price. . . . Subaru and Mercedes, two of the finest engineered cars around. One sells for 8 times the price of the other. The choice is yours." (Advertisement for Subaru.)*
>
> COMMENT: *The advertisement would have us believe that our choice of a well-engineered car reduces to either Mercedes or the cheaper Subaru. No doubt, Ford, G.M., and Chrysler would object to this characterization, and rightly so. The ad is a blatant reduction of many options to just two.*
>
> EXAMPLE: *The lead-in for an article about "Society and Sex Roles":*

"Economics, not biology, may explain male domination."
(Reported in Howard Kahane. Logic and Contemporary
Rhetoric. Belmont, Calif.: Wadsworth, 1980, p. 81.)

COMMENT: Are there just two possible explanations for male domination, biology and economics? What about social custom,
religious conviction, and various combinations of economic and biological factors? The quote invites readers to
ignore other possible explanations and thus commits the
fallacy of false dilemma.

NOVELTY

The fallacy of novelty consists of assuming that something is good simply
because it is new. For example, in the elections of 1980 a number of candidates argued: "It's time for a change" and "Let's try something different." To
many people this meant a change in economic and social philosophy. There
may have been solid reasons for so altering the nation's course, but change for
the sake of change was not one of them. Every policy, law, idea, program, or
action requires justification independent of its novel character. That a politician represents a "new face" or a proposal offers a "new approach" is not a
logical defense, though admittedly it is an appealing one.

Again, during the heated debate on the proposed 1981 federal budget,
critics of the program were often accused of "not wanting to try something
different." Perhaps they were guilty as charged. But should one endorse
something just because it's different or new? The relative novelty of the
program, compared with other budgets of recent decades, did not in itself
prove it was better than the alternatives or that it would work.

EXAMPLE: Copy for an advertisement featuring Leonard Nimoy (television's "Mr. Spock") pictured beside an hourglass in a paint-
ing reminiscent of one by the famed surrealist Salvador
Dali: "The picture of reliability. To Magnavox, it's the idea
that every time you turn on one of our color television sets,
you know it's going to do what you bought it to do.

"Our Star® System color television sets combine advanced design concepts, high technology and new manufacturing systems to deliver the highest level of reliability in
Magnavox history.

"Magnavox. For a picture as reliable as it is bright and
clear. Time after time.

"Magnavox—the brightest ideas in the world are here
today." (Advertisement for Magnavox.)

266

COMMENT: *The beauty of this kind of ad is that it capitalizes on the reasonable assumption that industry spends time, money, and energy developing new products because of the desire to make them better and thus sell more than the competition. But, although it's true that many new things are better, not every new thing is better. The only way to determine whether a particular new product is better than the old ones is to examine the specifics. Unfortunately, this ad lacks specificity. Indeed, even the television set that was shown carried this disclaimer in tiny print beneath it: "Model 4265, 19-inch diagonal measurement with remote control. TV picture and wood-grain cabinet simulated." It's hard to see, then, how this ad is anything more than a strict appeal to novelty.*

SPECIAL PLEADING

The fallacy of special pleading consists of assuming that a person is special and therefore subject to a different standard from the one being proposed. Here are some brief examples:

> "You know, you just can't trust anybody today. I peeked at my roommate's diary the other night, and you wouldn't believe the nasty stuff she's written about me. And I thought she was my friend!"

> "I know what it means to be generous, but Charlie is just a spend-thrift."

> "Did you see how dirty the Falcons played us? We played tough, but fair."

In each of these examples the speakers seem to hold someone accountable to a standard to which they claim personal exception.

In the hands of propagandists, special pleading can be highly effective in molding public opinion. Recall the earlier-cited euphemisms that characterized the Vietnam War. The U.S. military and most of the American press employed special pleading in "distinguishing" between the enemy's action and ours. Thus, when the North Vietnamese or Vietcong killed civilians, their actions were often described as "massacres"; the U.S. killings, in contrast, were termed "free-fire-zone actions." When enemy troops moved into Cambodia and Laos, their action was called an "invasion"; the U.S. action was termed an "incursion." Commenting on the double standard implied in this selective use of language, the journalist and student of language Edwin Newman has written:

267

The grim distinction between incursion and invasion was a distinction without a difference, in grammar and in fact. The incursion into, or invasion of, Cambodia in 1970 enormously increased death and destruction there, and the incursion into, or invasion of, Laos increased death and destruction there. It is not the business of news people to exaggerate any of this, but it is not their business to water it down either.[4]

Here are additional examples of special pleading, with comment:

EXAMPLE: **Jeff:** *I used to feel safe about depositing my money in the bank. Not any more. Frankly, I'm just not sure that our banks are sound.*
Joy: *That's a terribly unpatriotic attitude.*
Jeff: *Well, I don't see you making any deposits.*
Joy: *Oh, didn't I tell you? I turned in my dollars for gold and shipped it to Switzerland.*

COMMENT: *Why is it disloyal for Jeff to question the soundness of American banks but not disloyal for Joy to convert her dollars into gold and ship it abroad? Clearly, Joy considers herself special and, therefore, not bound by the same standard of patriotism as Jeff.*

EXAMPLE: *Earlier in the chapter, in the section on questionable classification, I referred to the confirmation hearing for William P. Clark, President Reagan's nominee for deputy secretary of state. In replying to committee charges that he was unqualified for the job, Clark said: "I bring to this committee . . . no formal training in foreign policy. I fully recognize that I must devote myself to accelerated study of substantive issues. I have begun that learning process." (William J. Eaton. "Clark Unqualified for State Department Post, Democrats Say." Los Angeles Times, February 5, 1981, p. 12.)*

COMMENT: *Clark is asking the committee to permit him to learn on the job. Although it's uncertain whether he himself favors this approach to such appointments, it's reasonable to assume that he does not. It also seems fair to assume that the normal standard against which candidates are judged includes a breadth of appropriate knowledge and experience, what Clark terms "formal training." By his own admission, Clark lacks this training, but he begs for special consideration.*

---

[4]Edwin Newman. *Strictly Speaking.* New York: Bobbs-Merrill, 1974, p. 53.

Exercise

8.6 A pre-med student gets a "C" in physiology. Concerned that this grade will hurt her chances of getting into medical school, she writes a brief letter to her instructor asking for reconsideration. The letter consists largely of special pleading. Pretend you are that student and write such a letter.

INCONSISTENCY

The fallacy of inconsistency consists of using contradictory premises in an argument. If two premises contradict each other, one must be false. So, even if an argument in which they appear is valid, we should not accept the argument, because it is inconsistent.

The fallacy of inconsistency occurs in several ways. First, arguers may contradict themselves in the same statement. For example, in the summer of 1981 Israel's Prime Minister Menachem Begin ordered the bombing of Beirut, Lebanon. As a result, the United States decided to withhold shipment of F-16 fighter planes to Israel. Commenting on the delay, Deputy Secretaty of State Clark said: "Mr. Begin is without question making it difficult to assist Israel. Our commitment is not to Mr. Begin but to the nation he represents."[5] But if the U.S. commitment was to Israel, why should any action of Begin's have made it difficult to assist Israel? Of course, it's impossible to make a simple distinction between a nation and its leader, as Clark himself later realized when he disavowed any intention to draw such a distinction between Begin and Israel.

Second, inconsistencies can result when people contradict themselves at different times without attempting to justify the change of mind. For example, at first Secretary of State Alexander Haig was reported to be opposed to Clark's appointment as deputy secretary of state. Later he enthusiastically backed him. Similarly, on July 23, 1981, Senator Barry Goldwater said that the director of central intelligence, William J. Casey, should resign or be fired for naming the extremely inexperienced Max Hugel to be the chief of U.S. clandestine intelligence. But just the week before, Goldwater had supported Casey's continuation in the top CIA post despite Hugel's resignation. Goldwater was to change his mind still another time and support Casey's continuation. Why all the turnabouts? Goldwater didn't say.

Third, inconsistencies can arise between words and action. For example, many times during his campaign and after his election President Reagan

---

[5]Oswald Johnston and George Skelton. "Weinberger Puts Blame on Israelis." *Los Angeles Times,* July 23, 1981, part 5, p. 1.

underscored the need for competition and deregulation. But his actions as president sometimes belied his commitment to either. Thus, in its first year the Reagan administration pressured Japan to adopt "voluntary" quotas on automobile imports. The president also appointed Riese H. Taylor to head the Interstate Commerce Commission. By his own admission Taylor was no devotee of deregulation, and, in fact, he was supported by the Teamsters union, which opposed deregulation.

Fourth, inconsistencies can result when people contradict the positions of their institutional affiliation. During his campaign Reagan declared that the United States had become second best militarily to the Soviet Union. About six months after the inauguration, however, Secretary of Defense Caspar Weinberger was warning Congress that the Russians *might* achieve "clear superiority" if they kept building their forces at current rates and if the United States didn't do more. He went on to say: "We will clearly be second in military power to the Soviet Union if the U.S. strategic forces are not improved."[6] Weinberger's views were not consistent with the administration position.

Similarly, on October 17, 1981, a spokesperson for the White House refused to admit that the U.S. economy was in a recession. The very next day Reagan surprised even his closest advisors by acknowledging that the country was indeed in a mild recession. Of course, the aides could not really be faulted, because the president had insisted all along, despite all the standard signs, that the country was not in a recession. Indeed, his October 18 admission was inconsistent with his prior assessments, since the economic facts were essentially the same as they had been for weeks.

CONCEALED EVIDENCE

The fallacy of concealed evidence consists of ignoring, suppressing, or unfairly minimizing evidence unfavorable to an assertion. For example, an investment counselor offers the generalization that municipal bonds, or mutual funds that invest exclusively in them, are good investments because they reduce one's income taxes. What this argument ignores is that (1) interest from municipal bonds is less than that from treasury or corporate bonds; (2) not all such interest may be tax free, since some or all of it may be taxable by the state; (3) municipal bonds carry risks: At one time potential default by New York City and other cities scared off some investors; (4) municipal bonds can be heavily discounted; that is, prices are often less than their face value. So, before investing in municipal bonds because they will reduce your income taxes, consider all the evidence. Otherwise, you may sadly discover that you've been victimized by the fallacy of concealed evidence.

---

[6]"Reagan Defense Buildup." *San Francisco Sunday Examiner and Chronicle*, July 26, 1981, p. A10.

Take as another illustration the Soviet Union's 1978 campaign against neutron weapons in which the Kremlin said that it had the capacity to build a similar weapon but for the time being would not. Presumably, this act of self-restraint was supposed to demonstrate the Soviet commitment to arms limitation and convince the United States to end its flirtation with the neutron bomb. But what the Soviets conveniently omitted was that they had no use for such a weapon, since it is designed to be used against overwhelming tank forces in Western and Eastern Europe.

Again in 1981, when the United States decided to start producing and stockpiling neutron warheads, the Kremlin portrayed neutron weapons as "colonial" or "capitalistic," because they were designed to kill people while sparing property. The Kremlin did not mention, however, that the people whom the United States had in mind were Soviet and Warsaw Pact tank crews, and the property consisted of European cities, including their civilian inhabitants. By the same token, State Department officials seemed to conceal evidence themselves when, announcing the U.S. intention to build neutron bombs, they insisted that the weapons would be produced and stockpiled in the United States but failed to mention that they were intended ultimately to be deployed in Europe.

Writers of argumentative essays are particularly susceptible to the fallacy of concealed evidence. In their zeal to win assent they can easily overlook or suppress damaging evidence. But this is fudging. In developing a position, confront *all* significant evidence. Raise contrary data before critics accuse you of lopsidedness. If your argument is sound, you should be able to rebuff the contrary evidence by showing that your position remains tenable, that the entire weight of evidence on balance supports your claim. Better yet, try to refute the opposed evidence. In any event, raising opposition gives you the appearance of being even handed and fair minded, and that's sure to win points with the audience.

EXAMPLE: *An argument for a bill restricting the giving of discount prices on beer to large wholesale purchasers: Discount prices to large retailers drive out of business "mom-and-pop" stores that so often depend on beer sales for part of their earnings. These stores aren't eligible for the volume discounts, which enable supermarkets to sell beer for lower prices.*

COMMENT: *The argument conceals at least three significant unfavorable points: (1) small stores could form cooperatives for volume purchase; (2) small stores have not gone under because of similar deregulation of wine and liquor sales; (3) small stores often survive more because of their location, hours, and general conveniences than because of their prices.*

271

Exercises

8.7 Show how an argument for or against the following proposals might conceal evidence: sex education in public schools; lie-detector test results as admissible evidence in all cases; tax penalties or "disincentives" for having more than two children; taxing the income and property holdings of religions; students' determining college curricula.

8.8 Report on the concealed evidence in a political speech, an editorial, a letter to the editor of a newspaper or magazine, or an advertisement.

UNKNOWN FACT

The fallacy of unknown fact consists of using premises that are unknowable either in principle or in a particular case. For example, according to James Usher, a sixteenth-century Anglican archbishop, and Dr. John Lightfoot, a seventeenth-century chancellor of St. Catherine's College in Cambridge, the earth was created at 9 A.M. London time, October 23, 4004 B.C. One could hardly take this assertion seriously, for no one can know precisely when creation occurred. (Of course, there's considerable dispute over whether creation, as these clergymen define it, ever occurred.)

Far more common than the mind-boggler that is unknown in principle is the assertion that, in principle, is knowable but probably is not known in a particular case. For example, the makers of Fleischmann's margarine once asserted: "Every fifteen seconds a doctor recommends Fleischmann's margarine." Granting that this assertion may be knowable, it is highly unlikely that Fleischmann knows this for a fact. Imagine the money, time, energy, and personnel it would take to find out. Lacking Fleischmann's method of discovery, we had best consider the assertion an unknown fact.

> EXAMPLE: *"Transportation Secretary Drew Lewis said today he believes the strike has shown there probably are 3,000 to 4,000 more controllers than are needed and that even with large numbers of dismissals the system can be run 'relatively well' for a year or two." ("Dismissal Threat Puts Air Travel in Doubt." Santa Barbara News Press, August 5, 1981, p. A16.)*

> COMMENT: *Lewis voiced this belief on the day after about 13,000 air traffic controllers walked off the job. Consequently, his*

judgment that the strike had shown that 3,000 to 4,000 controllers were not needed was premature. Beyond this, he certainly was in no position to know the status of the system in a year or two, his weasel "relatively well" notwithstanding. In fact, within three months some government officials were admitting that the only way to restore full air service would be to rehire a large number of the 13,000 controllers, who, of course, had been fired after they struck.

EXAMPLE: *"80's strongest investment: Mexico's 50-peso Centenario. . . . Take advantage of the temporary low gold market and protect yourself against inflation." (Advertisement for the International Gold Bullion Exchange appearing in various newspapers and magazines during the summer of 1981.)*

COMMENT: *It is true that in the eighteen months between January 1980 and July 1981 gold lost about half its value. But the International Gold Bullion Exchange couldn't know that the 1981 price of gold would be a "temporary low." Nor could it know that in 1981 gold would be the strongest investment of the 1980s or that gold would be a safeguard against inflation. In fact, during the same eighteen-month period anyone who put $10,000 in, say, treasury notes or saving certificates did far better than someone who invested in gold, inflation notwithstanding.*

TRIVIAL OBJECTIONS

The fallacy of trivial objections consists of trying to defeat a proposal by raising insignificant points against it and failing to weigh in the balance the objections to the alternatives. Jack is in love with Lynn. He thinks he may want to marry her. But on second thought he decides, "I'd better wait until I have a good job." Shortly thereafter, Jack lands a good job with a future and again contemplates marriage. "No," he decides, "I'd better wait until I get more money." When he gets enough money to get married, he then worries that Lynn may reject his proposal. Satisfied that he won't be rebuffed, he wonders whether Lynn is really the woman he wants to marry. We needn't go on with this sorry tale; the point should be clear: Jack will continuously raise objections until he is sure that he will never propose marriage or that, by the time he's ready, Lynn will have found someone else.

Don't misunderstand. This is no plea for hasty marriages or ill-conceived actions. But in the complexity of human affairs, few positions are so well considered, so airtight, that they brook no objections. Quite the reverse: Objections can almost always be raised. The issue, therefore, is which decision or action the weight of evidence suggests—not which of the alternatives is objection free. It is a sad fact of life, but nonetheless a fact, that people often must choose between the lesser of the evils. True, we may reject all proposals, but failure to decide is still a decision, albeit by default.

Opponents of measures often capitalize on the common incapacity to decide in favor of a plan by raising incessant objections until defeat is assured. The job of the audience is to weigh these objections against the objection to the alternatives. When we fail to weigh in the balance the objections to the alternatives, when we harp on comparatively insignificant objections, we commit the fallacy of trivial objections.

EXAMPLE: *In a case decided in 1980 (Richmond Newspapers, Incorporated v. Virginia) the U.S. Supreme Court decided that the First Amendment gives the public an implicit right to have open criminal trials. But some lawyers continue to press for closed proceedings. One of the most common objections to open criminal trials is that they make it difficult, maybe impossible, to establish an atmosphere in which jurors can fully and freely answer questions about their personal life and their feelings about the criminal justice system without embarrassment.*

COMMENT: *Although in some cases open trials might inhibit some jurors, there is the First Amendment to be considered. Are we to elevate the personal feelings of some jurors above the public's constitutional right to have open criminal trials? Again, are we to diminish the principle of open justice because some jurors might be inhibited by public exposure? Finally, and most importantly, are we to consider more important the speculation that open trials produce a chilling judicial atmosphere than the certainty that closed proceedings violate a constitutional right? If this analysis is fair and correct, then this particular argument against open trials fails to weigh in the balance the objections to the alternatives, and it thus commits the fallacy of trivial objections.*

Exercise

8.9 *You have fallen in love with a person of another race. In fact, the two of you are anticipating marriage. When you break the news to your parents, a heated debate erupts in which your parents try to convince you that you're about to make a terrible mistake. Much of their opposition, you feel, is based on trivial objections. In a paragraph or two, recreate your parents' position.*

HYPOTHESIS CONTRARY TO FACT

*The fallacy of hypothesis contrary to fact consists of making a weakly sup-
ported assertion about what might have happened if conditions had been
different or what might happen should certain conditions prevail.* For example, a sportscaster breezily announces, "If Moose had been in the lineup
today, the Bears would have won the game." The hypothesis ("If Moose had
been in the lineup") contradicts the fact that Moose was not in the lineup.
Having contradicted the fact, the sportscaster then draws a certain conclusion. But the conclusion is far from certain. Had Moose been in the lineup, any
number of things still could have happened that would have spelled defeat for
the Bears. True, the Bears might have had a better chance to win with Moose;
but it does not necessarily follow that they would have won. The sportscaster
would speak just as fallaciously by asserting, "If Moose is back in the lineup
next week, the Bears will win."

Again, a student says, "If I only had had more time to study, I would have
passed that test." Maybe so. But as it now stands, the conclusion is unconvinc-
ing because the hypothesis is not of itself sufficient for establishing the
conclusion. The student wants us to accept a contention that contradicts fact
as a basis for a conclusion. But where the contention is weakly supported, as
here, accepting it makes us guilty of the hypothesis contrary to fact.

Of course, there are times when the connection between hypothesis and
assertion, or the context of the assertion, provides strong support for the
assertion. Suppose a doctor tells a patient with syphilis, "If you hadn't come
into contact with someone with venereal disease, you wouldn't have syphilis." Although the doctor's hypothesis contradicts fact (the person has, in fact,
come into contact with a diseased person), the conclusion is warranted,
because direct contact is a necessary condition for syphilis. So the physician's
assertion is legitimate.

Similarly, a lawyer might tell a client who, in a fitful rage, struck someone
and is now being sued: "If you had just kept your temper, you wouldn't be in
this jam." Given the situational context, it's a safe bet that had the client
remained cool, he wouldn't have slugged his adversary and subsequently
been sued.

Whenever we come across or set up a condition that contradicts fact, then,
we must be careful to ensure that the conclusion is warranted. So, in reading
or writing hypotheses contrary to fact, scrutinize the connection between
hypothesis and assertion and the context in which the assertion is made.
Either may provide strong evidence for a conclusion. But where the hypothesis needs support, the conclusion is not warranted, and the fallacy of hypothesis contrary to fact results.

EXAMPLE: *A doctor, commenting on the death of Howard Hughes,
observed that the multimillionaire became addicted to mor-
phine in the hospital and later substituted Emperin and
codeine, injected subcutaneously. According to the doctor,*

the phemacetin in the codeine led to kidney failure and Hughes's death. Regarding Hughes's apparent abuse of these drugs, the doctor said: "He did not have people who knew how to manage his case or he would be alive today running his empire."[7]

COMMENT: Even if Hughes had had people who "knew how to manage his case" with respect to drugs, that would have been no guarantee that he would still be alive. He still could have died from a variety of conditions over which even the best medical attention has no control. Beyond this, who can say that Hughes would still be running his empire? Hughes died in 1976, evidently after thirty years of drug addiction. Assuming that he'd never become addicted to drugs, who is to say what his life-style might have been? As for Hughes's "empire," he might have sold it, turned it over to someone else, bankrupted it, or done any number of things with it. The physician's hypothesis seems weak; additional evidence is needed to support his assertions.

SUMMARY

Fallacies of presumption are arguments in which relevant facts have not been represented correctly in the premises or in which the premises are based on quesionable, although sometimes popular, principles or assumptions. The following are common fallacies of presumption:

1. **Misapplied generalization:** assuming that what is true under certain conditions must be true under all conditions.   EXAMPLE: "Since narcotics are addictive, they will addict the terminally ill patient."

2. **Hasty generalization:** drawing a conclusion based on insufficient evidence or on atypical cases.   EXAMPLE: A person concludes on the basis of one sour romance that no member of the opposite sex can be trusted.

3. **Questionable classification:** categorizing somebody or something on the basis of insufficient evidence.   EXAMPLE: The characterization of a group of civil disobedients as "malcontents."

4. **Begging the question:** asserting in the premises what is asserted in the conclusion.   EXAMPLES: "User's fees should be tacked on to the purchase of certain goods and services, since that would generate tax revenue" (circular reasoning). "A baby shouldn't have to suffer and die at a mother's convenience. Thus, abortion is wrong."

5. **Evading the issue:** ignoring all or part of an issue. EXAMPLE: Interior Secretary Watt's reply to a question about his ability to operate

---

[7]Beverly Beyette. "Anti-Drug Fervor Gone Too Far, Doctor Says." *Los Angeles Times*, July 29, 1981, part 5, p. 1.

in the face of mounting criticism: "I have one loyalty and that's to the President and to the oath of office and to the American people."

6. **Is/ought:** assuming that, because something is the case, it ought to be the case.   EXAMPLE: "Certainly, there's something wrong with growing marijuana for sale. If there weren't, it wouldn't be illegal."

7. **Wishful thinking:** assuming that, because we want something to be the case, it is or will be the case.   EXAMPLE: President Reagan's comment to the Future Farmers of America: "There's not anything we can't do if we set our minds to it."

8. **False dilemma:** erroneously reducing the number of possible positions or alternatives on an issue.   EXAMPLE: "At Mercedes Benz, they engineer a great car, without regard to price. Subaru engineers a great car, with regard for price. . . . Subaru and Mercedes, two of the finest engineered cars around. One sells for 8 times the price of the other. The choice is yours."

9. **Novelty:** assuming that something is good simply because it is new.   EXAMPLE: "The president's budget should be adopted, because it represents a new fiscal philosophy."

10. **Special pleading:** assuming that a person is special and therefore subject to a different standard from the one being proposed. EXAMPLE: William P. Clark, deputy secretary of state: "I bring to this committee . . . no formal training in foreign policy. I fully recognize that I must devote myself to accelerated study of substantive issues. I have begun that learning process."

11. **Inconsistency:** using contradictory premises. Inconsistency can occur when (1) arguers contradict themselves in the same statement, (2) arguers contradict themselves at different times without attempting to justify the change, (3) actions belie words, and (4) people contradict the position of their institutional affiliation.   EXAMPLE: Reagan's espousing of competition and deregulation and then appointing no friend of deregulation, Riese H. Taylor, as head of the Interstate Commerce Commission.

12. **Concealed evidence:** ignoring, suppressing, or unfairly minimizing evidence unfavorable to an assertion.   EXAMPLE: Arguing that municipal bonds are good investments, because they reduce one's income taxes.

13. **Unknown fact:** asserting premises that are unknowable either in principle or in a particular case.   EXAMPLE: Contending in 1981 that Mexico's 50-peso Centario is the strongest investment of the 1980s and that the depressed gold market is only temporary.

14. **Trivial Objections:** seeking to defeat a proposal by raising insignificant points against it and failing to weigh in the balance the objections to the alternatives.   EXAMPLE: Objecting to open criminal trials, because jurors would be reluctant to speak openly.

15. **Hypothesis contrary to fact:** Making a weakly supported assertion

about what might have happened if conditions had been different or what might happen should certain conditions prevail.   EXAMPLE: Arguing that Howard Hughes would be alive today, running his empire, if he had had people who knew how to manage his case.

Exercise

8.10 *Identify the fallacies of presumption, if any, in the following passages. A passage may contain more than one fallacy and possibly even fallacies of ambiguity.*

1. *"According to folk wisdom in many cultures, redheaded people tend to be a bit temperamental. An Israeli researcher believes there may be something to the ancient prejudice. At the Honolulu conference, psychiatrist Michael Bar, of Israel's Shalvata Psychiatric Center, reported a study showing that redheaded children are three or four times more likely than others to develop 'hyperactive syndrome'—whose symptoms include overexcitability, short attention span, quick feelings of frustration, and, usually, excessive aggressiveness.*

   "Bar arrived at his conclusion after matching the behavior of 45 redheaded boys and girls between the ages of six and twelve against that of a control group of nonredheaded kids. Though the evidence was far from conclusive, Bar believes the study points to a genetic connection between red hair and hyperactive behavior." (Time, September 12, 1977.)

2. *"The union's [Professional Air Traffic Controllers Organization] demands were excessive, pointing as they did toward pay and working hours comparable to those of airline pilots, including $10,000 salary increases and 32-hour work weeks."* ("Flying into Rough Weather." Los Angeles Times, August 16, 1981, part 2, p. 6.)

3. *"Mr. Wilson thought I made too much fuss about casualties in Vietnam. 'Now, every man wants to live,' he said. 'But the trouble is we're all born to die. So what the hell is the difference if we die when we're eighty or if we die when we're twenty-six?'"* (Gloria Emerson. Winners and Losers: Battles, Retreats, Gains, Losses and Ruins from a Long War. New York: Random House, 1976, pp. 261–262.)

4. On July 2, 1973, a decade after the product first appeared in stores, the Food and Drug Administration removed Pertussin Medicated Vaporizer from the market. The FDA had associated the product with eighteen deaths, which evidently resulted from inhaling the product's propellents and solvents. The manufacturers made no mention of these deadly ingredients on the can's label.

5. As a presidential candidate, Ronald Reagan opposed extending the

Voting Rights Act of 1965, including the controversial section that imposed additional sanctions on nine states and parts of thirteen others that have a history of ballot discrimination against minorities. Reagan said it was unfair to require only twenty-two of the country's political jurisdictions to obtain prior approval of changes in their election laws from a federal court or the Justice Department (preclearance). If the requirement is a good one, he asserted, it should be applied everywhere. In June 1981, Reagan reiterated his stand, arguing that, if maintained, preclearance requirements should be applied to all states, even though that would probably nullify their enforcement because of the many changes in state election laws every few years. In August, Reagan came out in favor of extending the Voting Rights Act for another ten years. He noted that applying it to fifty states would make it cumbersome and ineffective.

6. The chief justice of the California Supreme Court, Rose Bird, objecting to the state attorney general's practice of holding some police intelligence files immune from public inspection: "How are you going to ensure the public concerns [for privacy] are not violated over and over again by an overzealous attorney general who may be eager to become governor?" ("Personal Feud Embroils State Legal System." Los Angeles Times, August 10, 1981, part 1, p. 3.)

7. Supreme Court Justice William H. Rehnquist, defending a majority vote upholding the nation's military draft law and rejecting arguments that the law was unconstitutional because it applied to men and not to women: "This is not merely a case involving the customary deference accorded congressional decisions. . . . The case arises in the context of Congress's authority over national defense and military affairs, and perhaps in no other areas has the court accorded Congress greater deference." (Jim Mann. "Court Upholds All-Male Draft." Los Angeles Times, June 26, 1981, part 1, p. 1.)

8. "I use toothpaste that is not advertised at all, locally or nationally, or any other way. It costs less than half the price of brands that do advertise heavily on TV. Either my toothpaste is only half as good, or the price of the other brands is inflated to that extent by 'promotional costs.' " (Letter to the editor. Christian Science Monitor, September 4, 1981, p. 22.)

9. Elisabeth Kübler-Ross, a psychiatrist and expert in the treatment of the terminally ill, commenting in a Playboy interview about her connection with a group of healers and spiritualists and the defection of many group members, who spoke of odd sexual activities involving the "spirits" and the guests:

Playboy: Why did the whole group of avid followers defect and turn against you if those things weren't really happening?

Kübler-Ross: It was a very small group of people who went totally the *other way; maybe 20 out of 200 became really destructive. A much bigger group just stayed away and don't want to be dragged into the negativity. But they write us beautiful letters of how much growth there was. They're just—I want to say chicken; they kind of sit and wait and see." ("Playboy Interview: Elisabeth Kübler-Ross." Playboy, May 1981, pp. 104, 106.)*

10. "America has always despised its teachers and, as a consequence, it has been granted the teachers it deserves. The quality of first-grade education that my son received, in a New Jersey town noted for the excellence of its public schools, could not, I suppose, be faulted on the level of dogged conscientiousness. The principal had read all the right pedagogic books, and was ready to quote these in the footnotes to his circular exhortations to parents. The teachers worked rigidly from approved rigidly programmed primers, ensuring that school textbook publication remains the big business it is. But there seemed to be no spark; no daring, no madness, no readiness to engage in the individual child's mind as anything other than raw material for statistical reductions. The fear of being unorthodox is rooted in the American teacher's soul: you can be fired for teaching the path of experimental enterprise." (Anthony Burgess. "Is America Falling Apart?" New York Times Magazine, November 7, 1971, p. 101.)

11. J. Clayburn LaForce, dean of the Graduate School of Management at the University of California, Los Angeles, arguing that the business of corporations does not include achieving the "wider goals of society": "If the 'corporate governance' and 'responsibility' issues succeed as other political fads have, and bureaucrats or their appointees enter the board room, the free market, or what is left of it, will be damaged beyond repair." (J. Clayburn LaForce, in a speech delivered to a group of executives, August 1979).

12. Shortly after his appointment as secretary of health and human services, Richard S. Schweiker called prevention the nation's highest health priority. In response to research findings about salt, Schweiker used his office to propagandize against it and prod food manufacturers to cut their use of salt and list salt content on their labels. Schweiker also defended a budget that cut $2 million from the $3 million a year that his department had spent to counter the tobacco industry's $1 billion-a-year advertising budget.

13. "The knee-jerk response to the increase in criminal convictions and overcrowded prisons will be to build more prisons. But building and staffing prisons is an expensive proposition whose main effect is to postpone rather than solve the problem. The more logical alternative is to make increased use of non-prison alternatives, at least for non-violent offenders." (William Raspberry. "We're Getting Spaced Out in Our Prisons, So . . . " Los Angeles Times, August 17, 1981, part 2, p. 7.)

14. Sportscaster Howard Cosell: "I'm not sitting here telling you that I'm

the most popular man in the world, though I believe, with Governor Carey [of New York] and Bob Strauss [then chairperson of the Democratic party], that I blew it. I think I would have beaten Buckley [then a Republican senator] 4–1 in New York!" (Bill Rhoden. "Howard Cosell Tells It Like It Is." Ebony, December 1976, p. 80.)

15. The Soviet sociologist Geunadi Gerasimov: "Communism will replace capitalism because private ownership of the means of production is obsolete." *(Howard Kahane.* Logic and Contemporary Rhetoric. *Belmont; Calif.: Wadsworth, 1980, p. 40.)*

16. *Letter to the media by a public-relations firm trying to promote the sale of a drug: "After 12 years of successful use by people in 21 countries around the world, America's asthma sufferers can now legally obtain and use the drug known as Ventolin (albuterol). The remarkable therapeutic affects of Ventolin finally have been recognized by the U.S. Food and Drug Administration. The significance of this new drug and its potential impact on their life style should be good news to 9 million Americans suffering from asthma." (Alan Parachin. "The Medical Community Ponders a 'Touchy Subject.' " Los Angeles Times, July 9, 1981, part 5, p. 1.) The letter didn't mention that (1) a competitor had been simultaneously authorized to sell a version of the same drug and (2) the FDA had classified albuterol as a new drug with little or no advantage in therapeutic benefit over asthma drugs already on sale.*

17. "Many of my colleagues in the press are upset about the growing practice of paying newsmakers for news. The auction principle seems to them to strike somehow at the freedom of the press, or at least the freedom of the poor press to compete with the rich press. But I find their objections pious and, in an economy where everything and everybody has its price, absurd. Nobody gives you information for nothing. It's quid pro quo all the way. If someone doesn't tell you his story for cash, he does it for publicity or credibility or an alibi; to make himself look good or his enemy look bad, to sell his record or hawk his new book, or get his kid a job." *(Shana Alexander. "Loew's Common Denominator."* Newsweek, *April 14, 1975, p. 96.)*

18. In June 1981, Los Angeles Deputy Police Chief Louis J. Reiter charged that his department was suffering from serious management problems, including a "siege mentality," "too many well-paid brass," "wasteful deployment of officers," and a "stifling of innovative management practices." Advised of Reiter's criticisms, Police Chief Daryl F. Gates acknowledged some as accurate. But he also threatened to bring Reiter up on a charge of "dereliction of duty" for telling the Los Angeles Times about racism problems, saying that Reiter should have told him instead. Gates said that, overall, Reiter's remarks amounted to "subversion." *(David Johnston. "LAPD's Problems Serious, Retiring Top Officer Says."* Los Angeles Times, June 19, 1981, part 1, p. 3.)

19. President Reagan, assuring an audience of Republicans that he indeed
    would be successful in cutting an additional $70 billion from the federal
    budget in fiscal 1983 and 1984: "We are going to do it because we have no
    choice. It has to be done." (Ed Manuson. "Could Be the Party's Over."
    Time, September 14, 1981, p. 12.)

20. Some people believe that residents themselves should decide whether a
    nuclear power plant should be built in an area. "So a newswoman
    yesterday asked Robert Burt, manager of the nuclear project [proposed
    for Kern County, California], 'Would that have any weight with you?'
    Burt responded: ' . . . the state as a whole voted last June whether nuclear
    power should proceed in the same manner which it has proceeded. . . .
    They voted not to stop the nuclear programs.' " ("LADWP Opposes Nu-
    clear Plant Vote." Bakersfield Californian, October 19, 1976, p. 12.)

21. "From the standpoints of contemporary graphics and good photo-to-
    editorial balance, you should have noticed a change in the past few
    issues, but if you haven't our subtle approach has worked as planned."
    (John Dianna. "Editorially Speaking." Hot Rod, January 1977, p. 4.)

22. Ira Lipman, president of Guardsmark, Incorporated, a security services
    company in Memphis: "If you could get rid of drugs [in the work place],
    we'd be far ahead of other countries in productivity." (Stanley Penn.
    "Losses Grow from Drug Use at the Office." Wall Street Journal, July 29,
    1981, p. 27.)

23. "Begin's Beirut Raid: Calculation or Rage?" (Title of article by Norman
    Kemster. Los Angeles Times, July 6, 1981, part 2, p. 1.)

24. Commerce Secretary Malcolm Baldridge started a campaign against
    government gobbledygook shortly after he took office in 1981. On his "hit
    list" were words such as delighted, finalize, glad, happy, hereinafter,
    hopefully, image, input, and institutionalize. One letter to a State Depart-
    ment official had Baldridge "gratified by your willingness to aid in this
    endeavor." Baldridge penciled in: " 'Just say I'm glad you want to help.' "
    ("Commerce Chief Lets the Word Go Forth—Don't!" Los Angeles Times,
    July 24, 1981, part 1, p. 13.)

25. "Is it true by Nuremberg statute, as well as domestic laws, that it is a
    criminal act to conspire to commit a crime? . . . We say the conspiracy is
    under way. The weapons are concocted, the plan is well advanced. . . . We
    claim that the most horrid crime in the history of humanity is being
    planned [at the Pentagon], a conspiracy to Hiroshimize every city of the
    world, to pulverize and vaporize all flesh and bones." (Daniel Berrigan,
    before an Alexandria, Virginia, court on civil disobedience charges fol-
    lowing a peaceful demonstration at the Pentagon; quoted in Colman
    McCarthy. "Disobedience Takes Drubbing in Plowshares Eight Case."
    Los Angeles Times, August 6, 1981, part 2, p. 7.)

26. The erstwhile leader of the Yippie movement, Abbie Hoffman, after six

years on the run, finally came out of hiding and faced charges of peddling cocaine. After his conviction Hoffman said New York Governor Hugh Carey should turn him loose because he (Hoffman) was suffering from "post-Vietnam syndrome." Hoffman went to prison despite his defense.

27. At about the same time that Hoffman was sentenced, President Reagan granted Mark Felt and Edward Miller unconditional pardons. They had been convicted of illegally authorizing FBI agents to break into the homes of friends and relatives of fugitive members of the Weather Underground, a violent radical organization. Reagan defended his action by saying that Felt and Miller had acted on high principle to bring an end to terrorism in the United States.

28. "During my 12 years in office as your supervisor, I have always tried to be fair. . . . During this period, I have supported the employees' quest for fair wages, fringe benefits, and working conditions. And during recent conversations with the County Employee unions I have again tried to be fair—but that wasn't good enough for them—they wanted bigger salaries, bigger staffs, and a bigger tax bill to pay for it." (LeRoy M. Jackson. "Open Letter: To the Citizens of the First District." Bakersfield Californian, October 19, 1976, p. 21.)

29. On President Reagan's four-week vacation on his ranch outside Santa Barbara, California: "It is comforting that in this plastic and synthetic age, the American people are being led by a man who prefers to spend some time in simple work and private communication with nature. It seems unreal that munching canapes in the Hamptoms (wherever that is) would be preferable to the glories of the out-of-doors." (Letter to the editor. Time, September 14, 1981, p. 4.)

30. "I also admit that there are people for whom even the reality of the external world and the identifications leading to it constitute a grave problem. My answer is that I do not address them, but that I presuppose a minimum of reason in my readers." (Paul Feyerabend. "Materialism and the Mind-Body Problem." The Review of Metaphysics, vol. 2., 1963, p. 28.)

31. "President Carter labored for four years to try to kill the Tennessee nuclear project, but he only managed to get the start of construction delayed. Then-Congressman David Stockman said in 1977 that the program is 'totally incompatible with our free-market approach to energy policy.' But now as Director of the Office of Management and Budget, Mr. Stockman and the rest of the administration bent to the fierce lobbying of Senate Majority Leader Howard Baker of Tennessee and backed the demonstrator reactor, which is estimated to cost at least $3.2 billion." ("Flowing Rivers." Wall Street Journal, July 29, 1981, p. 24.)

32. Reaction to the late Anwar Sadat's angry blast at the press for reporting his jailing of members of the opposition in Egypt: "Can you imagine the

uproar, in the United States and Israel, if Begin reacted to criticism that way? But Good-Guy Dictator Sadat gets a free press, exemplified in a 'suppression notwithstanding' editorial in the New York Times: ' . . . his present troubles cry out for understanding.' " (William Safire. "Thanks, Menachem, for Keeping Cool; and, Uh, Anwar, Glad You're Reading My Column." Los Angeles Herald Examiner, September 14, 1981, p. A11.)

33. An imprisoned Socrates, explaining to his friend Crito why he (Socrates) will not try to escape from prison, even though he has been unjustly sentenced to die: "Compared with your mother and father and all the rest of your ancestors, your country is something far more precious, more venerable, more sacred, and held in greater honor both among gods and among all reasonable men. Do you not realize that you are even more bound to respect and placate the anger of your country than your father's anger? That if you cannot persuade your country you must do whatever it orders, and patiently submit to any punishment that it imposes, whether it be flogging or imprisonment? And if it leads you out to war, to be wounded or killed, you must comply, and it is right that you should do so; you must give way or retreat or abandon your position. Both in war and in the lawcourts and everywhere else you must do whatever your city and your country commands, or else persuade it in accordance with universal justice; but violence is a sin even against your parents, and it is a far greater sin against your country." (Socrates. "Crito." In Plato: The Last Days of Socrates. Trans. Hugh Tredennick. Harmondworth, England: Penguin, 1961, p. 91.)

ADDITIONAL EXERCISES
BASED ON READINGS

"Morality and Manipulation: Which Will Wither First, the New Right or the Bill of Rights?" by Birch Bayh (Chapter 3)

1. Does paragraph 2 contain an inconsistency?
2. Does sentence 2 of paragraph 3 beg the question?

"Human Rights: No More Small Men" by Michael Novak (Chapter 3)

1. Does the author use a hypothesis contrary to fact in paragraph 6?

2. Does any of the assumptions that underlie paragraphs 11 and 12 conceal evidence?
3. Is there a begging-the-question fallacy in paragraph 20?

"Abscam's Ominous Legacy" by Richard Reeves (Chapter 3)

1. Do you think the classification of television cameras as "Little Brother" is warranted (paragraph 4)?
2. The author deplores the showing on national television of a congresssional representative taking a bribe. He calls this the "modern equivalent of pillory." He also mentions the person's name three times in the essay. Is this inconsistent?
3. In paragraph 7 Reeves says that "American justice was set back about three hundred years" as a result of televising the apparent unseemly behavior of some of our elected officials. Presumably, the following two sentences are reasons for this opinion. Do you think that in giving these reasons the author begs the question; or does he establish his point?
4. Do you agree with the author's interpretation of the impact of the televised Abscam tapes (paragraph 8)?
5. Do you think any evidence is being concealed in paragraph 9?
6. The author detects some concealed evidence in the reply of the demonstrator of the voice analyzer (paragraph 10). What is it?
7. Do you think Reeves provides enough evidence for the generalization "The people who go to security-industry trade shows seem different from me and you" (paragraph 10)?
8. Is the author guilty of slippery slope in paragraph 11?

"Lifeboat Ethics: The Case Against Helping the Poor" by Garrett Hardin (Chapter 4)

1. Do you think that in applying the Christian ideal of "our brother's keeper" (paragraph 6), Hardin is misapplying a generalization?

"Censorship: It's 'a Choking Grip' " by Isaac Asimov (Chapter 4)

1. Do you think "New Puritans" (paragraph 2) is a questionable classification?
2. Does Asimov set up a false dilemma in paragraph 5?
3. Do you think Asimov's conclusion (last paragraph) is justified? Or is it a hasty generalization?

"Teen Pregnancies Involve More than Sex"
by Caryl Rivers (Chapter 5)

1. Do you think that the author has provided enough evidence to warrant the generalization that "girls get more approval when they ask for help than boys do" (paragraph 8)?

2. Underlying the essay are a number of implied assumptions that boys learn to build confidence and deal with disapproval more than girls and that boys receive more training in independence and assertion than girls. Rivers also assumes that teenage boys are driven by libido and do not tend to devalue themselves, as girls supposedly do. Do you agree with these generalizations?

3. The author presumably feels that, if girls were more independent and had a better sense of self-value, the incidence of teenage pregnancies would decline. Do you agree, or do you think that this is a case of wishful thinking?

"The Burnout of Almost Everyone"
by Lance Morrow (Chapter 6)

1. Do you agree that "today burnout is a syndrome verging on a trend" (paragraph 2)? Or do you think this is a hasty generalization?

2. What evidence does the author provide for the generalization "Burnout runs through the teaching profession like Asian flu" (paragraph 3)? Do you think this evidence warrants the generalization?

3. Identify all the generalizations in paragraph 3. Should any of them be qualified?

4. The author refers to burnout as "psychobabble." Do you think that this is a questionable classification? Is the assertion based on provincialism? Inasmuch as two authors cited by the author define burnout in terms of five distinct stages (paragraph 5), is the label inconsistent with cited literature about burnout?

5. In the first sentence of paragrah 7 the author says, "Despite the psychiatrists' exertions, the malady is utterly subjective and therefore unpredictable." What assumption, together with the premise stated, entails this conclusion? Is the assumption a true generalization? Is the assertion that burnout is utterly subjective a known fact, or is it unknown?

6. Do you agree that "hyperbole and narcissism working in tandem" are "an American habit"? Or is this a questionable classification? In making such a contention, is the author guilty of the very things he is asserting—namely, hyperbole and narcissism?

"Cop-Out Realism" by Norman Cousins (Chapter 6)

1. In assessing the effect of the legalization of gambling in New York, does Cousins conceal any evidence? (For example, is it possible that such legislation has had some good effects?)

2. In explaining why some schools are allowing youngsters to smoke on campus, does Cousins conceal any evidence? (Is it possible that other reasons help explain these school policies?)

9. Relevance

*Y*ou will probably recall reading the following passages in a high school literature course. They are from Shakespeare's *Julius Caesar* (act 3, scene 2).

Recall that Caesar's assassins, thinking that Mark Antony will sympathize with their cause, have asked Antony to address the people. Just before he does, Brutus, one of the conspirators, declaims so persuasively that he slew Caesar for the good of Rome that the crowd wants him to be the next Caesar. With false modesty Brutus demurs, urging instead that the crowd hear Antony eulogize the fallen emperor. Antony agrees to speak. But far from condoning the assassination, he condemns it. Indeed, he does it so expertly that by the time he has finished the crowd literally thirsts for the blood of Brutus and the other conspirators.

At one dramatic point in his oration, Antony alludes to Caesar's will. The mob wants it read. For the moment Antony resists. He tells the crowd:

> Have patience, gentle friends, I must not read it.
> It is not meet you know how Caesar loved you.
> You are not wood, you are not stones, but men;
> And being men, hearing the will of Caesar,
> It will inflame you, it will make you mad:
> 'Tis good you know not that you are his heirs.
> For if you should, O, what would come of it!

The mob grows restless. It insists on a reading of the will. Antony relents: Make a ring about the corpse of Caesar/So that they may see him that made the will. The people do so.

Having set the stage, Antony is ready to let the scene unfold. He shows the people Caesar's bloody cloak, each dagger hole made by the assassins. He reminds them of when Caesar first wore it: 'Twas on a summer's evening, in his tent/The day he overcame the Nervii. The eyes of the citizens rivet on Caesar's gory body. Their wills have become so much putty in the hands of Antony, who is about to deliver the coup de grace that will set the horde on a course of bloody revenge. Using the cloak as his prop, Antony speaks:

> Look, in this place ran Cassius's dagger through.
> See what rent the envious Casca made.
> Through this the well-beloved Brutus stabb'd,
> And as he pluck'd his cussed steel away,
> Mark how the blood of Caesar follow'd it,
> As rushing out-of-doors, to be resolved
> If Brutus so unkindly knock'd, or no.
> For Brutus, as you know, was Caesar's angel:
> Judge, O you gods, how dearly Caesar loved him!
> This was the most unkindest cut of all,
> For when the noble Caesar saw him stab,
> Ingratitude, more strong than traitors' arms,
> Quite vanquish'd him. Then burst his mighty heart;
> And in his mantle muffling up his face,
> Even at the base of Pompey's statue,
> Which all the while ran blood great Caesar fell.
> O, what a fall was there, my countrymen!
> Then I, and you, and all of us fell down.
> Whilst bloody treason flourished over us.

Well, we all know the outcome: Thanks to Antony, Brutus and company got theirs. But did Antony make a sound case against the conspirators? Certainly not, judged by the standards of proper argument. He cast logic to the winds, disregarded the intelligence of his audience, and relied exclusively on emotionalism. Was his tack effective? Consummately, given that his purpose was to move the audience to a predetermined course of action. In short, as argument Antony's speech was as full of holes as Caesar's mantle; but as persuasion it was as sharp, pointed, and well-aimed as the conspirators' daggers.

Although Antony's oration is a classic example of persuasion, the line between persuasion and argument cannot be sharply drawn. More often than not, the arguments we meet and make carry persuasive elements, not unlike Antony's. In the two preceding chapters we have examined two categories of these psychological and emotional devices, ambiguity and presumption. In this chapter we consider yet a third group, fallacies of relevance.

Fallacies of relevance are arguments whose premises are logically irrelevant to their conclusions. Irrelevant premises, as much as ones that are ambiguous or presumptuous, do not establish the truth of a conclusion. Thus, the fallacy. Antony made skillful use of one fallacy of relevance, the mob appeal. But there are others that readers and writers of argument should be aware of.

GENETIC FALLACY

There are a number of fallacies of relevance that take the form of personal attacks. One of them is called the genetic fallacy.

The genetic fallacy consists of attempting to prove a conclusion by condemning its source, or genesis. How an idea originates or who holds it is irrelevant to an idea's worth. Thus, it is always fallacious to reject a conclusion by condemning its source.

For example, suppose Grey argues against a national health insurance program on the ground that such a program smacks of socialism. Granted, guaranteeing all people access to medical care despite their ability to pay may be decidedly socialistic. But that in itself does not prove that the United States should not have such a program. Again, Grey summarily dismisses an argument against gun control because it is put forth by the National Rifle Association (NRA). True enough, the NRA has a vested interest in opposing gun-control laws. But that in itself does not disprove its argument. Thus, although it would be wise to withhold a judgment pending further consideration of the facts, it would be fallacious to reject the argument outright simply because the NRA drafted it.

Here is a further example of the genetic fallacy, with comment:

EXAMPLE: *"Every criminal, every gambler, every thug, every libertine, every girl ruiner, every home wrecker, every wife beater, every dope peddler, every moonshiner, every crooked politician, every pagan Papist priest, every shyster lawyer, every K. of C.. [Knights of Columbus, a Roman Catholic organization of laymen], every white slaver, every brothel madam, every Rome controlled newspaper, every black spider—is fighting the Klan. Think it over. Which side are you on?" (From a Ku Klux Klan circular. Reported in S. Morris Engel. Analyzing Informal Fallacies. Englewood Cliffs, N.J.: Prentice-Hall, 1980, p. 171.)*

COMMENT: Simply because the groups cited may be "fighting the Klan" does not prove that the Klan should not be fought. The real issue is why these groups oppose the KKK. Intelligent people decide according to the issues, not who stands beside them.

AD HOMINEM

Ad hominem is Latin for "to the man." When we argue ad hominem, we argue "to the man," not the argument; that is, we attack the person rather than the person's argument. *The fallacy of ad hominem, then, consists of attacking the person who makes an assertion rather than his or her argument.* There are two versions of the ad hominem fallacy, abusive and circumstantial.

Abusive

The abusive ad hominem consists of an attack on the person's character—in brief, character assassination. Like the genetic fallacy, the abusive ad hominem attacks the source, or origin. But in addition it heaps abuse on the source. The preceding example serves to illustrate. Notice how Roman Catholicism is being attacked not only genetically but also abusively, by being placed squarely within so unsavory a lineup.

As another example, suppose that in rejecting a charge of malfeasance of office Comptroller White replied: "My accusers are blackguards whose connections to organized crime are a matter of record. What's more, it's common knowledge that they have been out to get me for years." In damning the sources of the charge, White would discredit them with allegations of underworld connections and ulterior motives.

Again, responding to a proposal to limit nuclear power, an energy expert, Black, says: "The people behind this proposal are wild-eyed environmentalists and fanatics." Like White, Black not only condemns the source but heaps abuse on it as well.

It is important to note that not every argument that takes account of the character and motives of parties to an argument is fallacious. Personal considerations are certainly relevant to deciding a person's reliability and willingness to tell the whole truth. If people have proved unreliable, we surely have a basis for holding what they say suspect. But suspecting their words is different from rejecting them. Weighing the reliability of a witness differs from assuming that personalities dispose of issues. If White's accusers are, in fact, out to get him, then their charges are suspect. We would be justified in not accepting their assertions without further confirmation. But, again, not accepting is not the same as rejecting. White would have his abusive ad hominems disprove the charges against him. They do not. If White's observations are true, they provide character evidence that may only justify *not accepting* the charges without seeking more evidence about the facts. Here's one final example of an abusive ad hominem:

> EXAMPLE: *"Mr. North, a fascist flunkey, wishes by means of his semantics to make meaningless not only the sacred deeds of heroism of the fighters against fascism, but the whole past and future struggle for liberty. But he only exposes his reactionary guts, his hatred for liberty and for social progress.*
>
> *"As a result of Mr. Stuart Chase's many years of activity in the American press, his ability to understand 'truth' and 'national honor' must have become atrophied; as for his ability to understand a 'classless society,' it is inherent with him.*
>
> *"Stuart Chase, the petty bourgeois American economist, who writes prescriptions for the diseases of capitalism, having read the writings of semanticists has lost the last remnants of common sense and has come forward with a fanatical sermon of the new faith, a belief in the magical power of words." (Bernard Emmanuilovich Bykhovsky. The Decay of Bourgeois Philosophy. Moscow: Mysl, 1947, p. 173.)*

> COMMENT: Rather than engaging the arguments of North and Chase, the author attacks them: North is a "fascist flunkey," Chase a "petty bourgeois American economist, who writes prescriptions for the diseases of capitalism." Such name-calling is always a dead giveaway for the abusive ad hominem.

Circumstantial

The circumstanstantial ad hominem consists of attacking the circumstances of a person's life. For example, someone disparages Jane Fonda's position on nuclear energy, because she happens to be an actress. The critic is not assassinating Fonda's character but calling attention to an aspect of her life that supposedly invalidates her views on nuclear energy. But Fonda's career is irrelevant to the contention that her views are unsound. The speaker is guilty of a circumstantial ad hominem. Here are some other examples, with comment:

EXAMPLE: **Jim:** *Now, Sue Ellen, I wouldn't be relying on that Dr. Spock's book to help raise the baby.*
Sue Ellen: *But why, Jim?*
Jim: *Why, darling, you know as well as I that more than once that man has led a protest march on Washington.*
Sue Ellen: *Oh, I'd forgotten.*

COMMENT: *It is true that Dr. Benjamin Spock has been active in a number of political and social issues over the past two decades. But that has nothing to do with his worth as a pediatrician.*

EXAMPLE: **Panel member 1,** a Roman Catholic priest: Divorce is objectionable for lots of reasons. For one thing, it undermines the family. For another, it weakens the fabric of society. But most of all, divorce usurps a divine function, for only God can dissolve the union that He has forged in the holy state of matrimony.
Panel member 2: Frankly, Father, I don't understand how you can speak so authoritatively on marriage. You are, after all, a celibate.

COMMENT: *Rather than addressing the priest's reasons, the second panel member attacks an aspect of the priest's life. But a celibate can have sound views on the social and spiritual impacts of divorce.*

EXAMPLE: *"Name calling, derogatory articles, and adverse propaganda are other methods used to belittle persons refusing to recommend refined foods. We have long been called crackpots and faddists regardless of training or of accuracy in reporting research. The words 'quack' and 'quackery' are now such current favorites that any one using them is receiving benefits from the food processors."*[1]

COMMENT: *Curiously, after pointing out the ad hominems used to discredit her and others recommending nonprocessed foods, nutritionist Adele Davis then engages in one of her own. Rather than responding to their specific charges, Davis*

---

[1]Adele Davis. *Let's Eat Right to Keep Fit.* Quoted in Howard Kahane. *Logic and Contemporary Rhetoric,* 3rd ed. Belmont, Calif.: Wadsworth, 1980, p. 68.

attacks them as hirelings of the food processors. Even if they are, that in itself does not discredit their views.

TU QUOQUE

Tu quoque means "you also" in Latin. *The tu quoque fallacy, another personal attack, consists of charging someone with acting in a way that is inconsistent with what he or she is advocating.* For example, concerned about the dangers of drug abuse, a mother tells her son to avoid drugs. The son replies, "How can you tell me not to use drugs when you and dad drink and pop all kinds of pills?" Though a clever ploy, the son's argument is logically irrelevant, because his parents' behavior has nothing to do with the issue, which presumably is the wisdom of drug use. Although the mother may not be practicing what she preaches, her inconsistency does not discredit her advice. She could easily argue that the drugs she and her husband take are no better than the ones she's warning her son to avoid but that she wants her son to avoid the folly of their ways.

Here's another example of tu quoque:

EXAMPLE: *"Like Socrates 2000 years before, Galileo too was threatened with execution if he did not repudiate his own teachings. Galileo gave in and was spared. Does Galileo merit moral censure? Since only those can criticize Galileo who have chosen as Socrates, we may dispense with moral appraisals of Galileo's choice."[2]*

COMMENT: *The argument here is that only those who, like Socrates, have chosen death rather than repudiate principle can legitimately criticize Galileo. Obviously, no one living falls into that category. Therefore, no one can legitimately appraise Galileo's expedience. But must a person be morally pure before making a moral judgment? Even if I haven't chosen death in situations like Socrates's or Galileo's, that does not prove that the death decision is the more noble. Nor does it mean that I have no basis for moral appraisal. The gap between intellect and will can be awesome; my moral reach often exceeds my grasp.*

POISONING THE WELL

The fallacy of poisoning the well, still another personal attack, *consists of trying to place one's opponents in a position from which they cannot reply.*

---

[2]Cited in Perry Weddle. *Argument: A Guide to Critical Thinking.* New York: McGraw-Hill, 1978, p. 86.

Metaphorically, the arguer "poisons the well" before anyone can drink from it.

For example, just before his election opponent is about to speak, Brown says to the audience: "Don't believe a word my opponent is about to say. She's a born liar!" Whatever the opponent now says will probably be suspect. Of course, Brown might have been more subtle and simply said: "Don't be taken in by my opponent's get-tough-on-crime rhetoric. It's become fashionable of late for even the most permissive of lawmakers to assume this pose, now that they know the public no longer will tolerate coddling of criminals." Brown's opponent will find it very difficult to convince her audience that she means what she says about criminals. Here's another example of poisoning the well, with comment:

EXAMPLE: *"Remember the plot to dose up Cuban Premier Fidel Castro so his beard would fall out? the contract with Mafia hit men to knock him off? the CIA agent who plugged in a lie detector machine and blew out all the lights in a dingy Singapore hotel? the clandestine military operations that backfired in Cuba, Laos and Iraq?*

"The James Bonds responsible for those slapstick misadventures are back in business. A few weeks ago, for example, a report appeared in print that the CIA was plotting a multiphase operation to rid the world of Libya's radical ruler, Moammar Khadafy."[3]

COMMENT: *After these opening words, columnist Jack Anderson proceeds to report a Central Intelligence Agency plan to assassinate Khadafy. Notice the untenable position into which the CIA is placed before the details of the plot have been sketched. (In fact, the column provided no hard facts about the alleged plot.) Also, imagine how difficult it will be for a reader to react objectively to the alleged plan. Although past CIA blunders are relevant to evaluating the advisability of the alleged plot, Anderson seems to use these "slapstick misadventures" to pollute the waters before anyone can drink from them. There is even more reason for believing this inasmuch as Anderson provides no hard facts about the plan.*

Exercise

9.1   *Devise an abusive assertion that the persons in the following situations might make.*

---

[3]Jack Anderson. "Slapstick Plots." *San Francisco Chronicle*, August 25, 1981, p. 41.

1. a proponent for a national health insurance program responding to opposition from a member of the American Medical Association (AMA) (assert a genetic appeal)

2. an environmentalist responding to the Secretary of the Interior's plan to open wilderness areas for mining (assert an abusive ad hominem)

3. a political candidate reacting to the views of a wealthy opponent (assert a circumstantial ad hominem)

4. wife responding to husband's charge of infidelity (assert a tu quoque)

5. a columnist's opening remarks about a proposal to reinstate the draft (assert a poisoning the well)

HUMOR   OR   RIDICULE

A common variation on the ad hominem is the appeal to humor and ridicule, the fallacy that consists of relying strictly on humor or abuse to discredit an argument. For example, a member of the British Parliament named Thomas Massey-Massey once introduced a bill to change the name of Christmas to Christide. He reasoned thus: Since mass is a Catholic term and since Britons are largely Protestant, they should avoid the suffix mass in Christmas. On hearing the proposal another member suggested that Christmas might not want its name changed. "How would you like it," he asked Thomas Massey-Massey, "if we changed your name to Thotide Tidey-Tidey?" The bill died in the ensuing laughter.[4]

Similarly, a story is told of an incident that occurred at the Yalta meeting of Franklin D. Roosevelt, Winston Churchill, and Joseph Stalin. Churchill reportedly mentioned that the Pope had suggested a particular course of action as right, whereupon Stalin is said to have replied: "And how many divisions did you say the Pope had available for combat duty?"

In both examples the respondents employ humor and ridicule to disparage the proposal. They do not engage the issues, but dismiss them with contempt. Given their entertainment quality, appeals to humor and ridicule can be extremely effective in persuasion, though never logically relevant.

MOB   APPEAL

The fallacy of mob appeal (or appealing to popular prejudice, grandstanding, demogoguery, jingoism, and playing to the gallery) consists of attempting to

---

[4]Reported in S. Morris Engel. With Good Reason. New York: St. Martin's Press, 1976, p. 109.

persuade by arousing a group's deepest emotions. In mob appeal one always tries to win support by exciting the deepest feelings and enthusiasms of the crowd, by playing to its culturally induced prejudices.

Antony's funeral oration is a perfect example of mob appeal. Indeed, mob appeal is especially favored by propagandists or demagogues.

But mob appeal need not come only from the mouths and pens of propagandists. In fact, it's a staple in advertisement, where heroic efforts are made to associate a product with whatever the public can be expected to approve of strongly—for example, patriotism, status, or sexual gratification. Here are two examples, with comment:

EXAMPLE: *Superimposed over a picture of the model Cheryl Tiegs, provocatively attired in a black velvet dress: "Isn't Black Velvet smooth? Just the thought of it can give you a good feeling. Black Velvet. Canadian Whiskey. The smooth Canadian." (Advertisement for Black Velvet.)*

COMMENT: *The advertiser tries to exploit the audience's sexual appetite by associating its product with sexual gratification. Since the whiskey market is predominantly male, a seductive female is used. Ads for alcoholic beverages with a sizable female market, such as wines, often picture women and men. Their pitch is to sexual intimacy.*

EXAMPLE: *"In 1904, Julie Kelly of the famous dance team of Kelly and Kelly lit up a cigarette in the wings of the Palace Theatre in Atlantic City, New Jersey. 30 seconds later Kelly & Kelly became Kelly and Schwartz [Presumably, Ms. Kelly was fired for smoking.]. . . . You've come a long way, baby. Virginia Slims. Slimmer than the fat cigarettes men smoke." (Advertisement for Virginia Slims.)*

COMMENT: *Tapping into the enormous female market for cigarettes, the advertiser associates product with sexual liberation. Smoking is portrayed as a symbol of the new, liberated woman. And Virginia Slims, differing as they do from the "fat cigarettes men smoke," are presumably distinctively feminine. Ironically, although slanted toward the "liberated woman," the ad uses the sexist word "baby." Thus, the modern, liberated female smokes Virginia Slims but does not relinquish her femininity. This ad is selling a lot more than a cigarette.*

Exercise

9.2 *Suppose you were writing for the following audiences. For each audience, indicate some of the things that you could expect them to approve of strongly.*

children	the elderly
teenagers	urban dwellers
college students	Middle Westerners
college females	farmers
young black professionals	union members
middled aged parents	business people

P I T Y

The fallacy of pity consists of using sympathy to advance a contention. For example, failing to turn in an assignment on time, students sometimes offer various "reasons": "I had to work last night," "I lost my assignment," "I tried to do it but I couldn't," or "My dog ate my essay." Indeed, some students have been known to invoke the death of a dearly loved relative as an alibi— sometimes the same relative several times. Such appeals are excuses, not reasons; they are intended to elicit sympathy and, it is hoped, pardon.

The courtroom is a rich spawning grounds for appeals to pity. Backed against the wall, the case in shambles, a defense attorney may introduce a defendant's misspent youth, wretched childhood, and irresponsible parents. Although such appeals can be relevant to demonstrating constraint or mitigating circumstances, they are usually irrelevant to the question of guilt. A classic example is seen in the defense offered by Clarence Darrow, perhaps the most famous defense attorney in U.S. history. In this instance, Darrow is defending Thomas Kidd against the charge of criminal conspiracy. Notice that, although Darrow's defense undoubtedly has psychological appeal, it fails to address the key issue: whether Kidd committed the crime.

> I appeal to you not for Thomas Kidd, but I appeal to you for the long line—the long, long line reaching back through the ages and forward to the years to come—the long line of despoiled and down trodden people of the earth. I appeal to you for those men who rise in the morning before daylight comes and who go home at night when the light has faded from the sky and give their life, their strength, their

toil to make others rich and great. I appeal to you in the name of those women who are offering up their lives to this modern god of gold, and I appeal to you in the name of those little children, the living and the unborn.[5]

Here's a sampling of other appeals to pity, with comment:

EXAMPLE: Superimposed over a picture of a homey elderly couple with dog, standing on their front porch: "Swing by home on your next business trip." (Advertisement for the Boeing Company.)

COMMENT: Whose heart is so hard as to resist the warmth of this pitch? Why, the models are everyone's mom and pop! Boeing could not have selected a more effective pity-triggering symbol to sell the idea of flying.

EXAMPLE: After shoving a television photographer against a hotel lobby wall, the U.S. ambassador to Mexico, John Gavin, apologized: He said that he was ill from food poisoning and that the press had caught him off guard.[6]

COMMENT: The ambassador's excuse begs for sympathy for his rather boorish behavior. The explanation is all the more feeble coming from a diplomat, one whose function calls for exercising self-restraint over the irritants that undo lesser mortals.

---

[5]Irving Stone. *Clarence Darrow for the Defense.* New York: Doubleday, 1941, p. 112.
[6]*Los Angeles Times*, July 29, 1981, part 2, p. 4.

FEAR OR FORCE

The fallacy of fear or force consists of using the threat of harm to advance the acceptance of a contention. Also known as "swinging the big stick," this fallacy is summed up in the adage: Might makes right. Of course, might doesn't make right; that's precisely the point.

For example, lobbyists like to remind legislators of the many voters that they, the lobbyists, represent. The message is clear: Vote my way or you'll be in trouble at the next election. Again, an employer "counsels" a worker about the "imprudence" of joining a union. Translation: If you join, you'll be fired. A male supervisor suggests to a female subordinate that she might "go further faster" if she were "a bit more cooperative." Translation: "Go to bed with me or else!" A member of a law-and-order group suggests to the judiciary that "being soft on crime" could prove "most unwise." Translation: "Get tough on criminals, or we'll hound you out of office." Here are two other examples of the appeal to fear or force, with comment:

> EXAMPLE: *A reaction to a decision to scrap the B-1 bomber project: "If your planet is subjected one day to the unimaginable horrors of a third world war, 1977 might be recorded as the year in which the seeds of defeat for the Western powers were sown."[7]*

> COMMENT: *By using the conditional "if" and the weasel "might," the author implies catastrophe without actually predicting it. Presumably, the audience should deplore the decision to scrap the B-1 because, as a result, the fall of the West could ensue. But much the same horrifying hypothesis could be applied to the abandoning of any sophisticated weapons system—for example, the MX missile.*

> EXAMPLE: *A Soviet official, commenting on the Reagan administration's apparent unwillingness to negotiate key issues, such as the location of the Soviet Union's SS-20 missiles and a new Strategic Arms Limitation Treaty: "We shall continue to urge real negotiations but our patience is not unlimited. This does not mean, of course, that we would start a war, but ultimately if there is no change we will have to counter measures being taken by your Administration with measures of our own. We don't want to do this. It can only result in a dangerous spiral. This would be a very dangerous development."[8]*

> COMMENT: *Although the speaker seemingly wants peace, he rattles*

---

[7]John W. R. Taylor. In Preface to *Jane's All the World's Aircraft.* London: Jane's Year Book, 1977. (The B-1 bomber project was resurrected in 1981.)

swords. The message is clear: Either the Reagan administration gets down to "real negotiations," or the Soviet Union will stiffen its forces, thus increasing the threat of war. Notice the persuasive "real" in "real negotiations," and the title of the article, which itself is an appeal to fear.

TWO   WRONGS   MAKE   A   RIGHT

The fallacy of two wrongs make a right consists of attempting to justify what is considered objectionable by appealing to other instances of the same action. For example, a police officer stops a speeding motorist. "Why stop me?" the motorist asks. "Didn't you see that Jaguar fly by at eighty miles an hour?" The motorist tries to justify his own infraction by citing the wrongdoing of another. But the speed of the other motorist is irrelevant; the issue is whether he himself was speeding.

When President Gerald R. Ford impounded funds voted by Congress, some critics contended that his action was unconstitutional. Maybe it was, maybe it wasn't. But Ford's defenders did little logically to help their case when they invoked a two-wrongs appeal by arguing that other recent presidents had acted similarly, including Richard M. Nixon, Lyndon B. Johnson, and John F. Kennedy.

Here's one final illustration of the two-wrongs appeal, with comment:

> EXAMPLE: *Lowell Ferguson, a pilot who in 1979 aimed his Western Airlines jet, carrying ninety-four passengers, at Sheridan,*

---

[8]Fred Warner Neal. "America Frustrates Soviets—And That's Dangerous." *Los Angeles Times,* July 31, 1981, part 2, p. 7.

Wyoming, and inadvertently landed short—thirty-five miles short—on a smaller, narrower runway at tiny Buffalo: "After this happened to me, I had three pilots tell me how they'd done the same thing in the military or under other circumstances. People who work in the environment realize problems can occur that lead to this. When we sighted the [Buffalo] runway from 9,000 feet, it was brightly lit and right in line with the airway. It hasn't been the first time that someone has mistaken Buffalo for Sheridan and without [public] exposure it won't be the last."[9]

COMMENT: *Although there have been other such instances of pilot error at these airports, they do not exonerate this pilot. At the same time, the frequency of such miscalculations might indicate a problem that is contributing to pilot error.*

A common variation on the two-wrongs theme is the fallacy of common practice. *The common-practice fallacy consists of attempting to justify wrongdoing on the basis of some practice that has become widely accepted.* For example, attempting to justify helping herself to company stationery and postage stamps for personal correspondence, a worker might say: "Why, everybody else does it." But even if everybody else behaves this way, that doesn't make the behavior right. The issue is whether the employer has given permission for personal use of the firm's property. The common practice of workers' helping themselves establishes neither explicit nor implied permission.

Common practice was evident when President Ronald Reagan appointed a longtime friend and personal lawyer, William French Smith, to be attorney general. Some critics charged "cronyism." The charge was a circumstantial ad hominem; after all, Smith could make a good attorney general, despite his longstanding association with the president. But some defenders of Smith and Reagan invoked a no less fallacious appeal in rebutting the charge. The attorney general's office, they pointed out, is commonly held by a close legal associate of the president, even a relative, as in the case of Robert Kennedy. Although their observation was true, the common-practice appeal was irrelevant to whether Smith was qualified for the office. A better defense would have begun by pointing out that association with a president is not in itself a sufficient ground to disqualify a candidate for office. Then Smith's qualifications for office could have been listed.

STRAW MAN

The straw man fallacy consists of so altering a position that the altered version is easier to attack than the original. The name of this fallacy bespeaks

---

[9]*Los Angeles Times,* July 20, 1981, part 5, p. 2.

what it accomplishes: It sets up a "straw" that is easy to "blow over." Of course, the straw version is not the original; but that's exactly the point. The altered version makes a far more inviting target. An unthinking audience can easily infer that the original argument is demolished when the straw is blown over.

See if you can spot the straw man in this dialogue:

> **Tom:** The theory of creationism should be taught in the public schools right along with biological evolution.
>
> **Trish:** Why do you say that?
>
> **Tom:** Well, prohibiting the teaching of creationism is precisely what is done in communist countries.
>
> **Trish:** Well, I certainly don't want our public schools acting like communist schools.
>
> **Tom:** That's my point.
>
> **Trish:** You know, I never thought of it that way. I'm going to write my legislators right away and have them look into this.

The real issue here is the teaching of creationism; the straw issue is communism. It is certainly much easier to get Americans to support a position against communism in public schools. Simply because communist countries prohibit the teaching of creationism doesn't mean that any system that does the same is communistic or shares communism's motives. For example, anti-creationists often invoke the doctrine of church/state separation to keep creationism out of the classroom. Or they assert that creationism properly falls under religion, not science. But such points are obscured once the prohibition of creationism is identified with communism.

Not all straw men are so transparent, as the following example illustrates.

EXAMPLE: The dean of a prestigious graduate school of business once objected to the inclusion of business ethics in the business curriculum. "Much can be said about the moral and ethical nature of an economic system," he admitted, "but by the time students get to graduate business schools, their moral and ethical standards have long been set. And I think it's quite presumptuous of us to tell them what's right and what's wrong."

COMMENT: This argument is psychologically persuasive, because it associates courses in business ethics with dictating morality to students. Since we don't want moral dogma taught in the classroom, we shouldn't want business ethics. But such business ethics courses needn't indoctrinate. Rather, they can investigate the possible bases for a just economic system; explore the relationship between business and var-

ious claimants, such as employees, stockholders, consumers, and government; and consider a variety of business issues within the framework of diverse ethical theories. The real issue, then, is whether such topics warrant a place in the business curriculum. If not, why? But it's far easier to undercut coverage of these topics by identifying business ethics with dogma than by demonstrating that these issues are not worthy of study in a graduate school. To this day, no such course is offered in this institution.

Exercise

9.3 For each of the following proposals, construct an argument, pro or con, and explain why your argument is a straw man.

1. establishment of day-care centers (facilities for looking after the children of working parents)
2. a law that requires physicians to obtain the permission of parents before issuing any female minor birth control devices
3. giving students college credit for relevant work experience
4. a constitutional amendment guaranteeing women equal rights
5. mandatory revocation of the driver's license of any driver convicted of drunk driving

---

INVINCIBLE IGNORANCE

The fallacy of *invincible ignorance* consists of insisting on the legitimacy of an idea or principle despite contradictory facts. For example, in response to the president's economic program, someone says: "I don't care what you say about the president's budget and tax cuts, they won't help curb inflation." The speaker is closed to any facts or points suggesting the effectiveness of the proposal. "Don't confuse me with facts," the person, in effect, is saying. "My mind is already made up." Such ignorance is unconquerable—thus the term *invincible* ignorance.

Invincible ignorance is sometimes signaled by phrases such as "I don't care what you say," "All that's well and good, *but* . . . ," or "Be that as it may, the fact remains. . . ." What follows the phrases is not a reasoned rejection but an appeal to invincible ignorance.

EXAMPLE: **Fred:** *What do you think of Norman Mailer's The Execu-tioner's Song?*
Tony: *Oh, I never read Mailer. I don't care what anyone says. He's not a good writer.*

EXAMPLE: **Meg:** *We've wasted a lot of money on space exploration.*
May: *But what about all the things the space program has given us?*
Meg: *Name one.*
May: *Weather satellites.*
Meg: *Name another.*
May: *Transistor technology.*
Meg: *Well, whatever it may have given us doesn't make any difference. As far as I'm concerned, it's still a waste of money.*

COMMENT: *In both cases the speaker's minds are closed even to the possibility that their views might be incorrect. Mailer and space exploration aside, the chronic use of invincible igno-rance can cut us off to the disclosure of the world and thus foreclose personal growth and enrichment.*

ARGUMENT FROM IGNORANCE

Not to be confused with invincible ignorance is another fallacy rooted in ignorance. *The argument from ignorance consists of using an opponent's inability to disprove an assertion as proof of the assertion's truth.* As an example, consider the following dialogue:

Smith: God exists.

Jones: I disagree.

Smith: OK, prove God doesn't exist.

Jones: I can't. Nobody can.

Smith: Well, if nobody can prove God doesn't exist, then He must exist.

Smith has used Jones's inability to disprove the existence of God as proof for God's existence. Such an appeal is irrelevant, because it shifts the burden of proof from the claimant to the audience. Surely we can't expect an audience to prove our point for us. That task always falls to those asserting the conten-tion.

Just as an inability to disprove a contention does not verify it, so an inability to prove a contention does not make it false. For example:

Smith: God exists.

Jones: Prove it.

Smith: I can't prove it. Nobody can.

Jones: The fact that nobody can prove God's existence is conclusive proof that God doesn't exist.

Jones overlooks the fact that a statement may be true or false apart from anyone's ability to prove it. "God exists (does not exist)," "There is (not) life in outer space," "Cancer is (not) caused by a virus," and similar statements are true or false regardless of our inability to verify them. Although knowledge presupposes truth, truth does not presuppose knowledge. When we assume that something is the case because it can't be disproved or that it is not the case because it can't be proved, we make the mistake of assuming that a state of affairs depends on confirmation. It doesn't; only our knowledge does. Thus, before the fifteenth century the statement "The earth is round" was true or false. An inability to prove the statement did not make it false; an inability to disprove it did not make it true. Our knowledge of the earth's shape awaited confirmation; but the earth's shape per se did not.

IMPOSSIBLE CONDITIONS

The fallacy of impossible conditions consists of setting up an impossible hypothesis as a legitimate objection to an action. Because the impossible hypothesis usually takes the form of a call for human perfection, this fallacy is also termed the call for perfection.

For example, in response to the assertion that society needs gun-control legislation, someone replies: "If people didn't go around shooting one another, there wouldn't be any need for gun control" or, more commonly, "Guns don't kill people, people do." These idle observations suggest that humankind somehow must be changed if we're to curb the incidence of gun-related violence. True enough, if people didn't shoot people, there would be no need for gun control. But people do shoot people, and they often use handguns to do it. So, until humankind reaches that state of moral perfection in which no one ever shoots anyone, gun control is at least an issue worth debating. To object to gun control on the ground that human nature is less than ideal is irrelevant to the issue of whether society should enact gun control.

> EXAMPLE: **Sue:** What do you think of busing children outside their neighborhoods in order to integrate the public schools?
> **Sam:** I'm against it.
> **Sue:** Why's that?
> **Sam:** Because only when people change their attitudes will racial segregation end.

306

COMMENT: *Sam is calling for perfection as a prerequisite to action aimed at mitigating racial segregation in public schools. Certainly, if humans weren't prejudiced, racial segregation wouldn't exist. But we are prejudiced, and our racial prejudices seem to have led to unfair discrimination in schools. Busing may be a bad idea. But calling for human perfection is irrelevant to that assertion. What's more, such an argument ignores the many factors that influence attitudes, values, and behavior, one of which is social policy and the laws that carry it out.*

IRRELEVANT REASON

The fallacy of irrelevant reason consists of presenting evidence that does not support a stated conclusion but a conclusion that may vaguely resemble it. For example, in charging an executive with embezzlement, a prosecutor quotes harrowing statistics about white-collar crime. Although her statistical appeal may influence the jury, it shouldn't, because it is logically irrelevant to establishing the guilt of the defendant. The alarming statistics indeed support the assertion that white-collar crime is a serious social problem and that we ought to take corrective action. But they do not support the charge that the defendant is guilty of embezzlement.

Again, Frank argues that the courts have treated newspaper reporters unfairly by imprisoning them for not revealing their sources of information. As support Frank points out: "Reporters help keep people informed and public officials honest." True enough, but such evidence only shows that reporters perform a useful public service. It does not demonstrate that the courts have been unfair to reporters. In order to establish that point, Frank might show that reporters cannot function without being permitted to protect their sources and that freedom of the press presupposes this journalistic right. Here are two other examples of irrelevant reasons, with comment:

EXAMPLE: *A Duke University historian, arguing for a proposal to locate Nixon's presidential archives library at Duke University: " 'Whether one approves or disapproves of Richard Nixon himself seems quite beside the point.' The Nixon documents 'are of critical importance for [the study of] the political and diplomatic history of the United States.' "* (Barry Jacobs. "Duke Academicians up in Arms over Nixon Library Plans." Christian Science Monitor, September 4, 1981, p. 5.)

COMMENT: *Granted, the Nixon documents are of political and historical value. But that would only argue for their being made accessible to scholars and other interested parties. The* issue is whether Nixon's presidential archives should be housed at Duke University. The professor's remark does not address that point.

EXAMPLE: A professor at Tufts University, Hugo Adam Bedau, opposing legislation to authorize the death penalty for certain crimes: "Many who defend the death penalty today believe that racially objectionable aspects of the death penalty in our past have disappeared. The latest evidence suggests the contrary." Professor Bedau went on to report the findings of a study that confirmed his observation. (Ellen Hume. "Blacks Likelier to Get Death than Whites." Los Angeles Times, April 28, 1981, part 1, p. 6.)

COMMENT: Considerable evidence supports the assertion that the death penalty is not applied equally to blacks and whites. Though appalling, this condition only points to a problem in our judicial system, albeit a profound one. That the death penalty is applied unequally, though a miscarriage of justice, is irrelevant to the assertion that the death penalty should not be authorized in certain crimes. Whether the death penalty is an appropriate punishment is a separate issue from whether it is applied equally. Bedau's evidence addresses the latter, not the former, assertion.

SUMMARY

Fallacies of relevance are arguments whose premises are logically irrelevant to their conclusions. The following are key fallacies of relevance:

1. **Genetic fallacy:** Attempting to prove a conclusion by condemning its source, or genesis.   EXAMPLE: Dismissing an argument against gun control because it is put forth by the National Rifle Association.

2. **Abusive ad hominem:** Attacking a person's character, not the argument.   EXAMPLE: Responding to a proposal to limit nuclear power by calling its sponsors "wild-eyed environmentalists and fanatics."

3. **Ad hominem circumstantial:** Attacking the circumstances of a person's life, not the argument.   EXAMPLE: Insisting that a Roman Catholic priest cannot have valid views about divorce, because he is a celibate.

4. **Tu quoque:** Charging someone with acting in a way that is inconsistent with what he or she is advocating.   EXAMPLE: Insisting that people cannot criticize Galileo because they themselves have not chosen death rather than repudiate principle.

5. **Poisoning the well:** Attempting to place one's opponents in a position from which they cannot reply.   EXAMPLE: Telling an audience: "Don't be taken in by my opponent's get-tough-on-crime rhetoric. It's become fashionable of late for even the most permissive of lawmakers to assume this pose, now that they know the public no longer will tolerate coddling of criminals."

6. **Humor or ridicule:** Relying strictly on humor or contempt to discredit an argument.   EXAMPLE: Stalin's asking Churchill, "And how many divisions did you say the Pope had available for combat duty?"

7. **Mob appeal:** Attempting to persuade by arousing a group's deepest emotions.   EXAMPLES: Antony's funeral oration; advertisements that appeal to sex and status.

8. **Pity:** Using sympathy to advance a contention.   EXAMPLE: Darrow's defense of Kidd.

9. **Fear or force:** Using the threat of harm to advance the acceptance of a contention.   EXAMPLE: Lobbyists' reminding legislators of the many voters they represent.

10. **Two wrongs make a right:** Trying to justify what is considered objectionable by appealing to other instances of the same action.   EXAMPLE: Contending that President Ford's impounding of funds voted by Congress was justified because other recent presidents acted similarly.

11. **Common practice:** Trying to justify wrongdoing on the basis of some practice that has become widely accepted (a variation of two wrongs).   EXAMPLE: Insisting that Reagan's appointment of his longtime friend and personal lawyer, William French Smith, was justified because the attorney general's office is commonly held by a close legal associate of the president.

12. **Straw man:** Altering a position so that the altered version is easier to attack than the original.   EXAMPLE: A dean's objection to the inclusion of business ethics in the business curriculum on the ground that it is presumptuous of colleges to tell students what is right and wrong.

13. **Invincible ignorance:** Insisting on the legitimacy of an idea or principle despite contradictory facts.   EXAMPLE: Contending that space exploration is a waste of money, despite the various benefits it has produced.

14. **Argument from ignorance:** Using an opponent's inability to disprove a contention as proof of the contention's truth.   EXAMPLE: Asserting that God exists because no one can prove that God does not exist or that God does not exist because no one can prove that God does exist.

15. **Impossible conditions:** Setting up an impossible hypothesis as a legitimate objection to an action.   EXAMPLE: Responding to a gun-control proposal by saying, "Guns don't kill people, people do."

16. **Irrelevant reason:** Presenting evidence that does not support a stated conclusion but a conclusion that vaguely resembles it.   EXAMPLE: Insisting that the Nixon documents should be housed at Duke University

because they are of critical importance for the study of the political and diplomatic history of the United States.

Exercise

9.4 Identify the fallacies of relevance, if any, in the following passages. Explain your answers. Remember that passages may contain more than one fallacy.

1. "Walk into any office, any meeting or conference with the Brandell leather attaché case and people will immediately recognize you for what you are, a person of importance and consequence." (Advertisement.)
2. "Maker's Mark is the most searched for whisky in America. . . . It tastes expensive and it is." (Advertisement.)
3. "If America wins the war on inflation, will your company be a casualty?" (Advertisement for Westinghouse Credit Corporation.)
4. "I've had it with your anti-gun garbage! There are 50 million handgun owners in this country, myself included, and we'll fight your nonsense to the end!" (Letter to the editor. Time, May 4, 1981, p. 4.)
5. "I trust that Lance Morrow [author of an article on gun control] will sleep well after having advocated violation of the constitutional rights of 50 million honest, law-abiding citizens. If we ban handguns, the criminal elements will take over even more." (Letter to the editor. Time, May 4, 1981, p. 3.)
6. "Experience the freedom of total control. The New Sony Betamax SL-5800 frees you from the restraints of time, memory, and circumstance. And makes you master of them all." (Advertisement.)
7. A spokesperson for Regimen weight-reducing tablets, in responding to Justice Department charges of deliberate misrepresentation and falsehood in advertising the product: "Thousands of other advertisers and agencies are doing the same thing." (Samm Sinclair Baker. The Permissible Lie. New York: World, 1968, p. 24.)
8. In the fall of 1970 Princeton University adopted a plan under which the university would schedule no classes for a short period before the congressional elections of 1970, thus enabling students to campaign for candidates if they so wished. The proposal came in the aftermath of the U.S. invasion of Cambodia in June 1970, which touched off a number of campus demonstrations. The Princeton administration thought its plan would help defuse any further unrest, even violence, that might result during the campaign among students who believed that they had no voice in the electoral process. The immediate reaction to the plan among other colleges was quite favorable, and it appeared that many other

institutions would adopt it. Learning of the plan, Senator Strom Thur-mond attacked it by asking the Internal Revenue Service to investigate how it might affect the tax-exempt status of institutions adopting it. In the aftermath of Thurmond's warning the American Council of Education cautioned member institutions to be careful about engaging in any "poli-tical campaign on behalf of any candidate for public office." Under tax laws, an institution may lose its tax-exempt status for engaging in parti-san political activity. As a result, very few institutions adopted the plan. (Reported in Howard Kahane. Logic and Contemporary Rhetoric, 2nd ed. Belmont, Calif.: Wadsworth, 1976, pp. 53–55.)

9. " 'Teenage Turn-On: Drinking and Drugs. Since your child won't tell you, we will. Kids aren't just using one drug at a time any more. Now it's deadly combinations of beer, pot, liquor, cocaine, and pills. And your child may be part of this enormous national problem without your even knowing about it. Tonight's ABC News Closeup includes a question-and-answer test that can help you determine whether your children are in this kind of trouble." (Commercial for ABC News.)

10. Socrates, during his trial in 399 B.C.: "My friend, I am a man, and like other men, a creature of flesh and blood, and not of wood or stone, as Homer says; and I have a family, yes, and sons, O Athenians, three in number, one almost a man, and two others who are still young; and yet I will not bring any of them hither in order to petition you for an acquittal." (Plato. "Apology" in Five Great Dialogues, B. Jowett. New York: Walter S. Black, 1942, p. 53.)

11. "Everybody complains about the U.S. mail these days—prices going up and service down. But our Postal Service seems like a winner compared with the Canadian one. In fact, our neighbors to the north have elevated post-office bashing into a national sport." ("The World." San Francisco Chronicle, July 26, 1981, p. 5. The article went on to catalogue deficien-cies in the Canadian postal system.)

12. "Repressive environmentalists and population and economic zero-growthers have requested President Reagan to oust James G. Watt as Secretary of the Interior. Those stop-all-progress destructionists have thick-skinned craniums. They lack the intelligence to realize that the United States of America is no longer a subsidiary of the baby-and-people hating and business-repressive do-gooders. President Reagan and Secretary Watt have done what should have been done long ago. Their critics can go to blazes on a one-way ticket." (Letter to the editor. Los Angeles Times, July 24, 1981, part 2, p. 6.)

13. "Two women said Douglas Forbes raped them; they said there was no doubt about it. One was a minister's wife, the other the mother of three children. So Forbes—a disabled veteran, church deacon, Sunday school teacher and father of six—went to jail in 1975, sentenced to 60 years. He

lost his car and the dream house he had built himself and he missed watching his children grow into teenagers.

"'I was sure he did it,' said Louis May, who prosecuted Forbes, a postman from Elizabethan, Tenn. 'There was no way it couldn't be him. Both women eyeballed him.' " (Michael Sneed. "Wrongfully Imprisoned, He's Released but Isn't Really Free." San Francisco Sunday Examiner and Chronicle, July 26, 1981, p. A4. Note: In November 1980 Forbes was set free. Louis May succeeded in getting Forbes a pardon after another man confessed to both crimes.)

14. "Victory floats by like the Goodyear blimp, familiar, benign, with no particular urgency. It does not feel like [the film director] John Huston at his most engaged; to tell the truth it feels like a film directed from a nearby parked car with the windows rolled up." (Sheila Benson. "Victory: Boiling War Down to Soccer Match." Los Angeles Times, July 31, 1981, part 6, p. 1.)

15. Comments on the air traffic controllers' strike of 1981, all but the last reported in Newsweek, August 17, 1981: President Reagan: "Dammit, the law is the law, and the law says they cannot strike. If they strike, they quit their jobs." (p. 19); an Indianapolis businessman, Joseph Horvath: "The controllers are idiots. When any group of people can paralyze the nation, they should all be fired and replaced." (p. 21); Robert Poli, president of the Professional Air Traffic Controllers Union (PATCO): "There's more effort going into busting our union than there is into fighting drug abuse or organized crime. We're a very small union." (p. 21); Lane Kirkland, AFL–CIO president, explaining why he refused to urge his foundation's member unions to back PATCO: "It's all very well to be a midnight-gin militant and call for a general strike. I am not going to make that appraisal" (p. 22). A controller, Thomas Connelly, explaining the refusal of some controllers to strike: "It's weakness of character. It's fear." (Paul Blustein. "Ideals, Self-Interest Both Work to Keep a Controller on the Job." Wall Street Journal, August 13, 1981, p. 1.)

16. "The prospective showdown [between strike-threatening air controllers and the federal government] will test the rights of the people against the power of the controllers union. If the controllers strike, in defiance of federal law, the whole might, majesty and power of the government must be immediately invoked. Such a strike would have to be crushed decisively, and the ring leaders fined or imprisoned. A temporizing response would serve only to invite further trouble later on.

"Thus we approach confrontation—the people's right to uninterrupted public service against the union's power to interrupt that service. 'The question is,' said Humpty-Dumpty, 'which is to be master—that's all.' To that question there can be one answer only." (James J. Kilpatrick. "Air Controllers: Enough Is Enough." Los Angeles Times, July 31, 1981, part 2, p. 7.)

17. "President Reagan is scheduled to sign his economic package into law in a ceremony that will celebrate his stunning political victory in Congress and give him a new opportunity to promulgate his political mythology. If his past performances are any guide, we will likely hear again how the people last November issued a mighty mandate for fundamental change in relations between citizens and their government, how they have begun triumphantly to have their will transformed into action and how, if they continue to support the administration, all the people will benefit together from the great new beginning that is under way in America. This is part of a larger effort by Mr. Reagan and his White House minions to create a legend around him." (Morton M. Kondracke. "Democrats Must Do More To Oppose Reagan." Wall Street Journal, August 13, 1981, p. 23.)

18. J. Allen Hynek, astronomer, lecturer, and author: "The paranormal or 'psychic' aspects of the UFO phenomenon have generally been taken as sufficient reason for dismissing the entire subject, but such dismissal smacks of scientific irresponsibility. . . ."

    "Hynek ought to know about scientific irresponsibility. Take, for example, his 1979 UFO talk during The Spiritual Frontiers Fellowship Retreat, held by a religious group involved with psychic phenomena and mystical experience. 'I am going to feel freer to discuss the more esoteric aspect [of UFOs] because you have . . . an awareness of the possibilities that the solely materialistically oriented person, like scientists in general, do not have. Talking to them about certain subjects would be like trying to explain calculus to a kindergarten student.'

    "Hynek appears to be in his element at psychic meetings, or as an adviser for a movie about a giant musical top crewed by a race of potato-headed creatures." ("Encountering Hynek." Discover: The News-magazine of Science, August 1981, p. 18.)

19. In the 1960 presidential primaries two Democratic senators, John F. Kennedy and Hubert H. Humphrey, engaged each other in West Virginia in what would prove to be a pivotal election. At the time, West Virginia had a large percentage of war veterans. To help Kennedy, Franklin D. Roosevelt, Jr., came into the state and spoke on his behalf. Noting Kennedy's splendid war record, Roosevelt observed: "There's another candidate in your primary. He's a good Democrat, but I don't know where he was in World War II." (Victor Lasky. "It Didn't Start with Watergate." Book Digest, November 1977, p. 48.)

20. Justice Lynn Compton of the California Court of Appeals, explaining her decision to overturn the conviction of a salesman in the rape of a waitress who was hitchhiking: "A woman who enters a stranger's car 'advertises' that she has less concern for the consequences than the average female." ("Rape and Culture." Time, September 12, 1977, p. 51.)

21. "Precisely what is Nixon accused of doing, if he actually did it, that his predecessors didn't do many times over? The break-in and wire-tapping

at the Watergate? Just how different was that from the bugging of Barry Goldwater's apartment during the 1964 presidential campaign?" (Victor Lasky. "It Didn't Start with Watergate." Book Digest, November 1977, p. 47.)

22. "Didn't evolution have to take place day by day, month by month and year by year? You never hear of anything about what happened on a year-to-year basis. I submit to you this: No evolution per year, multiplied by however many millions of years you wish, still equals no evolution." (Letter to the editor. Science Digest, September 1981, p. 10. Note: Here's an excerpt from Origin of Species by Charles Darwin: "It may be said that natural selection is daily and hourly scrutinizing throughout the world, every variation, even the slightest; rejecting that which is bad, preserving and adding up all that is good. . . . We see nothing of these slow changes or progress, until the hand of time has marked the long lapses of the ages, and then so imperfect is our view into the long past geological ages, that we only see that the forms of life are now different from what they formerly were." (From Great Books of the Western World, vol. 49. Chicago: Encyclopedia Britannica, 1952, p. 101.)

ADDITIONAL EXERCISES BASED ON READINGS

"Morality and Manipulation: Which Will Wither First, the New Right or the Bill of Rights?" by Birch Bayh (Chapter 3)

1. Identify all uses of ad hominem appeal.
2. Does the opening paragraph poison the well?
3. Does the author ever resort to mob appeal?
4. What fallacies are evident in paragraphs 10 and 11?
5. In paragraphs 9–13 Bayh argues that there is nothing "new" about "the New Right." He then proceeds to demonstrate his point. Consult a dictionary and determine the various meanings of new. Is Bayh employing one of these meanings, or has he taken new to mean brand new or unprecedented? If he has, would you say that, by so doing, he has raised a straw man that he then blows over with some historical examples?

"Abscam's Ominous Legacy: Videotapes Can Convict As Surely As a Jury" by Richard Reeves (Chapter 3)

1. Does Reeves appeal to fear anywhere in his essay?
2. On what fallacy does the Panasonic ad capitalize (paragraph 3)?

3. What fallacies underlie the sentence "Little Brother is watching" (paragraph 4)?

4. Is the reference to "Walter Cronkite and friends" ridicule (paragraph 7)?

5. Is there any mob appeal in paragraph 9?

6. What fallacy does the demonstrator of the voice analyzer commit in the second sentence of his reply to Reeves (paragraph 10)?

7. Is there a genetic fallacy implied in the question "Why not use tapes done by outsiders with an ax to grind, maybe a clerk somewhere who thinks his boss is on the take?" (paragraph 11)?

"Lifeboat Ethics: The Case Against Helping the Poor"
by Garrett Hardin (Chapter 4)

1. In paragraph 2 Hardin states: "The spaceship metaphor can be dangerous when used by misguided idealists to justify suicidal policies for sharing our resources through uncontrolled immigration and foreign aid." Do you know of *anyone* who supports a policy of "uncontrolled immigration and foreign aid"? Do you think that Hardin is setting up a straw man that would make his lifeboat metaphor more palatable than it otherwise might be?

2. In paragraph 4 Hardin says that "the current energy crisis has shown in some ways we have already exceeded the carrying capacity of our land." Since the essay was written in 1974, Hardin probably is referring to the oil shortage and accompanying inconveniences of that year. If he is, does his conclusion follow? Or is the reason (current energy crisis) irrelevant to the conclusion (we have exceeded our carrying capacity)?

"Censorship: It's 'a Choking Grip' "
by Isaac Asimov (Chapter 4)

1. Does Asimov rely on humor and ridicule in the first two paragraphs?

2. Are "New Puritans" (paragraph 3) and "purity brigade" (paragraph 4) ad hominem appeals?

3. Is applying economic pressure to advertisers in the hope of influencing programming tantamount to censorship and "the choking grip of orthodoxy," as the author suggests (paragraph 5)? Or is Asimov setting up a straw man that he then blows over with some historical examples?

4. Is any evaluation of orthodoxy ultimately based on provincialism?

5. Is the phrase "the choking grip of orthodoxy" (paragraph 5) calculated to produce fear? Does Asimov evoke appeals to fear in his essay?

6. Asimov implies that, if certain groups succeed in pressuring advertisers to reevaluate their programs, then "unbridled repression" will follow. Is this a slippery slope?

"Living with Terrorism" by Douglas Davis (Chapter 5)

1. Does the author use mob appeal in the first paragraph?
2. Do you think that the author's proposal in the last paragraph sufficiently deals with the problem of managing overwhelming numbers of people? If not, would it be fair to call the proposal irrelevant to the problem of terrorism?
3. Somebody might argue: "The author clearly believes that human beings are innately aggressive and brutal. But I disagree with that view, and so reject his analysis." Do you think that Davis holds the view that human nature is basically aggressive? Or has the critic set up a straw man?

"Cop-Out Realism" by Norman Cousins (Chapter 6)

1. Does Cousins rely on humor and ridicule in making his point about serving alcoholic drinks at school?
2. When school officials permit students to smoke, are the officials in effect approving of smoking? Or is Cousins's assertion a straw man?

EXTENDED   ARGUMENTS   FOR   ANALYSIS

The following essays are provided to give you additional practice in dealing with extended arguments. In each case: (1) identify the author's thesis, main points, and organizational structure; (2) indicate the kind of assertion the author is advancing; (3) list the sources the author uses in developing support material; (4) identify developmental patterns (fact and opinion, comparison and analogy, cause and effect, definition) and associated fallacies; and (5) pick out fallacies of ambiguity, presumption, or relevance. For your convenience, the following is an alphabetical listing of all informal fallacies covered in this text. The number in parentheses indicates the chapter where the primary discussion of the fallacy can be found.

accent (7)	composition (7)
ad hominem (9)	concealed evidence (8)
amphiboly (7)	division (7)
argument from ignorance (9)	emotive language (7)
begging the question (8)	equivocation (7)
biased question (3)	evading the issue (8)
biased sample (3)	false analogy (4)
causal oversimplification (5)	false authority (3)
circular definition (6)	false dilemma (8)

faulty denotation (6)

fear or force (9)

genetic (9)

hasty generalization (8)

humor or ridicule (9)

hypostatization (7)

hypothesis contrary to fact (8)

impossible conditions (9)

incomplete comparison (4)

inconsistency (8)

innuendo (7)

invincible ignorance (9)

irrelevant reason (9)

is/ought (8)

misapplied generalization (8)

mob appeal (9)

neglect of a common cause (5)

novelty (8)

pity (9)

poisoning the well (9)

popularity (3)

post hoc (5)

provincialism (3)

question-begging definition (6)

questionable cause (5)

questionable classification (8)

questionable evaluation (3)

selective comparison (4)

slippery slope (5)

special pleading (8)

straw man (9)

tradition (3)

trivial objections (8)

tu quoque (9)

two wrongs make a right (9)

unknown fact (8)

wishful thinking (8)

Bring Back the Draft[9]

Jim Wright

1   It may be swimming against the tide to say so, but on one defense issue Jimmy Carter was right and Ronald Reagan is wrong: the draft.
2   Amid all the debate and economic crosstalk about defense hardware and its cost, we need to remember that item of defense equipment without which all the high-tech gadgetry is merely junk: the human being, the man or woman willing to devote an important part of a life to defending the rest of us.
3   In the later stages of the Vietnam War, both liberals and conservatives came to favor the idea of the all-volunteer army, a professional force that would not need to depend on conscription.
4   Liberals liked the idea because they thought it would diminish the influence of the military. Conservatives liked it because they believed it would reduce turnover and training costs and produce a smaller but more effective military. Both probably liked the idea that their own youngsters

[9]From *The Dallas Morning News*, August 30, 1981. Reprinted by permission of the author and publisher.

would no longer have to serve a year or two before getting on with their civilian careers.

5   But those who favored one or the other reason for an all-pro army did not foresee that the great American middle class would pretty well shrug off its share of personal responsibility for defense. That means the people who have benefited most from our system have turned over to the poor, the have-nots, the task of protecting it from destruction.

6   The first, and most obvious, flaw in the arrangement is that it is patently unjust. Furthermore, the middle class has failed even to keep its initial bargain with the professionals. The all-pro concept was launched with all sorts of blood oaths that military pay would be brought up to civilian levels and kept there. In fact, the military professionals have seen their pay fall farther and farther behind pay civilians get for easier jobs with better working conditions.

7   The second great drawback is that the middle class is increasingly ignorant of even the most basic facts of miltary life. The military is a different sort of society, necessarily authoritarian and dedicated to the well-being of the country rather than the individual. Preceding generations of Americans who served in World War II, Korea and Vietnam not only saw this but were able to grasp why it was true. Today's young adults haven't a clue, other than what they have read or seen in the movies, about what makes the military tick.

8   Since the middle class furnishes not only most of the civilian leaders but most of the voters who select them, this is a serious lack of knowledge and experience for a democracy. Those whose decisions will determine whether, when and where American soldiers will fight not only will not do the fighting themselves, they won't know much about the problems of those who do.

9   Of the 103 members of the last Congress who were of the age group that furnished soldiers during the Vietnam War, only 14 percent had served on active duty anywhere. Twice that share, 28 percent, of their generation as a whole served.

10   Author James Fallows points out that two-thirds of the senators born before 1939 have served on active duty, while only one-third of the congressmen born after that year have ever served in any way, even on reservist rosters.

11   Finally, even as it is a valuable experience for the middle-class youth to serve in the one institution that cuts across all regions, classes and races, so does the military itself benefit. The 1-hitch trooper or young officer who enters the service for one term and then resumes his civilian career provides the services with the full diversity, imagination and fresh intelligence they need to avoid mental stagnation. An army or navy that includes people from the full range of backgrounds within American society can best defend that society.

12   Ronald Reagan has opposed a return to the draft. But this is one area in which he is out of step with the voters. A Gallup poll last year found that 53 percent of the whites and 53 percent of the blacks in America think the time has come to demand that all classes be called to the defense of their country.

13   To be sure, we must eliminate from any conscription system the loopholes and escape hatches that existed during the Vietnam era. A lottery selection might be used. And it seems to me that those who go and do their duty should be given a place at the head of every line for every benefit from tuition assistance to home loans.

14   The responsibility of the citizen involves more than just paying taxes to buy defense hardware. He should also be prepared to spend time driving it or flying it or carrying it when and where needed.

Old Glory[10]

By Arthur Hoppe

1   The Reverend Jerry Falwell has sent me an American Flag decal in the mail. In addition to a donation to the Moral Majority, he asks me to pledge I will display the flag decal on my bumper in honor of the Fourth of July.

2   I won't. I'd be ashamed to.

3   It wasn't always this way. When I was young, the Fourth was bedecked with flags. The acrid smell of burning punk, the bang of cannon crackers, the sweet taste of lemonade on the porch and Old Glory flying bravely from the white pole on the lawn—that was the Fourth, second only to Christmas in the excited heart of childhood.

4   Summer was the season for flags: Memorial Day, Flag Day . . . And how proud you were in summer camp to be chosen to raise the flag at Morning Assembly or lower it at dusk. Don't let it touch the ground! If even a tiny corner touched the ground, you deserved to die a coward's death.

5   Then came World War II: the despicable swastika, the loathed rising sun, and the Stars and Stripes, gallantly streaming. All over the world, the Stars and Stripes triumphantly streaming.

6   What a shining flag it was, a big, honest, red-white-and-blue flag, made of real cloth that snapped in the wind. Not a tiny rectangle of plastic with a sticky back. What happened to our flag? I used to love it so.

7   I suppose it started in the McCarthy era. There were those who stuck flag decals on their bumpers to prove they weren't Communists. For those were the hysterical days when you had to prove you weren't a member of a perfectly legal political party.

---

[10]From the *San Francisco Chronicle*, July 3, 1981. Copyright 1981 Chronicle Publishing Company. Reprinted by permission of the author and publisher.

8   And it seemed as though these people were using the flag to attack the very civil liberties which that flag symbolized.

9   Then came Vietnam. That dirty little war. In their anger, the young radicals burned and desecrated the flag. What sad sights to see. In reaction, there were those who displayed the flag to show their support "for our boys in Vietnam."

10   And it seemed as though they were using the flag to cover up a dirty little war.

11   Now we have the "new right" and the Reverend Mr. Falwell, who uses the flag to raise money and justify his crusade against gays, feminists, libertines and intellectuals.

12   It is patriots like Mr. Falwell, I think, who have brought our flag into disrepute. It is they who have shrunk its grandeur, plasticized its glory and commercialized its appeal.

13   Oddly enough, I still love the sight of a real flag whipping in the breeze. I still believe in the real ideals for which it stands.

14   But I would be ashamed to put a plastic decal on my bumper. I would be afraid I would be thought self-righteous, simplistic and intolerant. That's the symbol that patriots like Mr. Falwell have made of our flag.

15   It's a damned shame.

Don't Deflate Auto Safety[11]

By the New York Times

1   Last April 21, Lawana Hansen lost control of her 1975 Oldsmobile on Interstate 15, near Salt Lake City. She plowed head-on into a tractor-trailer at a combined speed of about 100 m.p.h. The car was demolished, but she and an 81-year-old passenger survived. She didn't know it when she bought the used car, but it contained inflatable air bags.

2   Few crash victims are that lucky. Only a few thousand cars built in the early 1970's came with these convenient, reliable safety devices. And if the auto industry gets its way—as now seems tragically likely—cars of the future won't come with either air bags or belt-type "passive restraints."

3   Combination shoulder and lap belts provide adequate protection in most crashes—but only one driver in eight bothers to snap them shut. Thus for years, the National Highway Traffic Safety Administration has pushed hard for cars to include restraints requiring no effort to use. The auto manufacturers managed to stall the process. And now the Reagan Administration, unabashedly eager to prove that this Government is a friend of business, seems inclined to surrender altogether.

4   The car companies say air bags are too expensive and that belt-type

[11]From The New York Times, September 23, 1981. © 1981 by The New York Times Company. Reprinted by permission of the publisher.

automatic restraints, like those on VW Rabbits, would be quickly sabotaged by owners. The manufacturers have found powerful philosophical allies among conservatives who argue that it is not the Government's business to protect people who could easily protect themselves with ordinary seat belts.

5   The economic arguments do not bear close examination. Confidential industry documents (confirmed by independent auto parts suppliers) show that front-seat air bags would not cost $500 to $800, as the companies assert, but $100 to $300. William Nordhaus, a Yale economist and no friend of regulation, estimates that the benefits of a passive restraint rule would far outweigh the costs: the estimated net reduction in injury costs for cars made in 1984 would exceed $30 billion.

6   The ideological arguments are just as flimsy. Individuals may have the right to risk their own lives. But few of us would defend the right of a parent to risk the life of a child when protection can be provided at low cost. Besides, most of the cost of injury damage is borne by all society. Why should those who do wear seat belts have to pay higher insurance bills because others won't? Why should taxpayer-financed medical and welfare programs pick up the tab when insurance doesn't?

7   The real mystery here is why the auto industry fights safety so hard. Passive restraints would hardly add enough to the sticker price to make a dent in car sales. Indeed, the cleaner look and freedom of movement that air bags offer might be a sales plus on expensive cars. And now that Detroit is committed to smaller cars, inherently less crashworthy, the added safety factor might be a prudent investment against product liability suits.

8   The explanation for the mystery may be as simple as it is sad: American auto makers, always ready to underestimate consumer sophistication and ever resentful of interference by Government, oppose air bags because they would give regulation a good name.

9   There is always the possibility that the Administration will have the courage and good sense to review its blanket opposition to auto safety regulation. A more realistic hope is that Japanese car companies will decide to do what Detroit won't—do well by doing good.

Dear Mr. President . . .
an Open Letter from Jack Anderson[12]

1   You made a campaign pledge to seek out the larceny that lurks in the compounds of government. You acted swiftly when, just one day after your inauguration, you fired all 15 of the federal inspectors general. You had reason to believe that many of them had obstructed the prosecution of white-collar crime.

---

[12]From *Parade*, April 26, 1981. Reprinted by permission of the author.

2   As a chronicler of government skullduggeries for the past 34 years, perhaps, in a small way, I can assist you, Mr. President, in your search for fraud and waste.

3   Without realizing it, you are already in the process of being bound up by the rope-knowing Lilliputians of the permanent bureaucracy. Even some of the men you fired have slithered back, in other guises, into the bureaucratic briar patch, where the work of obstruction goes on.

4   As you are no doubt aware, when government officials investigate one another, they seldom seek the whole truth, opting instead to exclude evidence that would endanger the predetermined verdict. Then a Boy Scout version of the offense is submitted to superiors, whose curiosity about wrongdoing is constrained by an awareness that it would only reflect on their administration.

5   Anyone who tries to name actual thieves and perjurers in government—rather than merely *lamenting* theft and perjury—becomes a target in place of the real culprits. This is not to say that the federal apparatus is in the hands of brigands. On the contrary, the leaders of government are people of impressive ability and decorum. But the shabbiness is so widespread that the majority have become resigned to it.

6   As I write, the Justice Department is in hot pursuit of 101 public officials. Another 27 have been indicted and are awaiting trial. Given the fact that only 3 percent of all criminals in the federal government are found out and brought to trial—not to mention the special difficulties of detecting the gossamer-like crimes of politicians and the advantages they have over ordinary felons in avoiding prosecution—I'm sure the public can visualize the hidden battalions which these 128 represent.

7   I would suggest, Mr. President, that one thing, above all, is imperative: You must cultivate that most valuable species of bureaucratic life—the whistle-blower. It usually takes an insider who knows the bureaucratic maze to uncover a government scandal.

8   It should be noted that federal officials, though efficient at burying scandals, are a timid, cautious lot. If a bad enough stink is made over the suppression of evidence, the guilty bureaucrat quietly disengages himself from the cover-up and often turns up on the side of justice.

9   He is not inclined, however, to forgive. If the federal managers cannot furtively suppress or publicly discredit a whistle-blower, they bide their time until public interest is at a low ebb. Then they retaliate against the lonely informer—an action intended to intimidate others from revealing official embarrassments.

10   I have documented some two dozen case histories of informants who had the toughness and courage to act on their better impulses, even in the worst weather. Here are a few of them:

11   Ernest Fitzgerald. He is the Air Force cost-cutter who exposed an overspending of $2 billion for the C-5A cargo plane. As his reward, he was hounded from his job and subjected to attacks on his reputation. He

fought back in the courts, which reinstated him in the Pentagon. But it was an empty victory. He was closeted in a tiny office and excluded from important matters.

12   Dr. Kurt Luedtke. He had a spotless record as chief of neuro-psychiatry at the Memphis Naval Station until he protested that his superiors were filling their recruitment quotas by enlisting men with histories of mental instability and violent behavior. Luedtke was abruptly hustled off to Bethesda Naval Hospital himself for mental tests. He was pronounced completely sane and sound. But the ordeal so disillusioned him that he resigned from the Navy.

13   Richard Floyd. He complained that the National Security Agency's contracting methods were plagued with conflicts and inefficiencies. In retaliation, superiors gave him adverse performance evaluations and directed him to see a psychiatrist. He appealed to a hearing examiner, who ruled in his favor. Nevertheless, he was stripped of his "green badge," the symbolic passport to sensitive assignments and promotions. Eventually, he was railroaded out of the agency.

14   William Clinkscales. In his former capacity as the General Services Administration's chief investigator, he helped to indict 130 GSA officials and contractors for cheating the taxpayers. His pursuit of wrongdoers offended superiors who had close ties to House Speaker Tip O'Neill. After a complaint from O'Neill to the White House, Clinkscales was stripped of his parking permit and exiled to a desk in a passageway.

15   C. O. Miller. He investigated air safety for the National Transportation Safety Board with a zeal that discomforted the aviation companies. He also protested that reports on engine problems and airplane accidents had been softened to spare some companies. His superiors filed a charge sheet critical of his performance. The record shows that he quit thereafter for "medical reasons." But the real reason, he confided, was that he could no longer stomach the "conflict between public service and political expediency."

16   William C. Bush. Six years ago, he told his bosses at the Marshall Space Flight Center that he wasn't doing enough work for the money they paid him and requested more duties. For his efforts, they claimed he was overpaid—not underemployed—demoted him by two salary levels and removed him from his engineering functions to an isolated assignment. Bush took his case to the Civil Services Administration, which found he was absolutely right and restored him to his position. But he is, alas, still underemployed.

17   Caleb Glass. As president of an employees union, he blew the whistle on waste and inefficiency at the Energy Department. He also cooperated with a Congressional investigation into suspicious dealings between private contractors and the department's managers. In retaliation, the managers unilaterally declared him out as union president and threatened to discharge him if he tried to continue as the union's democratically elected leader.

18   David Stith. He alienated upper echelons at the Department of Housing and Urban Development by reporting, through channels, evidence of multimillion-dollar ripoffs in the government's subsidized housing program in North Carolina. Although an official investigation substantiated Stith's charges, he was removed from Greensboro and appointed to the obscure post of flood control official in Denver.

19   Mahlon DeLong. For resisting a political purge in the Farmers Home Administration, he was removed as the Maine state director and given a do-nothing job in Washington. He was shunted from one unheated office to another, with no duties except briefly to run a United Way fund drive. At last, he was assigned the menial work of a mail clerk at the executive salary of $47,000, which under law could not be taken away from him.

20   Dr. J. Anthony Morris. An eminent microbiologist, he challenged the government's 1976 swine flu immunization program. He was proved right in warning that the predicted epidemic would not occur and that mass inoculations would prove hazardous. Many who submitted to the shots suffered serious side effects. Some died. Damage suits against the government have totaled more than $3 billion. For trying to prevent this disaster, Morris was locked out of his laboratory and fired. He is now blackballed from further government employment.

21   Mr. President, I believe that exposure of the bad and inculcation of the good is not a hopeless goal. You need not be bound by the Lilliputians.

22   But you must keep a light burning for the storm-tossed whistle-blower. Somewhere within the federal labyrinth is someone who knows how money is being wasted and how the public is being cheated. There is always someone—somewhere.

23   I have been cultivating whistle-blowers for 34 years. I know something about the psychology of one who has a dangerous secret and is teetering on the awful brink of disclosing it. He may be seeking to protect the public from fraud, to advance a good cause or to avenge a personal grievance. Whatever the motive, to the committed reformer it should be secondary, except as it bears upon the validity of the information.

24   The whistle-blower is often a stranger to the glare of publicity and full of doubt and fear. He doesn't always know whom to go to or whether his disclosure will be deemed worthy of investigation. Will Administration officials just yawn or even laugh at him for trying to peddle such trivial stuff? Then he will have taken a risk for nothing. He fears that exposure could cost him his livelihood and lay him open to depressing harassments.

25   Most of the time, he never comes forward; and even when he does, he may turn back. I have had informants before me who, in the midst of their story, have begun to jabber, broken out in a sweat and edged for the door.

26   I believe, Mr. President, that you want right to be done, that you want

to do good—not in the well-intentioned way of the half-committed, but effectively. You can succeed, I believe, in curbing government waste and wrongdoing. But first, you must convey to the doubters out there—the potential whistle-blowers who want to help you—that the door is open to them.

Going Beyond the Point When Life Begins[13]

By Simon M. Lorne

1   Few topics of debate seem to arouse the passions of the protagonists as much as the abortion issue. Too often, but not surprisingly, those passions tend to dissolve arguments into rhetoric, with the result that rational discussion becomes impossible. The recent Senate Judiciary subcommittee hearings on the "human life bill," although themselves somewhat inflammatory, suggest the basis for responsible discussion.

2   The bill, sponsored by Sen. Jesse Helms (R-N.C.) and approved by the subcommittee on separation of powers, has as its primary focus the time at which human life begins. This is a question that the Supreme Court, by its own admission, avoided in its historic 1973 decision establishing the unrestricted right of women to obtain abortions during the first trimester of pregnancy. (In the words of the court, "The judiciary . . . is not in a position to speculate as to the answer.") The Helms bill would establish that, under the 14th Amendment to the Constitution, life begins at conception. It would have the effect of giving the states the duty, and opportunity, to determine the circumstances under which abortions should be permitted or prohibited.

3   While there are some questions about the bill's constitutionality— equally eminent authorities disagree, and only the Supreme Court can ultimately decide—its proponents believe that it is within the congressional authority granted by the 14th Amendment to "enforce, by appropriate legislation, the provisions of" the amendment.

4   What gives rise to the hope that the bill may establish a rational basis for discussion of the abortion issue is the scientific testimony that has been presented to date. It tends to fall into one of two categories. One group, represented by authorities such as geneticist Dr. Jerome Lejeune, asserts that "the human nature of the human being from conception to old age is not metaphysical contention, it is plain experimental evidence." Dr. Leon Rosenberg, a geneticist opposed to the bill, expresses the other view. While saying that it is "incontrovertible" that "the fertilized human egg is a living cell with the potential for human life," he also asserts that "concepts such as humanness are beyond the purview of science," so that "when actual life begins is not a scientific matter."

---

[13]From the *Los Angeles Times*, July 19, 1981. Reprinted by permission of the author and publisher.

5   Surely, this is sophistry reminiscent of Lewis Carroll's Humpty Dumpty, who told Alice that "a word means what I choose it to mean—neither more nor less." Scientific inquiry now appears to make clear that conception creates a cell that is undeniably alive. That cell is also undeniably human in nature. It is foolish to enter into debate about when we choose to call this life "human."

6   The real issue, which for some reason we have been afraid or ashamed to confront directly, is not whether abortion involves the destruction of human life. Rather, it is what reasons our society is willing to accept as sufficient to justify that destruction.

7   To so phrase the question should not be shocking. As a society, we already accept a variety of reasons as sufficient to justify the destruction of life. Self-defense is an obvious example. War, and penalties for some crimes, are others that we currently accept (although not without protest). Other societies have been more "liberal" in this regard, permitting or even requiring the sacrifice of children to various gods, or the abandonment of "unnecessary" infants and elderly people to death by the elements.

8   The question that we should properly debate is whether and under what circumstances social needs and concerns should cause us to permit the destruction of a life. There are a variety of reasons frequently advanced for the legitimacy of abortion. If we are a rational society—one that values life more than self-comfort—we would examine those reasons individually, and decide which of them justify abortion.

9   At present, we cannot meaningfully enter that debate; the current state of the law tends to force us to be "for" or "against" abortion per se, with little ability to discriminate. One columnist vilifies the pro-life movement because he believes that abortion may be important, if not essential, in the case of pregnancy following rape. Another demands the availability of abortion to prevent the birth of a deformed child.

10   Without question, these, and others like them, are serious and sensitive concerns that should be examined and weighed. But in the present environment, we do not accept only the reasons that some people consider compelling; our society also accepts the abortion of a girl fetus because the mother prefers to bear a boy, or abortion by a woman who doesn't want her vacation interrupted by morning sickness. Is abortion no more than an alternative—in some ways a more efficient—form of birth control? I think not. I think that few of us are morally comfortable with the notion that abortion should be within the absolute discretion of the woman carrying the fetus, unfettered by the laws that society customarily adopts to express its moral conclusions. Yet we have implicitly encouraged thousands of women to choose abortion when they might have chosen otherwise if our society had not advanced the convenient view that fetal life is not fully human.

11   I think it true that the vast majority of Americans, if forced to focus

upon the life process, would find that there is no clear point of initiation other than conception. I understand why we avoid that focus. Pregnancies often can be unwelcome events, and it is certainly more comfortable to ignore the humanity of the unseen life than to deal with it for what it is. But a society should not allow itself to avoid difficult problems by pretending that they don't exist.

12   Only when we recognize that to abort is to interrupt the life process of an existing person can we begin to address which factors we should properly recognize as sufficiently compelling to legitimate that interruption. The "human life bill" contains the potential for having us confront that question, for moving us beyond the semantic subterfuge of deciding whether to choose to call "human" a life whose existence, even to opponents of the bill, is "incontrovertible."

Scam, Impure and Simple—That's Human-Life Bill[14]

By Ellen Goodman

1   It sounded more like a high-school biology class than a Senate hearing.

2   For two days, the judiciary subcommittee room was filled with all sorts of lessons about the facts of life, the birds and the bees, the sperm and the ovum.

3   For two days, freshman Sen. John P. East (R-N.C.) conducted hearings on a piece of legislation known as the human-life bill. This is the bill that could outlaw abortion, by definition, without even bothering with a constitutional amendment.

4   The scam is a pretty simple one. First Congress pretends that the Supreme Court didn't know the medical facts when it decided in 1973 to decriminalize abortion. Then Congress in its wisdom "helps" the court by defining "person" as a fertilized egg.

5   As East explained it when he opened the hearings on the origin of life: "If life does commence at conception, then the unborn person is protected under the Constitution . . . Roe v. Wade would be negated."

6   This human-life bill, sponsored by Sen. Jesse Helms (R-N.C.), framed the abortion question—and I use the word "framed" advisedly—in terms of genetics rather than law or politics. That accomplished, East ran the hearings like a block meeting of the Friends of the Fetus.

7   On the first morning, five scientists, all apparently instructed never to use the word abortion, limited their testimony to the prescribed subject—simply to define the word "person" in biological terms. They talked about chromosomes, zygotes, fetuses, Fallopian tubes—everything but pregnant women.

---

[14]From the *Los Angeles Times*, April 28, 1981. © 1981 by The Boston Globe Newspaper Company/ Washington Post Writers Group. Reprinted by permission.

8   One of the witnesses, Dr. Jerome Lejeune of Paris, highlighted the event with a lyric description of transcontinental cattle-breeding. What you do is transport a fertilized cow ovum across the ocean in the Fallopian tube of a rabbit and then transplant the ovum back into a cow uterus. (What you get, by the way, is a calf and not a cabbit.)

9   By the end of the first morning, to no one's surprise, the doctors had testified that biological life begins at conception. Eureka! Stop the presses!

10   Had anyone doubted it? Even the most ardent pro-choice advocate will willingly confess that he or she was once a zygote.

11   East, however, maintained the charade that he was conducting a serious medical inquiry into the origin of life, instead of an end run around the abortion issue. In his best schoolboy manner, he earnestly asked the witnesses whether they were absolutely sure of their testimony. Finally, in exasperation, Mayo Clinic Dr. Hymie Gordon said, "This is the first time I've ever been called on to argue the unarguable."

12   The Senate hearings were clearly set up to ask the wrong questions. They answered them in utterly predictable ways.

13   The human-life measure raises a host of sticky constitutional issues about the relationship between Congress and the courts. Congress is trying to dictate law to the courts. For this reason, the Conference of Catholic Bishops has opposed the legislation, and even Sen. Orrin G. Hatch (R-Utah) has come down with a case of the qualms. He dropped out of co-sponsoring the hearings.

14   East has promised to call witnesses about these issues later, but the prospects for meaningful testimony are slim.

15   The deck is stacked by the language of the proposed legislation. The fierce, unabating abortion controversy in this country is not over the moment one biological life commences. It's over the tragic moment when two rights conflict.

16   It's not about whether a fetus has a claim to protection. It's about whether the fetus' claim is greater than the woman's. Does the Constitution protect the zygote over the woman? At what point in gestation does the state have a compelling interest in the unborn?

17   There are those who define "person" in strict biological terms, and those who define "person" in more complex legal and philosophical ways.

18   There are those who believe that a woman forced to maintain a pregnancy against her will is nothing more than a vessel, and there are those who believe that a woman who has an abortion is a murderer.

19   But, in the Senate chamber, all these deep political, legal and philosophical concerns were ignored. Finally, even one of the witnesses sighed, "I don't know why I'm here." He wasn't the only one.

Abortion—A Form of Violence?[15]

By Colman McCarthy

1   Unlucky in his chromosomes, Mike Skinner, a 3-month-old infant, was lucky medically. A month before his birth in early May, doctors in San Francisco discovered fetal abnormalities. They operated, successfully.

2   Surgery on unborn patients is such a new art that prenatal medicine commands front-page news stories. The healthiness of the Skinner baby—"the doctors were all smiling and I was overjoyed," his mother said—was reported not long after hearings before Senate subcommittee on when human life begins.

3   The clamor aroused by pro-abortion forces opposed to the hearings was an eruption of controversy that pushed aside, once again, the central issue of the abortion debate: What are the rights of human beings not yet born?

4   The parents of Mike Skinner, as well as their doctors and the medical ethicist they consulted, believed that this unborn person had quite a few rights, beginning with the one to be born alive. Other couples, like the one in Boston that discovered the mother was carrying a Down's syndrome fetus and therefore ordered it to be killed through the heart with a needle, believe that you have a right to be born only if you are healthy.

5   This group is among the more reflective of the abortion advocates. At least it gives signs that it is wrestling with the ethics and morality of the question. Others, content with stridency and sloganeering, won't even get into the ring. They are well-represented by Kathy Wilson, the new chairwoman of the National Women's Political Caucus. In a recent speech, she denounced Ronald Reagan as "a President who encourages Congress to nationalize a woman's body. . . ."

6   Dumping on Reagan is a sure applause line among many feminists. But it does no more than create a standoff with antiabortionists who win cheers among their faithful for blasting the Supreme Court as baby-killers for its 1973 decision. Despite the prepackaged cant, women's bodies aren't being nationalized, and the chamber of Justice Harry A. Blackmun, who wrote the decision, is not a torture chamber.

7   All that's relevant is what kind of protection we give to life, from the first stirrings to the final groan. Or, to turn it around, is death to be an acceptable solution to social and personal problems that are overbearing?

8   To raise the question is not to minimize the immense cost paid by those faced with what is overbearing. I, for one, am not so sure of my abilities to face, much less overcome, life's cruelties and mysteries that I would tell the parents of a Mongoloid fetus to rise up to the challenge ahead because raising a retarded child will be spiritually enhancing.

---

[15]From the *Los Angeles Times*, August 18, 1981. © 1981 by The Washington Post Company. Reprinted by permission.

9   It may be for some parents, but to others the opposite is true. In a remarkably candid letter to the Los Angeles Times the other day, a man began: "I am writing to tell the other side regarding the letters on the killing of the unborn fetus. I have a 30-year-old mentally retarded son whose life has been nothing but grief for him and us. . . . Every time I read letters from all those busy-bodies who would tell someone else how to live their lives and the decisions they should make, I wish I could send them my son for a month. Let them live with the problems that never end, the grief you feel, have always felt, and will until you die."

10   This is a persuasive plea that we should all have a merciful regard for the weight of the next person's cross. But it is no justification for abortion. Alternatives short of death are available, even if these alternatives are remote and rare.

11   Although it is depressingly true that few neighbors or institutions offer meaningful help to parents of the retarded, or rape victims, or pregnant teen-agers, that is no license to abandon the search for nonviolent alternatives.

12   That becomes despair. It sanctions the political and social system that has made it acceptable for the nation to rely on violent solutions to other problems that seem overbearing: capital punishment for despicable murderers, arms shipments to friendly Latin American dictators, the stockpiling of weapons to wipe out Russia should the need arise.

13   Life is sacred, everyone agrees, except when . . .

14   This list of "except whens" is a display of double standards. Either all of life is worth protecting, prenatal life included, or none is. When it's done, rationales replace moral absolutes. One group can say that we need more bombs to preserve peace, while another holds that fetal life can be destroyed because a woman doesn't want her body nationalized.

Confess to Your Corporate Father

By Peter Schrag[16]

1   By the time Linda Davis was halfway through the first set of 100 questions in the blue-covered booklet, her palms and fingers had begun to sweat. Maybe it was the heat in the little room in the back of the store where she was taking this test. Maybe it was something else. *I always get nervous taking tests,* she tells herself. But she has never taken a test like this before.

2   "Do you think most companies take advantage of people who work for them when they can?"

3   "Did you ever think about stealing money from places where you have worked?"

4   "Do you believe you are too honest to steal?"

---

[16]From *Mother Jones*, August 1978. Reprinted by permission.

5   *This is stupid,* she thinks. *The same question over and over.* She looks across at the young black man who is also applying for a sales clerk's job in the same store and who is taking the same test, but there is no eye contact, and she turns back to her booklet and to the pink-and-white machine-scored answer sheet.

6   "If you knew a member of your family was stealing from a place where he works, do you think you would report it to the owner of the company?"

7   "Were you ever tempted to take company money without actually taking any?"

8   "Do you keep out of trouble at all costs?"

9   "Do you think it okay to get around the law if you don't actually break it?"

10   The test, called the Reid Report, is one of about a dozen similar pre-employment screens now on the market for use in examining job applicants in discount and drug stores, banks, brokerage houses, fast-food restaurants and, as in Linda Davis' case, The Gap, a chain of some 300 mod clothing outlets specializing in Levi's jeans, shirts and jackets. The Gap likes to look hip, and in its use of the Reid Report it is in the very vanguard of what's known as "loss control."

11   The wave of the future. In a survey of 1,200 corporate executives conducted by the *Harvard Business Review* in 1974, 24 percent reported that their firms use "locker searches"; 46 percent of the firms use "package checks"; 30 percent use "electronic surveillance of high-risk areas"; 52 percent use "personality tests—tests that measure characteristics, not abilities"; ten percent use handwriting analysis in screening applicants for some jobs. Yet in the past few years probably the fastest-growing techniques for screening out so-called "dishonest employees" are polygraph tests—currently given some 500,000 workers a year, either on the job or before hiring—and paper-and-pencil tests like the Reid Report, now being given to some 250,000 job applicants annually. These tests supposedly can discern the 40 percent of the population who, in the estimate of Reid's director of research, will steal if they have the need and the opportunity.

12   "How much money do you pay each month as a result of divorce or separate maintenance for the support of your wife and/or children?"

13   "In the past five years about how much money, if any, have you gambled?"

14   "Did you wrongly take anything from a store without paying for it in the last three years?"

15   "Did you wrongfully take merchandise from other companies where you worked in the past three years?"

16   The questions go on and on—questions about debts and loans and outside income, about drug and drinking habits, about theft and

embezzlement. *The same question over and over. You have to be pretty stupid or pretty dishonest not to pass. If you said you'd turn in a member of your family if you learned he was stealing from his employer, they'd have to think you were pretty weird.* Yet by the time Linda answers all of the questions she will have revealed to her prospective employer nearly every important detail of her financial situation; her personal habits; her criminal record, if any; her mental and physical health; and, along the way, a considerable amount about her spouse and children. More important, she will also have accepted the idea that it's proper for her employers to know those things about her.

17   When Linda Davis turns in her booklet and answer sheet, they are sent to Reid and Associates, the Chicago polygraph firm that created the test and that will score it and report back to The Gap that the applicant is either "recommended for employment," "qualifiedly recommended," or "not recommended." In some cases it gives "no opinion." The report to the employer also includes a score indicating Reid's estimate of the chances that the applicant "would be involved in undesirable behavior." The inventory of Linda Davis' attitudes about theft—the first 100 questions she answered—is retained by Reid, but the evaluation and a 93-item factual questionnaire with the data on her alimony, debts and drug habits are returned to the employer for his personnel files.

18   After she completed the test—she was eventually hired—Linda Davis says she spent most of her testing time "psyching out the people who were trying to psych me out." But Reid claims that the test can't be psyched out—that thieves, like anyone else, believe that what they do is commonplace and normal and will, in the very process of "psyching out" the test, confess all sorts of dishonesty. "The typical view," according to Philip Ash, Reid's director of research, "is that an applicant will 'see through' the test and 'fake good.' In fact, this does not seem to happen. Although it may seem incredible, applicants in significant numbers admit to all kinds of delinquencies, defalcations and crimes. Hard data are not yet available to prove why this should be the case, but at least two important human tendencies seem to be at work. In the first place, in contemporary American society, there exists a strong tendency toward confession. . . . Confession reduces guilt; the act itself seems to mitigate the offense confessed. In the second place, response to the questions in the Reid Report is strongly determined by the individual's own practices. For example, someone who steals will approve of punishment only for thefts greater than his own."

19   Reid claims that, in screening out dishonest job applicants, the Report is almost as accurate as the polygraph (which, Reid says, is accurate nearly 95 percent of the time when used by a qualified examiner). The Report's major advantages are that it is cheaper than a polygraph test and is not covered by the statutes that, in 17 states, restrict or prohibit the use of electronic "lie detectors" in employment screening.

What is certain is that in the past decade the use of both polygraphs and paper-and-pencil tests has been growing at a phenomenal rate; that the subjects include a disproportionate number of blacks, Chicanos and other minorities who constitute the basic non-union, high-turnover, minimum-wage force in discount stores and fast-food restaurants; and that those who take them are often so desperate for work that they can't afford the luxury of refusing to take a test. The choice, as one woman said after refusing to take a polygraph test, "is starvation or submission."

20   The personnel directors and the "loss control" managers who require tests like the Reid Report and the Stanton Survey, a similar instrument published by another Chicago firm, insist that such tests are far less intrusive than the polygraph because they can't be used (as polygraphs sometimes are) to make one employee turn in another, to dredge up irrelevant personal information or to elicit personally embarrassing data that is sometimes sold to employers, credit companies or anyone else in the market for dirt. Yet the principle and objectives are the same: to get the subject to reveal himself, to psych him out through the very process that makes him think he's psyching the test out.

21   "It's uncanny," said Carl Klump, a former Reid employee who developed the Stanton Survey. "Crooked people speak alike and write alike." In Klump's test the applicant is allowed to explain certain answers—essentially to free-associate. "Ninety percent of the people who say 'Honesty is the best policy' are honest. But of those who say 'I don't like stealing, it makes me feel guilty,' 75 percent are crooked. The people who rationalize by denying their own responsibility tend to be dishonest.

22   "You can also learn a lot from people's fantasies. We ask, among other things, what the applicant would like to do if he had a chance to train for any kind of job. We found that, of the people who say they'd be nurses, twice as many are honest as those who say they'd be airline stewardesses. And look out for the young man who fantasizes about being a welder or a carpenter. I'm not saying that welders and carpenters are dishonest. I'm saying that those who fantasize about it tend to be dishonest."

23   The manufacturers of these tests insist that they work, and they provide extensive anecdotal and statistical data to support their case. Klump reports that 77 percent of high-risk applicants admit shoplifting in the Stanton Survey, compared with fewer than two percent of the low-risk applicants. He talks about one firm that reduced its inventory shrinkage from 9.1 percent to 1.5 percent in two years with the Stanton Survey, then found the shrinkage increasing again when it temporarily stopped using the test. And both Reid and Stanton publish validation studies indicating that the paper-and-pencil tests compare favorably with polygraph results.

24   Yet the accuracy of the polygraph itself continues to be challenged—indeed, can be challenged even if one accepts the industry's own data about its accuracy. In a study conducted by Frank S. Horvath

and John E. Reid (a pioneer in the polygraph field) of Reid and Associates, roughly six percent of "innocent" people tested by the most highly trained examiners were found to be "guilty." (When inexperienced examiners gave the same test, 16 percent were falsely judged "guilty.") What these percentages mean is that, of the 300,000 honest people given polygraph examinations every year (a crude estimate based on industry figures), even the most experienced examiners—which most are not—will label 18,000 dishonest. Considering the fact (acknowledged by most of the test manufacturers) that the paper-and-pencil instruments are less accurate than the polygraph, the percentage of "false positives"—people falsely judged dishonest—is likely to be considerably higher. Many firms, like The Gap, say they use the tests in combination with interviews and other data to make a judgment about an applicant—that they do not blindly follow the recommendation of the test manufacturers. But most acknowledge that the recommendation is, at the very least, an important factor.

25   The professional polygraphers—they like to call themselves "detectors of deception"—argue that such devices are not aimed at honest workers. In the words of a statement by the American Polygraph Association: "All intelligent people endorse the right of the innocent to prove their innocence, the right of the employer to protect his business—*and his honest employees*—from the occasional dishonest worker." The association believes that these honest employees "have a very personal stake in preserving the polygraph technique . . . so that their reputations, jobs and public safety and welfare can be protected."

26   Although the novel idea that the innocent have to prove their innocence isn't yet a formal part of American jurisprudence, it is *all* workers who are being tested and screened, all who come under scrutiny. All are being taught that, in their relationship with their employer (and sometimes with their union), their records, personalities, behavior, credit ratings, mental health, drug habits and, in some cases, their living arrangements and sexual preferences, are not private, and that if they lie about them they will be found out and fired.

27   The industry claims that tests like the polygraph and the Reid Report are necessary to reduce theft, particularly where there is high employee turnover and when references and other background data are hard or expensive to get. Employee theft, according to the industry, amounts to somewhere around $24 billion a year; any company (in Carl Klump's words) "that doesn't use one of these tests is foolish."

28   All sorts of explanations have been offered for the apparent rise in such crime, most of them predictable; yet employee theft clearly reflects a decline in conventional sources of loyalty and discipline. Where the worker once identified with his employer, or where he once worked in the expectation that good work would eventually be rewarded with higher pay or a better job—where he trusted the system to function as advertised

or to be mutable through labor unions or political action—he now attempts to beat it with a sort of freelance economic guerrilla warfare. The employer, in turn, responds with counter-insurgency tactics and counter-insurgency technology: closed-circuit television monitors, bugs, infrared sensors and other electronic devices to watch stores, warehouses and offices. The pre-employment screen, in that context, is just another weapon in the arsenal.

29   Yet the power of the instrument to find liars and cheats and thieves, however accurate, may not be nearly so important as the presumption behind the instrument's use: that the innocent have to prove their innocence, that 40 percent of all workers will steal given "need and opportunity" and that confession is the best test of truth. In that respect, the Reid Report may merely institutionalize the presumption of dishonesty among workers that fosters the theft problem in the first place. People like Klump, and the personnel managers who require such tests, say that applicants rarely refuse to take them. Yet those who will not sacrifice their privacy or relinquish their principles—those who are not willing or not hungry enough to submit to the indignities of proving their honesty—will never get the jobs or, in many cases, will never even apply for them.

30   By their very nature, questionnaires and tests that intrude into the private lives, thoughts and attitudes of the individual favor the docile, the obedient and the desperate. And that, in the final analysis, may be their real effect, if not their intended function. They condition the individual to accept the questions of official snoops, to defer, to regard such intrusions as normal—as one of the necessary conditions of modern life. The fact that potential employees have to answer those questions is both an expression and a confirmation of the inequities of power and position.

Research

10. The Research Paper

*W*hat do you think of when you hear the word *research*? A white-smocked scientist working in a laboratory amidst vials, containers, and white mice? A scholar poring over some musty tomes in the library stacks? A smiling interviewer accosting you in the dairy section of the supermarket with samples of a new cheese? Actually, each of these activities represents research, insofar as each involves careful, serious, and systematic investigation.

As these activities suggest, research takes various forms according to the aim of those doing it. For example, those doing *pure research* aim to discover new knowledge about a subject. Today, for instance, we send spacecraft millions of miles in the hope of increasing our knowledge about the universe. Those engaged in *applied research* aim to make practical use of what is already known. For example, once the laser beam had been invented, scientists started looking for ways to apply it, as in determining the distances to the planets, improving weapons, and performing delicate eye surgery. Those doing *market research* study consumer needs and desires in order to produce new products. Remote control devices for television sets, flip-top cans, escort services, and even textbooks such as this one are among the multitude of goods and services developed because research showed that consumers wanted them.

Then there is *scholarly research*. Scholarly research resembles pure research in that it aims to increase the store of knowledge about a subject, even though the knowledge may be of no immediate or practical use beyond the knowing itself. But whereas pure research is ordinarily associated with the natural sciences (biology, chemistry, geology, physics) and deals with materials of the physical world, scholarly research can be conducted within any field and deals primarily with written records. A historian who publishes a work on the New Deal, a philosopher who writes an article on theories of social justice, a sociologist who does an article on the social impact of divorce, and someone in business who delivers a speech on the merits of "trickle-down" economics are all doing scholarly research. Students are often required to do scholarly research, as, for example, when they are asked to prepare a research paper, or term paper, the subject of this chapter.

For most students the research paper is probably the most dreaded of all academic exercises. The announcement of a required research paper often sends students scurrying off in search of an alternative course without such a requirement. The reasons for this student fright and flight are understandable enough. For one thing, many students have trouble enough writing a short essay, let alone a long one. For another, there is the unsettling thought of having to choose a subject, do research, and then organize a mountain of material. What to write about? Where to get the information? How to evaluate, organize, and present the data? Still another problem is the time factor. Research is time consuming and painstaking. It is not something that can be done in a free hour or at a cafeteria table. Research requires considerable field work—usually, but not always, in the college library. With the other academic and personal demands on their time, students worry about how they can budget time for a research paper, perhaps for several of them. Such concerns are real and pressing.

But, like it or not, the research paper remains a fact of student life. Although there is no easy way to allay the anxiety you may feel, you can help yourself by cultivating a positive attitude toward the research paper.

The research paper promises many benefits for those who diligently undertake it. First, it allows you to explore a subject that interests you. Very often students complain about having no voice in selecting course content. Professors choose the topics to be covered and the books to be read. The research paper gives you the opportunity to pursue some aspect of a course with particular appeal to you or even a subject outside the course content.

Looked at this way, the research project is a rare opportunity for self-direction and personal expression.

Second, the research paper allows you to plumb a subject. So often in courses and textbooks, time limitations encourage only surface coverage. As a result, students leave with a sketchy knowledge of a subject. The research paper can serve as an antidote to this superficiality, which is especially embedded in survey courses. It allows you to deepen and broaden your understanding of a subject, to give focus and definition to what otherwise might remain blurred and amorphous.

Third, the research paper is a wonderful opportunity for you to develop skills for lifelong learning. One of these is the ability to dig out and use diverse sources of information. It is far better for you to acquire this ability now in an academic setting than later in a professional one, where people are not likely to be as sympathetic to your research inadequacies as your professors are. Another important skill is the ability to distinguish between significant and insignificant data. In large part, the research paper is an exercise in critical judgment. It not only requires that you exercise critical thinking but also helps you develop and refine this ability. Learning to think critically has great carry-over value in making speeches; in writing reports, letters, and articles; and in doing graduate studies. Still another skill that the research paper sharpens is your organizational ability. Professional people often have an impressive mastery of facts but are unable to communicate them effectively for lack of organizational ability. The research paper forces you to assemble a large body of material in a clear, logical way.

Fourth, the research paper is an invitation to discovery. The discovery takes the form of recognizing links and relations among seemingly discrete data. It also takes the form of realizing, perhaps for the first time, the worth and impact of what you have been studying. You might even discover things that help shape your future course of study or occupational goals.

Fifth, and perhaps most important, the research paper offers you opportunities for self-satisfaction. It gives you the joy of working independently to fulfill a goal. It promises the satisfaction that follows from having written something good, of having worked to the current limits of your ability, and of knowing that you are steeped in a topic.

As for the concerns of this text, this chapter can be viewed as a capstone to our study of good reason for writing. It draws together what we have previously said about argument, argumentative essays, developmental patterns, and fallacies by showing their interplay with research and the research paper. Indeed, if you have diligently studied the previous chapters, you are well on your way toward doing a good research paper.

I should hasten to note, however, that it is beyond the scope of this text to cover all the important technical aspects of writing a research paper—for example, taking notes, inserting quotations, providing footnotes, presenting a bibliography, and so on. Rather, this chapter relates the concerns of our study to the basic steps of a research paper: (1) choosing the topic, (2) collecting the information, (3) evaluating the materials, (4) organizing the ideas, and (5) writing the paper. Before taking up these steps, we will consider what a research paper is and what it is not.

WHAT THE RESEARCH PAPER IS
AND WHAT IT IS NOT

The research paper we are considering closely resembles the writing you have been doing throughout this course. In fact, the research paper can be viewed as an extended argument. Like the other argumentative essays you've studied, the research paper aims to win audience assent or consent. In other words, it has an argumentative point, a persuasive point, or both. Accordingly, it has a thesis, main points, and organization, and it relies on various developmental patterns (fact and opinion, comparison and contrast, analogy, cause and effect, and definition). Furthermore, as with any other argumentative essay, the effectiveness of the research paper depends in part on the avoidance of common fallacies.

There are, however, some differences between the research paper and shorter essays. One difference is length: The typical student research paper runs from 1,500 to 3,000 words, or from six to twelve typewritten pages. A more significant difference lies in the actual form of the research paper. Whereas an ordinary theme has little if any documentation, the research paper fully identifies sources, usually in footnotes, and often lists them again in a bibliography (an alphabetical listing of all sources used in the project). The main difference between the research paper and the ordinary theme, then, is that in the research paper you must make available to the readers all the sources on which you based your presentation. This allows readers to check your sources and to look for things such as balance, fairness, completeness, and accuracy in your presentation.

Although the research paper can be looked on as an extended argument, it does have three characteristics that you must keep in mind to avoid writing something that is not a research paper.[1] The research paper (1) is a *synthesis,* (2) shows *originality,* and (3) provides *documentation.*

The research paper is, ideally, a synthesis of your ideas and the material supplied to you by others. Accordingly, it brings together your discoveries about a topic and your evaluation of those discoveries. It is true that the discoveries largely consist of the thoughts, findings, ideas, and words of authorities that you have investigated. But *you* must evaluate all these data.

This evaluation involves you intimately in the creation of the paper. It is you who must decide what all the information means and what point of view

---

[1]See Audrey J. Roth. *The Research Paper: Form and Content,* 3rd ed. Belmont, Calif.: Wadsworth, 1978, p. 8.

it suggests. And you must decide how to organize and present this information. Thus, although writing a research paper may not be as creative an exercise as composing a poem or short story, it does require highly original activities, which in the broadest sense do require creativity.

The third characteristic of the research paper is that it documents source material. It clearly and completely credits those from whose work you have drawn. There are several ways to provide documentation. Your instructor will inform you of the method to follow.

Knowing what a research paper is, we can now distinguish it from pieces of writing that try to pass as research papers. First, a summary of an article or book is *not* a research paper. A research paper embraces numerous sources, not just a single one. Second, merely repeating the ideas of others is *not* a research paper. Remember the personal process involved: *You* must examine critically the thoughts of others and draw your own conclusions from that analysis. If you don't do this, you will succeed only in writing a report, perhaps a book report. Third, a string of quotations, no matter how artfully rendered, is not a research paper. Yes, quotations have a definite role in the research paper, but they function to support *your* discoveries about a topic and *your* evaluation of these discoveries. Fourth, unsupported personal opinion does not constitute a research paper. Although it is true that your evaluations are opinions, they must be based on your careful sifting of the available data. In order for readers to evaluate your judgments, they must have access to the information on which you based them. Fifth, using other people's work without acknowledging them is not research but plagiarism, a subject about which your instructor will undoubtedly have more to say.

With these preliminary remarks behind us, let's now turn to the basic steps in writing a research paper: choosing a topic, finding material, evaluating the material, organizing the material, and writing the paper.

STEP ONE: CHOOSING A TOPIC

There are two basic tasks that face you in this first step. One concerns the type of subject assigned, and the other deals with a procedure for selecting a topic.

Types of Subject

There are three kinds of research subject: assigned subjects, which are selected by the instructor (often together with the actual topics); field-of-study subjects, which are chosen by you and related to the course for which the paper is required; and free-choice subjects, which are chosen by you from whatever area you like.[2] Since field-of-study and free-choice subjects give students the most trouble, we will concentrate on them.

---

[2]Roth. *The Research Paper*, pp. 11–38.

Field-of-Study Subjects By definition, field-of-study subjects must deal with the subject matter of the course. Therefore, you must know something about that subject matter before you can make any progress in the research paper. In all likelihood, the paper will be assigned early in the term. If you're lucky, you may know enough about the course content at that point to select a subject. But it is more likely that you will know next to nothing about the course. If so, you face a dilemma. On the one hand, you can begin work on the research paper as early in the term as possible in order to allow yourself the necessary time for research and writing. But how can you do this when you don't know enough about a course to select a subject? On the other hand, you can delay beginning the paper until well into the term. By that time you will be informed enough to select an appropriate subject, but you may not have enough time to write an effective paper.

If you are one of those wise and conscientious students who want to begin as early as possible but don't know how to identify a subject, there are a couple of things you can do. First, you can turn to a myriad of printed aids. Second, you can look to your own interests.

1. *There is an abundance of printed material that can help you choose a subject.* Your own textbook, encyclopedias, library card catalogs, and periodical indexes are just some. The textbook of your course has a table of contents that lists chapter titles and issues covered, both of which are rich sources of subjects. For example, suppose that you are taking a course entitled Business and Social Responsibility. On the first day of class the instructor announces a field-of-study research paper requirement. That night you examine the table of contents of the text. Although you know nothing about the course's content, some of the entries in the table of contents pique your interest. Indeed, you find the subject matter of Chapter 5 particularly interesting (see page 345, top).

There is much in this entry of potential use to you. For one thing, it suggests a broad area for your research: privacy. For another, it suggests narrower subjects that fall under privacy, such as obtaining information without consent and invading personal decisions. Indeed, topics are suggested under these subjects (for example, legitimate areas of organizational influence, polygraph tests, and submission to mental health therapy).

Further, this table of contents indicates the presence of case presentations, which can be a most valuable source of additional subjects, particularly controversial issues, and approaches to certain problems. For example, you turn to the case entitled "She Snoops to Conquer." You find that it deals with a department store manager who, faced with the problem of employee theft of merchandise in the jewelry department, decides to install cameras and microphones in employee locker rooms, lounges, and restrooms. After reading the brief case, you wonder how much spying on employees and customers actually goes on in retail business. This may be a subject you want to pursue further. The point is simple but important: Don't overlook cases and other exercises

5. ORGANIZATIONAL INFLUENCE IN PRIVATE LIVES
    Privacy
        Spheres of Privacy: Psychic, Physical, Social
        Legitimate Areas of Organizational Influence
        Legitimate Interference
    Obtaining Information without Consent
        Polygraph Tests
        Personality Tests
        Monitoring Employees
    Invasion of Personal Decisions
        Contributions to Charities
        Membership in Civic Organizations
        Submissions to Mental Health Therapy
        Participation in Consciousness-Raising Workshops
    Case Presentations
        "Speak, If You Dare"
        "Foreign Cars: Keep Out"
        "She Snoops to Conquer"
    Readings
        "Your Employees' Right to Blow the Whistle" by Kenneth D. Walters
        "Polygraph Usage Among Major U.S. Corporations" by John A. Belt
          and Peter B. Holden
        "Privacy Versus Intrusion: Darkness at Noon?" by David W. Ewing
    Bibliography

included in texts. Frequently they key on controversial issues and approaches to specific problems in a field. As such, they are subject sources worth exploiting.

Furthermore, the reading selections contained in the chapter on privacy are potentially of enormous help in choosing a subject. Even their titles suggest areas, indeed topics (for example, "whistle-blowing" or polygraphs). Suppose further that this text contained a name index, as do many books. Here you would find a list of people mentioned in the text. Done properly, a study of the work or contributions of any of these figures could lead to an acceptable field-of-study research paper. And don't forget the bibliography and glossary. They can serve the same purpose by providing key terms, issues, and concepts related to the course. In short, the table of contents, exercises, reading selections, bibliography, indexes, and glossary of your text constitute a menu of subject possibilities.

Besides your text, there are other good printed aids to subject selection. One is an encyclopedia. Reading an article on the subject of a course or on a related subject provides an overview that can go far toward suggesting a research subject and topic. Another printed aid is the card catalog of your library. It contains at least three card entries for each nonfiction work in the library: one filed by author, another by title, and still another by subject. Start your search in the subject catalog. For example, if you think you want to do your paper for the Business and Social Responsibility course on the subject of privacy, look under "Privacy." There you will not only find that many books on privacy are listed but also discover that the subject is divided into various subheadings. The many periodical indexes housed in the library are still another useful source of field-of-study research ideas. These list magazine and journal articles. For example, looking under "Privacy" in an issue of the *Readers' Guide to Periodical Literature,* you will discover various subheadings that may suggest a subject. I will say more about periodical indexes presently.

2. *Your own interests are a valuable source of research subjects.* One author has suggested that, by associating words related to a course with your vocational or avocational interests, you can devise relevant subjects.[3] For example, you have an interest in real estate. Draw a vertical line. On one side, write *real estate;* on the other write all the words you can think of that relate to the course. Use words from the table of contents, words associated with subdivisions within the course, or words devised by free association with the course material. Here's what you might get for the course under discussion.

hiring	
promotions	
discipline	
discharge	
function of work	
wages	
work conditions	
job content	
privacy	real estate
polygraphs	
personality tests	
bribes and kickbacks	
antitrust and securities	
consumerism	
women	
minorities	
environment	
theories of social justice	

By combining each word on the left with the one on the right, you might so relate course content to individual interest that a subject is suggested. Accordingly, you might make a connection between consumerism and selling real estate such that the following subject emerges: "Consumer Rights in Real Estate Transactions." Similarly, you might connect wages and real estate to

---

[3]Roth. *The Research Paper,* pp. 19–22.

suggest this subject: "Alternatives to the Standard Real Estate Commission." Again, you might connect the environment with real estate to produce the subject "Environmental Pollution and Land Development."

Naturally, the connection between course material and personal interest is not always as apparent as in this example. For instance, courses in logic, political science, or astronomy might pose a real challenge. Still, with industry and imagination you could relate the concerns of these areas to real estate. Thus, for logic: "The Use of Emotional Appeals in Selling Real Estate"; for political science: "Property Ownership in Democratic Capitalism"; and for astronomy: "Land Ownership in Outer Space."

So, although a field-of-study research assignment may at first intimidate you, it needn't. Available to you are numerous printed aids and personal interests waiting to be enlisted in your search for a subject.

Free-Choice Subjects Sometimes an instructor gives you freedom in choosing a subject for the paper. If you are invited to choose a subject of your own, one not necessarily related to the course, the sky is the limit. But the complete freedom of choice may be too much for you. Faced with no subject constraints, you may falter and flounder. But you needn't despair, for there are several antidotes to this paralysis of imagination.

First, you can select something that you are familiar with and about which you would like to learn more. Perhaps you've had a health course and learned something about vitamin therapy in the treatment of disease. If you want to learn more, why not make vitamin therapy your research subject? Or maybe you recently read a newspaper article entitled "The American Indian: The Forgotten Minority." You remember being moved by the piece and wishing that you had the time to explore the plight of American Indians further. Here again is a possible research subject. Or perhaps one of your outstanding gripes with colleges is the weight that admissions officers sometimes place on standardized tests. If you want to learn more about the pros and cons of such testing, make it the subject of your paper.

Second, you can choose a subject that you know nothing about but would like to investigate. A good place to begin is with terms you encountered once and glossed over, such as *supply-side economics, circles of work, Big Bang, astral plains,* or *cybernetics.* Such terms are potential subjects for research.

Similarly, subjects can originate in conversations you've had. A few years ago a student did a research paper on what some experts on organizational psychology and management term "Z Theory," which is a way of approaching and structuring work that is new to the United States but has been common throughout Japan for decades. When asked how he decided on such an unusual subject, the student explained that some time before he had struck up a conversation with a passenger on a flight from San Francisco to Los Angeles. As it happened, the exchange turned to the subject of work and young people's attitudes toward it. The passenger thought that the Japanese approach to work organization might be more appealing to young American workers and help improve U.S. productivity. The flight ended before the passenger could explain very much about this approach. The student said he didn't think much more about it until, a few months later, he was asked to write a free-choice research paper. Recalling the conversation, he discovered his research subject.

Third, you can skim newspapers, magazines, and other periodicals for possible subjects. A good newspaper (sometimes even a poor one) is a treasure trove of research subjects. Daily columns, commentaries, and editorials abound with information about current events, science, medicine, the arts, sports, religion, and education. In fact, brief news reports often inspire a research subject. Another enterprising student once chanced upon an item about how the Food and Drug Administration had banned for sale in the United States an intrauterine device called the Dalkon Shield. A few weeks later the student came across another item, concerning the export of the Dalkon Shield for sale abroad. She found this odd and began to wonder how many other products that were banned in the United States were being shipped overseas for sale. "Why not write a paper on this subect?" she thought. She did, and was it an eye-popper!

Fourth, you can consult the library for a subject of interest. Because the card catalogs contain information on every subject, merely perusing them should yield a clutch of ideas.

After you have chosen a subject, you must identify possible topics and then select one and narrow it.

Selection Procedure

The same procedure for topic selection that was sketched in Chapter 2 can be applied to the research paper. Recall that topic selection consists of (1) selecting a subject, (2) identifying possible topics, and (3) selecting and limiting a topic to write on. Presumably you have been using this procedure, or a comparable onc, throughout this course. So, there is no need to belabor it here. But it might be useful to provide one final example of this process as it applies to a research paper. For illustrative purposes, let's return to the earlier example involving a field-of-study idea for your Business and Social Responsibility course. Suppose that, after scanning the table of contents of your text, you decide to research the subject of privacy. Here are some possible broad topics and limited ones:

Subject	*Broad Topics*
Privacy	Use of information to invade it
	Impact of the new technology on it
	Effect on the quality of life at work

Broad Topics	*Limited Topics*
Use of information	How information gathered from applications, interviews, and other personnel data can be used to invade privacy

Broad Topics	Limited Topics
Impact of technology	The social effects of computers, electronic surveillance, and various monitoring devices
Quality of life at work	The impact of dictating employee manners, dress, and life-style

Notice again that the suggested limited topics contain a useful way of controlling your research: dividing it into parts. It's quite possible that you will be unable to do this until you have done some preliminary research. But you should select and limit the topic as soon as possible to direct the research and thus save time and work.

Were you writing a short essay, at this point you would determine your attitude toward the topic and write the thesis statement. The danger of doing that at this point in the research-paper process is that you will end up consulting and using only sources that confirm your presuppositions. Ideally, you should approach the research without any predetermined attitudes or conclusions about the topic. So, having decided on a topic, you should then start collecting information about it. A careful study of this information will give rise to your attitude, which, when combined with the limited topic, will yield the thesis.

At the same time, there is something that you can and should decide at this point: the approach that you will take toward the topic. *Approach* here refers to the method you will use to deal with the material. Although there are several approaches to a research paper, we will assume an argumentative approach, which is consistent with the focus of this book.

Exercises

10.1 *Perhaps you have to do a field-of-study research paper for a course that you are taking. If not, pretend that you do, and select four different subjects for possible investigation: (1) select a subject based on material that you find in the course's text; (2) select a subject based on an encyclopedia article; (3) select a subject based on entries in the library card catalog; and (4) select a subject based on listings in the Readers' Guide.*

10.2 *For each of the four subjects that you have selected, identify possible topics and limit each.*

10.3 Choose still another subject for a field-of-study paper by associating words pertaining to the course with your own vocational or avocational interests.

10.4 Suppose that you have been assigned a free-choice subject in a course you are taking. Identify four different subjects: (1) select something you are familiar with and about which you would like to learn more; (2) select something you know nothing about but would like to investigate; (3) select something from a newspaper, magazine, or other periodical; and (4) select something you discovered in the library.

10.5 Identify possible topics for each of the four free-choice subjects, and limit those topics.

STEP TWO: FINDING THE MATERIALS

Once you have decided on a topic, you must then look for material about it. There are two kinds of sources that you can consult: primary and secondary.

Primary sources are the most direct information you can obtain. They consist of legal documents, letters, diaries, notes, autobiographies, eyewitness reports, transcripts of speeches and interviews, reports on experiments, established surveys, and the like. In doing papers on literature and the other arts, primary sources also include novels, short stories, plays, poems, films, and paintings. *In contrast, secondary sources are other authors' accounts and interpretations of primary materials.* Secondary sources commonly take the form of evaluations, commentaries, and summaries.

In doing your paper you will be relying on both kinds of sources. Therefore, a few guidelines are in order. First, because primary sources are closer to unedited firsthand facts, using them gives your paper the authoritative clout it requires. Thus, if you are dealing with President Jimmy Carter's social-welfare policies, don't just rely on what others say about them; go to Carter's speeches themselves. If you're doing a paper on the work of the novelist Kurt Vonnegut, Jr., don't just rely on others' comments; consult Vonnegut's stories. In taking you closer to unedited firsthand facts, the inclusion of primary sources lowers the risk that your paper will be larded with questionable assertions, unsubstantiated opinions, and appeals to false authorities.

Second, don't prematurely give up on finding primary materials. It is true that primary sources are sometimes difficult to track down, especially in the limited time you will have to do your paper. But be imaginative. Remember, interviews and letters are primary sources. Thus, if you were doing research on the rising rate of rapes, you might call on a police chief, a judge, or personnel at a local rape crisis center or women's center for their opinions. Again, in doing the aforementioned paper on informational privacy, you could collect job applications from various local businesses to see what questions are typically asked. Also, you could interview personnel directors to find out how they use information. Similarly, if you were doing a paper on the merits of a proposed nuclear power plant, you could write to an officer with the utility company and to an environmentalist with special expertise on the subject.

Whether the material you seek is primary or secondary, you must know where this information can be obtained. We have already suggested some of these sources, but there are many more.

Sources

The library is where you will do most of your research. It contains a number of vital sources of information. Among the sources are *generalized reference works* such as the following:

1. *Encyclopedias.* An encyclopedia provides a summary of what is known on a subject. As such it can serve to launch your research. Among the popular and creditable encyclopedias are the *Encyclopaedia Britannica*, the most authoritative and general one; the *Encyclopedia Americana*, which is especially good for science and biography; *Collier's Encyclopedia*, which is written in a popular style; and the *Columbia Encyclopedia*, which provides a readable, concise view of subjects. Although encyclopedias are useful sources for beginning your research, they are only a beginning. Never end your research with the reading of an encyclopedia article.

2. *Bibliographies.* As indicated earlier, many encyclopedia entries provide a short list of important books and other sources of information. The books themselves will ordinarily contain a more detailed bibliography, as will your course text. The *Book Review Digest*, which contains short book reviews, is another useful bibliographic source. Read first those books that a bibliography labels "standard," "indispensable," or "the best introduction" to your subject. If no such description is provided, read those books most frequently mentioned in the bibliographies.[4]

3. *Periodical indexes.* Most research papers call for the most up-to-date information available. Magazine articles are one of the best sources of current information on an issue. You can find lists of individual articles in the periodical indexes. These are published monthly or semimonthly and then

---

[4]Hans Guth, *Words and Ideas*, 5th ed. Belmont, Calif.: Wadsworth, 1980, p. 199.

combined in large volumes, each listing articles for a period of a year or more. The best known of these indexes is the previously mentioned *Readers' Guide to Periodical Literature*. Under author and subject headings, it lists articles appearing in more than 100 general magazines. The *Social Science Index* (formerly *International Index*) lists articles contained in more scholarly magazines, such as sociological and psychological journals. The *Humanities Index* also focuses on more scholarly work.

4. *Newspaper indexes.* Newspaper indexes are another good source of information about current events, as well as issues that never appear in other kinds of periodicals. The most useful of these are the indexes published by the *New York Times*, the *Christian Science Monitor*, and the *Wall Street Journal*. In using indexes and bibliographies, always read their introductory pages and their lists of abbreviations. Also, always study the list of periodicals indexed, for they may not include a magazine that you have been referred to elsewhere. Finally, look at the same entries to study the listing of individual articles and the system of cross references.

Besides generalized reference works, such as the aforementioned, the library also contains *specialized reference works*, which are useful in special areas of study. Every major area (business, economics, education, geography, history, political science, psychology, sociology, art and architecture, literature, music and dance, philosophy, and religion) has its own specialized reference books: year books, encyclopedias, dictionaries of names and technical terms, and general bibliographies. Constance M. Winchell's *Guide to Reference Books,* or some such general guide, will help you find specialized books relevant to your research paper.

Also available are various reference works that include biographical entries. For example, *Who's Who in America* and the *Dictionary of American Biography* contain accounts of the lives of important people. *Biography Index* is a guide to biographical material in books and magazines.

Besides these generalized and specialized reference materials, your library, of course, contains card catalogs. Sometimes your research will involve simply tracking down an author or title. More likely, you will have to be conscientious and inventive in researching material by looking under relevant subject headings.

Although the library contains most of the materials you need for your project, there are other sources to consider. For example, interviews can be useful. So can questionnaires that you prepare, administer, and evaluate. If you employ this primary source, be careful how you construct it: Remember how easy it is to introduce bias into a questionnaire. Still other good nonlibrary sources are letters, radio and television programs, reports, pamphlets, and booklets.

Looking in the places cited is only one part of collecting information. You also need to record the results of the search in some way. This calls for the formulating of what is usually called a preliminary bibliography, which is a recording of each likely looking resource, typically written on index cards.

Your instructor will probably provide more information about how you should construct your preliminary bibliography. You will be using these records in the next step of the research paper: evaluating materials.

Exercise

10.6 *If you successfully completed the preceding exercises in this chapter, you should now have nine different topics for possible investigation—five field-of-study and four free-choice. Of these nine, choose four that you are particularly interested in—two field-of-study and two free-choice. Find five major sources for each of these topics. (Following your teacher's instructions, prepare a preliminary bibliography card for each source.)*

STEP THREE: EVALUATING THE MATERIALS

In evaluating the materials that you have collected, you are faced with two jobs: (1) identifying the most useful and informative sources for your purposes and then (2) taking notes from these sources.

Identifying the Best Sources

I noted at the beginning of this chapter that one of the benefits of doing a research paper is that it helps and requires you to exercise critical thinking and the logical skills you've developed in this course. In identifying the best sources, you must read over your research materials and decide which are the most helpful and reliable. Regarding helpfulness, keep your topic foremost in mind. Even though all of the materials you've collected presumably bear in some way on the topic, some works will be more relevant than others. As for their reliability, you must select those works that are dependable and truly informative. This calls for selecting authoritative sources and evaluating conflicting evidence. Although the judgments you must make about research materials are not easy, they are based on similar principles that you have used in collecting materials for other kinds of writing and in evaluating the essays in this text and elsewhere. Specifically, when evaluating your sources, keep the following questions in mind:

1. *Which authors seem outstanding in the field?* As you gather information, you will probably notice that some names recur or that some authors have written extensively in a field. The chances are good that these people are reliable sources, or sound authorities.

2. *Is a particular author an expert in the field?* This question addresses one of the basic criteria for a legitimate appeal to authority. Since your paper will rely so heavily on authoritative appeals, it is vital that you scrupulously apply the standards for judging reliable authority. Generally speaking, a book written by someone outside a field is not considered as authoritative as one by someone within the field, especially if the field is a highly technical one. Often the dust jacket provides professional information about the author. If the author is not identified in some way within the publication, you may be able to discover some information by consulting a biographical reference, such as *Who's Who in America* or *Contemporary Authors*.

3. *Does a source seem credible?* Simply because an author is an expert in the field does not make the person's work reliable. If your resource is a book, check some reviews. How a piece of scholarship is reviewed by critics is one good way to evaluate it. Also, consider the publisher. A book from a well-known publisher may be more credible than a privately published one. Also, you may be aware of some bias a publisher has that impugns a book's credibility. This is especially true of periodical publications. Many magazines have been founded expressly for advancing a particular political, social, or religious philosophy. Although this alone doesn't discredit a source, it should alert you to the presence of provincialism and the need to weigh the material contained in balance with counterevidence, perhaps from a publication that doesn't share the bias. Finally, the completeness of material in the introduction, preface, index, and bibliography is a further evidence of scholarship, and, therefore, credibility.

4. *Is a source long on evidence rather than opinion?* Because your project will require substantial facts, you will want sources that are muscled with useful data and information. Many books, even those that read well, serve up opinion at the expense of fact. Be careful of these. Used indiscriminately, they can pitch your paper into the realm of sheer opinion and questionable assertions.

5. *Is a source fair-minded and balanced?* Elsewhere in this text, fair-mindedness and balance have been held up as ideals that good argumentative writers try to attain. These ideals apply equally to your source material. Biased and unbalanced sources give you a lopsided view of things. If you rely exclusively on them, then your paper will be "loaded." This doesn't mean that you shouldn't use highly opinionated works. On the contrary, often a field's leading experts write the most inflammatory works. As long as the authors show that they have carefully considered the findings of other authorities, they constitute useful sources for your paper.

6. *Does an author settle important questions by going to primary sources?* Since, as noted, primary sources take us close to unedited firsthand fact, they are generally more reliable than secondary sources. It follows that the author who attempts to resolve crucial issues by harking back to primary source material is providing a more solid basis for judgment than one who chooses to stand on the more tenuous ground provided by secondary sources.

Again, this is why it's important for you to use some primary sources in your project.

7. *Is a work recent?* That a work was published, say, more than ten years ago does not make it unreliable. To assume so is a version of the appeal to novelty. The fact is that primary source material is frequently far older than a mere decade. And yet, the older a work, the more likely it is to contain dated material, even inaccuracies. Conversely, the more recent, the more likely it is to have profited from current research and the shortcomings of others. Furthermore, recent works generally summarize older, important works before charting what may be a new course. Reading good current scholarship, then, is one way to become acquainted with older works. All of this suggests that the wise researcher, although not ignoring the past, pays special attention to the newest work in a field, certainly in a scientific or technical field.

8. *What does the language used tell you about a source?* A careful inspection of the language used in a source can be most enlightening. For one thing, it can tell you for whom the work is written—a specialized audience or a lay one. For another, it can reveal bias or the lack of it. Recall what was said earlier about the emotive use of language. Unbiased scholarship avoids using emotive language. Again, however, simply because a work shows bias in its use of language does not mean that it is an unreliable source. But it does mean that you must be aware of the bias in using the material and drawing conclusions from it.

9. *What facts recur in your reading?* Every good writer can distinguish the important from the trivial, the more relevant from the less relevant. Without this ability, one omits the important and includes the insignificant. Although there is no sure way to acquire or sharpen this ability to discriminate, being attentive to recurring facts, ideas, themes, and observations is one good way to separate the wheat from the chaff. It's a safe bet that what you keep running across in your reading is important and, therefore, should find a place, perhaps a central one, in your paper.

10. *Does an author rely excessively on fallacies?* If an author relies on fallacies of ambiguity, presumption, or relevance to make a point, the source probably isn't very reliable. Certainly, it isn't one you can invoke in any detail without yourself committing the fallacies. This doesn't mean that a work must be fallacy free, for that is as rare as a dog without fleas. But there is a difference between a book containing an occasional fallacious appeal and one that relies on them excessively. Faced with the author who chronically casts reason to the winds in favor of ambiguity, presumption, and irrelevance, seek truth and wisdom elsewhere.

Taking Notes

Once you have decided which sources will probably be the most useful and informative for your purposes, you are ready to read the individual works

closely enough to take notes on them. Note taking is itself part of the evaluative process, because it calls for extraction of the materials that you will use to
write the research paper. If the information you cull from your reading is
trivial or irrelevant or if you record inaccurately, these defects will show up in
your paper. There are three kinds of notes that you will take: summaries,
paraphrases, and direct quotations. Although much can be said about the
techniques involved in each, our brief remarks will be essentially cautionary.

A summary is a report written in your own words. Summaries typically
contain examples, explanations, and other forms of elaboration that appeared
in the original source. Most important, a summary records *only* what another
has said, not your interpretation of it. In writing summaries ensure accuracy
and completeness. You don't want to be left with notes that are misrepresentative or insufficient for making a point. Also, distinguish between facts and
opinions, so that you can later indicate to the reader the nature of the material
you are presenting.

A paraphrase is a note that repeats, phrase by phrase, what an author has
written, but in your own words. The paraphrase is particularly useful in
translating technical material into ordinary language. Unlike a summary, a
paraphrase is not a condensation of lengthy material but is approximately the
same length as the original. But, like the summary, it does restate the material
without interpreting it. Again, therefore, it is important to ensure accuracy
and completeness in paraphrasing and to distinguish between fact and
opinion.

Direct quotations, or verbatim quotes, are records of the actual words the
author uses. Students have a tendency to quote extensively, perhaps because
the direct quote is the easiest note to take. You should resist this temptation,
because ultimately you may be left with little more than a string of quotes,
which will hardly produce an original paper. Direct quotations are useful,
however, when (1) you want to record characteristic or vivid phrases, (2) the
material is so significant or controversial that it must be stated with utmost
accuracy, or (3) you want to show that you are sticking close to firsthand
sources. If you apply these three principles to the selection and use of direct
quotations, you can preclude quoting inappropriately. Finally, in quoting out
of context, make sure that you do not misrepresent an author's remarks by
concealing additional, relevant material.

Exercises

10.7 Evaluate the sources that you collected in answering Exercise 10.6.

10.8 For each source write three notes: a summary, a paraphrase, and a
direct quotation.

STEP FOUR: ORGANIZING THE MATERIAL

When you have finished evaluating your materials, you then face what may be the most challenging part of the process—evaluating your notes to select and organize the material that will be included in your paper. This step can be viewed as consisting of three parts: (1) evaluating your bibliography and notes, (2) structuring the content, and (3) outlining the paper. All of this once again requires you to use your critical faculties. You must choose and interpret materials and eventually bring them together into a unified and cohesive whole.

1. *Evaluating the bibliography and notes.* In studying your bibliography materials and notes, you must ensure completeness. Specifically, be able to answer yes to the following questions:

1. Have I consulted a variety of sources?
2. Have I avoided relying on encyclopedias and other general reference works?
3. Have I used primary sources when possible, as well as secondary ones?
4. Have I consulted both books and periodicals?
5. Have I consulted articles from scholarly periodicals when possible, as well as those from more popular sources?
6. Have I taken complete and accurate notes?

Satisfying yourself on these points is the best way to ensure that your paper will contain enough of the right kind of information on which you can base your conclusions.

When satisfied that your bibliography and notes are adequate, you must then evaluate your notes to determine what you can use and how it will fit into the overall plan. As you sort out your notes, keep in mind that you will want your research paper to show that you understand the research process, have carefully examined your subject, have weighed your information, have taken a particular point of view, and have presented the material successfully.[5]

The process of evaluating your materials will have three results. First, your attitude toward the topic will emerge, and with it your thesis. Second, the main points that you will want to emphasize will become evident. Third, the arrangement for your material will become apparent. This third result brings us to the question of how to structure the content.

2. *Structuring the content.* In Chapter 2 we distinguished between organizing an essay around a series of independent reasons (series structure) or around a closely linked chain of interdependent reasons (chain structure). You should review these general organizational methods, which apply as much to the research paper as to the ordinary theme. Also, keep in mind the specific organizational structures: (1) inductive, (2) pro-and-con, (3) cause-

---

[5]Roth. *The Research Paper,* p. 77.

and-effect, and (4) analysis-of-alternatives. The kind of assertion that your thesis makes (meaning, value, consequence, policy, or fact) can indicate the appropriate organizational structure for your material. For example, a pro-and-con or inductive structure is especially useful for controversial assertions of value or policy; a cause-and-effect structure is helpful for assertions of consequence. Whatever your choice of organization, remember that you want to choose one that follows a logical pattern that guides your reader to the same conclusions you have reached.

3. *Outlining the material.* A choice of organizational method is important in ordering your materials and suggesting an outline for your paper. An outline is a written, orderly plan showing the division and arrangement of ideas. The main purpose of an outline is to show the relationship of these ideas to one another. An outline enables you to see the effectiveness of your organization and the relative strengths of your paper, thereby allowing you to make adjustments. Given its purpose and benefits, then, you should never attempt to write a research paper without first constructing an adequate outline.

Probably you have already had instruction in a proper method of outlining; if not, your instructor will show you what it involves. In any event, it is beyond the scope of this text to teach outlining.

STEP FIVE: WRITING THE PAPER

Once you have completed the preceding four steps, you will be ready to write your paper. As with any ordinary theme, you must begin, develop, and end your research paper.

Beginning It

In previous chapters I have suggested strategies for developing specific kinds of essay. In keeping with that approach, it is fitting that I provide some suggestions for writing the openings to research papers. What follow, then, are ways that you can open your paper.

1. *Clarify your topic. Illustration* (from a paper linking the media with widespread anxiety): "It is little wonder that many people today show intense anxiety and worry. An uncertain economy makes them wonder whether they will be able to maintain themselves and their families. The deplorable state of the environment makes them question whether the struggle for survival is even worth it. The worsening of international relations leaves them fearful that the world is headed for a nuclear holocaust. In all this, the media play a crucial role in producing anxiety."

2. *Indicate your feelings about the topic. Illustration* (from a paper opposing pornography): "Rarely do we consider it politically interesting whether men and women find pleasure in performing their duties as citizens, parents, and spouses; or, on the other hand, whether they derive pleasure from watching their laws and customs ridiculed on stages, in films, or in books. Nor do we consider it politically relevant whether the relations between men and women are depicted in terms of an eroticism separated from love and calculated to undercut the family. Nevertheless, much of the obscenity from which so many of us derive pleasure today is expressly political."

3. *Relate your topic to something current or well known. Illustration* (from a paper dealing with the evolution of the term *competition*): "In the winter of 1982, two monumental antitrust cases came to an end. In the first, AT&T (American Telephone and Telegraph) agreed to divest itself of a score of subsidiaries; in the second, the Justice Department dropped its suit against IBM (International Business Machines). Some heralded these events as a great victory for the free-enterprise system. Others deplored them as a defeat for free enterprise at the hands of big business. Whether one sees these cases as good or bad for free enterprise depends very much on one's definition of *competition*, a concept whose current meaning does not always parallel its eighteenth century classical formulation."

4. *Challenge a generally held assumption about your topic. Illustration* (from a paper on the virtues of not voting): "In the last presidential election, at least half of those eligible did not vote. These nonvoters faced the combined scorn of political parties, school teachers, chambers of commerce, Leagues of Women Voters, and sundry high-minded civic groups and individuals. In upcoming elections we can expect to see these same forces again heroically trying to 'get out the vote.' Yet the notion that 'getting out the vote' makes for better election results is not nonpartisan, patriotic, or logical."

5. *Show something paradoxical about your topic. Illustration* (from a paper on the deficiencies in textbooks): "Textbooks certainly are one of the most influential factors in an individual's intellectual, cultural, and social development. Yet, though they are called 'educational,' textbooks often teach little. Although they are thought 'liberalizing,' they sometimes inculcate narrow-mindedness and intolerance. Though they are viewed as disseminating American values, they sometimes work to undermine them. Yes, textbooks are influential, but not always in a positive way."

6. *State some striking facts or statistics related to your topic. Illustration* (from a paper dealing with the overconsumption of medical drugs in the United States): "The volume of drug business in the U.S. has grown by a factor of one hundred during the twentieth century. Twenty thousand tons of aspirin are consumed per year, about 225 tablets per person. Central-nervous-system agents are the fastest-growing sector of the pharmaceutical market, now making up 31% of total sales. Dependence on prescribed tranquilizers

has risen about 290% since 1962. Medicalized addiction has outpaced all self-chosen forms of creating well-being, such as marijuana or alcohol."[6]

Developing It

In developing your research paper, you will be arguing your thesis, using the material you have gathered to make your points and referring to the sources that you have consulted. Just as in an ordinary argumentative theme, be conscious of the need to support your statements with facts, illustrations, and examples and to avoid fallacies of ambiguity, presumption, and relevance. Your paper will certainly include a mix of fact and opinion. Therefore, you must be careful to distinguish between them and to avoid the fallacies associated with them—false authority, popularity, and tradition—and the misuses of statistics, surveys, and polls. If you invoke comparison or analogy, beware of faulty comparison and false analogies, as well as the fallacies of hasty generalization, concealed evidence, and false dilemma. Should you employ cause and effect, make sure you clarify the causal concept you have in mind as necessary, sufficient, necessary and sufficient, or contributory. Also, avoid fallacies associated with faulty causation: questionable cause, causal over-simplification, neglect of common cause, post hoc, and slippery slope.

You will probably have reason to define some key terms. Indeed, a portion of your paper may require extensive definition. In any event, make sure that you define key terms and concepts and that you adhere to the conventions of good definitions and avoid related fallacies, such as semantical ambiguity and circularity. If you use a term in a special way, stipulate it; if you define persuasively, be careful not to argue erroneously through persuasive definition.

Finally, since you want to guide the reader through an orderly arrangement of ideas, be sure that your paper is coherent—that it all hangs together. Helpful in this regard is the use of signal words (*nevertheless, however, therefore, as a result,* and the like). These terms will show readers the logical connections among your ideas and help guide them to the conclusions that you have drawn.

Ending It

The conclusion of your paper should reinforce your thesis, tie your paper together, and emphatically end it. Here are three strategies for ending the research paper:

1. *Make some statement about your thesis rather than merely repeating it. Illustration:* "In their editorial decisions, communication methods, and

---

[6]Ivan Illich. *Medical Nemesis.* New York: Bantam Books," 1976, pp. 63–64.

marketing devices, the media contribute dramatically to our individual and collective anxiety. For those in print and electronic journalism to ignore or minimize this psychological impact or glibly subordinate it to some lofty mission guaranteed by the Constitution seems irresponsible. To be sure, we need an unfettered press. But we also need a citizenry that is self-confident, optimistic, and panic-free."

2. *Show how you have proved, disproved, or enlarged on your thesis. Illustration:* " 'Getting out the vote,' then, does not necessarily make for better election results. On the contrary, it is always partisan, insofar as a calm and dignified effort benefits the party in power and a frenetic one benefits the party out of power. By the same token, it is no more patriotic than the time-honored American attitude of 'a plague on both your houses.' Nor is it logical. Inasmuch as a successful 'getting out the vote' campaign generates votes from the poorly informed, uninformed, misinformed, and the down-right indifferent and ignorant, it undercuts the votes of the intelligent elector-ate. No, let's not get out the vote; let's get out the *informed* vote."

3. *Tie your paper to something known or a future possibility. Illustration:* "When classical capitalists such as Adam Smith talked about competition, they did so in a social and economic atmosphere quite different from today's. Whereas the economy of the industrial revolution was characterized by a comparatively free and open market system, the economy of the twentieth century is made up of relatively few enormous holding companies that can secretly fix prices, eliminate smaller companies, and monopolize an industry. Ironically, through intense competition such corporate giants have reached a point at which they can now make a mockery of the classical doctrine of competition. The challenge that lies ahead for society and government is to redefine competition in such a way that the classical notion is integrated into present-day realities. As the AT&T and IBM cases well illustrate, this is no mean undertaking."

Exercises

10.9 Using the strategies provided, try to write an opening for each of the four topics you have selected.

10.10 Using the strategies provided, try to write a conclusion for each of the four topics.

SUMMARY

Research is careful, serious, and systematic investigation. The research paper involves scholarly research and promises the following benefits if you do it well:

1. It allows you to investigate a subject that interests you.
2. It allows you to study a subject in depth.
3. It allows you to develop and refine important research skills and critical judgment.
4. It lets you discover links and relations among seemingly disparate material and discover the importance of a field.
5. It offers you self-satisfaction.

In that the argumentative research paper aims to win audience assent or consent and has a thesis, main points, organization, and developmental patterns, it resembles an ordinary argumentative theme. It differs, however, in length and form: The typical student research paper runs between 1,500 and 3,000 words (about six to twelve typewritten pages) and fully documents its sources and lists a bibliography. Ideally, a research paper has three character- istics. First, it is a synthesis of your ideas and the materials supplied by others. Second, it shows originality. Third, it provides documentation. The research paper is not an article or book summary, a mere repeating of the ideas of others, a string of quotations, or unsupported personal opinion.

There are five steps in doing a research paper: (1) choosing a topic, (2) finding the material, (3) evaluating the material, (4) organizing the material, and (5) writing the paper. Step one, choosing a topic, involves two tasks. One concerns the type of subject—assigned, field-of-study, or free-choice. Printed aids such as the following are useful sources of field-of-study subjects: text- books, encyclopedias, library card catalogs, and periodical indexes. Also of help are those interests of yours that can be related to the course content. Regarding free-choice subjects, you can (1) select something you are familiar with and about which you would like to learn more; (2) choose a subject that you know nothing about but would like to investigate; (3) skim newspapers, magazines, and other periodicals for possible subjects; or (4) consult the library for a subject of interest.

The second task in choosing a topic involves a topic selection procedure. A useful one suggested in Chapter 2 consists of selecting a subject, identifying possible topics, and selecting and limiting a topic to write on.

Step two of the research paper, finding the materials, involves a search for primary and secondary sources. Primary sources, the most direct kind of information you can find, include legal documents, letters, diaries, notes, autobiographies, eyewitness reports, transcripts of speeches and interviews, reports, surveys, works of fiction, films, and paintings. Secondary sources are other authors' accounts and interpretations of primary materials. A good research paper contains both primary and secondary sources. Because primary sources are closer to unedited firsthand facts, you should use them whenever possible.

Your library is a rich source of both primary and secondary sources. Specifically, it contains generalized reference works—such as encyclopedias, periodical indexes, and newspaper indexes—and specialized reference works pertaining to specific fields such as business, political science, and literature. Further, there are useful nonlibrary sources: interviews, questionnaires, letters, radio and television programs, reports, pamphlets, and booklets.

Step three, evaluating materials, requires that you identify the most useful and informative sources and take notes from them. Use the following questions to help discriminate among the materials:

1. Which authors seem outstanding in the field?
2. Is a particular author an expert in the field?
3. Does a source seem credible?
4. Is a source long on evidence and short on opinion?
5. Is a source fair-minded and balanced?
6. Does an author settle important questions by going to primary sources?
7. Is the work recent?
8. What does the language used tell you about a work?
9. What facts recur in your reading?
10. Does an author rely excessively on fallacies?

Once you have identified the most useful sources, you must study them and take notes from them. There are three kinds of notes: summaries, paraphrases, and direct quotations. In each case be sure your notes distinguish fact from opinion and are accurate and complete.

Step four, organizing the material, consists of evaluating your bibliographic materials and notes, structuring the content, and outlining the paper. In evaluating the bibliography and notes, satisfy yourself that you can answer the following questions affirmatively:

1. Have I consulted a variety of sources?
2. Have I avoided relying on encyclopedias and other generalized reference works?
3. Have I used primary sources when possible as well as secondary ones?
4. Have I consulted books and periodicals?
5. Have I consulted articles from scholarly periodicals when possible as well as those from more popular sources?
6. Have I taken complete and accurate notes that distinguish fact from opinion?

In structuring the content, keep in mind the four basic organizational patterns: inductive, pro-and-con, cause-and-effect, and analysis-of-alternatives. Finally, do not try to write the paper without first outlining it.

Step five, writing the paper, requires that you think carefully about a good opening, development, and closing. In beginning your paper, reflect on the following strategies:

1. Clarify your topic.
2. Indicate your feelings about the topic.
3. Relate your topic to something current or well known.
4. Challenge a generally held assumption about your topic.
5. Show something paradoxical about your topic.
6. State some striking facts or statistics related to your topic.

In developing your paper you will be advancing your argumentative thesis by using the materials you have researched to make your main points and by referring to those sources that you have consulted. In using specific developmental patterns, such as fact and opinion, comparison and analogy, definition, and cause and effect, adhere to conventional practices and avoid related fallacies, as well as others. Also, make generous use of signal words (also, because, for, thus, and others) to ensure overall coherence and logic of development.

The conclusion of your paper should reinforce your thesis, tie your paper together, and emphatically end it. Three strategies are particularly useful here:

1. Make some statement about your thesis, rather than merely repeating it.
2. Show how you have proved, disproved, or enlarged on your thesis.
3. Tie your paper to something known or a future possibility.

SAMPLE RESEARCH PAPER FOR ANALYSIS

The Role of Secondary Providers in Health Care

Thesis: Three secondary providers--medical schools, professional organizations, and drug suppliers--are the most influential force in shaping the health care system in the United States.

Outline

I. Illustrative case

II. "Health care system" defined as including:

    A. Secondary providers

    B. Primary providers

    C. Financing mechanisms

    D. Consumer patients

III. Key secondary providers

    A. Medical schools described:

      1. As transmitting knowledge and skills

      2. As imparting values, group identity, and a sense of autonomy

      3. As determining the technology to be used and the nature of health care itself

      4. As helping shape various healing professions

    B. A professional association--the AMA--described:

      1. As setting standards

      2. As protecting the interests of itself and its members

      3. As exercising control over various health groups

    C. Drug suppliers described:

      1. As making big money selling drugs

      2. As advancing and protecting their own financial interests

IV. The illusion of patient autonomy

PART FOUR   RESEARCH

The Role of Secondary Providers in Health Care

Between 1973 and 1976, 1,978 patients died in a California state hospital. One hundred and twenty of the deaths occurred under questionable
circumstances.[1] In 1977 the state of California attempted to get to the
bottom of these deaths by stationing an investigator at each of the state
hospitals. But the authority of the special investigators was immediately
undercut by the medical lobby in the legislature, thus igniting a wave of
resentment among the investigators. In the spring of 1980, a publication
of the state's medical association paranoically denounced the investigation
as "shades of 1984" and a "symbol of the totalitarian spectre."[2] A month
after this article appeared, a state senator introduced a resolution calling
for an end to the reviewing by special investigators of deaths in state
hospitals. Instead, the resolution said, the state medical staff should
conduct an investigation of its members under a peer review system. The
state association drafted the resolution, and the senator introduced it,
virtually word for word, as it was given to him. Within a month it passed
through the Senate Health and Welfare Committee and passed the full Senate
39-0.

The preceding case says a good deal about the health care system--how
it is organized and operates. It especially underscores the key role that
secondary providers play in the system.

---

[1]Jim Lewis. "Records Law Blocked Probe of Hospital Deaths." Sacramento Bee, December 28, 1980, p. A3.

[2]Jim Lewis. "Doctors Battle Hospital Investigations." Sacramento Bee,
December 29, 1980, p. A1.

The social scientist C. W. Aakster refers to a system as "a relatively stable whole composed of various parts which are integrated and coordinated in their activities by some kind of communications network."[3] Systems can be natural or human made. For example, a human being could be looked on as a natural system within a hierarchy of other natural systems, which range from the biosphere to subatomic particles. Falling within this hierarchy of natural systems are culture and society, which include numerous human-made systems. Included among these human-made systems are educational, legal, and health care systems.

Like all complex systems, the health care system is made up of inter-related parts, each of which is a system in its own right as well as part of a greater system. Both the parts and the whole are goal directed, the primary goal being the delivery of health care. In addition, each of the health system's components can itself be broken down into smaller and sim-pler systems, thus forming a hierarchy of systems ranging from the complex to the simple. We can define the health care system, then, as a distinct, separable, and permanent part of our society, consisting of an elaborate set of arrangements and interrelated parts, whereby the technology of the health sciences is made available to us.[4] The bewildering variety of its parts and their interrelationships makes it difficult to provide a sketch of the health system that is complete, but just being aware of its main compo-nents serves as a useful departure point for understanding the whole system.

---

[3] C. W. Aakster. "Psychosocial Stress and Health Disturbances." Social Science in Medicine, February 1974, p. 77.

[4] David B. Smith and Arnold D. Kaluzny. The White Labyrinth: Under-standing the Organization of Health Care. Berkeley, Calif.: McCutchan Publishing, 1975, p. 5.

In general, any health care system can be visualized as consisting of three major elements: people and equipment, the organization of these two, and the financial arrangements between suppliers and consumers.[5] Specifically, the health system consists chiefly of secondary and primary providers, financing mechanisms, and consumer patients.

Secondary providers are those who, though not providing direct patient care, shape the system in which health services are delivered and organized. They supply the human resources, the technology, and the overall coordination of health services. Among the most important secondary providers are medical and nursing schools, as well as other professional training programs; professional associations; pharmaceutical companies; equipment suppliers; and various planning agencies. Although the influence of these secondary providers may not be apparent to outsiders, these institutions, agencies, and associations dominate the health care system in the United States. As a result, one cannot understand the system without understanding the influential role played by secondary providers in shaping it. Stated another way, understanding the influential role of secondary providers provides insight into why the system operates as it does, why health care professionals face the problems they do, and why and how their capacity to manage these problems is often constrained.

Primary providers, the second component, are those who provide direct patient care in an office, health center, institution, or clinic. They can be distinguished on the basis of the kind of service rendered: institutional, ambulatory, and community. Thus, institutional providers treat

---

[5]Duane F. Stroman. The Medical Establishment and Social Responsibility. Port Washington, N.Y.: Kennikat Press, 1976, p. 12.

patients confined within the institution. Hospitals, nursing homes, and

extended and home care programs are among the chief institutional providers.

In contrast, ambulatory care provides health services within the context of

a physician's office, a hospital outpatient clinic or emergency room, or one

of the many group practices that are emerging. And community or public

health care focuses on the treatment of the community rather than the indi-

vidual. Local health departments and public health agencies carry out most

of the activities in this area.

The third key component in the health system is the elaborate set of

mechanisms for financing primary providers. Among these would fall private

and public charities, Blue Cross-Blue Shield, commercial insurance, Medicaid

and Medicare, and other federal subsidies. Traditionally, primary providers,

especially physicians, have viewed the emergence of these "third parties"

with considerable suspicion and distrust, even hostility. Their fear is

that these financing mechanisms will wrest financial control of the system

from primary providers. As a result, the third-party mechanisms that have

developed have been largely controlled by primary providers.

Consumers represent the final component in the health system. Unfortu-

nately, they exercise very little influence over the other parts, and thus

their influence on the system is negligible. In effect, consumers of health

services accept what is offered and use what is available. Most of their

costs are subsidized by Social Security and payroll deductions. It is sad

but true that consumers rarely understand precisely how these federal subsi-

dies apply to health care, nor do they exercise any control over how the

contributions withheld are to be used.

The health care system, then, can be viewed as an interaction among

providers, financing mechanisms, and consumers. The interaction is such

369

that the inputs of each are combined in various services, such as treatment
or therapy. These services provide specific outputs, such as health, death,
profit, loss, morale, staff turnover, and so on. These outputs, in turn,
interact with the four major components of the system to produce new inputs,
such as more or fewer financial and human resources, governmental policies,
malpractice suits, and so forth. The system must then process and adapt to
these new inputs, in such a way that a dynamic equilibrium is maintained and
the basic character of the system is preserved. All the rules, regulations,
standards, policies, and procedures that health care professionals labor
under are presumably part of the adaptive mechanism by which the stability
and nature of the system are established and maintained. Although no single
entity is solely responsible for managing the system, secondary providers
have traditionally exercised most control. Today, their influence is
rightly being challenged on several fronts, but they continue to play a
formidable part in shaping health care in the United States.

Although secondary providers consist of a number of individuals and
entities, three exercise enormous influence in shaping the system: medical
schools, professional organizations, and drug companies. Medical schools
are institutions that train physicians. So defined, medical schools help
shape the health system in several important ways. First, they produce the
essential work force for the system. Second, they shape the technology of
the system. Third, they determine the technology that is appropriate to
the provision of health care. Fourth, they define the standards of health
care. Fifth, they serve as models for the education of nonphysician health
professionals. Sixth, they help shape these professionals by influencing
their licensing and accrediting procedures.

But the training of both physicians and nonphysician health professionals goes beyond teaching them skills and imparting the knowledge necessary for practice. In fact, such training attempts to impart a system of values, a sense of professional loyalty, and a profound commitment to independence and self-determination. This attempt to transmit a distinctive group identity and a homogeneous set of values, which underlies the lengthy isolated training period of medical students (and to a lesser extent the training of other health professionals and paraprofessionals), has far-reaching implications for how health personnel will subsequently fit into the system and interact with patients. Commenting on this phenomenon, two authors in the field of public health express its significance this way:

> This helps to justify and at the same time increase the
> autonomy and insulation of the professional groups from
> outside pressures and control. From the point of view of
> the student, the process comes close to that experienced
> by all those processed by "total institutions."[6] His ex-
> perience has certain similarities with that of a prisoner
> in a concentration camp, a new recruit in an army boot camp,
> and, ironically enough, a patient in a large hospital. He
> is placed in a tightly scheduled, isolated environment under
> careful surveillance. He is stripped of his previous iden-
> tity, often goaded and humiliated, and given restricted
> opportunities for contact with those outside the institu-
> tional framework. He is given a new identity, one that he

---

[6]For a discussion of "total institutions," see: Erving Goffman. <u>Asylums</u>. Garden City, N.Y.: Doubleday (Anchor Books), 1961.

371

shares with his peers, all of whom are treated the same
way. His dependence on the institution and the profession
is emphasized at each stage of indoctrination. Such a
process helps induct the individual into a tight, cohesive,
and insulated social world. He learns to function well
in such a world and to adhere to norms that go far beyond
the limited confines of technical proficiency.[7]

So, medical schools clearly exert influence that extends far beyond
transmitting a body of necessary knowledge and skills. They impart values,
group identity, and a sense of autonomy. They also determine the technology that is used in health care and define the nature of health care
itself. Finally, they help shape the various healing professions as well
as determine who will be admitted to them.

Another key secondary provider is the various professional associations, which, in large part, function to advance the interests and standing
of their members. Again, as in the education of all health professionals
and paraprofessionals, the medical profession has made its formidable
presence felt; for the AMA (American Medical Association) serves as the
model professional health association. It also exercises immense influence
over secondary providers generally.

Although the AMA claims the membership of only about half of today's
physicians and its membership figures continue to decline, by numerous
indexes it wields power far beyond its numbers. Thus, in organizational
stability, membership size, percentage of total practitioners, stability

---

[7]Smith and Kaluzny. The White Labyrinth, pp. 27-28.

of membership, fidelity of members, status, wealth, and numbers and circulation of associational periodicals, the AMA remains the dominant medical organization among all the health care professions. As one author puts it, "while the medical establishment dominates health care, the AMA dominates the medical establishment."[8]

Organized medicine, as embodied in the AMA, has numerous professional and public functions. But the professional and public functions of organized medicine do not always run parallel. For example, zealously guarding physician autonomy and financial interests is not always compatible with providing health care to all who need it. Again, inculcating professional loyalty among membership is not always consistent with public service. The fact is that organized medicine, operating through the AMA, has opposed most major health bills for over fifty years. Indeed, the only major pieces of legislation it has supported have been for federal funds for hospital construction and medical research.[9]

One of the important functions of organized medicine that is most relevant to all nonphysician health professionals is its effort to coordinate the training programs and activities of various health groups. The groups include specialists and their boards, nurses' associations, the American Hospital Association, and a large number of allied health organizations. For example, the AMA's Council on Medical Education is responsible for approving curriculum and training programs and for certifying a whole smorgasbord of occupational titles.

---

[8] Stroman. The Medical Establishment, p. 100.

[9] Ibid., p. 193.

A number of social and professional concerns arise out of this discussion, all of which involve the issue of raw power. First, given the enormous influence of the AMA and its functions, the public interest cannot be best served. A second concern relates to professional and personal autonomy. Again, given this physician-dominated organization, how much autonomy do other health care professions and professionals have? Very little. But how much ought they have? Third, a similar question can be asked about health care consumers. Given the virtually complete control that organized medicine has over who will practice health care, what services will be permitted and what institutions, treatments, and therapies will be licensed, how much autonomy in health matters do consumers have? How much ought they have? Again, such questions deserve an airing, for at the very least they raise serious social and moral issues about whether we want a system based on paternalism or individual choice.

A third secondary provider that interacts with enormous day-to-day influence on the provision of health care is drug suppliers. To get some idea of the extent of their influence, consider that, in 1971, 1.5 billion prescriptions were filled in the United States, an average of twenty per family and an increase of 150 percent in prescriptions per capita in a ten-year period. In 1972, $11 billion out of a total of $70 billion spent for health care was for drugs, medical supplies, and equipment.[10] Today the figures are even greater. But this is only part of the picture.

Drug companies must market prescription drugs. In order to do that they spend a whopping $1.5 billion a year hawking their products, a figure that represents roughly one out of every four dollars they make wholesale

---

[10]J. L. Goddard. "The Medical Business." Scientific American, September 1973, p. 161.

for their products and nearly four times what they spend yearly on research and development.[11] This advertising is aimed not at the patient but primarily at the physician and pharmacist. The marketing effort includes thousands of drug hucksters who visit physicians, pharmacists, and institutional purchasers to sell their company's products. Those contacts and the advertising that appears in professional journals are the primary ways that physicians become aware of new pharmaceutical products as well as new applications for old ones.

To get some idea of the money involved, consider that one pharmaceutical company, Hoffman-La Roche, spent $200 million in ten years and engaged about 200 physicians a year to produce scientific articles extolling the benefits of Valium.[12] Similarly, in 1973 the drug industry spent about $4,500 per physician for advertising and promotion, which was roughly the equivalent of the cost of a year in medical school. In the same year the industry contributed less than 3 percent of the budget of American medical schools.[13] What is more, industry estimates peg Hoffman-La Roche's profits from minor tranquilizers (Valium, Librium, Dalmane, and others) at about $100 million in 1978.[14]

Unquestionably, then, the pharmaceutical industry has a huge financial investment in the health care system. Naturally enough, it will seek to protect this interest by influencing the nature of health care delivery.

---

[11]Ibid., p. 162.

[12]Ivan Illich. Medical Nemesis: The Expropriation of Health. New York: Bantam Books, 1976, p. 66.

[13]Ibid., p. 66.

[14]Richard Hughes and Robert Breuin. The Tranquilizing of America. New York: Harcourt Brace Jovanovich (Warner Books), 1979, p. 21.

This alone would be objectionable, but there are additional concerns about the impact of drug suppliers on the health system. The availability of so many drugs produces reliance on drug technology to solve health problems. Also, the involvement of monstrous commercial interests represents an immoral distribution of society's resources and demonstrates that the primary concern is not with people but with profit. Furthermore, since physicians' drug selections are based on the saturation advertising in medical journals and the pitches of drug salespeople, one must conclude that many prescriptions are inappropriate,.even harmful. A case in point can be found in the history of the drug Chloromycetin.

During the 1960s chloramphenicol was packaged as Chloromycetin by Parke, Davis. It yielded about one-third of the company's overall profits. Even then it was known that people who take chloramphenicol stand a chance of dying of aplastic anemia, an incurable blood disease, and that typhoid is almost the only disease that warrants such a risk. Nonetheless, through the 1950s and early 1960s, Parke, Davis spent large sums of money to promote the drug. The promotion worked, for physicians in the United States prescribed chloramphenicol to almost 4 million people per year to treat acne, sore throat, and the common cold. Given that typhoid is rare in the United States, it can safely be assumed that only a small fraction of patients actually needed the drug.[15]

A footnote to the chloramphenicol tale underscores the power that the drug industry wields not only in health care but also in the area of government control of dangerous drugs. At the same time it raises another moral

---

[15]U.S. Senate Select Committee on Small Business, Subcommittee on Monopoly. Competitive Problems in the Drug Industry, 1967-1968, part 2, p. 565.

dimension to the issue of pharmaceutical influence. Shortly after the

dangers of chloramphenicol were exposed by a congressional hearing, its use

dwindled. Parke, Davis was forced to insert strict warnings about its

hazards, but such warnings did not extend to exports. As a result, the

drug continued to be used indiscriminately in Mexico, thus breeding a drug-

resistant strain of typhoid bacilli that today not only infects Central

America but is spreading to the rest of the world.[16]

The reasons for the widespread use of drugs in the United States are

complex. In all likelihood, though, it is the result of a health care system

that is tightly organized around what some authors have termed "an unbreak-

able drug-dispensing circle."

> This circle consists of a profit-motivated drug manufac-
>
> turer that must spend heavily to develop new drugs and
>
> spend equally heavily to promote them; an often harried
>
> physician who has read drug ads and believes in them; and
>
> a patient who is seeking and has come to believe it is
>
> right to receive instant relief for whatever problem,
>
> mental or physical, plagues him. All play equal roles
>
> in this circle, and until the circle is broken, the use
>
> of psychoactive drugs--and the problems associated with
>
> them--will continue to grow.[17]

Of all the components in the health care system, then, three key

secondary providers wield the most influence. Medical schools not only

---

[16]Illich. Medical Nemesis, p. 62.

[17]Hughes and Breuin. The Tranquilizing of America, p. 31.

transmit knowledge and skills but also shape the values and attitudes of their students and determine what technology will be available to consumer patients. The American Medical Association not only sets standards of practice but zealously guards its own interests and those of its members. Drug suppliers make billions from selling their products while at the same time contributing to our overconsumption of drugs. Although patient consumers may think that they exercise great control over their personal health decisions, in fact they do not. In the last analysis the health services available to them, the attitudes of those who care for them, and even the concept of health offered to them are shaped by these key secondary providers of health care in the United States.

Bibliography

Aakster, C. W. "Psychosocial and Health Disturbances." Social Science
    Medicine, February 1974.

Alford, R. R. Health Care Politics: Ideological Interest Group Barriers to
    Reform. Chicago: University of Chicago Press, 1975.

Goddard, J. L. "The Medical Business." Scientific American, September
1973, pp. 161-165.

Goffman, Erving. Asylums. Garden City, N.Y.: Doubleday (Anchor Books),
    1961.

Hughes, Richard, and Breuin, Robert. The Tranquilizing of America. New
    York: Harcourt Brace Jovanovich (Warner Books), 1979.

Illich, Ivan. Medical Nemesis: The Expropriation of Health. New York:
    Bantam Books, 1976.

Lewis, Jim. "Doctors Battle Hospital Investigations." Sacramento Bee,
    December 29, 1980, pp. A1, A12, A14.

_____. "Records Law Blocked Probe of Hospital Deaths," Sacramento Bee,
    December 28, 1980, p. A3, A11, A14.

Ostheimer, N., and Ostheimer, J., eds. Life or Death--Who Controls? New
    York: Springer, 1976.

Smith, David B., and Kaluzny, Arnold D. The White Labyrinth: Understanding
    the Organization of Health Care. Berkeley, Calif.: McCutchan
    Publishing, 1975.

Stevens, Rosemary. American Medicine and the Public Interest. New Haven,

Conn.: Yale University Press, 1971.

Stroman, Duane F. The Medical Establishment and Social Responsibility.

Port Washington, N.Y.: Kennikat Press, 1976.

U.S. Senate Select Committee on Small Business, Subcommittee on Monopoly.

Competitive Problems in the Drug Industry, 1967-1968, part 2, p. 565.

QUESTIONS FOR ANALYSIS

1. Do you think the topic is sufficiently narrow?
2. What kind of assertion is the thesis?
3. What strategy does the writer use in opening the paper? Choose another strategy, and write a different beginning.
4. What organizational structure does the writer use?
5. Identify all the primary sources.
6. In paragraph 1, which sentences report facts? Which mix facts with opinions? Rewrite the fact/opinion sentences so that they are opinion free.
7. Do you think the author generally has avoided emotive language and stayed close to the facts?
8. Identify all signal words in paper. Are there places where you think transitions are needed but do not appear? If so, provide them.
9. Does the case cited in paragraph 1 strike you as typical or atypical?
10. Suppose someone complained: "Why, the first paragraph does nothing more than poison the well. The writer has loaded the deck before even dealing the cards." Would you agree or disagree with this criticism?
11. Paragraph 2 draws some conclusions based on the case presentation in paragraph 1. Do you think the conclusions are warranted? Or would you consider at least some of them hasty generalizations?
12. Is the reference to C. W. Aakster in paragraph 3 a legitimate appeal to authority?
13. What kind of definition of "system" is given in paragraph 3—denotative, logical, stipulative, or persuasive?
14. What kinds of definition of "natural" and "human made systems" are given in paragraph 3?
15. What kind of definition of "health care system" does the writer provide in paragraph 4?
16. Write a syllogism that combines sentences 4 and 5 of paragraph 6.
17. Does the writer make effective use of denotation in defining the components of the health system (paragraphs 6–9)?
18. Sentences 3 and 4 (especially 4) of paragraph 8 are controversial value judgments. Does the writer support them? Is sentence 4 a questionable cause?
19. Does the author mix fact and opinion in paragraph 9?
20. Does paragraph 10 contain jargon? If so, rewrite the paragraph so that it is more understandable.

21. Does the last sentence of paragraph 10 mix fact and opinion? If so, how would you rid the sentence of the opinion?

22. In paragraph 12, the writer appeals to authority in the form of an extended quotation. The authors of the quote compare the medical trainee variously to a prisoner in a concentration camp, a new recruit, and a patient in a large hospital. Do you think the comparisons are good ones?

23. Would you say that the author's inferences in paragraph 13 logically follow from the discussion that preceded them?

24. Is there a clear, logical connection between paragraphs 15 and 16? If not, provide one. Should the author have defined "organized medicine"?

25. In paragraph 16, the writer does not mention that the AMA also sets ethical standards for its members, provides resources for the maintenance of professional skills, and tries to protect the interests of society. Is it fair to say, then, that the writer, by concealing evidence, presents a biased and unbalanced view? Rewrite the paragraph so that it contains the suppressed facts while still making its point.

26. Is "raw power" in the first sentence of paragraph 18 emotive? Would "power" have been sufficient?

27. In the second sentence of paragraph 18, the author implies that the "enormous influence" and functions of the AMA are incompatible with the public interest. Is this necessarily true, or is it a questionable assertion? Rewrite the sentence so that the connection is qualified.

28. In the same paragraph, does the writer make use of innuendo?

29. Is the last sentence of the same paragraph a false dilemma? If so, rewrite the sentence so that a false dilemma is avoided.

30. Are statistics used correctly and effectively in paragraphs 19, 20, and 21?

31. Is the meaning of "average" in paragraph 19 clear?

32. Paragraph 22 contains many value judgments. Evaluate them.

33. In paragraph 22, what kind of causal relationship is implied between the availability of drugs and overdependence on drugs? Do you think the writer is guilty of causal oversimplification? If so, rewrite the sentence so that the assertion is qualified.

34. Should the Chloromycetin example be viewed as typical or atypical?

35. Does the last sentence of paragraph 24 contain a causal oversimplification? If so, rewrite it to avoid the fallacy but preserve the essential meaning.

36. Are the first two sentences of paragraph 25 consistent? If not, rewrite one or the other to make them compatible.

37. Is the second sentence of paragraph 25 a causal oversimplification? If so, rewrite to avoid the fallacy.

38. What strategy does the writer use in ending the paper? Choose another strategy, and write a different ending.

39. Would you say that the writer understands the research process?

40. Do you think the writer has examined the topic thoroughly?

41. Has the writer carefully weighed the information?

42. Has the writer taken a particular point of view?

43. Has the writer presented the material successfully—that is, has the person succeeded in demonstrating the thesis?

RESEARCH PAPER ASSIGNMENT

Using the steps sketched in this chapter and following the directions of your instructor, write a research paper. Perhaps a good place to begin is with the materials you have developed by doing the chapter exercises. Thus, you may wish to investigate further one of the four topics you have selected. If you do and if you have properly limited the topic, you are ready for step two of the research paper process: finding the materials.

Index